Data Mining with Ontologies:
Implementations, Findings, and Frameworks

Héctor Oscar Nigro
Universidad Nacional del Centro de la Provincia de Buenos Aires, Argentina

Sandra Elizabeth González Císaro
Universidad Nacional del Centro de la Provincia de Buenos Aires, Argentina

Daniel Hugo Xodo
Universidad Nacional del Centro de la Provincia de Buenos Aires, Argentina

INFORMATION SCIENCE REFERENCE

Hershey · New York

Acquisitions Editor:	Kristin Klinger
Development Editor:	Kristin Roth
Senior Managing Editor:	Jennifer Neidig
Managing Editor:	Sara Reed
Copy Editor:	Katie Smalley
Typesetter:	Jamie Snavely
Cover Design:	Lisa Tosheff
Printed at:	Yurchak Printing Inc.

Published in the United States of America by
Information Science Reference (an imprint of IGI Global)
701 E. Chocolate Avenue, Suite 200
Hershey PA 17033
Tel: 717-533-8845
Fax: 717-533-8661
E-mail: cust@igi-pub.com
Web site: http://www.igi-pub.com/reference

and in the United Kingdom by
Information Science Reference (an imprint of IGI Global)
3 Henrietta Street
Covent Garden
London WC2E 8LU
Tel: 44 20 7240 0856
Fax: 44 20 7379 0609
Web site: http://www.eurospanonline.com

Library of Congress Cataloging-in-Publication Data

Date mining with ontologies : implementations, findings and frameworks / Hector Oscar Nigro, Sandra Gonzalez Cisaro, and Daniel Xodo, editors.

p. cm.

Summary: "Prior knowledge in data mining is helpful for selecting suitable data and mining techniques, pruning the space of hypothesis, representing the output in a comprehensible way, and improving the overall method. This book examines methodologies and research for the development of ontological foundations for data mining to enhance the ability of ontology utilization and design"--Provided by publisher.

Includes bibliographical references and index.

ISBN 978-1-59904-618-1 (hardcover) -- ISBN 978-1-59904-620-4 (ebook)

1. Data mining. 2. Ontologies (Information retrieval) I. Nigro, Hector Oscar. II. Cisaro, Sandra Gonzalez. III. Xodo, Daniel.

QA76.9.D343D39 2008

005.74--dc22

2007007283

British Cataloguing in Publication Data
A Cataloguing in Publication record for this book is available from the British Library.

Table of Contents

Section III
Frameworks

Detailed Table of Contents

Section I
Implementations

Chapter I

In this chapter we study how we can organize the continuously proliferating Web content into topical categories, also known as Web directories. In this respect, we have implemented a system, named TODE that uses a topical ontology for directories' editing. First, we describe the process for building our on-tology of Web topics, which are treated in TODE as directories' topics. Then, we present how TODE in-teracts with the ontology in order to categorize Web pages into the ontology's topics and we experimentally study our system's efficiency in grouping Web pages thematically. We evaluate TODE's performance by comparing its resulting categorization for a number of pages to the categorization the same pages display in the Google directory as well as to the categorizations delivered for the same set of pages and topics by a Bayesian classifier. Results indicate that our model has a noticeable potential in reducing the human-effort overheads associated with populating Web directories. Furthermore, experimental results imply that the use of a rich topical ontology increases significantly classification accuracy for dy-namic contents.

Chapter II

This chapter introduces Raising as an operation that is used as a preprocessing step for data mining. In the Web Marketing Project, people's demographic and interest information has been collected from the Web. Rules have been derived using this information as input for data mining. The Raising step takes advantage of an interest ontology to advance data mining and to improve rule quality. The definition and implementation of Raising are presented in this chapter. Furthermore, the effects caused by Raising are analyzed in detail, showing an improvement of the support and confidence values of useful association rules for marketing purposes.

Chapter III

This chapter proposes an original approach for ontology management in the context of Web-based information systems. Our approach relies on the usage analysis of the chosen Web site, in complement of the existing approaches based on content analysis of Web pages. Our methodology is based on the knowledge discovery techniques mainly from HTTP Web logs and aims at confronting the discovered knowledge in terms of usage with the existing ontology in order to propose new relations between concepts. We illustrate our approach on a Web site provided by French local tourism authorities (related to Metz city) with the use of clustering and sequential patterns discovery methods. One major contribution of this chapter, thus, is the application of usage analysis to support ontology evolution and/or Web site reorganization.

Chapter IV

Clustering similar documents is a difficult task for text data mining. Difficulties stem especially from the way documents are translated into numerical vectors. In this chapter, we will present a method that uses Self Organizing Map (SOM) to cluster medical documents. The originality of the method is that it does not rely on the words shared by documents, but rather on concepts taken from an ontology. Our goal is to cluster various medical documents in thematically consistent groups (e.g., grouping all the documents related to cardiovascular diseases). Before applying the SOM algorithm, documents have to go through several preprocessing steps. First, textual data have to be extracted from the documents, which can be either in the PDF or HTML format. Documents are then indexed, using two kinds of indexing units: stems and concepts. After indexing, documents can be numerically represented by vectors whose dimensions correspond to indexing units. These vectors store the weight of the indexing unit within the document they represent. They are given as inputs to a SOM, which arranges the corresponding documents on a two-dimensional map. We have compared the results for two indexing schemes: stem-based indexing and conceptual indexing. We will show that using an ontology for document clustering has several advantages. It is possible to cluster documents written in several languages since concepts are language-independent. This is especially helpful in the medical domain where research articles are written in different languages. Another advantage is that the use of concepts helps reduce the size of the vectors, which, in turn, reduces processing time.

Section II
Findings

Chapter V

Ontology-Based Interpretation and Validation of Mined Knowledge:
Normative and Cognitive Factors in Data Mining / *Ana Isabel Canhoto*

The use of automated systems to collect, process, and analyze vast amounts of data is now integral to the operations of many corporations and government agencies, in particular it has gained recognition as a strategic tool in the war on crime. Data mining, the technology behind such analysis, has its origins in quantitative sciences. Yet, analysts face important issues of a cognitive nature both in terms of the input for the data mining effort, and in terms of the analysis of the output. Domain knowledge and bias information influence, which patterns in the data are deemed as useful and, ultimately, valid. This chapter addresses the role of cognition and context in the interpretation and validation of mined knowledge. We propose the use of ontology charts and norm specifications to map how varying levels of access to information and exposure to specific social norms lead to divergent views of mined knowledge.

Chapter VI

Data Integration Through Protein Ontology / *Amandeep S. Sidhu,*
Tharam S. Dillon, and Elizabeth Chang

Traditional approaches to integrate protein data generally involved keyword searches, which immediately excludes unannotated or poorly annotated data. An alternative protein annotation approach is to rely on sequence identity, structural similarity, or functional identification. Some proteins have a high degree of sequence identity, structural similarity, or similarity in functions that are unique to members of that family alone. Consequently, this approach can not be generalized to integrate the protein data. Clearly, these traditional approaches have limitations in capturing and integrating data for protein annotation. For these reasons, we have adopted an alternative method that does not rely on keywords or similarity metrics, but instead uses ontology. In this chapter we discuss conceptual framework of protein ontology that has a hierarchical classification of concepts represented as classes, from general to specific; a list of attributes related to each concept, for each class; a set of relations between classes to link concepts in ontology in more complicated ways then implied by the hierarchy, to promote reuse of concepts in the ontology; and a set of algebraic operators for querying protein ontology instances.

Chapter VII

TtoO: Mining a Thesaurus and Texts to Build and Update a Domain Ontology /
Josiane Mothe and Nathalie Hernandez

This chapter introduces a method re-using a thesaurus built for a given domain, in order to create new resources of a higher semantic level in the form of an ontology. Considering ontologies for data-mining tasks relies on the intuition that the meaning of textual information depends on the conceptual relations between the objects to which they refer rather than on the linguistic and statistical relations of their content. To put forward such advanced mechanisms, the first step is to build the ontologies. The originality of the method is that it is based both on the knowledge extracted from a thesaurus and on the knowledge semiautomatically extracted from a textual corpus. The whole process is semiautomated and experts' tasks are limited to validating certain steps. In parallel, we have developed mechanisms based on the obtained ontology to accomplish a science monitoring task. An example will be given.

This chapter investigates different aspects in the construction of a domain ontology to a content-based recommender system. The recommender systems suggests textual electronic documents from a digital library, based on documents read by the users and based on textual messages posted in electronic discussions through a Web chat. The domain ontology is used to represent the user's interest and the content of the documents. In this context, the ontology is composed by a hierarchy of concepts and keywords. Each concept has a vector of keywords with weights associated. Keywords are used to identify the content of the texts (documents and messages), through the application of text mining techniques. The chapter discusses different approaches for constructing the domain ontology, including the use of text mining software tools for supervised learning, the interference of domain experts in the engineering process and the use of a normalization step.

Section III
Frameworks

This chapter introduces the problem of mining frequent geographic patterns and spatial association rules from geographic databases. In the geographic domain most discovered patterns are trivial, non-novel, and noninteresting, which simply represent natural geographic associations intrinsic to geographic data. A large amount of natural geographic associations are explicitly represented in geographic database schemas and geo-ontologies, which have not been used so far in frequent geographic pattern mining. Therefore, this chapter presents a novel approach to extract patterns from geographic databases using geo-ontologies as prior knowledge. The main goal of this chapter is to show how the large amount of knowledge represented in geo-ontologies can be used to avoid the extraction of patterns that are previously known as noninteresting.

This chapter introduces an ontology-based framework for automated construction of complex interactive data mining workflows as a means of improving productivity of Grid-enabled data exploration systems. The authors first characterize existing manual and automated workflow composition approaches and then present their solution called GridMiner Assistant (GMA), which addresses the whole life cycle of the knowledge discovery process. GMA is specified in the OWL language and is being developed around a novel data mining ontology, which is based on concepts of industry standards like the predictive model markup language, cross industry standard process for data mining, and Java data mining API. The ontology introduces basic data mining concepts like data mining elements, tasks, services, and so forth. In addition, conceptual and implementation architectures of the framework are presented and its application to an example taken from the medical domain is illustrated. The authors hope that the further research and development of this framework can lead to productivity improvements, which can have significant impact on many real-life spheres. For example, it can be a crucial factor in achievement of scientific discoveries, optimal treatment of patients, productive decision making, cutting costs, and so forth.

Several issues of database organization of petroleum industries have been highlighted. Complex geo-spatial heterogeneous data structures complicate the accessibility and presentation of data in petroleum industries. Objectives of the current research are to integrate the data from different sources and connect them intelligently. Data warehousing approach supported by ontology, has been described for effective data mining of petroleum data sources. Petroleum ontology framework, narrating the conceptualization of petroleum ontology and methodological architectural views, has been described. Ontology-based data warehousing with fine-grained multidimensional data structures, facilitate to mining and visualization of data patterns, trends, and correlations, hidden under massive volumes of data. Data structural designs and implementations deduced, through ontology supportive data warehousing approaches, will enable the researchers in commercial organizations, such as, the one of Western Australian petroleum indus-tries, for knowledge mapping and thus interpret knowledge models for making million dollar financial decisions.

Pattern base management systems (PBMS) have been introduced as an effective way to manage the high volume of patterns available nowadays. PBMS provide pattern management functionality in the same way where a database management system provides data management functionality. However, not all the extracted patterns are interesting; some are trivial and insignificant because they do not make sense according to the domain knowledge. Thus, in order to automate the pattern evaluation process, we need to incorporate the domain knowledge in it. We propose the integration of PBMS and ontologies as a solution to the need of many scientific fields for efficient extraction of useful information from large databases and the exploitation of knowledge. In this chapter, we describe the potentiality of this integration and the issues that should be considered introducing an XML-based PBMS. We use a case study of data mining over scientific (seismological) data to illustrate the proposed PBMS and ontology integrated environment.

Preface

Data mining, also referred to as knowledge discovery in databases (KDD), is a process of finding new, interesting, previously unknown, potentially useful, and ultimately understandable patterns from very large volumes of data. Data mining is a discipline which brings together database systems, statistics, artificial intelligence, machine learning, parallel and distributed processing and visualization between other disciplines (Fayyad et al., 1996; Hand & Kamber, 2001; Hernadez Orallo et al., 2004).

Nowadays, one of the most important and challenging problems in data mining is the definition of the prior knowledge; this can be originated from the process or the domain. This contextual information may help select the appropriate information, features or techniques, decrease the space of hypothesis, represent the output in a most comprehensible way and improve the whole process.

Therefore we need a conceptual model to help represent to this knowledge. According to Gruber's ontology definition—explicit formal specifications of the terms in the domain and relations among them (Gruber, 1993, 2002); we can represent the knowledge of knowledge discovery process and knowledge about domain. Principally, ontologies are used for communication (between machines and/or humans), automated reasoning, and representation and reuse of knowledge (Cimiano et al., 2004). As a result, ontological foundation is a precondition for efficient automated usage of knowledge discovery information.

Thus, we can perceive the relation between Ontologies and data mining in two manners:

- From ontologies to data mining, we are incorporating knowledge in the process through the use of ontologies, i.e. how the experts comprehend and carry out the analysis tasks. Representative applications are intelligent assistants for discover process (Bernstein et al., 2001, 2005), interpretation and validation of mined knowledge, Ontologies for resource and service description and knowledge Grids (Cannataro et al., 2003; Brezany et al., 2004).
- From data mining to Ontologies, we include domain knowledge in the input information or use the ontologies to represent the results. Therefore the analysis is done over these ontologies. The most characteristic applications are in medicine, biology and spatial data, such as gene representation, taxonomies, applications in geosciences, medical applications and specially in evolving domains (Langley, 2006; Gottgtroy et al., 2003, 2005; Bogorny et al., 2005).

When we can represent and include knowledge in the process through ontologies, we can transform data mining into knowledge mining.

Figure 1. General framework of data mining with ontologies

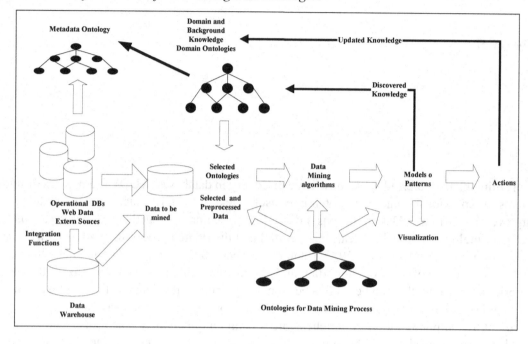

DATA MINING WITH ONTOLOGIES CYCLE

Figure 1 shows our vision of data mining with ontologies cycle.

- **Metadata ontologies:** These ontologies establish how this variable is constructed i.e. which was the process that permit us to obtain its value, and it can vary using another method. Of course this ontology must also express general information about the variable as is treated.
- **Domain ontologies:** These ontologies express the knowledge about application domain.
- **Ontologies for data mining process:** These ontologies codify all knowledge about the process, i.e., select features, select the best algorithms according to the variables and the problem, and establish valid process sequences (Bernstein, 2001, 2005; Cannataro, 2003, 2004).

According with Gomez-Perez and Manzano-Macho (2003) the different methods and approaches, which allow the extraction of ontologies or semantics from database schemas can be classified on three areas, main goal, techniques used and sources used for learning. With regard to the attributes of each area they are the following for summary of ontology learning methods from relational schema are:

- **Main goal**
  - To map a relational schema with a conceptual schema
  - To create (and refine) an ontology
  - To create ontological instances (from a database)
  - Enhance ad hoc queries

- **Techniques used**
  - ○ Mappings
  - ○ Reverse engineering
  - ○ Induction inference
  - ○ Rule generation
  - ○ Graphic modeling
- **Sources used for learning**
  - ○ Relational schemas (of a database)
  - ○ Schema of domain specific databases
  - ○ Flat files
  - ○ Relational databases

In next paragraphs we explain in more detail these three classes of ontologies based on earlier works from different knowledge fields.

Domain Ontology

The models on many scientists work to represent their work hypotheses are generally cause effect diagrams. Models make use of general laws or theories to predict or explain behavior in specific situations. Currently these cause effect diagrams can be without difficulty translated to ontologies, by means of conceptual maps which discriminate taxonomy organized as central concepts, main concept, secondary concepts, specific concepts.

Discovery systems produce models that are valuable for prediction, but they should also produce models that have been stated in some declarative format, that can be communicated clearly and precisely, which helps people understand observations, in terms that they find well known (Bridewell, 2006; Langley, 2002, 2006). Models can be from different appearances and dissimilar abstraction level, but the more complex the fact for which they account, the more important that they be cast in some formal notation with an unambiguous interpretation. And of course these new knowledge can be easily communicated and updated between systems and Knowledge databases. In particular into data mining field knowledge can be represented in different formalisms, e.g. rules, decision trees, cluster, known as models. Discovery systems should generate knowledge in a format that is well known to domain users.

There are an important relation between knowledge structures and discovery process with learning machine. The formers are important outputs of discovery process, and are important inputs to discovery (Langley, 2000). Thus knowledge plays as crucial a role as data in the automation of discovery. Therefore, ontologies provide a structure capable of supporting the knowledge representation about domain.

Metadata Ontologies

As Spyns et al. (2002) affirm ontologies in current computer science language are computer-based resources that represent agreed domain semantics. Unlike data models, the fundamental asset of ontologies is their relative independence of particular applications, i.e., an ontology consists of relatively generic knowledge that can be reused by different kinds of applications/tasks.

In opposition a data model represents the structure and integrity of the data elements of the, in principle "single", specific enterprise application(s) by which it will be used. Consequently, the conceptualization and the vocabulary of a data model are not intended a priori to be shared by other applications (Gottgtroy et al., 2005).

Similarly, in data modeling practice, the semantics of data models often constitute an informal accord between the developers and the users of the data model—including when a data warehouse is designed-and, in many cases, the data model is updated as it evolves when particular new functional requirements pop up without any significant update in the metadata repository. Both ontology model and data model have similarities in terms of scope and task. They are context dependent knowledge representation, that is, there doesn't exist a strict line between generic and specific knowledge when you are building ontology. Moreover, both modeling techniques are knowledge acquisition intensive tasks and the resulted models represent partial account of conceptualizations (Gottgtroy et al., 2003).

In spite of the differences, we should consider the similarities and the fact of data models carry a lot of useful hide knowledge about the domain in its data schemas, in order to build ontologies from data and improve the process of knowledge discovery in databases. Due the fact data schemas do not have the required semantic knowledge to intelligently guide ontology construction has been presented as a challenge for database and ontology engineers (Gottgtroy et al., 2003).

Ontologies for Data Mining Process

Vision about KDD process is changing over time. In its beginnings the main objective was to extract a valuable pattern from a fat file as a play of try and error. As time goes by, researchers and fundamentally practitioners discuss the importance of a priori knowledge, the knowledge and understandability about the problem, the choice of the methodology to do the discovery, the expertise in similar situations and an important question arises up to what existent is such inversion on data mining projects worthwhile?

As practitioners and researchers in this field we can perceive that expertise is very important, knowledge about domain is helpful and it simplify the process. To do more attractive the process to managers the practitioners must do it more efficiently and reusing experience. So we can codify all statistical and machine learning knowledge with ontologies and use it.

Bernstein et al. (2001) have developed the concept of intelligent assistant discovery (IDA), which helps data miners with the exploration of the space of valid data mining processes. It takes advantage of an explicit ontology of data-mining techniques, which defines the various techniques and their properties. Main characteristics are (Bernstein et al., 2005).

- A systematic enumeration of valid DM processes, so they do not miss important, potentially fruitful options.
- Effective rankings of these valid processes by different criteria, to help them choose between the options.
- An infrastructure for sharing data mining knowledge, which leads to what economists call network externalities.

Cannataro and colleagues have done another interesting contribution to this kind of ontologies. They developed an ontology that can be used to simplify the development of distributed knowledge discovery applications on the Grid, offering to a domain expert a reference model for the different kind of data mining tasks, methodologies and software available to solve a given problem, helping a user in finding the most appropriate solution (Cannataro et al., 2003, 2004). Authors have adopted the Enterprise Methodology (Corcho et al., 2003).

RESEARCH WORKS IN THE TOPIC

The next paragraphs will describe the most recently research works in data mining with ontologies field.

Singh, Vajirkar, and Lee (2003) have developed a context aware data mining framework which provide accuracy and efficacy to data mining outcomes. Context factors were modeled using ontological representation. Although the context aware framework proposed is generic in nature and can be applied to most of the fields, the medical scenario provided was like a proof of concept to our proposed model.

Hotho, Staab and Stumme (2003) have showed that using ontologies as filters in term selection prior to the application of a K-means clustering algorithm will increase the tightness and relative isolation of document clusters as a measure of improvement.

Pand and Shen (2005) have proposed architecture for knowledge discovery in evolving environments. The architecture creates a communication mechanism to incorporate known knowledge into discovery process, through ontology service facility. The continuous mining is transparent to the end user; moreover, the architecture supports logical and physical data independence.

Rennolls (2005, p. 719) have developed an intelligent framework for data mining, knowledge discovery and business intelligence. The ontological framework will guide to user to choice of models from an expanded data mining toolkit, and the epistemological framework will assist to user in interpreting and appraising the discovered relationships and patterns.

On domain ontologies, Pan and Pan (2006) have proposed ontobase ontology repository. It is an implementation, which allows users and agents to retrieve ontologies and metadata through open Web standards and ontology service. Key features of the system include the use of XML metadata interchange to represent and import ontologies and metadata, the support for smooth transformation and transparent integration using ontology mapping and the use of ontology services to share and reuse domain knowledge in a generic way.

Recently, Bounif et al. (2006) have explained the articulation of a new approach for database schema evolution and outline the use of domain ontology. The approach they have proposed belongs to a new tendency called the tendency of a priori approaches. It implies the investigation of potential future requirements besides the current requirements during the standard requirements analysis phase of schema design or redesign and their inclusion into the conceptual schema. Those requirements are determined with the help of a domain ontology called "a requirements ontology" using data mining techniques and schema repository.

BOOK ORGANIZATION

This book is organized into three major sections dealing respectively with implementations, findings, and frameworks.

Section I: Implementations includes applications or study cases on data mining with ontologies.

Chapter I, *TODE: An Ontology-Based Model for the Dynamic Population of Web Directories* by Sofia Stamou, Alexandros Ntoulas, and Dimitris Christodoulakis studies how we can organize the continuously proliferating Web content into topical categories, also known as Web directories. Authors have implemented a system, named TODE that uses Topical Ontology for Directories' Editing. Also TODE's performance is evaluated; experimental results imply that the use of a rich topical ontology significantly increases classification accuracy for dynamic contents.

Chapter II, *Raising, to Enhance Rule Mining in Web Marketing with the Use of an Ontology* by Xuan Zhou and James Geller introduces Raising as an operation which is used as a preprocessing step for data mining. Rules have been derived using demographic and interest information as input for data mining. The Raising step takes advantage of interest ontology to advance data mining and to improve rule quality. Furthermore, the effects caused by Raising are analyzed in detail, showing an improvement of the support and confidence values of useful association rules for marketing purposes.

Chapter III, *Web Usage Mining for Ontology Management* by Brigitte Trousse, Marie-Aude Aufaure, Bénédicte Le Grand, Yves Lechevallier, and Florent Masseglia proposes an original approach for ontology management in the context of Web-based information systems. Their approach relies on the usage analysis of the chosen Web site, in complement of the existing approaches based on content analysis of Web pages. One major contribution of this chapter is then the application of usage analysis to support ontology evolution and/or web site reorganization.

Chapter IV, *SOM-Based Clustering of Multilingual Documents Using an Ontology* by Minh Hai Pham, Delphine Bernhard, Gayo Diallo, Radja Messai, and Michel Simonet presents a method which make use of Self Organizing Map (SOM) to cluster medical documents. The originality of the method is that it does not rely on the words shared by documents but rather on concepts taken from ontology. The goal is to cluster various medical documents in thematically consistent groups. Authors have compared the results for two indexing schemes: stem-based indexing and conceptual indexing.

Section II: Findings comprise more theoretical aspects of data mining with ontologies such as ontologies for interpretation and validation and domain ontologies.

Chapter V, *Ontology-Based Interpretation and Validation of Mined Knowledge: Normative and Cognitive Factors in Data Mining* by Ana Isabel Canhoto, addresses the role of cognition and context in the interpretation and validation of mined knowledge. She proposes the use of ontology charts and norm specifications to map how varying levels of access to information and exposure to specific social norms lead to divergent views of mined knowledge. Domain knowledge and bias information influence which patterns in the data are deemed as useful and, ultimately, valid.

Chapter VI, *Data Integration Through Protein Ontology* by Amandeep S. Sidhu, Tharam S. Dillon, and Elizabeth Chang discuss conceptual framework of Protein Ontology that has a hierarchical classification of concepts represented as classes, from general to specific; a list of attributes related to each concept, for each class; a set of relations between classes to link concepts in ontology in more complicated ways than implied by the hierarchy, to promote reuse of concepts in the ontology; and a set of algebraic operators to query protein ontology instances.

Chapter VII, *TtoO: Mining a Thesaurus and Texts to Build and Update a Domain Ontology* by Josiane Mothe and Nathalie Hernandez introduces a method re-using a thesaurus built for a given domain, in order to create new resources of a higher semantic level in the form of an ontology. The originality of the method is that it is based on both the knowledge extracted from a thesaurus and the knowledge semiautomatically extracted from a textual corpus. In parallel, authors have developed mechanisms based on the obtained ontology to accomplish a science-monitoring task. An example is provided in this chapter.

Chapter VIII, *Evaluating the Construction of Domain Ontologies for Recommender Systems Based on Texts* by Stanley Loh, Daniel Lichtnow, Thyago Borges, and Gustavo Piltcher, investigates different aspects in the construction of domain ontology to a content-based recommender system. The chapter discusses different approaches so as to construct the domain ontology, including the use of text mining software tools for supervised learning, the interference of domain experts in the engineering process and the use of a normalization step.

Section III: Frameworks includes different architectures for different domains in data warehousing or mining with ontologies context.

Chapter IX, *Enhancing the Process of Knowledge Discovery in Geographic Databases Using Geo-Ontologies* by Vania Bogorny, Paulo Martins Engel, and Luis Otavio Alvares introduces the problem of mining frequent geographic patterns and spatial association rules from geographic databases. A large amount of natural geographic associations are explicitly represented in geographic database schemas and geo-ontologies, which have not been used so far in frequent geographic pattern mining. The main goal of this chapter is to show how the large amount of knowledge represented in geo-ontologies as prior knowledge can be used to avoid the extraction of patterns previously known as noninteresting.

Chapter X, *Ontology-Based Construction of Grid Data Mining Workflows* by Peter Brezany, Ivan Janciak, and A Min Tjoa, introduces an ontology-based framework for automated construction of complex interactive data mining workflows. The authors present their solution called GridMiner Assistant (GMA), which addresses the whole life cycle of the knowledge discovery process. In addition, conceptual and implementation architectures of the framework are presented and its application to an example taken from the medical domain is illustrated.

Chapter XI, *Ontology-Based Data Warehousing and Mining Approaches in Petroleum Industries* by Shastri L. Nimmagadda and Heinz Dreher. Complex geo-spatial heterogeneous data structures complicate the accessibility and presentation of data in petroleum industries. Data warehousing approach supported by ontology will be described for effective data mining. Ontology based data warehousing framework with fine-grained multidimensional data structures facilitates mining and visualization of data patterns, trends, and correlations hidden under massive volumes of data.

Chapter XII, *A Framework for Integrating Ontologies and Pattern-Bases* by Evangelos Kotsifakos, Gerasimos Marketos, and Yannis Theodoridis propose the integration of pattern base management systems (PBMS) and ontologies. It is as a solution to the need of many scientific fields for efficient extraction of useful information from large databases and the exploitation of knowledge. Authors use a case study of data mining over scientific (seismological) data to illustrate their proposal.

BOOK OBJECTIVE

This book aims at publishing original academic work with high quality scientific papers. The key objective is to provide to data mining students, practitioners, professionals, professors and researchers an integral vision of the topic. This book specifically focuses on those areas that explore new methodologies or examine real study cases that are ontology-based

The book describes the state-of-the-art, innovative theoretical frameworks, advanced and successful implementations as well as the latest empirical research findings in the area of data mining with ontologies.

AUDIENCE

The target audience of this book is readers who want to learn how to apply data mining based on ontologies to real world problems. The purpose is to show users how to go from theory and algorithms to real applications.

The book is also geared toward students, practitioners, professionals, professors and researchers with basic understanding in data mining. The information technology community can increase its knowledge and skills with these new techniques.

People working on the Knowledge Management area such as engineers, managers, and analysts can read it, due to the fact that data mining, ontologies and knowledge management areas are linked straightforwardly.

REFERENCES

Bernstein, A., Hill, S., & Provost, F. (2001). *Towards intelligent assistance for the data mining process: An ontology-based approach.* CeDER Working Paper IS-02-02, New York University.

Bernstein, A., Provost, F., & Hill, S. (2005). Towards intelligent assistance for the data mining process: An ontology-based approach for cost/sensitive classification. In *IEEE Transactions on Knowledge and Data Engineering, 17*(4), 503-518.

Bogorny, V., Engel, P. M., & Alvares, L.O. (2005). Towards the reduction of spatial join for knowledge discovery in geographic databases using geo-ontologies and spatial integrity constraints. In M. Ackermann, B. Berendt, M. Grobelink, & V. Avatek (Eds.), *Proceedings ECML/PKDD Second Workshop on Knowledge Discovery and Ontologies* (pp. 51-58).

Bounif, H., Spaccapietra, S., & Pottinger, R. (2006, September 12-15). *Requirements ontology and multi-representation strategy for database schema evolution.* Paper presented at the 2nd VLDB Workshop on Ontologies-based techniques for Databases and Information Systems. Seoul, Korea.

Brezany, P., Janciak, I., Woehrer, A., & Tjoa, A.M. (2004). *GridMiner: A framework for knowledge discovery on the Grid from a vision to design and implementation.* Cracow Grid Workshop. Cracow, Poland: Springer.

Bridewell, W., Sánchez, J. N., Langley, P., & Billwen, D. (2006). An Interactive environment for the modeling on discovery of scientific knowledge. *International Journal of Human-Computer Studies*, 64, 1009-1014.

Cannataro, M., & Comito, C. (2003, May 20-24). *A data mining ontology for Grid programming.* Paper presented at the I Workshop on Semantics Peer to Peer and Grid Computing. Budapest. Retrieved March, 2006, from http://www.isi.edu/~stefan/SemPGRID

Cannataro, M., Congiusta, A. Pugliese, A., Talia, D., & Trunfio, P. (2004). Distributed data mining on Grids: Services, tools, and applications. *IEEE Transactions on Systems, Man and Cybernetics, Part B, 34*(6), 2451-2465.

Cimiano, P., Stumme, G., Hotho, A., & Tane, J. (2004). Conceptual knowledge processing with formal concept analysis and ontologies. In *Proceedings of The Second International Conference on Formal Concept Analysis (ICFCA 04)*.

Corcho, O., Fernández-López, M., & Gómez-Pérez, A. (2003). Methodologies, tools and languages for building ontologies: where is their meeting point? *Data & Knowledge Engineering 46*(1), 41-64. Amsterdam: Elsevier Science Publishers B. V.

Fayyad, U., Piatetsky-Shiapiro, G., Smyth, P., & Uthurusamy R. (1996). *Advances in knowledge discovery and data mining*. Merlo Park, California: AAAI Press.

Gómez Pérez, A., & Manzano Macho, D., (Eds.) (2003). *Survey of ontology learning methods and techniques*. Deliverable 1.5 OntoWeb Project Documentation. Universidad Politécnica de Madrid. Retrieved November, 2006, from http://www.deri.at/fileadmin/documents/deliverables/Ontoweb/D1.5.pdf

Gottgtroy, P., Kasabov, N., & MacDonell, S. (2003, December). An ontology engineering approach for knowledge discovery from data in evolving domains. In *Proceedings of Data Mining 2003 Data Mining IV*. Boston: WIT.

Gottgtroy, P., MacDonell, S., Kasabov, N., & Jain, V. (2005). *Enhancing data analysis with Ontologies and OLAP*. Paper presented at Data Mining 2005, Sixth International Conference on Data Mining, Text Mining and their Business Applications, Skiathos, Greece.

Gruber, T. (1993). A translation Approach to Portable Ontology Specification. *Knowledge Acquisitions*, 5(2), 199-220.

Gruber, T. (2002). *What is an ontology?* Retrieved November, 2006, from http://www-ksl.stanford.edu/kst/what-is-an-ontology.html

Han, J., & Kamber, M. (2001). *Data mining: Concepts and techniques*. Morgan Kaufmann.

Hernández Orallo, J., Ramírez Quintana, M., & Ferri Ramirez, C. (2004). *Introducción a la Minería de Datos*. Madrid: Editorial Pearson Educación SA.

Hotho, A., Staab, S., & Stumme, G. (2003). Ontologies improve text document clustering. In *Proceedings of the 3rd IEEE Conference on Data Mining*, Melbourne, FL, (pp.541-544).

Langley, P. (2000). The computational support of scientific discovery. *International Journal of Human-Computer Studies*, 53, 393-410.

Langley P. (2006). *Knowledge, data, and search in computational discovery*. Invited talk at International Workshop on feature selection for data mining: Interfacing machine learning and statistics, (FSDM) April 22, 2006, Bethesda, Maryland in conjunction with 2006 SIAM Conference on data mining (SDM).

Pan, D., & Shen, J. Y. (2005). Ontology service-based architecture for continuous knowledge discovery. In *Proceedings of International Conference on Machine Learning and Cybernetics*, 4, 2155-2160. IEEE Press.

Pan, D., & Pan, Y. (2006, June 21-23). Using ontology repository to support data mining. In *Proceedings of the Sixth World Congress on Intelligent Control and Automation*, Dalian, China, (pp. 5947-5951).

Rennolls, K. (2005). An intelligent framework (O-SS-E) For data mining, knowledge discovery and business intelligence. Keynote Paper. In *Proceeding 2nd International Workshop on Philosophies and Methodologies for Knowledge Discovery*, PMKD'05, in the DEXA'05 Workshops (pp. 715-719). IEEE Computer Society Press. ISBN 0-7695-2424-9.

Singh, S., Vajirkar, P., & Lee, Y. (2003). Context-based data mining using ontologies. In Song, I., Liddle, S. W., Ling, T. W., & Scheuermann, P. (Eds.), *Proceedings 22nd International Conference on Conceptual Modeling*. Lecture Notes in Computer Science (vol. 2813, pp. 405-418). Springer.

Spyns, P., Meersman, R., & Jarrar, M. (2002). Data modeling versus ontology engineering, *SIGMOD Record Special Issue on Semantic Web, Database Management and Information Systems*, 31.

Acknowledgment

First, we wish to express our sincere gratitude to Dr. Mehdi Khosrow-Pour, senior academics editor, and Jan Travers, managing director for the opportunity they give us, and whose enthusiasm motivated our accepting their invitation for taking on this project.

Special thanks also to all the staff at IGI Global, whose contribution throughout the whole process from inception of the initial idea to final publication have been invaluable. In particular, to Kristin Roth, development editor and Meg Stocking, assistant development editor for their helpful advise on how to solve some problems and for their guidance and professional support. We thank our first assigned assistant development editor, Lynley Lapp, as well.

We deeply appreciate the support of Laura Rivero, Viviana Ferraggine and Jorge Doorn. They have provided unconditional assistance, and they have also offered their inestimable experience as editors.

Most of the authors of the chapters included in this book also served as referees for articles written by other authors, without whose support the project could not have been satisfactorily completed. Special thanks go to all those who provided constructive and comprehensive reviews.

External reviewers who provided comprehensive, critical, and constructive comments were Paulo Gottgtroroy and Stephen MacDonell of Knowledge Engineering and Discovery Research Institute, School of Computer and Information Sciences, Auckland University of Technology.

Once again, as editors, we would like to thank the contributor's authors for their excellent papers and patience with the process. Making this kind of compilation is a huge responsibility and it has brought about people with varied experience and analysis.

Finally, we want to thank our families for their love and support throughout this project.

Héctor Oscar Nigro
Sandra González Císaro
Daniel Xodo
Tandil, Argentina, May 2007

Section I
Implementations

Chapter I
TODE:
An Ontology-Based Model for the Dynamic Population of Web Directories

Sofia Stamou
Patras University, Greece

Alexandros Ntoulas
University of California Los Angeles (UCLA), USA

Dimitris Christodoulakis
Patras Univeristy, Greece

ABSTRACT

*In this chapter we study how we can organize the continuously proliferating Web content into topical categories, also known as Web directories. In this respect, we have implemented a system, named TODE that uses a **T**opical **O**ntology for **D**irectories' **E**diting. First, we describe the process for building our ontology of Web topics, which are treated in TODE as directories' topics. Then, we present how TODE interacts with the ontology in order to categorize Web pages into the ontology's topics and we experimentally study our system's efficiency in grouping Web pages thematically. We evaluate TODE's performance by comparing its resulting categorization for a number of pages to the categorization the same pages display in the Google directory as well as to the categorizations delivered for the same set of pages and topics by a Bayesian classifier. Results indicate that our model has a noticeable potential in reducing the human-effort overheads associated with populating Web directories. Furthermore, experimental results imply that the use of a rich topical ontology increases significantly classification accuracy for dynamic contents.*

INTRODUCTION

Millions of users today access the plentiful Web content to locate information that is of interest to them. However, as the Web grows larger the task of locating relevant information within a huge network of data sources is becoming daunting. Currently, there are two predominant approaches for finding information on the Web, namely searching and browsing (Olston & Chi, 2003). In the process of searching, users visit a Web search engine (e.g., Google) and specify a query that best describes what they are looking for. During browsing, users visit a Web directory (e.g., the Yahoo! directory), which maintains the Web organized in subject hierarchies, and navigate through these hierarchies in the hope of locating the relevant information. The construction of a variety of Web directories in the last few years (such as the Yahoo! directory (http://yahoo.com), the Open Directory Project (ODP) (http://dmoz.org), the Google directory (http://dir.google.com) etc.) indicates that Web directories have gained popularity as means for locating information on the Web.

Typically, the information provided by a Web search engine is automatically collected from the Web without any human intervention. However, the construction and maintenance of a Web directory involves a staggering amount of human effort because it is necessary to assign an accurate subject to every page inside the Web directory. To illustrate the size of the effort necessary, one can simply consider the fact that Dmoz, one of the largest Web directories, relies on more than 65,000 volunteers around the world to locate and incorporate relevant information in the directory. Given a Web page, one or more volunteers need to read it and understand its subject, and then examine Dmoz's existing Web directory of more than 590,000 subjects to find the best fit for the page. Clearly, if we could help the volunteers automate their tasks we would save a lot of time for a number of people.

One way to go about automating the volunteers' tasks of categorizing pages is to consider it as a classification problem. That is, given an existing hierarchy of subjects (say the Dmoz existing hierarchy) and a number of pages, we can use one of the many machine learning techniques to build a classifier which can potentially assign a subject to every Web page. One problem with this approach however, is that in general it requires a training set. That is, in order to build an effective classifier we need to first train it on a set of pages which have already been marked with a subject from the hierarchy. Typically this is not a big inconvenience if both the collection that we need to classify and the hierarchy are static. As a matter of fact, as shown in (Chakrabarti et al., 1998a; Chen & Dumais, 2000; Huang et al., 2004; Mladenic, 1998), this approach can be quite effective. However, in a practical situation, neither the Web nor the subject hierarchies are static. For example, previous studies have shown that eight percent of new pages show up on the Web every week (Ntoulas et al., 2004) and Dmoz's subject hierarchy is undergoing a variety of changes every month[1]. Therefore, in the case of the changing Web and subject hierarchy, one would need to recreate the training set and re-train the classifier every time a change was made.

In this chapter, we present a novel approach for constructing a Web directory, which does not require a training set of pages, and therefore can cope very easily with changes on the Web or the subject hierarchy. The only input that our method requires is the subject hierarchy from a Web directory that one would like to use and the Web pages that one would like to assign to the directory. At a very high level our method proceeds as follows: first, we enrich the subject hierarchy of the Web directory by leveraging a variety of resources created by the natural language processing community and which are freely available. This process is discussed in Section 2. Then, we process the pages one by one and identify the most important terms inside every page and we link them together, creating "lexical chains," which we will describe in Section 3. Finally, we use the enriched hierarchy and the lexical chains to compute one or more subjects to assign to every page, as shown in Section 4. After applying our method on a real Web directory's hierarchy and a set of 320,000 Web pages we conclude that, in certain cases, our method has an accuracy of 90.70 percent into automatically assigning the Web pages to the same category that was selected by a human. Our experimental results are presented in Section 5.

In summary, we believe that our work makes the following contributions:

- **Untangling the Web via an ontology:** We introduce an ontology[2] that has been designed to serve as a reference guide for grouping Web pages into topical categories. In particular, we report on the distinct knowledge bases that have been merged together to form the ontology. The resulting joint ontology was further augmented with a top level of topics, which are borrowed from the Google directory subject hierarchy. We explore the ontology's lexical hierarchies to compute chains of thematic words for the Web pages. Dealing with lexical chains rather than full content, reduces significantly both the categorization process overhead and the computational effort of comparing pages, as we will shown in Section 4.
- **Bringing order to directories' contents:** We use the ontology to deliver a comprehensive ordering of Web pages into directories and to prune directories' overpopulation. In particular, we introduce DirectoryRank, a metric that sorts the pages assigned to each directory in terms of both their relatedness to the directory's topic and their correlation to other "important" pages grouped in the same directory.
- **Keeping up with the evolving Web:** The immense size of the Web is prohibitive for

thoroughly investigating the information sources that exist out there. Our model enables the incremental editing of Web directories and can efficiently cope with the evolving Web. The efficiency of our system is well supported by empirical evidence, which proves that it gives good results and scales well. Therefore, directories remain "fresh" upon index updates and newly downloaded pages are accessible through Web catalogs, almost readily.

To the best of our knowledge, our study is the first to make explicit use of an ontology of Web-related topics to dynamically assign Web pages to directories. Our goal reaches beyond classification per se, and focuses on providing the means via which our ontology-based categorization model could be convenient in terms of both time and effort on behalf of Web cataloguers in categorizing pages. In particular, we show that our approach can serve as a good alternative to today's practices in populating Web directories.

We start our discussion by presenting how to enrich an existing subject hierarchy with information from the suggested upper merged ontology (http://ontology.teknowledge.com), WordNet (http://www.cogsco.princeton.edu/~wn) and MultiWordNet Domains (http://wndomains.itc. it). Construction of lexical chains is presented in Section 3, while Section 4 shows how to employ the lexical chains to assign Web pages to the subject hierarchy. Our experimental results are shown in Section 5 and we conclude our work in Sections 6 and 7.

BUILDING AN ONTOLOGY FOR THE WEB

Traditionally, ontologies are built in order to represent generic knowledge about a target world (Bunge, 1977). An ontology defines a set of representational terms, referred to as concepts, which describe abstract ideas in the target world and which can be related to each other. For example, in an ontology representing all living creatures, "human" and "mammal" might be two of the concepts and these two concepts might be connected with a relation "is-a" (i.e., human "is-a" mammal). Typically, ontologies' concepts are depicted as nodes on a graph and the relations between concepts as arcs. For example, Figure 1 shows a fraction of an ontology for the topic *Arts*, represented as a directed acyclic graph, where each node denotes a concept that is interconnected to other concepts via a specialization ("is-a") relation, represented by the dashed arcs. Concepts that are associated with a single parent concept via an "is-a" link are considered disjoint.

Depending on the application, there are different ways of developing an ontology. The usefulness, however, of an ontology lies in the fact that it presents knowledge in a way easy to understand by humans. For our purpose of generating a Web directory, we chose to develop an ontology that would describe humans' perceptions of the most popular topics that are communicated via the Web. Consequently, we define our ontology as a hierarchy of topics that are currently used by Web cataloguers in order to categorize Web pages in

topics. To ensure that our ontology would define concepts that are representative of the Web's topical content, we borrowed the ontology's top level concepts from the topic categories of the Google directory. Moreover, to guarantee that our ontology would be of good quality, we preferred to obtain our ontology's conceptual hierarchies from existing ontological resources that have proved to be richly encoded and useful. In order to build our ontology we used three different sources:

1. The suggested upper merged ontology (SUMO). SUMO is a generic ontology of more than 1,000 domain concepts that have been mapped to every WordNet synset that is related to them.

2. WordNet 2.0. WordNet is a lexical network of more than 118K synonym sets (synsets) that are linked to other synsets on the basis of their semantic properties and/or features.

3. The MultiWordNet Domains (MWND). MWND is an augmented version of Word-Net; a resource that assigns every WordNet[3] synset a domain label among the total set of 165 hierarchically structured domains it consists of.

Figure 1. A portion of the ontology for the Arts topic category

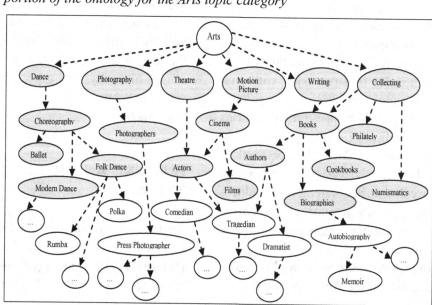

The reason for using the above resources to build our ontology is the fact that they have been proven to be useful in resolving sense ambiguities, which is crucial in text categorization. Additionally, because the above resources are mapped to WordNet, our task of merging them into a common ontology is easier. Part of our ontology is illustrated in Figure 1. Our ontology has three different layers: the top layer corresponds to topics (arts in our case), the middle layer to subtopics (for example photography, dance, etc.) and the lower level corresponds to WordNet hierarchies, whose elements are hyponyms of the middle level concepts. We describe the selection of the topics in every layer next.

The Top Level Topics

The ontology' top level concepts were chosen manually and they represent topics employed by Web cataloguers to categorize pages by subject. In selecting the topical categories, we operated based on the following dual requirement: (1) our topics should be popular (or else useful) among the Web users and (2) they should be sufficiently represented within WordNet, in order to guarantee that our ontology would be rich in concept hierarchies. To that end, we borrowed topics from the Google directory taxonomy, thus satisfying our popularity requirement. Subsequently, we manually checked the topics against WordNet hierarchies and all Google directory topic concepts found in WordNet and which had deep and dense

Table 1. The ontology's root concepts

First Level Topics	
Arts	News
Sports	Society
Games	Computers
Home	Reference
Shopping	Recreation
Business	Science
Health	

subordinate hierarchies were retained, thus fulfilling the WordNet representation requirement. Eventually, we came down to totally 13 Google directory first level topics, for which there was sufficient information within the WordNet hierarchies. These topics formed the ontology's root concepts and are shown on Table 1.

The Middle and Lower Level Concepts

Middle level concepts were determined by merging MWND and SUMO into a single combined resource. Merging SUMO hierarchies and MWND domains into a common ontology was generally determined by the semantic similarity that the concepts of the distinct hierarchies exhibit, where semantic similarity is defined as a correlation of: (1) the length of the path that connects two concepts in the shared hierarchy and (2) the number of common concepts that subsume two concepts in the hierarchy (Resnik, 1999).

The parent concept of every merged hierarchy was then searched in the ontology's 13 top level topics (borrowed from the Google directory) and if there was a matching found, this merged hierarchy was integrated with this top level concept For instance, consider the SUMO hierarchies of the domain "swimming" and the hierarchies that have been assigned the MWND domain "sport." Due to their hierarchies' overlapping elements in WordNet, "sport" and "swimming" were integrated in a common parent concept, that is, "sport." Because this parent concept is also a top level topic (*Sports/Athletics*), the merged hierarchies are assigned to the ontology's topic *Sports/Athletics*.

If no matching was found between the merged hierarchy's parent concept and the ontology's topics, the direct hypernyms of the parent concept were retrieved from WordNet and searched within the ontology's 13 top level topics. If there was a matching found, the merged hierarchy was integrated with the top level topic via the "is-a" relation. This way the joint hierarchy's parent concept becomes a subdomain in one of the ontology's 13 topics, and denotes a middle level concept in the ontology. As an example, consider the SUMO domain concept "computer program," whose corresponding hierarchies have been integrated with the hierarchies of the MWND domain "applied science." Following merging, the joint hierarchies' parent concept was searched in the ontology's top level concepts. Because this parent concept was not among the ontology's topics, its WordNet direct hypernyms were retrieved and searched in the ontology's topics. Among the hypernyms of the concept "applied science" is the concept "science," which is also a top level topic in the ontology. As such, the hierarchies merged into the "applied science" concept, were integrated into the *Science* topic, and their common parent concept becomes a middle level concept in the ontology.

Following the steps previously described, we integrated in the ontology's top level topics all SUMO and MWND hierarchies for which there was sufficient evidence in WordNet to support our judgments for their merging. The hierarchies that remained disjoint at the end of this process were disregarded from the ontology. Although, we could have examined more WordNet hypernyms (i.e., higher level concepts), in an attempt to find a common parent concept to merge the remaining SUMO and MWND disjoint hierarchies, we decided not to do so, in order to weed out too abstract concepts from the ontology's middle level concepts. Our decision was based on the intuition that the higher a concept is in a hierarchy, the greater the likelihood that it is a coarse grained concept that may lead to obscure distinctions about the pages' topics. At the end of the merging process, we came down to a total set of 489 middle level concepts, which were subsequently organized into the 13 top level topics, using their respective WordNet relations. The resulting upper level ontology (i.e., top and middle level concepts) is a directed acyclic graph with maximum depth 6

and branching factor, 28 (i.e., number of children concepts from a node). Finally, we anchored to each middle level concept all WordNet hierarchies that encounter a specialization link to any of the ontology's middle level concepts. The elements in WordNet hierarchies formed our ontology's lower level concepts.

REDUCING PAGES TO LEXICAL CHAINS

In this section, we show how to leverage the ontology that we generated, in order to detect which of the Web pages' words are informative of the page's theme. At a high level, we explore the ontology's concepts while processing Web pages in order to find the pages' thematic words. This results into generating for every page a sequence of lexical elements, known as lexical chains. Lexical chains communicate the pages' thematic contents and they will be used later on to determine the Web pages' topical categories.

Finding Web Pages' Thematic Words

The main intuition in our approach for categorizing Web pages is that topic relevance estimation of a page relies on the page's lexical coherence, that is, having a substantial portion of words associated with the same topic. To capture this property, we adopt the lexical chaining approach and, for every page, we generate a sequence of semantically related terms, known as lexical chain.

The computational model we adopted for generating lexical chains is presented in the work of Barzilay and Elhadad (1997), and it generates lexical chains in a three steps approach: (1) select a set of candidate terms[4] from the page, (2) for each candidate term, find an appropriate chain relying on a relatedness criterion among members of the chains, and (3) if it is found, insert the term in the chain and update accordingly. The relatedness factor in the second step is determined by

Figure 2. A lexical chain example

Lexical chain
system $_{s6}$ → network $_{s4}$
system $_{s6}$ → sensor $_{s1}$
system $_{s6}$ → weapon $_{s2}$ → missile $_{s1}$
system $_{s6}$ → surface $_{s1}$ → net $_{s2}$

the type of the links that are used in WordNet for connecting the candidate term to the terms that are already stored in existing lexical chains. Figure 2 illustrates an example of the lexical chain generated for a text containing the candidate terms: system, network, sensor, weapon, missile, surface, and net. The subscript *si* denotes the id of the word's sense within WordNet[5].

Having generated lexical chains, we disambiguate the sense of the words inside every chain by employing the scoring function *f*, introduced in Song et al., (2004), which indicates the probability that a word relation is a correct one. Given two words, w_1 and w_2, their scoring function *f* via a relation *r*, depends on the words' association scores, their depth in WordNet, and their respective relation weight. The association score (*Assoc*) of the word pair (w_1, w_2) is determined by the words' co-occurrence frequency in a generic corpus that has been previously collected. In practice, the greater the association score between a word pair w_1 and w_2 is, the greater the likelihood that w_1 and w_2 refer to the same topic. Formally, the (*Assoc*) score of the word pair (w_1, w_2) is given by:

$$Assoc(w_1, w_2) = \frac{\log\,(p\,(w_1, w_2) + 1)}{N_s\,(w_1) \cdot N_s\,(w_2)}$$

where $p(w_1, w_2)$ is the corpus co-occurrence probability of the word pair (w_1, w_2) and $N_s(w)$ is a normalization factor, which indicates the number of WordNet senses that a word *w* has.

Given a word pair (w_1, w_2) their *DepthScore* expresses the words' position in WordNet hierarchy and is defined as:

$$DepthScore(w_1, w_2)$$
$$= Depth(w_1)^2 \cdot Depth(w_2)^2$$

where *Depth* (*w*) is the depth of word *w* in WordNet and indicates that the deeper a word is in the WordNet hierarchy, the more specific meaning it has.

Within the WordNet lexical network two words w_1 and w_2 are connected through one or more relations. For example, the words "computer" and "calculator" are connected through a synonymy relation, while the words "computer" and "server" are connected through a hyponymy relation. In our framework, semantic relation weights (*RelationWeight*) have been experimentally fixed to 1 for reiteration, 0.2 for synonymy and hyper/ hyponymy, 0.3 for antonymy, 0.4 for mero/holonymy and 0.005 for siblings. The scoring function *f* of w_1 and w_2 is defined as:

$$f_s(w_1, w_2, r) = Assoc\,(w_1, w_2)$$
$$\cdot DepthScore(w_1, w_2) \cdot \mathrm{Re}\,lationWeight\,(r)$$

The value of the function *f* represents the probability that the relation type *r* is the correct one between words w_1 and w_2. In order to disambiguate the senses of the words within lexical chain C_i we calculate its score, by summing up the f_s scores of all the words w_{j1} w_{j2} (where w_{j1} and w_{j2} are successive words) within the chain C_i. Formally, the score of lexical chain C_i, is expressed as the sum of the score of each relation r_j in C_i.

$$Score(C_i) = \sum_{r_j\,in\,C_j} f_s\,(w_{j1}, w_{j2}, r_j)$$

Eventually, in order to disambiguate, we will pick the relations and senses that maximize the *Score* (C_i) for that particular chain.

To compute a single lexical chain for every downloaded Web page, we segment the latter into shingles (Broader et al., 1997), and for every shingle, we generate scored lexical chains, as described before. If a shingle produces multiple chains, the lexical chain of the highest score is considered as the most representative chain for the shingle. In this way, we eliminate chain ambiguities. We then compare the overlap between the elements of all shingles' lexical chains consecutively. Elements that are shared across chains are deleted so that lexical chains display no redundancy. The remaining elements are merged together into a single chain, representing the contents of the entire page, and a new $Score(C_i)$ for the resulting chain C_i is computed.

POPULATING WEB DIRECTORIES

We have so far described how Web pages are reduced into sequences of thematic words, which are utilized by our model for categorizing Web pages to the ontology's topics. Here, we analyze how our model (TODE) populates topic directories and we evaluate its efficiency in categorizing roughly 320,000 real Web pages.

Assigning Web Pages to Topic Directories

In order to assign a topic to a Web page, our method operates on the page's thematic words. Specifically, we map every thematic word of a page to the hierarchy's topics and we follow the hierarchy's hypernymic links of every matching topic upwards until we reach a root node. For short documents with very narrow subjects this process might yield only one matching topic. However, due to both the great variety of the Web data and the richness of the hierarchy, it is often the case that a page contains thematic words corresponding to multiple root topics.

To accommodate multiple topic assignment, a *Relatedness Score* (*RScore*) is computed for every Web page to each of the hierarchy's matching topics. This *RScore* indicates the expressiveness of each of the hierarchy's topics in describing the page's content. Formally, the *RScore* of a page represented by the lexical chain C_i to the hierarchy's topic D_k is defined as the product of the chain's $Score(C_i)$ and the fraction of the chain's elements that belong to topic D_k. We define the *Relatedness Score* of the page to each of the hierarchy's matching topics as:

$$RScore\ (i,\ k) =$$

$$\frac{Score(C_i) \cdot \#of\ C_i\ elements\ of\ D_k\ matched}{\left| \#of\ C_i\ elements \right|}$$

The denominator is used to remove any effect the length of a lexical chain might have on *RScore* and ensures that the final score is normalized so that all values are between 0 and 1, with 0 corresponding to no relatedness at all and 1 indicating the category that is highly expressive of the page's topic. Finally, a Web page is assigned to the topical category D_k for which it has the highest relatedness score of all its *RScores* above a threshold T, with T been experimentally fixed to $T = 0.5$. The page's indexing score is:

$$IScore\ (i,\ k) = \max RScore\ (i,\ k)$$

Pages with chain elements matching several topics in the hierarchy, and with relatedness scores to any of the matching topics below T, are categorized in all their matching topics. By allowing pages to be categorized in multiple topics, we ensure there is no information loss during the directories' population and that pages with short content (i.e., short lexical chains) are not unquestionably discarded as less informative.

Ordering Web Pages in Topic Directories

Admittedly, the relatedness score of a page to a directory topic does not suffice as a measurement for ordering the pages that are listed in the same directory topic. This is because *RScore* is not a good indicator of the amount of content that these pages share. Herein, we report on the computation of semantic similarities among the pages that are listed in the same directory topic. Semantic similarity is indicative of the pages' correlation and helps us determine the ordering of the pages that are deemed related to the same topic.

To estimate the semantic similarity between a set of pages, we compare the elements in a page's lexical chain to the elements in the lexical chains of the other pages in a directory topic. Our intuition is that the more elements the chains of two pages have in common, the more correlated the pages are to each other. To compute similarities between pages, P_i and P_j that are assigned to the same topic, we first need to identify the common elements between their lexical chains, represented as PC_i and PC_j respectively. Then, we use the hierarchy to augment the elements of the chains PC_i and PC_j with their synonyms. Chain augmentation ensures that pages of comparable content are not regarded unrelated if their lexical chains contain distinct but semantically equivalent elements (i.e., synonyms). The augmented elements of PC_i and PC_j respectively, are defined as:

$$AugElements(PC_i) = C_i \bigcup SynC_i$$

and

$$AugElements(PC_j) = C_j \bigcup SynC_j,$$

where, $SynC_i$ denotes the set of the ontology's concepts that are synonyms to any of the elements in C_i and $SynC_j$ denotes the set of the ontology's concepts that are synonyms to any of the elements in C_j. The common elements

between the augmented lexical chains PC_i and PC_j, are determined as:

$$ComElements(PC_i, PC_j)$$
$$= AugElements_i \bigcap AugElements_j$$

We formally define the problem of computing pages' semantic similarities as follows: if pages P_i and P_j share elements in common, produce the correlation look up table with triples of the form *<AugElements (PC_i), AugElements (PC_j), ComElements>*. The similarity measurement between the lexical chains PC_i, PC_j of the pages P_i and P_j is computed as follows:

$$\sigma_S(PC_i, PC_j) = \frac{2 \cdot \left| ComElements \right|}{\left| AugElements_i \right| + \left| AugElements_j \right|}$$

where, the degree of semantic similarity is normalized so that all values are between zero and one, with 0 indicating that the two pages are totally different and 1 indicating that the two pages talk about the same thing.

Ranking Pages in Directories

Pages are sorted in directory topics on the basis of a DirectoryRank metric, which defines the importance of the pages with respect to the particular topics in the directory. Note that in the context of Web Directories, we perceive the amount of information that a page communicates about some directory topic to be indicative of the page's importance with respect to the given topic.

DirectoryRank (*DR*) measures the quality of a page in some topic by the degree to which the page correlates to other informative/qualitative pages in the given topic. Intuitively, an informative page in a topic, is a page that has a high relatedness score to the directory's topic and that is semantically close (similar) to many other pages in that topic. *DR* defines the quality of a page to be the sum of its topic relatedness score and its overall similarity to the fraction of pages with which it correlates in the given topic. This way, if a page is highly related to topic D and also correlates highly with many informative pages in D, its DR score will be high.

Formally, consider that page p_i is indexed in directory topic T_k with some $RScore\ (p_i, T_k)$ and let $p_1, p_2, ..., p_n$ be pages in T_k with which p_i semantically correlates with scores of $\sigma_s (PC_1, PC_i)$, $\sigma_s (PC_2, PC_i),..., \sigma_s (PC_n, PC_i)$, respectively. Then, the directoryRank (DR) of p_i is given by:

$$DR\ (p_i, T_k)\ =\ RScore\ (p_i, T_k)$$
$$+\ \left[\sigma_s\ (PC_1, PC_i)\ +\ \sigma_s\ (PC_2, PC_i)\right.$$
$$+\ ......\ +\ \left.\sigma_s\ (PC_n, PC_i)\right]\ /\ n$$

where n corresponds to the total number of pages in topic T_k with which p_i semantically correlates. High DR values imply that: (1) there are some "good quality" sources among the data stored in the directory, and that (2) more users are likely to visit them while browsing the directory's contents. Lastly, it should be noted that similarities are computed offline for all the pages in a directory's topics, regardless of the pages' $RScore$.

EXPERIMENTAL STUDY

We have implemented the experimental TODE prototype using a Pentium 4 server at 2.4 GHz, with 512 MB of main memory. For fast computations of the lexical chains, we stored the ontology's top and middle level (sub)-topics in main memory, while WordNet hierarchies were stored on disk and were accessed through a hashtable whenever necessary. Moreover, words' co-occurrence statistics were precomputed in the corpus and stored in inverted lists, which were again made accessible upon demand. Of course, the execution time of TODE's categorizations

depends on both the number of pages considered and the ontology's coverage. In our experimental setup it took only a few hours to categorize our whole dataset. In order to study the efficiency of our approach in populating Web directories, we conducted an experiment in which we supplied TODE with roughly 320K Web pages, inquiring that these are categorized in the appropriate top or middle level ontology's concepts.

Experimental pages were obtained from the Google directory, because of the Google directory topics' compatibility with our ontology's topics. A less decisive factor for picking our data from the Google directory is because the latter maintains a ranked list of the pages associated with each category. At the end of the experiment, we compared our model's resulting categorizations to the categorizations the same pages displayed for the same topics in Google directory, as well as to the categorizations delivered for the same set of pages and topics by a Naïve Bayes classifier. In this section, we present our experimental data and we discuss TODE's classification performance based on experimental results.

Experimental Data

In selecting our experimental data, we wanted to pick a useful yet representative sample of the Google directory content. By useful, we mean that our sample should comprise Web pages with textual content and not only links, frames or audiovisual data. By representative, we mean that our sample should span those Google directory categories, whose topics are among the top level topics in our subject hierarchy.

In selecting our experimental data, we picked pages that are categorized in those topics in Google directory, which are also present in our hierarchy. Recall that we borrowed our hierarchy's 13 top-level topics form Google directory.

Out of all the subtopics organized in those 13 top-level topics in Google directory, 156 were

Table 2. Statistics on the experimental data

Category	# of documents	# of subtopics
Arts	28,342	18
Sports	20,662	26
Games	11,062	6
Home	6,262	7
Shopping	52,342	15
Business	60,982	7
Health	23,222	7
News	9,462	4
Society	28,662	14
Computers	35,382	13
Reference	13,712	10
Recreation	8,182	20
Science	20,022	9
Total	318,296	156

represented in our hierarchy. Having determined the topics, whose set of pages would be categorized by our system, we downloaded a total number of 318,296 pages, categorized in one of the 156 selected topics, which in turn are organized into the 13 top-level topics. Table 2 shows the statistical distribution of our experimental pages in the selected top level topics in Google directory.

We parsed the downloaded pages and generated their shingles after removing HTML markup. Pages were then tokenized, part-of-speech tagged, lemmatized, and submitted to our classification system, which, following the process described previously, computed and weighted a single lexical chain for every page. To compute lexical chains, our system relied on a resources index, which comprised (1) the 12.6M WordNet 2.0 data for determining the semantic relations that exist between the pages' thematic words, (2) a 0.5GB compressed TREC corpus from which we extracted a total of 340MB binary files for obtaining statistics about word co-occurrence frequencies, and (3) the 11MB top level concepts in our hierarchy.

Since we were interested in evaluating the performance of our approach in automatically categorizing web pages to the ontology's topics, our system generated and scored simple and augmented lexical chains for every page and

based on a combined analysis of this information it indicates the most appropriate topic in the hierarchy to categorize each of the pages.

To measure our system's effectiveness in categorizing Web pages, we experimentally studied its performance against the performance of a Naïve Bayes classifier, which has proved to be efficient for Web scale classification (Duda & Hart, 1973). In particular, we trained a Bayesian classifier by performing a 70/30 split to our experimental data and we used the 70 percent of the downloaded pages in each Google directory topic as a learning corpus. We then tested the performance of the Bayesian classifier in categorizing the remaining 30 percent of the pages in the most suitable Google directory category. For evaluating the classification accuracy of both the Bayesian and our classifier, we used the Google directory categorizations as a comparison testbed, that is, we compared the classification delivered by each of the two classifiers to the classification done by the Google directory cataloguers for the same set of pages. Although, our experimental pages are listed in all subcategories of the Google directory's top level topics, for the experiment presented here, we mainly focus on classifying the Web pages for the top-level topics.

Directories' Population Performance

The overall accuracy results are given in Table 3, whereas Table 4 compares the accuracy rates for each category between the two classifiers. Since our classifier allows pages with low *RScores* to be categorized in multiple topics, in our comparison

Table 3. Overall accuracy results of both classifiers

Classifier	Accuracy	Standard Error Rate
Bayesian	65.95%	0.06%
Ours	69.79%	0.05%

Table 4. Comparison of average accuracy rates between categories for the two classifiers

Category	Bayesian classifier	Our classifer
Arts	67.18%	90.70%
Sports	69.71%	75.15%
Games	60.95%	64.51%
Home	36.56%	40.16%
Shopping	78.09%	71.32%
Business	82.30%	70.74%
Health	64.18%	72.85%
News	8.90%	55.75%
Society	61.14%	88.54%
Computers	63.91%	74.04%
Reference	20.70%	69.23%
Recreation	54.83%	62.38%
Science	49.31%	71.90%

we explored only the topics of the highest *RScores*. Note also that we run the Bayesian classifier five times on our data, every time on a random 70/30 split and we report on the best accuracy rates among all runs for each category.

The overall accuracy rates show that our method has improved classification accuracy compared to Bayesian classification. The most accurate categories in our classification method are *Arts* and *Society*, which give 90.70 percent and 88.54 percent classification accuracy respectively. The underlying reason for the improved accuracy of our classifier in those topics is the fact that our hierarchy is rich in semantic information for those topics. This argument is also attested by the fact that for the topics *Home* and *News*, for which our hierarchy contains a small number of lexical nodes, the classification accuracy of our method is relatively low, that is, 40.16 percent and 55.75 percent, respectively. Nevertheless, even in those topics our classifier outperforms the Bayesian classifier, which gives for the above topics a classification accuracy of 36.56 percent and 8.90 percent. The most straightforward justification for the Bayesian's classifier low accuracy in the topics *Home* and *News* is the limited number of pages that our collection contains about those two topics. This is also in line with the observation that the Bayesian classifier outperforms our

classifier when (1) dealing with a large number of documents, and/ or (2) dealing with documents comprising specialized terminology. The previously mentioned can be attested in the improved classification accuracy of the Bayesian classifier for the categories *Business* and *Shopping*, which both have many documents and whose documents contain specialized terms (e.g., product names) that are underrepresented in our hierarchy.

A general conclusion we can draw from our experiment is that, given a rich topic hierarchy, our method is quite promising in automatically classifying pages and incurs little overhead for Web-scale classification. While there is much room for improvement, and further testing is needed before judging the full potential of our method, nevertheless, based on our findings, we argue that the current implementation of our system could serve as a Web cataloguers' assistant by delivering preliminary categorizations for Web pages. These categorizations could be then further examined by human editors and reordered when necessary. Finally, in our approach, we explore the pages' classification probabilities (i.e., *RScore*) so that, upon ranking, pages with higher *RScores* are prioritized over less related pages. This, in conjunction with the pages' semantic similarities, forms the basis of our ranking formula (DirectoryRank).

RELATED WORK

The automated categorization of Web documents into predefined topics has been investigated in the past. Previous work mainly focuses on using machine learning techniques to build text classifiers. Several methods have been proposed in the literature for the construction of document classifiers, such as decision trees (Apte et al., 1994), Support Vector Machines (Christianini & Shawe-Taylor, 2000), Bayesian classifiers (Pazzani & Billsus, 1997), hierarchical text classifiers (Boypati, 2002; Chakrabarti et al., 1998a; Chen & Dumais, 2000; Huang et al., 2004; Koller & Sahami, 1997; Mladenic, 1998; Ruiz & Srinivasan, 1999; Stamou et al., 2005; Nigam et al., 2000). The main commonality in previous methods is that their classification accuracy depends on a training phase, during which statistical techniques are used to learn a model based on a labeled set of training exampled. This model is then applied for classifying unlabeled data. While these approaches provide good results, they are practically inconvenient for Web data categorization, mainly because it is computationally expensive to continuously gather training examples for the ever-changing Web. The distinctive feature in our approach from other text classification techniques is that our method does not require a training phase, and therefore it is convenient for Web scale classification.

An alternative approach in categorizing Web data implies the use of the Web pages' hyperlinks and/or anchor text in conjunction with text-based classification methods (Chakrabarti et al., 1998b; Furnkranz, 1999; Glover et al., 2002). The main intuition in exploring hypertext for categorizing Web pages relies on the assumption that both the links and the anchor text of Web pages communicate information about the pages' content. But again, classification relies on a training phase, in which labeled examples of anchor text from links pointing to the target documents are employed for building a learning model. This model is subse-

quently applied to the anchor text of unlabeled pages and classifies them accordingly. Finally, the objective in our work (i.e., populating Web Directories) could be addressed from the agglomerative clustering perspective; a technique that treats the generated clusters as a topical hierarchy for clustering documents (Kaufman & Rousseeuw, 1990). The agglomerative clustering methods build the subject hierarchy at the same time as they generate the clusters of the documents. Therefore, the subject hierarchy might be different between successive runs of such an algorithm. In our work, we preferred to build a hierarchy by using existing ontological content, rather than to rely on newly generated clusters, for which we would not have perceptible evidence to support their usefulness for Web data categorization. However, it would be interesting for the future to take a sample of categorized pages and explore it using an agglomerative clustering module.

CONCLUDING REMARKS

We have presented a method, which uses a subject hierarchy to automatically categorize Web pages in directory structures. Our approach extends beyond data classification and challenges issues pertaining to the Web pages' organization within directories and the quality of the categorizations delivered. We have experimentally studied the effectiveness of our approach in categorizing a fraction of Web pages into topical categories, by comparing its classification accuracy to the accuracy of a Bayesian classifier. Our findings indicate that our approach has a promising potential in facilitating current tendencies in editing and maintaining Web directories. It is our hope therefore, that our approach, will road the map for future improvements in populating Web directories and in handling the proliferating Web data.

We now discuss a number of advantages that our approach entails and which we believe could be fruitfully explored by others. The implications of our findings apply primarily to Web cataloguers and catalogue users. Since cataloguers are challenged by the prodigious volume of the Web data that they need to process and categorize into topics, it is of paramount importance that they are equipped with a system that carries out on their behalf a preliminary categorization of pages. We do not imply that humans do not have a critical role to play in directories' population, but we deem their "sine-qua-non" involvement in the evaluation and improvement of the automatically produced categorizations, rather than in the scanning of the numerous pages enqueued for categorization. In essence, we argue that our approach compensates for the rapidly evolving Web, by offering Web cataloguers a preliminary categorization for the pages that they have not processed yet. On the other side of the spectrum, end users are expected to benefit from the Directories' updated content. Given that users get frustrated when they encounter outdated pages every time they access Web catalogs to find new information that interests them, it is vital that directories' contents are up-to-date. Our model ensures that this requirement is fulfilled, since it runs fast and scales up with the evolving Web, enabling immediacy of new data.

FUTURE RESEARCH DIRECTIONS

In the previous sections, we discussed how we can use a topical ontology in order to automatically categorize Web pages to directory structures. Our main contribution is a new ranking function that exploits the ontology along with the semantic similarity between one or more Web pages in order to organize the pages within a directory structure according to their relevance to the directory's underlying topics.

In this section we discuss some further research avenues that could benefit from our proposed method and enable the users better organize and process textual information. At a high level, we believe that our TODE framework can be useful in the following areas: (1) Web search personalization, (2) duplicate page detection, (3) managing of bookmarks. We briefly discuss each one of these areas below.

In the area of Web search personalization, we believe that our ontology can contribute both towards the automatic identification of the user search-interests and the automatic filtering of the retrieved results according to these interests. Our main idea is to leverage the ontology for estimating a user's past preferences based on his past searches, i.e. previously issued queries and pages visited for those queries. We could then explore the semantic correlation between that user's current query and the query-matching pages in order to identify the user's current topic preference and based on the knowledge accumulated about the user's learnt past and current topic preferences personalize the user's search accordingly. We are currently experimenting with applying the various techniques of TODE in the area of Web search personalization and we are building a research prototype to validate our ideas. We plan to report our findings in a future work.

On the Web it is commonplace to find certain kinds of pages replicated a number of times. Such pages are, for example, the python documentation, or parts of Wikipedia etc. These pages are a nuisance for search engines since they contribute to waste of storage space, and crawling bandwidth. We believe that our ontology combined with the semantic similarity metric that we defined in Section Ordering Web Pages in Topic Directories can contribute towards detecting pages of identical (or near-identical) content. Our main idea is to directly compare the semantic similarity scores among a set of pages in order to define the degree of common information that the pages share.

Finally, we plan to investigate ways that TODE can assist the users in managing personal textual Web repositories, such as collections of bookmarks/favorites. The idea here is to employ the categorization techniques described in Section 4.1 in order to organize a given user's Web favorites into topics and subtopics in a meaningful and useful way. Our goal is to allow the users focus on what is important during their work on the Web by minimizing the effort of maintaining the bookmarks in an orderly manner.

It is our hope that our work will pave the way for Web applications that will focus on assisting both Web users and Web content-providers to improve the overall Web experience.

REFERENCES

Apte, C., Damerau, F., & Weiss, S.M. (1994). Automated learning of decision rules for text categorization. *ACM Transactions on Information Systems, 12*(3), 233-251.

Barzilay, R., & Elhadad, M. (1997). *Lexical chains for text summarization*. Master's thesis, Ben-Gurion University.

Boyapati, V. (2002). Improving text classification using unlabeled data. In *Proceedings of the ACM Special Interest Group in Information Retrieval (SIGIR) Conference* (pp. 11-15).

Broader, A.Z., Glassman, S.C., Manasse, M., & Zweig, G. (1997). Syntactic clustering of the web. In *Proceedings of the 6th International World Wide Wweb (WWW) Conference* (pp.1157-1166).

Bunge, M. (1977). *Treatise on Basic Philosophy. Ontology I. The Furniture of the World. Vol. 3*, Boston: Reidel.

Chakrabarti, S., Dom, B., Agraval, R., & Raghavan, P. (1998a). Scalable feature selection, classification and signature generation for organizing large text databases into hierarchical topic taxonomies. *Very Large DataBases (VLDB) Journal, 7*, 163-178.

Chakrabarti, S., Dom, B., & Indyk, P. (1998b). Enhanced hypertext categorization using hyperlinks. In *Proceedings of the ACM's Special Interest Group on Data on Data Management (SIGMOD) Conference.*

Chen, H., & Dumais, S. (2000). Bringing order to the web: Automatically categorizing search results. In *Proceedings of the SIGCHI Conference on Human Factors in Computing Systems* (pp. 145-152).

Christianini, N., & Shawe-Taylor, J. (2000). *An introduction to support vector machines*. Cambridge University Press.

Duda, R.O., & Hart, P.E. (1973). *Pattern classification and sense analysis*. Wiley & Sons.

Furnkranz, J. (1999). Exploring structural information for text classification on the WWW. In *Intelligent data analysis* (pp. 487-498).

Glover, E., Tsioutsiouliklis, K., Lawrence, S., Pennock, M., & Flake, G. (2002). Using web structure for classifying and describing Web pages. In *Proceedings of the 11th International World Wide Web (WWW) Conference.*

Huang, C.C., Chuang, S.L., & Chien, L.K. (2004). LiveClassifier: Creating hierarchical text classifiers through web corpora. In *Proceedings of the 13th International World Wide Web (WWW) Conference* (pp. 184-192).

Kaufman, L., & Rousseeuw, P.J. (1990). *Finding groups in data: An introduction to cluster analysis*. New York: John Wiley & Sons.

Koller, D., & Sahami, M. (1997). Hierarchically classifying documents using very few words. In *Proceedings of the 14th International Conference on Machine Learning (ICML)* (pp. 170-178).

Mladenic, D. (1998). Turning Yahoo into an automatic web page classifier. In *Proceedings of the 13th European Conference on Artificial Intelligence* (pp. 473-474).

Nigam, K., McCallum, A.K., Thrun, S., & Mitchell, T.M. (2000). Text classification from labeled and unlabeled documents using EM. In *Machine Learning, 39*(2-3) 103-134.

Ntoulas, A., Cho, J., & Olston, Ch. (2004). What's new on the web? The evolution of the web from a search engine perspective. In *Proceedings of the 13ᵗʰ InternationalWorld Wide Web (WWW) Conference* (pp. 1-12).

Olston, C., & Chi, E. (2003). ScentTrails: Intergrading browsing and searching. *ACM Transactions on Computer-Human Interaction, 10*(3), 1-21.

Pazzani, M., & Billsus, D. (1997). Learning and revising user profiles: The identification of interesting Web sites. *Machine Learning Journal, 23,* 313-331.

Resnik, Ph. (1999). Semantic similarity in a taxonomy: an information based measure and its application to problems of ambiguity in natural language. *Journal of Artificial Intelligence Research,* 11, 95-130.

Ruiz, M.E., & Srinivasan, P. (1999). Hierarchical neural networks for text categorization. In *Proceedings of the ACM's Special Interest Group in Information Retrieval (SIGIR) Conference* (pp. 281-282).

Song, Y.I., Han, K.S., & Rim, H.C. (2004). A term weighting method based on lexical chain for automatic summarization. In *Proceedings of the 5ᵗʰ Conference on Intelligent Text Processing and Computational Linguistics (CICLing)* (pp. 636-639).

Stamou, S., Krikos, V., Kokosis, P., & Christodoulakis, D. (2005). Web directory construction using lexical chains. In *Proceedings of the 10ᵗʰ International Conference on Applications of Natural Language to Information Systems (NLDB).*

ADDITIONAL READING

Budanitsky, A., & Hirst, G. (2006) Evaluating WordNet based measures of lexical semantic relatedness. *Computational Linguistics, 32*(1), 13-44.

Deerwester, S., Dumais, S., Furnas, G., Landauer, T., & Harshman, R. (1990). Indexing by latent semantic analysis. *Journal of the American Society for Information Science, 41*(6), 391-404.

Fridman, N., & Musen, M. (2000). PROMPT: Algorithm and tool for automated ontology merging and alignment. In *Proceedings of the 7ᵗʰ National Conference on Artificial Intelligence and 12ᵗʰ Conference on Innovative Applications of Artificial Intelligence,* Austin, Texas (pp. 450-455).

Gliozzo, A., Strapparava, C., & Dagan, I. (2004). Unsupervised and supervised exploitation of semantic domains in lexical disambiguation. In *Computer Speech and Language, 18*(3), 275-299.

Kleinberg, J. (1999). Authoritative Ssources in a hyperlinked environment. *Journal of the ACM, 46*(5), 604-632.

Kotis, K., Vouros, G., & Stergiou, K. (2005). Towards automatic merging of domain ontologies: The HCONE merge approach. *Informational Journal of Web Semantics (IJWS).*

Lenat, D.B. (1995). Cyc: A large-scale investment in knowledge infrastructure. *Communications of the ACM, 38*(11), 33-38.

Magnini, B., Strapparava, C., Pezzulo, G., & Gliozzo, A. (2002). The role of domain information in word sense disambiguation. *Natural Language Engineering, 8*(4), 359-373.

Nigam, K., McCallum, A.K., Thrun, S., & Mitchell, T.M. (2000). Text classification from labeled and unlabeled documents using EM. *Machine Learning, 39*(2-3), 103-134.

Pretschner, A., & Gauch, S. (1999). Ontology-based personalized search. In *Proceedings of the 11ᵗʰ IEEE International Conference on Tools with Artificial Intelligence* (pp. 391-398).

Resnik, Ph. (2005). Using information content to evaluate semantic similarity in a taxonomy. In *Proceedings of the 14ᵗʰ International Joint Conference on Artificial Intelligence* (pp. 448-453).

Richardson, M., & Domingos, R. (2002). The intelligent surfer: Probabilistic combination of link and content information in PageRank. In *Advances in Neural Information Processing Systems*. MIT Press.

Sebastiani, F. (2002). Machine learning in automated text categorization. In *ACM Computing Surveys, 34*(1).

Sowa, J. (2000). *Knowledge representation.* Brooks/Cole: Pacific Grove, CA.

Woods, W. (1999). *Conceptual indexing: A better way to organize knowledge.* Technical Report of Sun Microsystems.

ENDNOTES

[1] This can be checked at: http://rdf.dmoz.org/rdf/catmv.log.u8.gz

[2] The word "ontology" and the phrase "subject hierarchy" are being used interchangeably in the chapter

[3] MWND labels were originally assigned to WordNet 1.6 synsets, but we augmented them to WordNet 2.0 using the mappings available at http://www.cogsci.princeton.edu/~wn/links.shtml

[4] Candidate terms are nouns, verbs, adjectives or adverbs

[5] For example, net_{s1} may refer to a fishing net while net_{s2} may refer to a computer network

Chapter II
Raising, to Enhance Rule Mining in Web Marketing with the Use of an Ontology

Xuan Zhou
VPIsystems Corporation, USA

James Geller
New Jersey Institute of Technology, USA

ABSTRACT

This chapter introduces Raising as an operation that is used as a preprocessing step for data mining. In the Web Marketing Project, people's demographic and interest information has been collected from the Web. Rules have been derived using this information as input for data mining. The Raising step takes advantage of an interest ontology to advance data mining and to improve rule quality. The definition and implementation of Raising are presented in this chapter. Furthermore, the effects caused by Raising are analyzed in detail, showing an improvement of the support and confidence values of useful association rules for marketing purposes.

INTRODUCTION

Marketing has faced new challenges over the past decade. The days of the mass market are definitely over. Consumers now are exposed to numerous cable channels and satellite channels. Many people do not get their information from TV at all, but use Web sites. The population has

also developed. Minorities have grown and asserted their own tastes and needs. A product that is attractive to the average white Anglo-Saxon or Italian citizen might be completely uninteresting to a first generation South American immigrant. Similarly, the market has split up by preferences. Chinese and Indian food have made major inroads and many consumers would like to cook the same food in their homes. In short, the mass market is dead, and marketers today face the problem of advertising to many disjoint niche markets.

With the increase in available, cheap data storage, companies are keeping terabytes of information about their customers. Today, it is not outrageous to talk about one-to-one marketing. However, marketers face two problems. They may have information about previous customers, but how could they get personal information about potential customers? Secondly, if information about individuals is truly not accessible, how could they classify such individuals into small categories and then market effectively to these small categories?

To provide a solution for these two problems, the Web Marketing Project (Geller, Scherl, & Perl, 2002; Scherl & Geller, 2002) was created. This project targeted millions of publicly accessible home pages on the Web, on which people freely express their likes and dislikes. These pages are a valuable source of data for marketing purposes. One approach is to use the contact information for direct (e-mail) marketing. For example, if someone expressed his interest as music, then he might be a potential customer of music CDs. Thus the marketing can be directed towards a very narrow niche. If someone lists very detailed interests, such as the TV comedy show *The Simpsons*, the Season 8 DVD released in August, 2006, could be one of his must-buy products.

A second important use of this data is for finding interesting marketing knowledge. The data may be mined for useful correlations between interests and also between interests and demographic categories. If someone is interested in *The Simpsons*, what is the likelihood that he is interested in another comedy? What age groups are interested in particular types of TV series? The available data can be used for such investigations. The results may again be useful for marketing.

In the Web Marketing Project, we collected people's demographic and interest information from home pages and stored them in a database.

There are six modules in this project, which are Web search, glossary-based extraction, database, data mining, ontology, and front end, as described in detail in Zhou (2006). In this chapter, we only focus on the ontology and data mining modules. The ontology consists of two taxonomies, one of which describes different customer classifications, while the other one contains a large hierarchy, based on Yahoo, which contains 31,534 interests. For the customer classification, an intersection ontology (Zhou, Geller, Perl, & Halper, 2006) was developed.

The data mining module uses well-known data mining algorithms to extract association rules from the given data. The WEKA (Witten & Frank, 2000) package was used at the beginning of the project. From the WEKA package, the Apriori algorithm (Agrawal & Srikant, 1994) for data mining was used. The real world data about real people tends to produce rules with unsatisfactory support values. Thus, in this research a method was developed for improving the support values of rules by using the existing ontology. This method is called "*Raising*" and will be discussed in depth later in this chapter. Moreover, due to the limitations of WEKA found during the project, the FP-Growth algorithm (Han, Pei, & Yin, 2000; Han, Pei, Yin, & Mao, 2004) was implemented and used in the second stage to correct some errors and improve the results.

The next section presents previous literature on ontologies used in rule mining. Following that, we introduce the Raising method and show how an ontology can be used to improve the support of mined rules. The effects caused by Raising on derived rules are discussed afterwards. At last, future trends and conclusions are presented at the end of this chapter.

BACKGROUND

A concept hierarchy is present in many databases either explicitly or implicitly. Some previous work utilizes a hierarchy for data mining. Han (1995) discusses data mining at multiple concept levels. His approach is to use associations at one level (e.g., milk → bread) to direct the search for associations at a different level (e.g., milk of brand X → bread of brand Y). As most of our data mining involves only one interest, the problem setting in this research is quite different. Han and Fu (1995) introduce a top-down progressive deepening method for mining multiple-level association rules. They utilize the hierarchy to collect large item sets at different concept levels. The approach in this research utilizes an interest ontology to improve support in rule mining by means of concept raising. To the best of our knowledge, the implementation of ontologies with association rule mining for the purpose of finding generalized rules with high support from sparse data has not appeared in the literature before our publication (Chen, Zhou, Scherl, & Geller 2003).

Fortin and Liu (1996) use an object-oriented representation for data mining. Their interest is in deriving multilevel association rules. As only one data item in each tuple is typically used for Raising, the possibility of multilevel rules does not arise in our problem setting. Srikant and Agrawal (1995) present cumulate and EstMerge algorithms to find associations between items at any level by adding all ancestors of each item to the transaction. In their research, items of different levels are added to candidates during the mining. Psaila and Lanzi (2000) describe a method how to improve association rule mining by using a generalization hierarchy in data warehouses. Páircéir, McClean, and Scotney (2000) also differ from the work of this research in that they are mining multilevel rules that associate items spanning several levels of a concept hierarchy. Data mining has been viewed as an operation with a query language in (Elfeky, Saad, & Fouad, 2000; Novacek, 1998).

Zaki and Hsiao (2002) present a method that greatly reduces the number of redundant rules generated by previous rule miners. They define closed frequent item sets, which are sufficient for rule generation, to replace traditional frequent item sets. They show that this may lead to a reduction of the frequent item sets by two orders of magnitude, for a given support value. The concern is not with the efficiency of generating association rules, but with the total support of the resulting rules. However, *any rule mining algorithm* may be plugged into the Web Marketing Project, as mining and Raising are performed in a modular way. Thus, the Web Marketing Project would benefit from the improved efficiency of a data mining algorithm such as CHARM (Zaki & Hsiao, 2002). Mannila, Toivonen, and Verkamo (1994) worked on improving algorithms for finding associations rules, by eliminating unnecessary candidate rules.

Berzal, Blanco, Sanchez, and Vila (2001) have worked on a problem that is in some sense the diametrical opposite of the problem in this research. They are trying to eliminate misleading rules that are the result of too high support values. The problem of generating association rules when the available support is too low to derive practically useful rules is being addressed here.

This work is similar to Zhou, Liu, Li, and Chua (2001) in that it incorporates prior knowledge into the rule mining process. Like Zhou et al., a directed acyclic graph structure is used to present such additional knowledge. However, this research is not using the numeric (probabilistic) dependencies of (Zhou et al., 2001).

Tsujii and Ananiadou (2005) compared the effect on text mining of using a thesaurus versus a logical ontology and argued that a thesaurus is more useful for text mining applications than formal ontologies. On the contrary, Missikoff, Velardi, and Fabriani (2003) did not focus on how to use an ontology for mining but how to build one by mining. *SymOntos*, an ontology management system, and the text mining approach were discussed to support ontology construction or updating.

Mädche and Volz (2001) have combined ontologies with association rules, but in a completely different way than what is done in this research. Their purpose is to semiautomatically construct ontologies. They are using an association rule miner in the service of this activity.

Li and Zhong (2006) have introduced an approach to automatically discover ontologies from data sets in order to build complete concept models for Web user information needs. They proposed a method for capturing evolving patterns to refine discovered ontologies and established a process to assess relevance of patterns in an ontology by the dimensions of *exhaustivity* and *specificity*.

Our approach is similar to Xodo and Nigro (2005), in that we are interested in potential customers as opposed to previous customers. However, their domain is tourism.

RAISING

Data mining has become an important research tool for the purpose of marketing. It makes it possible to draw far-reaching conclusions from existing customer databases about connections between different products commonly purchased. If demographic data are available, data mining also allows the generation of rules that connect them with products. However, companies are not only interested in the behavior of their existing customers. They would also like to find out about potential future customers. Typically, there is no information about potential customers available in a company database, which can be used for data mining. However, it is possible to perform data mining on potential customers when people express their interests freely and explicitly on their home pages and there is a close relationship between specific interests and potential purchases.

Applying well-known data mining algorithms to the data extracted from the Web and stored in the database, association rules representing marketing knowledge are derived in this research for marketing purposes. However, when mining this data for association rules, what is available is often too sparse to produce rules with reasonable support values. Thus, when we initially derived rules by data mining, we found some rules which were interesting but with fairly low support values. In other words, those rules were not representative enough to predict future purchases. Since an interest ontology was created in the project, taking advantage of the ontology hierarchy provided a path to solve this problem.

Using Raising to Improve Support

The Raising method has been introduced in Chen et al., (2003). A formal definition of **raising a tuple to its parents** and **raising a tuple to a level k** was given in (Geller, Zhou, Prathipati, Kanigiluppai, & Chen, 2005). However, in Geller et al. (2005), the definition was given based on the implementation using the WEKA package (Witten & Frank, 2000). In order to use WEKA, an Attribute-relation File Format (ARFF) format input file is required. In an ARFF file, all the attributes together with all their possible values need to be listed before the data. Thus, once an attribute has a large number of values, such as the 31,534 interests in our case, the input file size becomes extremely large. Moreover, the ARFF format does not allow multiple values for an attribute, which happened in our database since people often express more than one interest. Due to the limitations of the ARFF format, every tuple only contains one interest (one value of the attribute *Interest*) in the ontology. Since people normally express more than one interest, such a representation brings about some spurious records after Raising, as described in (Geller et al., 2005). More details about the ARFF limitations and effects can be found in (Zhou, 2006). Realizing this, here we introduce the revised definition of **raising a tuple to a level k** to better represent the situation of multiple interests.

For convenience, it is assumed that every interest in the hierarchy is assigned a level L by a revised breadth-first search algorithm, LEVEL-

BFS(), as described in (Zhou, 2006, pp. 24-25). Then the level function L(T) is defined to return this level as a number. Interests nearer to the root have lower level numbers. The root is by definition at level 0. Lower levels in the diagram correspond to higher level numbers. In a DAG, such as Figure 1, the concept V is at level 3 and has parents at two different levels, X at level 1 and W at level 2.

The major difference between the previous definitions in (Geller et al., 2005) and this revised definition is the format of the input and the output. The input of the previous definition only contains one single term (interest) due to the limitations of the ARFF format. In the new definition, the input contains a set of terms, which are used for multiple interests of one person. For the output, the previous definitions returned a set of tuples, which mistakenly added spurious people into the dataset after Raising. However, the new definition only returns one tuple for each person.

Definition: An **operation R^k**, called **raising a tuple to the level k**. Given is a data tuple $T = <N_s, D>$ where N_s is a set $\{N_1, N_2, ..., N_n\}$ of interests. D stands for one or several items of demographic information. N_i is derived from a rooted ontology O. In O, each N_i has a uniquely determined, ordered sequence of m_i ($m_i \geq 1$) parents$<A^k_{i\_1}, A^k_{i\_2}, .., A^k_{i\_mi}>$, all at level k. If N_i is at a higher level with a number less than k, it does not have an ancestor at level k. In this case, $A^k_{i\_1} = N_i$. Therefore, R^k is defined as the operation that takes T as input and returns the raised tuple (please see equation (1)) as output for every T, except for the tuple $<Root(O), D>$. For the latter $R^k(T)$ is undefined. Moreover, a duplication check is performed during Raising. Thus, every $A^k_{i\_j}$ that appears in T^k is unique and all the duplicates have been removed. Also, as the result for every T, all the $A^k_{i\_j}$ in T^k are at a level with a number less than or equal to k.

Because N_i has m_i ancestors at level k, the result of Raising T, namely $R^k(T)$, is a new tuple with $\sum m_i + n_D$ terms, one for each ancestor at level k. The term n_D is added for the items of demographic information D. The sum assumes a case with no duplicates. For the previous example (Figure 1):

$$R^2(<V, D>) = <W, D>$$

but

$$R^1(<V, D>) = <X, Y, D>$$

For example, if the given tuple T says that one male (M) in the age range 20-24 is interested in Jennifer Lopez and Richard Gere:

T = < LOPEZ_JENNIFER, GERE_RICHARD, M, (20-24)>

and the interest LOPEZ_JENNIFER has two ancestors at level 3, ACTRESS and SINGER while GERE_RICHARD has only ACTOR as a level 3 ancestor, then the result of Raising to level 3 is:

Figure 1. Example of parents at different levels

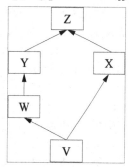

Equation 1.

$$T^k = R^k(T) = < A^k_{1\_1}, A^k_{1\_2}, .., A^k_{1\_m1}, A^k_{2\_1}, A^k_{2\_2}, .., A^k_{2\_m2}, .., A^k_{n\_1}, A^k_{n\_2}, .., A^k_{n\_mn}, D >$$

R^3 (*T*) = <ACTRESS, SINGER, ACTOR, M, 20-24>

meaning that one person of male gender in the age group (20-24) is interested in actress, singer, and actor. One issue arising at this point is whether we accept the generalization that has occurred. This was described in (Geller et al. 2005) and will also be discussed further below.

After having raised the data item <N_s, *D*>, any traditional association rule mining algorithm may be applied to the result of Raising, instead of applying it to the original data item <N_s,*D*>. Thus, Raising replaces a data item by its ancestors before performing rule mining.

An Example of Raising

Here is an example to illustrate how the Raising method works to improve the quality of derived association rules. The following dataset is the input to a data mining algorithm and is going to be raised to level 3. Each tuple, that is, each line, stands for one interest instance with demographic information. As before, the values of three attributes (age, gender and interest) are all included in each tuple. Age values are represented as a range while Gender values of male and female are abbreviated as M and F. Text after a double slash (//) is not part of the data. It contains explanatory remarks.

(20-29), M, BUSINESS_FINANCE   //level=1
(40-49), M, METRICOM_INC   //level=8
(50-59), M, BUSINESS_SCHOOLS   //level=2
(30-39), F, ALUMNI   //level=3
(20-29), M, MAKERS   //level=4
(20-29), F, INDUSTRY_ASSOCIATIONS
        //level=2
(30-39), M, AOL_INSTANT_MESSENGER
        //level=6
(30-39), F, INTRACOMPANY_GROUPS
        //level=3

Once this original dataset is fed into a data mining algorithm, the best association rules, as measured by support value, that can be derived are {(20-29)}→{M} and {(30-39)}→{F}. Both rules have confidence values of 0.67 and support values of 2. This is also an example of sparse data. Every interest only appears once in the dataset. Though rules with a confidence of 1.0 can be derived from the data, such as {(50-59), M}→{BUSINESS_SCHOOLS}, as discussed before, the low support value of 1 does not make these rules useful for marketing purposes.

While performing Raising, ancestors are found at level 3 of the interests in the data. Table 1 shows all ancestors of the interests from levels below 3 such that the ancestors are at level 3. Table 1 is based on the DAG hierarchy in Figure 2. As seen in Figure 2, among the eight interests in eight tuples, two of them (ALUMNI, INTRA-COMPANY_GROUPS) are already at level 3, and three of them (BUSINESS_FINANCE, BUSINESS_SCHOOLS, INDUSTRY_ASSO-CIATIONS) are at levels above. Therefore, the Raising process will only function on the other

Table 1. Relevant ancestors

Interest Name	Its ancestor(s) at Level 3
METRICOM_INC	COMPUTERS, COMMUNICATIONS_AND_NETWORKING
MAKERS	ELECTRONICS
AOL_INSTANT_MESSENGER	COMPUTERS, INSTANT_MESSAGING

three interests (METRICOM_INC, MAKERS, AOL_INSTANT_MESSENGER) which are at levels 4, 6 and 8 respectively. Table 1 lists their ancestors at level 3. The interest ontology is not a tree but a DAG. Some interests have more than one parent and thus more than one ancestor at a certain level. While the interest MAKERS has only one ancestor (parent) at level 3, the other two interests METRICOM_INC and AOL_IN-STANT_MESSENGER both have two ancestors at level 3. The Raising to level 3 then replaces all the interests below level 3 in the original dataset by their ancestors at level 3. By doing so, all the interests in the new dataset are at level 3 or above. Thus, the new dataset after being raised to level 3 becomes:

(20-29), M, BUSINESS_FINANCE
(40-49), M, COMMUNICATIONS_AND_NET-WORKING, COMPUTERS
(50-59), M, BUSINESS_SCHOOLS
(30-39), F, ALUMNI

(20-29), M, ELECTRONICS
(20-29), F, INDUSTRY_ASSOCIATIONS
(30-39), M, INSTANT_MESSAGING, COM-PUTERS
(30-39), F, INTRACOMPANY_GROUPS

By feeding the new dataset as input to the data mining algorithm, a new association rule, with a support value greater than 1, is derived, other than the two demographic rules derived before:

{M}→{COMPUTERS}
Confidence: 0.5 Support: 2

The overall Raising procedure is performed in the following steps (Zhou, 2006, pp. 74-75):

- Data Preparation
- Raising Operation
- Rule Generation
- Result Analysis

Figure 2. An example of raising to level 3

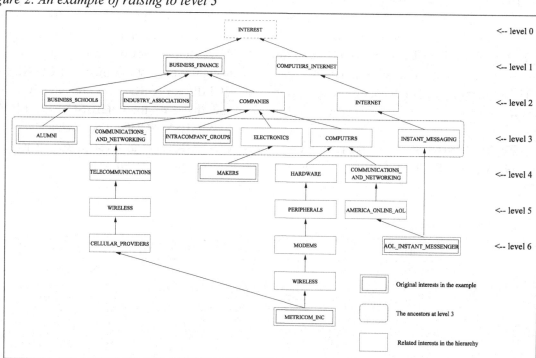

Effects of Generalization

Raising does lose detail and specificity during the process by replacing interests by their ancestors. This is a fact that has positive and negative consequences. A disadvantage would be the missing details due to replacing interests by their ancestors. Those details could have been used as direct business act indicators about a product. Thus, a rule which involves deep-level interests can explicitly express a connection between customers and products. Such a rule might connect a specific movie DVD with a demographic group. It is, of course, possible to perform data mining before Raising. Thus, no real loss occurs. However, if a confidence and a support threshold are given, any rule has to *qualify* to appear in the results. That is, a rule must have a greater confidence value and a greater support value than the thresholds to qualify. Once a rule *qualifies*, it will appear in the results no matter whether Raising is used later or not. Many rules that are mined before Raising tend to have low support values. Thus these rules would not show up anyway. Thus, no new loss is introduced due to Raising. If a rule is not *qualified*, it does not meet the expectations of a *useful* rule. Therefore, to discard such a rule of *little use* and to lose those details is reasonable.

On the other hand, the generalization has the advantage that it provides better indicators for new product promotions. A new product would never appear in any existing rule, thus no exact match can be found. However, it is not a hard problem to categorize the new product into an existing category, or a higher level interest. For example, the 2005 TV comedy "American Dad" had not been listed in Yahoo at the time of this research, that is, no rule can be found for it by mining. If the FOX TV network would like to attract a potential audience for the new show, the rules involving the interest "television comedy" would be a nice option to consider. Thus, Raising can help to generalize the information from specific interests such as "The Simpsons" or "Family Guy" (two other TV comedies) to "television comedy," if such a rule is not there before Raising. Even if this rule exists before Raising, the new increased support value after Raising would bring about a better rule quality.

As a conclusion, the Raising operation is not meant to replace the existing mining result rules. Instead, Raising is used to strengthen the derived rules and to provide more possible rules by generalizing detail information.

Results of Raising

The Raising method has been implemented using the new definition, as described earlier in this chapter. This implementation avoids the problems caused by spreading out interests of one person over several lines in the ARFF format, applying the previous definitions, and makes it possible to derive better rules. An FP-Growth mining program was implemented in this research, using JAVA. The input specifies a file which has to be formatted as required for *set-based input mining*, that is, a person's record is in a single line, including age, gender and all his/her interests. For example, some lines in the input file after Raising at level 6 in the category "BUSINESS & FINANCE" are as follows:

B,FEMALE,1600840341,1602248651,
C,MALE,1600000236,1600001222,1600909559,
1600909561,
C,MALE,1600840352,1602216980,1602216981,
1602219139,1602236895,
D,MALE,1600000393,1600001278,1600001779,
1600193918,

The letters A to F are used to represent age ranges. For example, B stands for an age range from 20 to 29 and D stands for a range of 40-49. A 10-digit number is a unique Yahoo ID for an interest in our ontology. For example, the Yahoo ID 1600840341 stands for the interest TUPPER-WARE.

The increments of support values after Raising are shown at the left side in Table 2. The increment percentage I_i is computed as the difference between the average support values of mining results from raised data at level i (S_{ai}) and from unraised data (S_b), at the lowest level appearing in this data, and then divided by Sb. Thus,

$$I_i = \frac{S_{ai} - S_b}{S_b} \times 100\% \qquad (1)$$

and Ii is the increment rate of the support value at level i relative to the original value before Raising. Since result level 1 only contains one interest and results from levels below level 5 contain sparse data or do not even exist, only level 2 to level 5 appear. The data show the concrete increments of support values from lower levels to higher levels. The right side of Table 2 shows the number of newly discovered {Interest}→{Interest} rules, which we could not derive using the WEKA implementation. For example, some rules mined from the input file raised to level 6 in category "BUSINESS & FINANCE" are as follows:

{INTERNET_MARKETING_AND_ADVERTISING}→{INTERNET_BUSINESS}
{HOME_BUSINESS, INTERNET_MARKETING_AND_ADVERTISING}→{INTERNET_BUSINESS}

{STARTUPS}→{INTERNET_BUSINESS}
{NETWORK_MARKETING}→{INTERNET_BUSINESS}
{INTERNET_BUSINESS, HOME_BUSINESS}→{INTERNET_MARKETING_AND_ADVERTISING}
{HOME_BUSINESS, SMALL_BUSINESS}→{INTERNET_BUSINESS}

This Raising implementation solves the problems caused by the WEKA ARFF implementation. It results in better performance while still improving support values over the previously published Raising method (Chen et al., 2003; Geller et al., 2005). It also eliminates in a natural way the duplication of tuples, which might occur during Raising when an ancestor is reachable by more than one path in a DAG. The application of the FP-Growth mining algorithm results in better efficiency than the previously used Apriori algorithm.

EFFECTS ON MINING RESULTS BY RAISING

Observations about Raising Results

To derive association rules, data are selected from the database and fed into data mining algorithms.

Table 2. Support value increments and new rule discovery

Category	Level 2	Level 3	Level 4	Level 5	Interest-Interest Rules
BUSINESS FINANCE	858.79%	371.90%	74.02%	5.60%	115
COMPUTERS INTERNET	946.25%	749.90%	97.66%	3.53%	26
FAMILY HOME	341.41%	146.17%	46.16%	0.15%	6
GOVERNMENT POLITICS	4084.36%	2320.00%	2090.90%	1119.50%	169
RECREATION SPORTS	853.49%	251.86%	64.35%	11.67%	2
SCHOOLS EDUCATION	877.91%	459.82%	249.03%	20.72%	23
SCIENCE	1661.34%	971.87%	894.58%	751.98%	13
Data mined at Confidence≥0.6, Support≥0.02					

In the Web Marketing Project, both the Apriori algorithm (Agrawal, Imielinski, & Swami, 1993, Agrawal & Srikant, 1994) from the WEKA package (Witten et al., 2000) and the FP-Growth algorithm (Han et al., 2000, Han et al., 2004) were used. By providing minimum support and confidence values as input parameters, the data mining algorithms return derived association rules based on the input. However, as we described in Chen et al., (2003), a problem in the derivation of association rules is that available data is sometimes very sparse and biased. For example, among over a million of interest records in the database of this research, only 11 people expressed an interest in RECREATION_SPORTS, and nobody expressed an interest in SCIENCE which is counter-intuitive.

Recall the Raising to level 3 example. The new rule "{M}→{COMPUTERS} Confidence: 0.5 Support: 2" is relatively more attractive for marketing purposes than the results from the original dataset, for the following reasons.

1. The new rule has a better support value, thus it is a rule of higher quality. The occurrence count of an interest at the raised level in the dataset is increased by replacing its descendants in all instances. During the replacement, the demographic information and the interests at levels above are not affected or updated. Thus, while the number of tuples in the dataset is still the same, the support value is improved.

2. The new rule connects demographic information with interest information. The rules derived originally, such as:

{20-29}→{M} Confidence: 0.67 Support: 2
{30-39}→{F} Confidence: 0.67 Support: 2
{F}→{30-39} Confidence: 0.67 Support: 2

only imply some connections between age and gender. Though those rules are valid, they do not contribute any useful insights for marketing purposes. For marketing usage, an interest should be included in the rules to predict future purchases of potential customers.

3. Last but not least, "brand-new" rules can be derived after Raising. Note that in the original dataset, the interest COMPUTERS did not exist at all. This interest at level 3 is introduced when several interests in the original dataset share it as ancestor. In other words, the newly appeared interest is a generalization of its descendants based on the interest ontology. In the example at the beginning of this section, just because people did not express interests with more general terms does not mean they are not interested. On the contrary, people prefer to express their interests more specifically. In the data file, there are 62,734 data items in the category of RECREATION_SPORTS. These thousands of people prefer saying something like "I'm interested in BASKETBALL and FISHING" instead of saying "I'm interested in RECREATION_SPORTS." By the Raising method, those wide-spread data can be collected and thus new rules can be derived to describe the situation by using high-level interests.

Effects on Support and Confidence of Different Rule Types

Since the inputs only include three attributes for each person's record, all the association rules are combinations of those attributes in their antecedents and consequents. For the age and gender attributes, only one single value is allowed for each attribute in every tuple, that is one person's record. However, since a person might have expressed more than one interest at the same time, the interest attribute may have multiple values. Here all the possible rule types based on this situation are listed. (The expression {Interest(s)} stands for one or more interests. For example, the rule

{Male} → {FISHING, POKER} is categorized by the rule type {Gender} → {Interest(s)}.) Rules with an empty antecedent or consequent are not interesting.

1. {Age} → {Gender}
2. {Age} → {Interest(s)}
3. {Age} → {Gender, Interest(s)}
4. {Age, Gender} → {Interest(s)}
5. {Age, Interest(s)} → {Gender}
6. {Age, Interest(s)} → {Interest(s)}
7. {Age, Interest(s)} → {Gender, Interest(s)}
8. {Age, Gender, Interest(s)} → {Interest(s)}
9. {Gender} → {Age}
10. {Gender} → {Interest(s)}
11. {Gender} → {Age, Interest(s)}
12. {Gender, Interest(s)} → {Age}
13. {Gender, Interest(s)} → {Interest(s)}
14. {Gender, Interest(s)} → {Age, Interest(s)}
15. {Interest(s)} → {Age}
16. {Interest(s)} → {Gender}
17. {Interest(s)} → {Interest(s)}
18. {Interest(s)} → {Age, Gender}
19. {Interest(s)} → {Age, Interest(s)}
20. {Interest(s)} → {Gender, Interest(s)}
21. {Interest(s)} → {Age, Gender, Interest(s)}

These 21 rule types include all the possibilities of derived association rules. By studying these rule types one by one in groups, all the rules which are not proper for marketing purposes are filtered out and the research focuses on the effect of Raising on the remaining rule types.

- **Group (A):** The rule types #1 and #9 only involve age and gender. As discussed before, such rules are not useful for marketing purposes and thus are filtered out.

- **Group (B):** The rules that are useful for marketing purposes should be those that connect a certain group of persons to a certain interest, or product. The types #2, #4, and #10 are exactly predicting the relationship between a group of persons and their interests. They tie people and their interests together. Moreover, type #4 is more specific than types #2 and #10. Once such rules with a high confidence and a high support value are found, the group of people described by the antecedent is more likely to make purchases related to the interest.

- **Group (C):** The types #15, #16, and #18 are the opposite of #2, #10, and #4. The attribute interest is in the antecedent while demographic attributes are in the consequent. The interpretation for such rule types is "If somebody is interested in A, this person is likely to be in a certain demographic group B." These rules describe the distribution of person groups within all those who are interested in an interest A. The types #5 and #12 can also be categorized in this group since there is only the demographic attribute in the consequents. These rule types are less useful for promotion purposes which this project is focused on.

- **Group (D):** The types #3 and #11 have only demographic attributes in the antecedents. In the consequents are the combinations of a demographic attribute and interest attributes. For example, #3 can be interpreted as, "If a person is in the age group B, there is a certain confidence that this person has a gender C and will be interested in the interest A." A more specific example is "If a person is a teenager, there is a confidence of 0.8 that it's a girl who is interested in SOFTBALL." By connecting the age attribute and gender attribute in the rules, the interpretation of these two types of rules is confusing and they appear not suitable for marketing.

- **Group (E):** The types #6, #8, #13, and #17 have only the interest attribute in the consequents. The rule type #17 implies a connection between two or more interests. The types #6, #8, and #13 are more specific formats of type #17 by including demographic groups. These kinds of rules are attractive for marketing purposes. When a retailer is going to promote a product, which is categorized by interest X, he might prefer association rules which can lead to persons grouped by age, gender, and so forth. However, there might not be a rule (due to insufficient support or confidence values during rule mining) of rule type #4 from Group (B). Therefore, rules in this group would greatly support his search as a complement of Group (B).

- **Group (F):** The types #7, #14, #19, #20, and #21 also contain a combination of demographic attribute and interest attribute in consequents, like the rule types in Group (D). The difference to Group (D) is that interest attributes appear in the antecedent. Type #7 and #14 are more specific formats of type #20 and #19 respectively. The usefulness of these rules for marketing is doubtful. For example, a rule could be "If a man is interested in FOOTBALL, there is a certain confidence that his age is 30 to 39 and he is also interested in BEER." These rule types try to connect interest attributes to demographic attributes and are hybrids of Group (C) and Group (E). However, for marketing purposes, these rule types are weaker than those in Group (E).

All the 21 rule types have been categorized into six groups. The effects of Raising can be analyzed group by group. Before Raising, a rule has a support value of $S_0 = Occ_{ante \& con}$ and the confidence value is calculated by $C_0 = \dfrac{S_0}{Occ_{ante}}$.

- **Group (A):** After Raising, since the instances of age and gender have not been changed and no interests occur, the confidence and support values are not affected.

$$S_{new} = S_0 \qquad\qquad (1)$$

$$C_{new} = C_0 \qquad\qquad (2)$$

- **Group (B):** After Raising, the occurrences of demographic information in the antecedents are not changed. However, the occurrences of interests in the consequent might be increased by replacing descendants by multiple ancestors. If there is no replacement needed, the occurrences stay unchanged. Thus, the support values always stay unchanged or are increased and the confidence values also stay unchanged or are increased accordingly. Suppose the increment of occurrence is Inc ($Inc \geq 0$), then

$$S_{new} = S_0 + Inc \geq S_0 \qquad\qquad (3)$$

$$C_{new} = \frac{S_0 + Inc}{Occ_{ante}} \geq C_0 \qquad\qquad (4)$$

- **Group (C):** After Raising, the occurrences of interests in the antecedent are increased. Suppose the increment of occurrences of the antecedent is Inc_{ante} ($Inc_{ante} \geq 0$). However, among all the tuples updated with these interests, the demographic information might not match those in the rule, thus the increment of occurrence of both antecedent and consequent will be a different variable, $Inc_{ante \& con}$ ($Inc_{ante} \geq Inc_{ante \& con} \geq 0$). Therefore,

$$S_{new} = S_0 + Inc_{ante \& con} \geq S_0 \qquad\qquad (5)$$

$$C_{new} = \frac{S_0 + Inc_{ante \& con}}{Occ_{ante} + Inc_{ante}} \qquad\qquad (6)$$

The comparison of C_{new} to C_0 depends on the two increments. If $Inc_{ante \& con}$ is much smaller than Inc_{ante}, C_{new} could be less than C_0. Otherwise, $C_{new} \geq C_0$. More specifically,

$$C_{new} - C_0 = \frac{S_0 + Inc_{ante \& con}}{Occ_{ante} + Inc_{ante}} - \frac{S_0}{Occ_{ante}}$$

$$= \frac{(S_0 + Inc_{ante\ \&\ con})Occ_{ante} - S_0(Occ_{ante} + Inc_{ante})}{Occ_{ante}(Occ_{ante} + Inc_{ante})}$$

$$= \frac{Inc_{ante\ \&\ con}Occ_{ante} - S_0 Inc_{ante}}{Occ_{ante}(Occ_{ante} + Inc_{ante})}$$

$$= \frac{\dfrac{Inc_{ante\ \&\ con}}{Inc_{ante}} - \dfrac{S_0}{Occ_{ante}}}{\dfrac{Occ_{ante}}{Inc_{ante}} + 1} \qquad (7)$$

Since all the values in the equation are non-negative, the value of the numerator in the Formula 1 shows which is greater, C_{new} or C_0. If the value is non-negative, C_{new} is greater than or equal to C_0. Otherwise, if the value is negative, C_{new} is less than C_0. Thus,

$$\frac{Inc_{ante\ \&\ con}}{Inc_{ante}} \geq \frac{S_0}{Occ_{ante}} \Rightarrow C_{new} \geq C_0 \qquad (8)$$

$$\frac{Inc_{ante\ \&\ con}}{Inc_{ante}} < \frac{S_0}{Occ_{ante}} \Rightarrow C_{new} < C_0 \qquad (9)$$

Notice that $C_0 = \dfrac{S_0}{Occ_{ante}}$. Let's take a look at $\dfrac{Inc_{ante\ \&\ con}}{Inc_{ante}}$. The numerator is the increment of the records which contain all the terms in both antecedent and consequent. The denominator is the increment of the records which contain all the terms in the antecedent. Thus, for $C_{Inc} = \dfrac{Inc_{ante\ \&\ con}}{Inc_{ante}}$, C_{Inc} is the confidence value of the rule mined from the subdataset which contains all the updated records, *i.e.* records which have interests being replaced by their ancestors, during Raising. In other words, the changes of confidence values before and after Raising are based on the confidence value from the subdataset which contains all the Raising-affected records.

Thus, if $C_{Inc} \geq C_0$ then $C_{new} \geq C_0$ and if $C_{Inc} < C_0$ then $C_{new} < C_0$.

- **Group (D):** As in Group (B), the occurrences of demographic information in the antecedents are not changed after Raising. The increment of occurrences of both antecedent and consequent $Inc_{ante\ \&\ con}$ ($Inc_{ante\ \&\ con} \geq 0$) depends on the increment of occurrence of interests.

$$S_{new} = S_0 + Inc_{ante\ \&\ con} \geq S_0 \qquad (10)$$

$$C_{new} = \frac{S_0 + Inc_{ante\ \&\ con}}{Occ_{ante}} \geq C_0 \qquad (11)$$

Therefore always: $S_{new} \geq S_0$ and $C_{new} \geq C_0$.

- **Group (E) and Group (F):** These two groups can be put together since the interest attributes appear in both antecedent and consequent. After Raising, the increment of occurrence of both antecedent and consequent is $Inc_{ante\ \&\ con}$ ($Inc_{ante\ \&\ con} \geq 0$). However, there is also an increment of occurrence of interests in the antecedent Inc_{ante} ($Inc_{ante} \geq Inc_{ante\ \&\ con}$). Unfortunately, these two increments $Inc_{ante\ \&\ con}$ and Inc_{ante} do not have any relationship to each other. Thus,

$$S_{new} = S_0 + Inc_{ante\ \&\ con} \geq S_0 \qquad (12)$$

$$C_{new} = \frac{S_0 + Inc_{ante\ \&\ con}}{Occ_{ante} + Inc_{ante}} \qquad (13)$$

Note the formulas are exactly the same as Formulas 5 and 6 in **Group (C)**. Therefore, the same Formula 7 can also be applied to the relationship between the confidence values before and after Raising for **Group (E)** and **Group (F)**. Thus the changes are also based on the Raising-affected data.

If $C_{Inc} \geq C_0$ then $C_{new} \geq C_0$ and if $C_{Inc} < C_0$ then $C_{new} < C_0$.

According to the case analysis, after Raising, the *support values* of all the association rules are *never decreased*, thus Raising guarantees higher or equal quality rules. For *confidence values*, the most important rule types for marketing purposes, Group (B), always have higher confidence values. This ensures high quality association rules with better support values and also better confidence values. The rule types in Groups (A), (C) and (D) are not proper for marketing purposes. Those rules are filtered out from the data mining results in a postprocessing step. The rule types in Groups (F) and (E) have increasing support values but undetermined changes of confidence values. However, as discussed before, those rule types are only used as complements for Group (B).

FUTURE WORK

In the processing of Raising, there is a duplication check performed while replacing the interests by their corresponding ancestors at a specific level. Such a check eliminates one interest if it would appear in somebody's interest list more than once. However, though it is the case that people will not express the same interest twice in an interest list, it is still possible that two siblings are expressed at the same time. When Raising is performed to the level where the two siblings' parent is located, the new interest list for this level only contains the parent once. One concern arises here whether this parent should be counted twice in the list since two of its children were originally expressed. In other words, should the interests in the list be assigned a weight in such situations? In that case, when somebody expressed those two siblings, one might want to stress his multiple interests in the same category. Should this stress also be considered in the new list after Raising?

To expand this idea to the supermarket shopping cart example, a weight could be assigned according to the values of products. Thus, should a product for which customers paid a lot be assigned a higher weight and function as more important in the mining than other products which cost less? A mining method with weighted items might be a solution. This kind of work has been done before. In 1998, Cai, Fu, Cheng, and Kwong introduced the MINWAL algorithm, which used a metric called *k-support bound* in the mining process. Wang, Yang, and Yu (2000) extended the traditional association rule problem by allowing a weight to be associated with each item in a transaction and then introducing the weight during the rule generation. Lu, Hu, and Li (2001) also presented an algorithm called MWAR to handle the problem of mining mixed weighted association rules. However, since all these approaches were based on the Apriori algorithm, we would like to include a weighted mining mechanism based on FP-Growth in future work.

The Raising method discussed here was applied to the domain of Web marketing. However, it is not limited to this single domain. The Raising method targets any input datasets, as long as the data items in the datasets use terms from an existing, well-structured ontology. The originality or the domain of the data is not important. By adapting the input formats, Raising can be applied to different domains with a corresponding ontology.

CONCLUSION

The Raising method uses an ontology to perform a preprocessing step on the input datasets before data mining. The preprocessed dataset can be used as input to any data mining algorithm to derive more and better association rules, with higher support values and higher confidence values. Again, we are not inventing a novel data mining algorithm but a preprocess to be applied to the input datasets of ANY data mining algorithm, once the input format is made compatible.

The Raising method takes advantage of the hierarchy structure of an ontology and collects instances at the lower levels of the hierarchy to enrich the derivation of the association rules which involves the ancestors of these instances. In our experiments, the support values of rule sets were greatly increased, up to 40 times. The effects of Raising on the confidence values were also analyzed based on each type of the possible derived rules. Though not all the confidence values for every rule type were increased during Raising, we found that the rule group (B), which is the most useful for marketing purposes, did have their confidence values increased by Raising. Thus Raising resulted in better rules with higher support and confidence values.

FUTURE RESEARCH DIRECTIONS

The work on Raising, presented in this chapter, relies on the close interplay of an ontology and a large set of instances. Traditionally, ontology researchers have preferred dealing with the engineering of abstract concept hierarchies and the properties of those concepts and hierarchies, possibly including reasoning rules. They leave the creation or classification of large sets of instances to "the users."

On the other hand, many data mining researchers are mostly interested in the efficient and effective processing of large, flat sets of real world instances. Our work is one of several existing approaches, which combine these two aspects into one coherent framework. In effect, by Raising, we are using the ontology as a mechanism for providing the user with an option to mine data at different levels. With Raising she/he can mine many sets, each with a few similar instances, or a few sets, each with many diverse instances. This is comparable to OLAP operations such as drill-down and roll-up. However, no aggregates

of raised instances are computed in our approach, except for the mined rules. In order to further investigate Raising and connections with OLAP, there is a great need for the development of interconnected test beds with *"large instance sets + large ontologies"* from the same domain.

We believe that in the future researchers will increasingly ignore the fine differences between terminologies, ontologies, concept hierarchies, controlled vocabularies, taxonomies, (combined) thesauri, etc., as long as these structures contain concepts organized by a hierarchy of IS-A / subclass / subconcept / a-kind-of links. Thus it will become more common to use, e.g., the unified medical language system (UMLS) Metathesaurus, created by the US National Library of Medicine, as an ontology. Because the UMLS is the largest existing, freely available ontology, with over one million concepts and over six million terms, it provides the "large ontology" needed. On the other hand, "large instance sets" may be derived from existing, extensive electronic medical records (EMR), as long as the privacy of personal data is assured.

We have not investigated the possibility of attaching mined rules to the individual concept nodes of the ontology at which the rules were mined. Doing so would, in effect, make the ontology an index for the mined rules. The rules themselves, together with the IS-A links, would form a rule generalization hierarchy. This would make it easier to select the right rules for each user need. We see this as another avenue for future research.

REFERENCES

Agrawal, R., Imielinski, T., & Swami, A.N. (1993). Mining association rules between sets of items in large databases. In *Proceedings of the 1993 ACM SIGMOD International Conference on Management of Data* (pp. 207-216). New York: ACM Press.

Agrawal, R., & Srikant, R. (1994). Fast algorithms for mining association rules in large databases. In *Proceedings of the 20th International Conference on Very Large Data Bases* (pp. 487-499). San Francisco: Morgan Kaufmann.

Berzal, F., Blanco, I., Sanchez, D., & Vila, M.-A. (2001). Measuring the accuracy and interest of association rules: A new framework. *Intelligent Data Analysis, 6*(3), 221-235.

Cai, C.H., Fu, A.W., Cheng, C.H., & Kwong, W.W. (1998). Mining association rules with weighted items. In *Proceedings of 1998 Internatinal Database Engineering and Applications Symposium,* (pp. 68-77).

Chen, X., Zhou, X., Scherl, R., & Geller, J. (2003). Using an interest ontology for improved support in rule mining. In *Proceedings of the 5th International Conference on Data Warehousing and Knowledge Discovery* ser. *Lecture Notes in Computer Science,* Vol. 2738 (pp. 320-329). New York: Springer Verlag.

Elfeky, M.G., Saad, A.A., & Fouad, S.A. (2001). ODMQL: Object data mining query language. In *Proceedings of the 2000 International Symposium on Objects and Databases* (pp. 128-140). New York: Springer Verlag.

Fortin, S., & Liu, L. (1996). An object-oriented approach to multilevel association rule mining. In *Proceedings of the 5th International Conference on Information and Knowledge Management* (pp. 65-72). New York: ACM Press.

Geller, J., Scherl, R., & Perl, Y. (2002). Mining the Web for target marketing information. In *Proceedings of the Collaborative Electronic Commerce Technology and Research (CollECTeR) Workshop*. Toulouse, France.

Geller, J., Zhou, X., Prathipati, K., Kanigiluppai, S., & Chen, X. (2005). Raising data for improved support in rule mining: How to raise and how far to raise. *Intelligent Data Analysis, 9*(4), 397-415.

Han, J. (1995). Mining knowledge at multiple concept levels. In *Proceedings of the 4th International Conference on Information and Knowledge Management* (pp. 19-24). New York: ACM Press.

Han, J., & Fu, Y. (1995). Discovery of multiple-level association rules from large databases. In *Proceedings of the 21st International Conference on Very Large Data Bases* (pp. 420-431). Zurich, Switzerland.

Han, J., Pei, J., & Yin, Y. (2000). Mining frequent patterns without candidate generation. In *Proceedings of the 2000 ACM SIGMOD International Conference on Management of Data* (pp. 1-12). New York: ACM Press.

Han, J., Pei, J., Yin, Y., & Mao, R. (2004). Mining frequent patterns without candidate generation: A frequent-pattern tree approach. *Data Mining and Knowledge Discovery, 8*(1), 53-87.

Li, Y., & Zhong, N. (2006). Mining ontology for automatically acquiring Web user information needs. *IEEE Transactions on Knowledge and Data Engineering, 18*(4), 554-568.

Lu, S., Hu, H., & Li, F. (2001). Mining weighted association rules. *Intelligent Data Analysis, 5*(3), 211-225.

Mädche, A., & Volz, R. (2001). The ontology extraction and maintenance framework Text-To-Onto. In *Proceedings of the ICDM'01 Workshop on Integrating Data Mining and Knowledge Management*. San Jose, CA.

Mannila, H., Toivonen, H., & Verkamo, A. (1994). Improved methods for finding association rules. In *Proceedings of the AAAI Workshop on Knowledge Discovery* (pp. 181-192). Finland.

Missikoff, M., Velardi, P., & Fabriani, P. (2003). Text mining techniques to automatically enrich a domain ontology. *Applied Intelligence, 18*(3), 323-340.

Novacek, V. (1998). Data mining query language for object-oriented database. In *Proceedings of the 2nd East European Symposium on Advances in Databases and Information Systems* (pp. 278-283). New York: Springer Verlag.

Páircéir, R., McClean, S., & Scotney, B. (2000). Discovery of multilevel rules and exceptions from a distributed database. In *Proceedings of the 6th ACM SIGKDD International Conference on Knowledge Discovery and Data Mining* (pp. 523-532). New York: ACM Press.

Portscher, E., Geller, J., & Scherl, R. (2003). Using internet glossaries to determine interests from home pages. In *Proceedings of the 4th International Conference on Electronic Commerce and Web Technologies* (pp. 248-258). Berlin: Springer Verlag.

Psaila, G., & Lanzi, P. L. (2000). Hierarchy-based mining of association rules in data warehouses. In *Proceedings of the 2000 ACM Symposium on Applied Computing* (pp. 307-312). New York: ACM Press.

Scherl, R., & Geller, J. (2002). Global communities, marketing and Web mining. *Journal of Doing Business Across Borders, 1*(2), 141-150.

Srikant, R., & Agrawal, R. (1995). Mining generalized association rules. In *Proceedings of the 21st International Conference on Very Large Data Base* (pp. 407-419). Zurich, Switzerland.

Tsujii, J., & Ananiadou, S. (2005). Thesaurus or logical ontology, which one do we need for text mining? *Language Resources and Evaluation, 39*(1), 77-90.

Wang, W., Yang, J., & Yu, P.S. (2000). Efficient mining of weighted association rules (WAR). In *Proceedings of the Sixth ACM SIGKDD International Conference* (pp. 270-274). Boston.

Witten, I.H., & Frank, E. (2000) *Data mining, practical machine learning tools and techniques with java implementations.* San Francisco: Morgan Kaufmann.

Xodo, D., & Nigro, H.O. (2005). Knowledge Management in Tourism. In L.C. Rivero, J.H. Doorn, & V.E. Ferraggine (Eds.). *Encyclopedia of database technologies and applications* (pp. 319-329). Hershey, PA: Idea Group Reference.

Zaki, M.J., & Hsiao, C.J. (2002). CHARM: An efficient algorithm for closed itemset mining. In *Proceedings of the 2nd SIAM International Conference on Data Mining.* SIAM.

Zhou, X., Geller, J., Perl, Y., & Halper, M. (2006). An application intersection marketing ontology. *Theoretical computer science: Essays in memory of Shimon Even. Lecture Notes in Computer Science,* Vol. 3895 (pp. 143-153). Berlin: Springer-Verlag.

Zhou, X. (2006). *Enhancing web marketing by using an ontology.* Doctoral dissertation, New Jersey Institute of Technology, Newark, NJ.

Zhou, Z., Liu, H., Li, S.Z., & Chua, C.S. (2001). Rule mining with prior knowledge: A belief networks approach. *Intelligent Data Analysis, 5*(2), 95-110.

ADDITIONAL READING

Adda M., Missaoui R., Valtchev P., & Djerba C. (2005). Recommendation strategy based on relation rule mining. In *Proceedings of the 3rd Workshop on Intelligent Techniques for Web Personalization, in conjunction with IJCAI'05,* Edinburgh, Scotland (pp. 33-40).

Ale, J.M., & Rossi, G. (2005) Discovering association rules in temporal database. *Encyclopedia of database technologies and applications* (pp. 195-200).

Becerra-Fernandez, I. (2006). Searching for experts on the Web: A review of contemporary expertise locator systems. *ACM Transactions on Internet Technology, 6*(4), 333-355.

Bernstein, A., Provost, F.J., & Hill, S. (2006). Toward intelligent assistance for a data mining process: An ontology-based approach for cost-sensitive classification. *IEEE Transactions on Knowledge and Data Engineering, 17*(4), 503-518.

Bonino, D., Corno, F., & Pescarmona, F. (2005). Automatic learning of text-to-concept mappings exploiting WordNet-like lexical networks. In *Proceedings of the 2005 ACM Symposium on Applied Computing SAC'05* (pp. 1639-1644).

Campbell, K.E., Oliver, D.E., & Shortliffe, E.H. (1998). The unified medical language system: Toward a collaborative approach for solving terminologic problems. *JAMIA, 5*(1), 12-16.

Cannataro, M., Guzzi, P.H., Mazza, T., Tradigo, G., & Veltri, P. (2007). Using ontologies for preprocessing and mining spectra data on the Grid. *Future Generation Computer Systems, 23*(1), 55-60.

Charest, M., & Delisle, S. (2006) Ontology-guided intelligent data mining assistance: Combining declarative and procedural knowledge. *Artificial Intelligence and Soft Computing*, 9-14.

Chen, L., Martone, M., Gupta, A., Fong, L., & Wong-Barnum, M. (2006). OntoQuest: Exploring ontological data made easy. VLDB'06, Seoul, Korea (pp. 1183-1186).

Choi, N., Song, I.-Y., & Han, H. (2006) A survey of ontology mapping. *ACM SIGMOD Record, 35*(3), 34-41.

Das, S., Chong, E. I., Eadon, G., & Srinivasan, J. (2004). Supporting ontology-based semantic matching in RDBMS. In *Proceedings of the 30th VLDB Conference*, Toronto (pp. 1054-1065).

Farzanyar, Z., Kangavari, M., & Hashemi, S. (2006). *A new algorithm for mining fuzzy as-sociation rules in the large databases based on ontology.* ICDM Workshops (pp. 65-69).

Furtado, V., Flavio de Souza, F., & Cirne, W. (2007). Promoting performance and separation of concerns for data mining applications on the Grid. *Future Generation Computer Systems, 23*(1), 100-106.

Geller, J., Perl, Y., & Lee, J. (Guest Eds.). (2003). Introduction to the special issue on ontologies: Ontology challenges. *A Thumbnail Historical Perspective, Knowledge and Information Systems (KAIS), 6*(4), 75-379.

Khasawneh, N., & Chan, C. (2006). Active user-based and ontology-based web log data preprocessing for web usage mining. *Web Intelligence*, 325-328.

Klusch, M., Fries, B., & Sycara, K. (2006). Automated Semantic Web service discovery with OWLS-MX. In *Proceedings of the Fifth International Joint Conference on Autonomous Agents and Multiagent Systems* (pp. 915-922).

Köhler, J., Philippi, S., Specht, M., & Rüegg, A. (2006). Ontology based text indexing and querying for the semantic web. *Knowledge-Based systems, 19*(8), 744-754.

Li, Y., & Zhong, N. (2004) Web mining model and its applications for information gathering. *Knowledge-Based Systems, 17*(5-6), 207-217.

Li, Y., Ma, Z., Xie, W., & Laing, C. (2006). Inspection-oriented coding service based on machine learning and semantic mining. *Expert Systems with Applications, 31*(4), 835-848.

Nemrava, J., & Svatek, V. (2005). Text mining tool for ontology engineering based on use of product taxonomy and web directory. In *Proceedings of the DATESO 2005 Annual International Workshop on DAtabases, Texts, Specifications and Objects*, Desna, Czech Republic (pp. 94-102).

Nenadic, G., Spasic, I., & Ananiadou, S. (2003). Terminology-driven mining of biomedical literature. *ACM Symposium on Applied Computing (SAC),* 83-87.

Perl, Y., & Geller, J. (Guest Eds.) (2003). Introduction to the special issue: Research on structural issues of the UMLS. Past, present and future. *Journal of Biomedical Informatics, 36*(6), 409-413.

Phillips, J., & Buchanan, B.G. (2001). Ontology-guided knowledge discovery in databases. In *Proceedings of the 1st International Conference on Knowledge Capture K-CAP '01* (pp. 123-130).

Singh, L., Scheuermann, P., & Chen, B. (1997). *Generating association rules from semistructured documents using an extended concept hierarchy, CIKM 1997,* pp. 193-200.

Stumme, G., Hotho, A., & Berendt, B. (2006). Semantic web mining, state of the art and future directions. *Web Semantics: Science, Services and Agents on the World Wide Web, 4*(2), 124-143.

Chapter III
Web Usage Mining for Ontology Management

Brigitte Trousse
INRIA Sophia Antipolois, France

Marie-Aude Aufaure
INRIA Sophia and Supélec, France

Bénédicte Le Grand
Laboratoire d'Informatique de Paris 6, France

Yves Lechevallier
INRIA Rocquencourt, France

Florent Masseglia
INRIA Sophia Antipolois, France

ABSTRACT

This chapter proposes an original approach for ontology management in the context of Web-based information systems. Our approach relies on the usage analysis of the chosen Web site, in addition to the existing approaches based on Web pages content analysis. Our methodology is based on knowledge discovery techniques mainly from HTTP Web logs and aims to confronting the discovered knowledge in terms of usage with the existing ontology in order to propose new relations between concepts. We illustrate our approach on a Web site provided by local French tourism authorities (related to Metz city) with the use of clustering and sequential patterns discovery methods. One major contribution of this chapter is, thus, the application of usage analysis to support ontology evolution and/or Web site reorganization.

INTRODUCTION

Finding relevant information on the Web has become a real challenge. This is partly due to the volume of available data and the lack of structure in many Web sites. However, information retrieval may also be difficult in well-structured sites, such as those of tourist offices. This is not only due to the volume of data, but also the way information is organized, as it does not necessarily meet Internet users' expectations. Mechanisms are necessary to enhance their understanding of visited sites.

Local tourism authorities have developed Web sites in order to promote tourism and to offer services to citizens. However, this information is scattered and unstructured and thus does not match tourists' expectations. Our work aims at to provide a solution to this problem by:

- Using an existing or semiautomatically built ontology intended to enhance information retrieval.
- Identifying Web users' profiles through an analysis of their visits employing Web usage mining methods, in particular automatic classification and sequential pattern mining techniques.
- Updating the ontology with extracted knowledge. We will study the impact of the visit profiles on the ontology. In particular, we will propose to update Web sites by adapting their structure to a given visit profile. For example, we will propose to add new hyperlinks in order to be consistent with the new ontology.

The first task relies on Web structure and content mining, while the second and the third are deduced from usage analysis. A good structure of information will allow us to extract knowledge from log files (traces of visit on the Web), extracted knowledge will help us update Web sites' ontology according to tourists' expectations. Local tourism authorities will thus be able to use these models

and check whether their tourism policy matches tourists' behavior. This is essential in the domain of tourism, which is highly competitive. Moreover, the Internet is widely available and tourists may even navigate pages on the Web through wireless connections. It is therefore necessary to develop techniques and tools in order to help them find relevant information easily and quickly.

In the future, we will propose to personalize the display, in order to adapt it to each individual's preferences according to his profile. This will be achieved through the use of weights on ontology concepts and relations extracted from usage analysis.

This chapter is composed of five sections. The first section presents the main definitions useful for the comprehension. In the second, we briefly describe the state-of-the-art in ontology management and Web mining. Then, we propose our methodology mainly based on Web usage mining for supporting ontology management and Web site reorganization. Finally, before concluding, we illustrate the proposed methodology in the tourism domain.

BACKGROUND

This section presents the context of our work and is divided into two subsections. We first provide the definitions of the main terms we use in this chapter, then we study the state-of-the-art techniques related to ontology management and to Web mining.

Definitions

- *Web mining* is a knowledge discovery process from databases (called KDD) applied to Web data. Web mining can extract patterns from various types of data; three areas of Web mining are often distinguished: Web content mining, Web structure mining and

Web usage mining (Kosala & Blockeel, 2000).

- *Web content mining* is a form of text mining applied to Web pages. This process allows reveals relationships related to a particular domain via co-occurrences of terms in a text for example.
- *Web structure mining* is used to examine data related to the structure of a Web site. This process operates on Web pages' hyperlinks. Structure mining can be considered as a specialisation of graph mining.
- *Web usage mining* is applied to usage data such as those contained in logs files. A log file contains information related to the queries executed by users on a particular Web site. Web usage mining can be used to support the modification of the Web site structure or to give some recommendations to the visitors. Personalization can also be enhanced by usage analysis (Trousse, Jaczynski, & Kanawati, 1999).
- A *thesaurus* is a *"controlled vocabulary arranged in a known order and structured so that equivalence, homographic, hierarchical, and associative relationships among terms are displayed clearly and identified by standardized relationship indicators."* (ANSI/NISO, 1993). The purpose of a thesaurus is to facilitate documents retrieval. The *WordNet* thesaurus organizes English nouns, verbs, adverbs, and adjectives into a set of synonyms and defines relationships between synonyms.
- *An ontology* aims to formalizing domain knowledge in a generic way and provides a common agreed understanding of a domain, which may be used and shared by applications and groups. According to Gruber, *"an ontology is an explicit specification of a conceptualization"* (Gruber, 1993).

In computer science, the word *ontology*, borrowed from philosophy, represents a set of precisely defined terms (vocabulary) about a specific domain and accepted by this domain's community. Ontologies thus enable people to agree upon the meaning of terms used in a precise domain, knowing that several terms may represent the same concept (synonyms) and several concepts may be described by the same term (ambiguity). Ontologies consist of a hierarchical description of important concepts and of each concept's properties. Ontologies are at the heart of information retrieval from nomadic objects, from the Internet and from heterogeneous data sources.

Ontologies generally are make up of a taxonomy or vocabulary and of inference rules.

- *Information retrieval* provides answers to precise queries, whereas *data mining* aims to discover new and potentially useful schemas from data, which can be materialized with metadata (which are data about data).
- A *user profile* is a set of attributes concerning Web sites' visitors. These attributes provide information that will be used to personalize Web sites according to users' specific needs. Two kinds of information about users—explicit and implicit—can be distinguished. Explicit knowledge about users may come for example from the user's connection mode (with or without a login), his status (e.g., subscription) or personal information (address, preferences, etc.). On the other hand, implicit knowledge—provided by log files—is extracted from users' visit on the Web. In this work, we mainly focus on implicit data extracted from the Web usage. Users' visits will be analyzed so as to be applied online —during the same session—or during future Web visits.
- A *user session/visit profile* corresponds to the implicit information about users based on user sessions or user visits (cf. definitions of 'Step 2' section of our methodology) for precise definitions).

State of the Art of Techniques Related to Ontology Management and to Web Mining

Ontology Management

Regarding ontology management, our state of the art focuses on ontology construction and evolution.

(a) Ontology construction

Methodologies for ontology building can be classified according to the use or non use of a priori knowledge (such as thesaurus, existing ontologies, etc.) and also to learning methods. The first ones were dedicated to enterprise ontology development (Gruber, 1993; Grüninger & Fox, 1995) and manually built. Then, methodologies for building ontologies from scratch were developed, which do not use a priori knowledge. An example of such a methodology is *OntoKnowledge* (Staab et al., 2001), which proposes a set of generic techniques, methods, and principles for each process (feasibility study, initialization, refinement, evaluation, and maintenance). Some research work is dedicated to collaborative ontology building such as *CO*4 (Euzenat, 1995) and (*KA*)2 (Decker et al., 1999). Another research area deals with ontology reengineering (Gòmez-Pérez & Rojas, 1999). Learning methodologies can be distinguished according to their input data type: texts, dictionaries (Jannink, 1999), knowledge bases (Suryanto & Compton, 2001), relational (Rubin et al., 2002; Stojanovic et al., 2002) and semistructured data (Deitel et al., 2001; Papatheodrou et al., 2002; Volz et al., 2003).

In the following subsections, we focus on the general dimensions implied in ontology learning, and describe some approaches for ontology learning from Web pages.

Existing methods can be distinguished according to the following criteria: learning sources, type of ontology, techniques used to extract concepts, relationships and axioms, and existing tools. The most recent methodologies generally use a priori knowledge such as thesaurus, minimal ontology, other existing ontologies, and so forth. Each one proposes different techniques to extract concepts and relationships, but not axioms. These axioms can represent constraints but also inferential domain knowledge. As for instance extraction, we can find techniques based on first order logic (Junker et al., 1999), on Bayesian learning (Craven et al., 2000), and so forth. We have to capitalize the results obtained by the different methods and characterize existing techniques, properties, and ways we can combine them. The objective of this section is to describe the characteristics of these methods.

Learning ontologies is a process requiring at least the following development stages:

- Knowledge source preparation (textual compilations, collection of Web documents), potentially using a priori knowledge (ontology with a high-level abstraction, taxonomy, thesaurus, etc.).
- Data source preprocessing.
- Concepts and relationships learning.
- Ontology evaluation and validation (generally done by experts).

The ontology is built according to the following characteristics:

- **Input type** (data sources, a priori knowledge existence or not, …).
- **Tasks involved for preprocessing:** Simple text linguistic analysis, document classification, text labeling using lexico-syntactic patterns, disambiguating, and so forth.
- **Learned elements:** Concepts, relationships, axioms, instances, thematic roles.
- **Learning methods characteristics:** Supervised or not, classification, clustering, rules, linguistic, hybrid.
- **Automation level:** Manual, semiautomated, automatic, cooperative.

- **Characteristics of the ontology to be built:** Structure, representation language, coverage.
- Usage of the ontology and users' needs (Aussenac-Gilles et al., 2002).

(b) Ontology Evolution

Since the Web is constantly growing and changing, we must expect ontologies to change as well. The reasons to update ontologies are various (Noy et al., 2004): there may have been errors in prior versions, a new terminology or way of modeling the domain may be preferred or the usage may have changed. Specification changes are due, for example, to the transformation of the representation language, while changes at the domain level are comparable to databases' schema evolution. Finally, modifications of conceptualization concern the application or the usage.

The W3C distinguishes ontology evolution and ontology extension. In the first case, a complete restructuring of the ontology is possible while ontology extension does not suppress or modify existing concepts and relations of the original ontology.

Ontology evolution can be achieved in different ways. This evolution may be linked to changes at the application level, which requires dealing with the integration of new data sources and their impact on the ontology. In this context, the challenge consists of specifying the way to link ontology evolution to corpus evolution or other resources which justify them—such as ontologies, thesauri, or text collections. Another possible case of evolution is when two versions of an ontology exist: differences are searched for with techniques quite similar to those used for semantic mapping between ontologies. Evolution and version management can fully take advantage of the numerous works achieved in the databases domain (Rahm & Bernstein, 2001). The issue of ontology evolution is essential for perennial applications.

The compatibility between various versions can be defined as follows:

- Instance preservation.
- Ontology preservation (any query result obtained with the new version is a superset of the old version's results, or the facts inferred with the old version's axioms can also be inferred with the new one).
- Consistency preservation (the new version does not introduce any inconsistency).

An open research problem in this area is the development of algorithms allowing an automatic detection of differences between various versions.

The area of ontology evolution is very active and a lot of work is being done in this domain (Castano et al., 2006; Flouris et al., 2006). The Boemie ("Boostrapping Ontology Evolution with Multimedia Information Extraction." http://www.boemie.org/) IST 6th Framework Programme Project (FP6-027538), which has started in March, 2006 (Spyropoulos et al., 2005), will pave the way towards automation of knowledge acquisition from multimedia content, by introducing the notion of evolving multimedia ontologies.

Web Mining

Web mining is a KDD process applied to Web data. Vast quantities of information are available on the Web, its lack of structure in which Web mining has to cope. A typical KDD process is made of four main steps (cf. Figure 1):

1. *Data selection* aims to extract from the database or data warehouse the information needed by the data mining step.
2. *Data transformation* will then use parsers in order to create data tables which can be used by the data mining algorithms.

3. *Data mining* techniques range from sequential patterns to association rules or cluster discovery.

4. Finally the last step will allow the re-use of the obtained results into a *usage analysis/ interpretation* process.

In such a KDD process, we insist on the importance of the preprocessing step composed of selection and transformation substeps. The input data usually comes from databases or from a file in a standard (such as XML) or private format. Then various data mining techniques may be used according to the data types in order to extract new patterns (association rules, sequential patterns, clusters). And finally some graphical tools and different quality criteria are used in the interpretation step in order to validate the new extracted patterns as new knowledge to be integrated.

In the context of Web usage mining, the data mining methods are applied on usage data relying, if possible, on the notion of user session or user visit. This notion of session enables us to act at the appropriate level during the process of knowledge extraction from log files (Tanasa, 2005; Tanasa & Trousse, 2004). Moreover, a Web site's structure analysis can make knowledge extraction easier. It may also allow us to compare usage analysis with information available on the site, which can lead to Web site and/or ontology updates.

WEB USAGE MINING FOR ONTOLOGY MANAGEMENT

This section presents the proposed methodology for supporting the management of Web sites' ontologies based on usage mining.

Based on the previous states of the art in the two communities—ontology management and Web mining—we can notice that there is a great synergy between content mining (or Web content mining) and ontology management. Indeed, ontologies could be built or updated through content mining in the context of Web sites. Web mining could be improved through the use of ontologies

Figure 1. Steps of the KDD Process

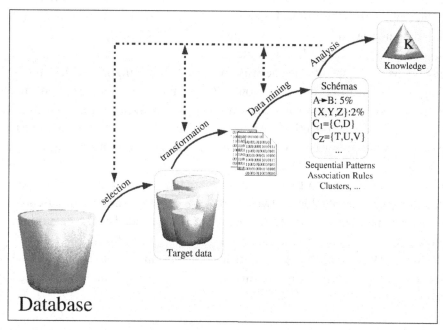

or Web semantics, also called "Semantic Web mining" by (Berendt et al., 2002; Berendt et al., 2005). On the contrary, the use of Web structure mining and Web usage mining are not really explored for supporting ontology construction and evolution. Below, we propose our methodology for supporting ontology extension and Web site reorganization based on Web usage mining techniques.

Proposed Methodology

Our methodology is divided into four steps:

- The first step consists of building the ontology of the considered Web sites—or in enriching the existing ontology if one is already available. The construction of this basic ontology can be achieved through knowledge extraction from Web sites, based on content and structure mining. In the experiment presented in the section entitled 'Illustration in the Tourism Domain,' we used an existing ontology and modified

it according to the structure of the studied Web sites.

- The second step consists of preprocessing the logs (raw data) in a rich usage data warehouse based on various notions such as user session, user visit and so forth.

- The third step aims to apply data mining techniques of users' visits on these Web sites through the analysis of log files in order to update the current ontology. Web usage mining techniques allow us to define visit profiles (or navigation profiles) and then to facilitate the emergence of new concepts, for example by merging several existing ones. Two different methods will be emphasized and used to analyze usage: *clustering* and *sequential pattern mining.*

- Finally, we combine the information obtained from these two methods. One expected result is the ability to update the basic ontology with respect to user visits.

The four steps of our methodology—as shown in Figure 2 (derived from (AxIS, 2005))—are detailed in the following subsections. We first

Figure 2. Steps of the proposed methodology

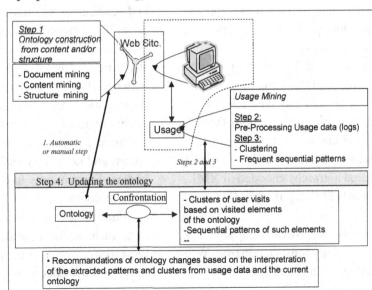

describe ontology construction and preprocessing methods applied to usage data in order to make them usable for analysis. Secondly, we describe two different techniques employed in Web usage mining: clustering and sequential pattern mining. Finally, we explain how to use Web mining to support ontology evolution.

Step 1: Ontology Construction Methods

Ontology construction can be performed manually or semiautomatically. In the first case, this task is hard and time consuming. This is the reason why many methods and methodologies have been designed to semiautomate this process. The data sources can be text, semistructured data, relational data, and so forth. In the following, we describe some methods dedicated to knowledge extraction from Web pages. A survey on ontology learning methods and tools can be found in the OntoWeb Web site (http://ontoweb.org/Members/ruben/Deliverable%201.5).

Many methods or methodologies have been proposed to enrich an existing ontology using Web documents (Agirre et al., 2000; Faatz & Steinmetz, 2002). However, these approaches are not specifically dedicated to Web knowledge extraction.

The approach proposed by Navigli and Velardi (2004) attempts to reduce the terminological and conceptual confusion between members of a virtual community. Concepts and relationships are learned from a set of Web sites using the *Ontolearn* tool. The main steps are: terminology extraction from Web sites and Web documents data warehouse, semantic interpretation of terms, and identification of taxonomic relationships.

Some approaches transform html pages into a semantic structured hierarchy encoded in XML, taking into account HTML regularities (Davulcu et al., 2003).

Finally, we can also point out some approaches only dedicated to ontology construction from Web pages without using any a priori knowledge.

The approach described in Sanchez and Moreno (2004) is based on the following steps: (1) extract some keywords representative of the domain, (2) find a collection of Web sites related to the previous keywords (using for example Google), (3) exhaustive analysis of each Web site, (4) the analyzer searches the initial keywords in a Web site and finds the preceding and following words; these words are candidates to be concepts, (5) for each selected concept, a statistical analysis is performed based on the number of occurrences of this word in the Web sites and finally, (6) for each concept extracted using a window around the initial keyword, a new keyword is defined and the algorithm recursively iterates.

In Karoui et al. (2004) a method is proposed to extract domain ontology from Web sites without using a priori knowledge. This approach takes the Web pages structure into account and defines a contextual hierarchy. The data preprocessing is an important step to define the more relevant terms to be classified. Weights are associated to the terms according to their position in this conceptual hierarchy. Then, these terms are automatically classified and concepts are extracted. In Ben Mustapha et al., (2006) the authors define an ontological architecture based on a semantic triplet, namely: semantics of the contents, structure and services of a domain. This chapter focuses on the domain ontology construction and is based on a metaontology that represents the linguistic structure and helps to extract lexico-syntactic patterns. This approach is a hybrid one, based on statistical and linguistic techniques. A set of candidate concepts, relationships and lexico-syntactic patterns is extracted from a domain corpus and iteratively validated using other Web bodies. Experiments have been realized in the tourism domain.

Many projects also include ontology construction, such as for example the French projects Picsel (http://www.lri.fr/~picsel/) or WebContent (http://www.Webcontent-project.org).

Step 2: Web Logs Preprocessing Methods
In order to prepare the logs for usage analysis, we used the methodology for multisites logs data preprocessing recently proposed by (Tanasa, 2005; Tanasa & Trousse, 2004).

Definitions
Given below are the main definitions extracted from (Tanasa, 2005, page 2), in accordance with the World Wide Web consortium's work on Web characterization terminology:

- A *resource*, according to the W3C's uniform resource identifier specification, can be "anything that has identity." Possible examples include an HTML file, an image, or a Web service.
- A *URI* is a compact string of characters for identifying an abstract or physical resource.
- A *Web resource* is a resource accessible through any version of the HTTP protocol (for example, HTTP 1.1 or HTTP-NG).
- A *Web server* is a server that provides access to Web resources.
- A *Web page* is a set of data constituting one or several Web resources that can be identified by a URI. If the Web page consists of n resources, the first $(n-1)^{th}$ are embedded and the nth URI identifies the Web page.
- A *page view* (also called an hit) occurs at a specific moment in time, when a Web browser displays a Web page.
- A *Web browser* or *Web client* is client software that can send Web requests, handle the responses, and display requested URIs.
- A *user* is a person using a Web browser.
- A *Web request* is a request a Web client makes for a Web resource. It can be *explicit* (user initiated) or *implicit* (Web client initiated). Explicit Web requests (also called *clicks*) are classified as *embedded* (the user selected a link from a Web page) or *user-input* (the user manually initiates the request—for

example, by typing the address in the address bar or selecting the address from the bookmarks or history). Implicit Web requests are generated by the Web client that needs the embedded resources from a Web page (images, multimedia files, script files, etc.) in order to display that page.

- A *Web server log file* contains Web requests made to the Web server, recorded in chronological order. The most popular log file formats are the *Common Log Format* (www.w3.org/Daemon/User/Config/Logging.html#common-logfile-format) and the *Extended CLF*. A line in the ECLF contains the client's host name or IP address, the user login (if applicable), the request's date and time, the operation type (GET, POST, HEAD, and so on), the requested resource's name, the request status, the requested page's size, the user agent (the user's browser and operating system), and the *referrer*. A given Web page's referrer is the URL of whatever the Web page which contains the link that the user followed to the current page. 192.168.0.1 - [03/Feb/ 2006:14:05:59 +0200] "GET /francais/geo/map.html HTTP/1.1" "Mozilla/4.0 (compatible; MSIE 6.0; Windows NT 5.2; .NET CLR 1.1.4322)"

- A user session is a delimited number of a user's explicit Web requests across one or more Web servers. User identification depends on the Web site policies. For Web sites requesting registration, the user identification task is straightforward. In other cases, we use the couple (IP, User Agent) for grouping requests in user session. So the couple (IP, user agent) associated to the set of requests is given an ID session. For instance, a user session S12 = < (192.168.0.1, "Mozilla/4.0 ...."), (['/english/geo/map.html', Fri Feb 3 14:05:59] ['/english/leisure/index.html', Tue Oct 3 14:06:17])> means that a user has requested URL '/english/geo/map.html' followed by

URL '/english/leasure/index.html' 18 seconds later.

- A *visit* (also called a *navigation*) is a subset of consecutive page views from a user session occurring *closely enough* (by means of a time threshold or a semantic distance between pages).

Classical Preprocessing and Advanced Preprocessing

The data preprocessing was done in four steps (cf. Figure 3.) as proposed in Tanasa and Trousse (2004): *data fusion, data cleaning, data structuration, data summarization.*

Generally, in the *data fusion* step, the log files from different Web servers are merged into a single log file. During the *data cleaning* step, the nonrelevant resources (e.g., jpg, js, gif files) and all requests that have not succeeded (cf. code status) are eliminated. In the *data structuration* step, requests are grouped by user, user session, and visit. Finally, after identifying each variable in the accessed URL and their corresponding descriptions, we define a relational database model to use. Next, the preprocessed data is stored in a relational database, during the *data summarization* step. Such a preprocessing process is supported by the AxISLogMiner toolbox (Tanasa, 2005, pp. 97-114).

Our database model for WUM is a star schema and it is implemented using the ACCESS software from Microsoft. The "base" table (cf. Log) is the main or fact table in this model and each line contains information about one request for page view from the provided log files. The dimension tables used are the tables "URL1" and "Navigation." The "URL1" table contains the list of the pages viewed with the decomposition of the file path associated to the page. The "Navigation" table contains the list of sessions, each session being described by many variables (date, number of requests, etc.).

Now we propose to extract through some queries a data table for our database (Sauberlich & Huber, 2001). The statistical units are the set of visits (i.e., navigations) which verify some properties. For each visit we associate the list of the visited pages which are weighted by the number of requests.

Step 3: Web Usage Mining Methods
In the following subsections, we describe the data mining methods we applied on Web usage data in order to illustrate our methodology.

Clustering Methods

Appropriate use of a clustering algorithm is often a useful first step in extracting knowledge from a

Figure 3. Four preprocessing steps

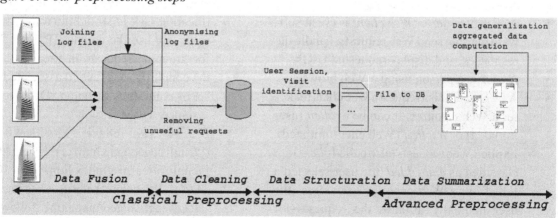

Figure 4. Relational model of the log database

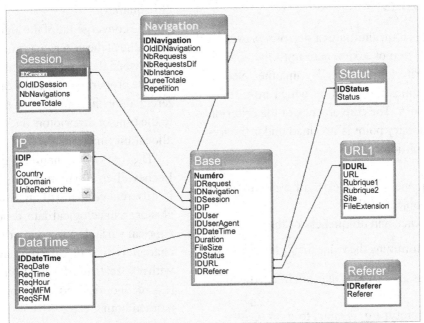

database. Clustering, in fact, leads to a classification, that is the identification of homogeneous and distinct subgroups in data (Bock, 1993; Gordon, 1981), where the definition of homogeneous and distinct depends on the particular algorithm used: this is indeed a simple structure, which, in the absence of a priori knowledge about the multidimensional shape of the data, may be a reasonable starting point towards the discovery of richer and more complex structures.

In spite of the great wealth of clustering algorithms, the rapid accumulation of large databases of increasing complexity raises a number of new problems that traditional algorithms are not suited to address. One important feature of modern data collection is the ever increasing size of a typical database: it is not unusual to work with databases containing from a few thousand to a few million items and hundreds or thousands of variables. Now, most clustering algorithms of the traditional type are severely limited as to the number of individuals they can comfortably handle (hundreds to thousands).

(a) General scheme of dynamical clustering algorithm

Let E be a set of n objects; each object s of E is described by p variables of V. The description space defined by the set of variables is D and x_s is the vector of description of object s in D. A weight $\mu_s > 0$ can be associated to the object s. The proposed clustering algorithm (Diday, 1975), according to the dynamical clustering algorithm, looks simultaneously for a *partition P* of E in k classes and for a *vector L* of k prototypes $(g_1, ..., g_i, ..., g_k)$ associated to the classes $(C_1, ..., C_i, ..., C_k)$ of the partition P that minimizes a criterion Δ:

$$\Delta(P^*, L^*) = Min \left\{ \Delta(P, L) \mid P \in P_k, L \in D^k \right\}$$

with P_k *the set of partitions* of E in k no-empty classes. Such criterion Δ expresses the fit between the partition P and the vector of the k prototypes. That is defined as the sum of the distances between all the objects s of E and the prototypes g_i of the nearest class C_i:

$$\Delta(P,L) = \sum_{i=1}^{k} \sum_{s \in C_i} \mu_s \psi^2(x_s, g_i) \quad C_i \in P, g_i \in D$$

The algorithm alternates a step of *representation* with a step of *assignment* until the convergence of criterion Δ. After N_r runs the selected partition comes the partition which minimizes the criterion Δ. The convergence of the criterion Δ to a stationary point is obtained under the following conditions:

- Uniqueness of the class of assignment of each object of E,
- Existence and uniqueness of the prototype g_C minimizing the value for $\sum_{s \in C} \mu_s \psi^2(x_s, g)$ all classes C of E. If ψ is Euclidian distance the prototype g_C is equal to $g_C = \dfrac{\sum_{s \in C} \mu_s x_s}{\sum_{s \in C} \mu_s}$

For more details on the chosen algorithm, see (Diday, 1975).

(b) The crossed clustering approach

Our aim is to obtain simultaneously a rows partition and a columns partition from a contingency table. Some authors (Govaert, 1977; Govaert & Nadif, 2003) proposed the maximization of the chi-squared criterion between rows and columns of a contingency table.

As in the classical clustering algorithm the criterion optimized is based on the best fit between classes of objects and their representation. In our analysis of the relations between visits and pages, we propose to represent the classes by prototypes which summarize the whole information of the visits belonging to each of them. Each prototype is even modeled as an object described by multicategories variables with associated distributions. In this context, several distances and dissimilarity functions could be proposed as assignment. In particular, if the objects and the prototypes are described by multicategories variables, the dissimilarity measure can be chosen

as a classical distance between distributions (e.g., chi-squared).

The convergence of the algorithm to a stationary value of the criterion is guaranteed by the best fit between the type representation of the classes and the properties of the allocation function. Different algorithms have been proposed according to the type of descriptors and to the choice of the allocation function.

The crossed dynamic algorithm (Verde & Lechevallier, 2003) on objects has been proposed in different contexts of analysis, for example: to cluster archaeological data, described by multicategorical variables; to compare social-economics characteristics in different geographical areas with respect to the distributions of some variables (e.g., economics activities; income distributions; worked hours; etc.).

Sequential Pattern Extraction Methods

Sequential pattern mining deals with data represented as sequences (a sequence contains sorted sets of items). Compared to the association rule extraction, a study of such data provides «intertransaction» analysis (Agrawal & Srikant, 1995). Due to the notion of time embedded in the data, applications for sequential pattern extraction are numerous and the problem definition has been slightly modified in several ways. Associated to elegant solutions, these problems can match real-life time stamped data (when association rules fail) and provide useful results.

(a) Definitions

Let us first provide additional definitions: the *item* is the basic value for numerous data mining problems. It can be considered as the object bought by a customer or the page requested by the user of a Website, etc. An *itemset* is the set of items that are grouped by timestamp (e.g., all the pages requested by the user on June 4, 2004). A *data sequence* is a sequence of itemsets associated to a customer. Table 1 gives a simple example of four customers and their activity over four days on the Web site of New York City. In Table 1, the data sequence of C2 is the following: «(Met, Subway) (Theater, Liberty) (Restaurant)», which means that the customer searched for information about the Metropolitan Museum and about the subway the same day, followed by Web pages on a theater and the Statue of Liberty the following day, and finally a restaurant two days later.

A *sequential pattern* is included in a data sequence (for instance «(Subway) (Restaurant)» is included in the data sequence of C2, whereas «(Theater) (Met)» is not, because of the time-stamps). The *minimum support* is specified by the user and stands for the minimum number of occurrences of a sequential pattern to be considered as *frequent*. A *maximal frequent sequential pattern* is included in at least «minimum support» data sequences and is not included in any other frequent sequential pattern. With a minimum support of 50% a sequential pattern can be considered as frequent if it occurs at least in the data sequences of 2 customers (2/4). In this case a maximal sequential pattern mining process will find three patterns:

- S1: «(Met, Subway) (Theater, Liberty)»
- S2: «(Theater, Liberty) (Restaurant)»
- S3: «(Bridge) (Central Park)»

One can observe that S1 is included in the data sequences of C2 and C4, S2 is included in those of C2 and C3, and S3 in those of C1 and C2. Furthermore the sequences do not have the same length (S1's length = 4, S2's length = 3 and S3's length = 2).

(b) Web usage mining based on sequential patterns

Various techniques for sequential pattern mining were applied on access log files (Bonchi et al., 2001; Masseglia et al., 1999; Masseglia et al., 2004; Nakagawa & Mobasher, 2003; Spiliopoulou et al., 1999; Tanasa, 2005; Zhu et al., 2002). The main interest in employing such algorithms for Web usage data is that they take into account the time-dimension of the data (Masseglia et al., 1999; Spiliopoulou et al., 1999).

The *WUM* tool (*Web Utilisation Miner*) proposed in (Spiliopoulou et al., 1999) allows the discovery of visit patterns, which are interesting either from the statistical point of view or through their structure. The extraction of sequential patterns proposed by *WUM* is based on the frequency of considered patterns. Other subjective criteria that can be specified for the visit patterns are, for example, the act of passing through pages with certain properties or a high confidence level between two or several pages of the visit pattern.

In Masseglia et al., (1999) the authors propose the *WebTool* platform. The extraction of sequential patterns in *WebTool* is based on PSP, an algorithm developed by the authors, whose originality is to propose a prefix tree storing both the candidates and the frequent patterns.

Unfortunately, the dimensionality of these data (in terms of different items—pages—as well as sequences) is an issue for the techniques of sequential pattern mining. More precisely,

Table 1. Data sequences of four customers over four days

Cust	June 04, 2004	June 05, 2004	June 06, 2004	June 07, 2004
C1	Met, Subway	Digital Camera	Bridge	Central Park
C2	Met, Subway	Theater, Liberty		Restaurant
C3	Theater, Liberty	Bridge	Restaurant	Central Park
C4		Met, Subway	Empire State	Theater, Liberty

because of the significant number of different items, the number of results obtained is very small. The solution would consist of lowering the minimum support used, but in this case the algorithms would not be able to finish the process and thus to provide results.

A proposal for solving this issue was made by the authors of Masseglia et al. (2004) who were interested in extracting sequential patterns with low support on the basis that high values of supports often generate obvious patterns. To overcome the difficulties encountered by sequential pattern mining methods when lowering the value of the minimum support, the authors proposed to address the problem in a recursive way in order to proceed to a phase of data mining on each subproblem. The subproblems correspond to the users' visits with common objectives (i.e., sublogs containing only the users, which passed through similar pages). The various patterns obtained are from to visit on a research team's tutorial by a set of hacking attempts, which used the same techniques of intrusion. Tanasa (2005) included these two proposals in a more general methodology of sequential pattern mining with low support.

Another solution is to reduce the number of items by using a generalization of URLs. In Fu et al. (2000) the authors use a syntactic generalization of URLs with a different type of analysis (clustering). Before applying a clustering with the *BIRCH* algorithm (Zhang et al., 1996), the syntactic topics of a level greater than two are replaced by their syntactic topics of a lower level. For example, instead of http://www-sop.inria.fr/axis/Publications/2005/all.html, they will use http://www-sop.inria.fr/axis/, or http://www-sop.

inria.fr/axis/Publications/. However, this syntactic generalization, although automatic, is naive because it is based only on the physical organization given to the Web site's pages. An improper organization will implicitly generate a bad clustering and thus generate results of low quality. In Tanasa and Trousse (2004), a generalization based on semantic topics is made during the preprocessing of Web logs. These topics (or categories) are given a priori by an expert of the field to which the Web site belongs. However, this is a time-consuming task both for the creation and for the update and maintenance of such categories.

For traditional Web usage mining methods, the general idea is similar to the principle proposed in Masseglia et al., (1999). Raw data is collected in a Web log file according to the structure described in Section 'Step 2: Definitions.' This data structure can be easily transformed to the one used by sequential pattern mining algorithms. A record in a log file contains, among other data, the client IP, the date and time of the request, and the Web resource requested. To extract frequent behaviors from such a log file, for each user session or visit in the log file, we first have to: transform the ID-Session into a client number (ID), the date and time into a time number, and the URL into an item number.

Table 2 gives a file example obtained after that preprocessing. For each client, there is a corresponding series of times along with the URL requested by the client at each time. For instance, the client 2 requested the URL "f" at time $d4$. The goal is thus, by means of a data mining step, to find the sequential patterns in the file that can be considered as frequent. The result may be, for instance, <(a)(c)(b)(c)> (with the file

Table 2. File obtained after a preprocessing step

Client	d1	d2	d3	d4	d5
1	a	c	d	b	c
2	a	c	b	f	c
3	a	g	c	b	c

illustrated in Table 2 and a minimum support given by the user: 100%). Such a result, once mapped back into URLs, strengthens the discovery of a frequent behavior, common to n users (with n the threshold given for the data mining process) and also gives the sequence of events composing those behaviors.

Nevertheless, most methods that were designed for mining patterns from access log files cannot be applied to a data stream coming from Web usage data (such as visits). In our context, we consider that large volumes of usage data are arriving at a rapid rate. Sequences of data elements are continuously generated and we aim to identify representative behaviors. We assume that the mapping of URLs and clients as well as the data stream management are performed simultaneously.

Step 4: Recommendations for Updating the Ontology via Web Mining

For supporting ontology management, we provide recommendations for updating the ontology via Web mining techniques, mainly via Web usage mining.

The result of Web mining applied to usage data provides classes of pages and visits. The clustering relies on the site's structure, visit classes (also called visit profiles) are based on clusters of visited pages and pages labeling is achieved syntactically with regard to the directories corresponding to the Web sites' structure. In order to see the impact on the ontology, a matching must be done between these syntactic categories and the ontology's semantic concepts.

Our updates mostly concern ontology extension which does not completely modify the initial ontology:

- Addition of a leaf concept in a hierarchy
- Addition of a subtree of concepts in the hierarchy

- Addition of a relation between two concepts

A new concept may appear as a consequence of the emergence of a class of user visits (from the classification process).

In the same way, a new relation between two concepts may be identified through the extraction of sequential patterns. The chosen example in the experimentation described in the following section allows us to illustrate the two first cases.

ILLUSTRATION IN TOURISM DOMAIN

The chosen application is dedicated to the tourism domain and is based on Web usage mining to evaluate the impact of the results of usage analysis on the domain ontology.

Web Site Description and Ontology Building

We analyzed the Web site of the French city of Metz (http://tourisme.mairie-metz.fr/) illustrated by Figures 5 and 6.

This Web site continues to develop and has been awarded several times, notably in 2003, 2004, and 2005 in the context of the "Internet City @@@@" label. This label enables local authorities to evaluate and to show the deployment of a local citizen Internet available to everyone for the general interest.

This Web site contains a set of headings such as events, hotels, specialties, etc. It also contains a heading visit where they exists many slides shows.

For this experiment, we used an existing ontology and modified it according to the structure of the studied Web site. This ontology was built according to the World Tourism Organization

Figure 5. The chosen tourism Web site (the general home page)

Figure 6. The chosen tourism Web site (the French home page)

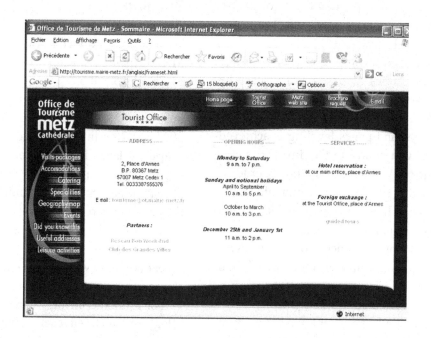

Figure 7. The domain ontology

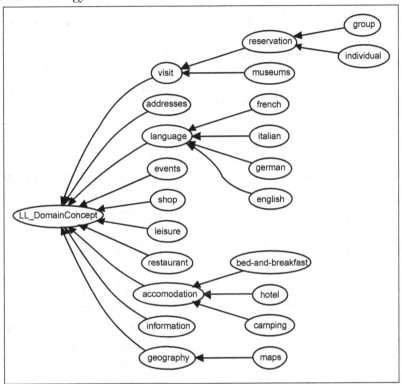

thesaurus. A thesaurus is a "controlled vocabulary arranged in a known order and structured so that equivalence, homographic, hierarchical, and associative relationships among terms are displayed clearly and identified by standardized relationship indicators" (ANSI/NISO, 1993). The main objective associated to a thesaurus is to facilitate documents retrieval. This ontology, edited with Protégé 2000, is represented on Figure 7.

Preprocessing Web Logs

The used log dataset consists in 4 HTTP log files with a total of 552809 requests for page views (91 MB). These requests were made from the Tourism office Web site from the Metz city. Each log file (corresponding to one week) contains all the requests covering a continuous 28-day period starting from 08:00AM 1st January 2006 until 06:21AM on the 29th January 2006.

The log files contain the following six fields (cf. Table 3):

- **IP address:** The computer's IP address of the user making the request
- **Date:** The Unix time of the request
- **Request:** The requested resource (page, picture,...) on the server
- **Status:** The HTTP status code returned to the client, such as success (200)
- Failure, redirection, forbidden access…
- **Size:** The content-length of the document transferred document
- **User Agent:** The user agent

During the preprocessing step, we thus grouped the 76133 requests remaining after preprocessing into 9898 sessions (i.e., sets of clicks from the same (IP, User Agent)). Each session is divided into several visits. A visit ends when at least a

Table 3. Format of the requests

IP	Date	Requests	Status	Size	User Agent
213.151.91.186	[25/ Sep/2005:07:45:49 +0200]	"GET /francais/ frameset.html HTTP/1.0"	200	1074	Mozilla 4.0
abo.wanadoo.fr	[25/ Sep/2005:07:52:23 +0200]	"GET /images/ backothtml.gif HTTP/1.1"	200	11588	Firefox 1.0

Table 4. Quantity of pages requested during each visit

visits	Pages (number of requests)
V_307(14)	tourisme.mairie-metz.fr(3) francais/frameset.html(2) francais/ot.html(3), ...
...	...
V_450(15)	anglais/frameset.html(2); anglais/geo/carte.html(1) anglais/manif/manif2006.html(1),..

30 minute interval exists between two consecutive requests belonging to the same session. The statistical unit for the analysis is the visit and the number of visits is equal to 11624. The number of distinct Urls' requested by users is 723.

For our analysis, we did not consider the status code and thus assumed that all requests had succeeded (code 200).

Afterwards, we generated from the relational database (cf. Figure 4 for the schema) the dataset used for the visit clustering, illustrated on Table 4. Here we have considered a crossed table where each line corresponds to a visit and the column describes one multicategorical variable, which represents the number of pages requested during each visit. We have limited our clustering analysis to the visits where the time is greater than 60 seconds and where more than 10 pages were visited.

We thus obtain 1852 visits (in different languages as shown on Table 5), 375 visited pages and 42238 requests on these pages.

Usage Analysis Results

Clustering Results

The confusion table (cf. Table 6) reports the results obtained after applying the crossed clustering method specifying 11 classes of visits and 10 classes of pages. The language is very important; the set of English pages is split into three classes (PEd_1, PE_2 and PE_3), the set of Germany pages into two classes (PGd_1 and PG_2), Italian into one (PI_1) and the set of French pages into three classes (PF_1, PFd_2 and PF_3), one class (PS_1) represents the set of organization pages (frame pages and home) and the set of pages which are used by all languages (address of hotel, restaurant).

It should be noted that the percentage of the clicks on the pages of English language is 10.6% and on the pages of German language is 22.7%. This proportion is the same for the entire set

Table 5. Linguistic distribution of the visits

language	Number of visits	proportion
English	194	10.5
German	400	21.6
Italian	28	1.5
French	1220	65.9
Multi Lang	10	0.5
Total	1852	100

of visits. It should be noted that the class of the slideshows exists in all the languages. The group of visits (VE_2) contains 52 visits, which contain mostly clicks on English pages (2138 out of 2304 clicks during these visits, accounting for 92.8% of the visited pages). We obtain similar results with the groups of visits of German language. For all the languages the average number of clicks during a visit belonging to the three groups of visits on the slideshows (labeled "d" for "diaporama" in French)that is (PEd_1, PGd_1 and PFd_2) is

identical (approximately 50 clicks per visit) and for it is much higher than the average calculated for the other groups of visits (between 15 to 20 clicks per visit).

42238 is the number of clicks realized by the set of selected visits. The group "V_1" contains 10 visits using multi languages and 28 clicks on the pages belonging to the page class "PE_2."

PEd_1 contains all the pages of English language associated with the slideshows of the site and PE_2 contains the other pages of English

Figure 8. Page groups and visit classes

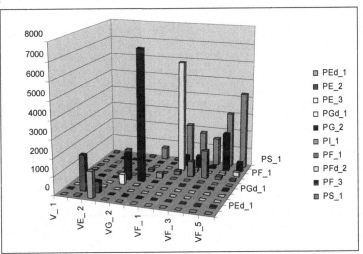

Table 6. Confusion table

Partition	PEd_1	PE_2	PE_3	PGd_1	PG_2	PI_1	PF_1	PFd_2	PF_3	PS_1	Total
V_1 (10)	0	28	0	0	32	44	8	0	7	*74*	193
VE_1 (142)	**76**	**1992**	**34**	0	38	1	16	0	7	*289*	2453
VE_2 (52)	**1464**	**606**	**68**	0	1	1	2	4	22	*136*	2304
VG_1 (37)	0	0	0	*566*	*1496*	0	14	0	1	*68*	2145
VG_2 (363)	11	48	3	*36*	*7278*	2	114	4	10	*669*	8175
VI_1 (28)	0	7	0	0	0	*279*	0	0	1	*33*	320
VF_1 (205)	0	13	0	0	8	11	218	6178	578	*2195*	9201
VF_2 (178)	0	25	0	0	15	2	848	100	643	*1803*	3436
VF_3 (205)	0	17	0	0	31	0	1553	12	116	*1527*	3256
VF_4 (320)	0	41	1	0	30	0	154	105	2122	*3067*	5520
VF_5 (312)	0	60	1	0	65	7	83	232	529	*4258*	5235
Total	1551	2837	107	602	8994	347	3010	6635	4036	14119	42238

language except some special pages, which belong to group PE_3 (these pages represent the activity of the "jewels"). We have a similar result for the German language, but PGd_1 contains only the pages of the slideshows that give a general

vision of the town of Metz. PFd_2 contains the French pages of the slideshows. The first group (PF_1) of the pages of French language contains the pages related to housing restoration. PF_3 contains the pages related to the two concepts

Figure 9. Factorial analysis between visits and visited pages

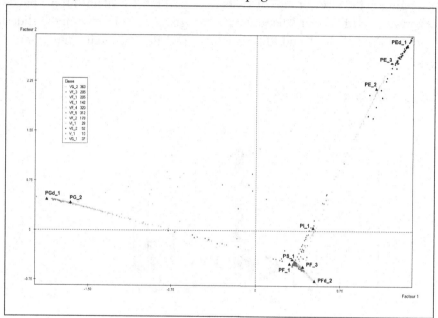

Figure 10. Relation between page classes and visit classes

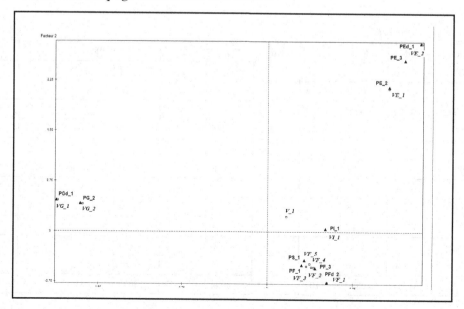

leisure (URL francais/loisirs/(velocation, shop, etc.)). HTML and the cultural or festive *events* (URL francais/manif/(manif2006,manif2005). html) and also pages to different regional specialties of the city (URL francais/specialites/(tartes, caramel, luth,...) html). Group (PS_1) contains the structuring pages (banner page, page related to the frames.) and the whole set of pages employed by the visitors (international hotel).

The factorial analysis (cf. Figure 9) shows that the visits associated with the pages related to the slideshows ('diaporama' in French) are at the border of the first factorial plan (PGd_1, PFd_2 and PEd_1) and the three directions represent the three languages (PGd_1 and PG_2 for the set of German pages, PE_1, PE_2 and PE_3 for the English pages and the PF_1, PFd_2 and PF_3 for the French pages).

Figure 10 shows the third axis related to the direction associated with the Italian pages (PI_1).

We can note that the V_1 group of the visits is a includes of the visits which includes pages of different languages. Figures 9 and 10 show that the groups of visits are very separate according to the language. The pages in French can be extracted for a specific analysis, for example to study how the vision of the slideshows can be connected to other activities (reservation of cultural activities, hotels and restaurants).

Sequential Pattern Extraction Results

After the preprocessing step, the log file of Metz city's Web site contains 723 URLs and 11624 visit sequences. These sequences have an average length of 6.5 itemsets (requested URLs). The extracted sequences reflect the frequent behaviors of users connected to the site. These have been obtained from the whole log file (including all the resources in all languages) with different minimum supports. We report in this section a few sequential patterns extracted from the log file:

Pattern 1:

http://tourisme.mairie-metz.fr/

→ http://tourisme.mairie-metz.fr/francais/frameset.html

→ http://tourisme.mairie-metz.fr/francais/resto/resto.html

→ http://tourisme.mairie-metz.fr/francais/resto/touresto.html

Support: 0.0238577

This behavior has a support of 2.38%. This means that it corresponds to 277 users of the Web site. These users are likely to be interested in finding a restaurant in Metz.

Pattern 2:

http://tourisme.mairie-metz.fr/francais/frameset.html

→ http://tourisme.mairie-metz.fr/francais/hebergement/heberg.html

→ http://tourisme.mairie-metz.fr/francais/geo/carte.html

Support: 0.0200722

This behavior has a support of 2%. Such a behavior corresponds to users interested by in lodging ("hebergement" in French), afterwards in a map ("carte" in French).

Results for Supporting the Update of the Ontology

The interpretation of usage analysis results from clustering and sequential pattern mining allow us to make suggestions in order to support ontology management and more precisely to update the ontology, as explained in this subsection.

Suggestion to add a concept derived from usage analysis (gathering several existing concepts): We observed that pages from the two concepts *leisure* and *events* and from regional specialties are grouped together (PE_3 group). First, the concept of *specialty* does not exist in our domain ontology and could be added as shown in Figure 11.

Figure 11. Updated ontology

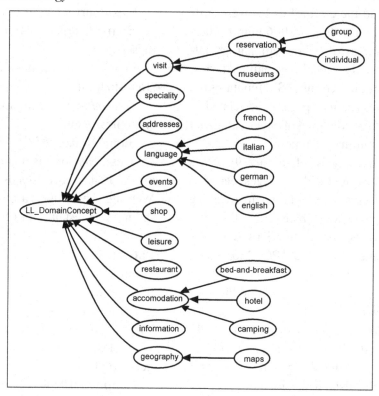

Moreover, as these notions seem to be frequently associated during visits, two evolutions of the ontology are possible:

- Relationships could be added between these three ontological concepts.
- These three concepts could become specializations of a new—more general—concept.

Let us note that there are many pages related to events (francais/specialites/fete.html, francais/specialites/galerie.html), which are stored in the repertory *specialites*.

Our goal is to suggest possible ontology evolutions consistent with usage analysis, but a validation from an expert is required to make a choice between different propositions.

We also note that *Slide show ("diaporama"* in French) represents 50% of pages from the « Visit »

category, and represents about one third of the pages globally visited on the site. The addition of a *Slide show* concept in the domain ontology could thus be suggested.

Suggestion to add a relation between concepts: The sequential pattern mining suggests that a relation exists between *accommodation* and *geography/maps* due to the extraction of various patterns linking a page of the concept *accommodation* and *maps* such as the frequent sequential pattern 2 previously described. This relationship extracted from usage analysis does not exist as a hyperlink on the Web site.

CONCLUSION

Ontology construction and evolution requires the extraction of knowledge from heterogeneous sources. In the case of the Semantic Web, the knowledge extraction is often done from the content of a set of Web pages dedicated to a particular domain. In this chapter, we considered another kind of pattern as we focused on Web usage mining. Web usage mining extracts visit patterns from Web log files and can also extract information about the Web site structure and visit profiles. Among Web usage mining applications, we can point out personalization, modification and improvement of Web pages, and detailed description of Web site usage.

In this chapter, we attempt to show the potential impact of Web usage mining on ontology updating. We illustrate such an impact in the tourism domain by considering the Web site of a French local authority; we start from a domain ontology—obtained through the adaptation of an existing ontology to the structure of the actual Web site. Then, we apply different Web usage mining techniques to the logs files generated from this site, in particular clustering and sequential pattern mining methods. Web usage mining provides relevant information to users and it is therefore a very powerful tool for information retrieval. As we mentioned in the previous section, Web usage mining can also be used to support the modification of the Web site structure or to give some recommendations to visitors.

Web mining can be useful to add semantic annotations (ontologies) to Web documents and to populate these ontological structures. In the experiment presented in this chapter, the domain ontology was manually built and we used usage mining to update it. In the future, we will combine Web content and structure mining for a semiautomatic construction of the domain ontology. Regarding the ontology evolution, we will still mainly exploit usage mining but we will also use content mining to confirm suggested updates. This combination of Web content and usage mining could allow us to build ontologies according to Web pages content and to refine them with behavior patterns extracted from log files.

Our ultimate goal is to mine all kinds of patterns—content, structure and usage—to perform ontology construction and evolution.

FUTURE RESEARCH DIRECTIONS

Many future research directions are possible related to ontology management. Considering ontology management as a complex and interactive process, we mention here two important directions: Semantic Web mining and Semantic Web visualisation.

First Semantic Web Mining aims to combine the two areas Semantic Web and Web Mining by using semantics to improve mining and using mining to create semantics (Berendt & al, 2005). More work is needed to realize such a convergence. See (Stumme & al, 2006) for a interesting survey and future directions in that area. In some domains consensual knowledge already exists and could be used for improving Web mining. But in many other domains it might be necessary to start from data and design the first version of ontology via ontology learning/construction. To achieve such learning, it is useful to combine Web usage mining with content and structure analysis in order to give sense to the observed extracted user behavior. New WUM approaches based on structure mining are needed for improving the recommendations to support the evolution of ontologies.

Another way to provide more accurate results is to involve users in the mining process, which is the goal of visual data mining. Ontologies (and other semantic formalisms, which create semantic graphs) are very powerful but they may be complex. Intuitive visual user interfaces may significantly reduce the cognitive load of users when working with these complex structures. Visualization is a promising technique for both enhancing users' perception of structure in large information spaces and providing navigation facilities. According to (Gershon&Eick, 1995), it also enables people to use a natural tool of observation and processing—their eyes as well as their brain—to extract knowledge more efficiently and find insights. The goal of semantic graphs visualization is to help users locate relevant information quickly and explore the structure easily. Thus, there are two kinds of requirements for semantic graphs visualization: representation and navigation. A good representation helps users identify interesting spots whereas an efficient navigation is essential to access information rapidly. We both need to understand the structure of metadata and to locate relevant information easily. A study of representation and navigation metaphors for Semantic Web visualization has been studied by (LeGrand & Soto, 2005) where the semantic relationships between concepts appear on the display, graphically or textually.

Many open research issues remain in the domain of Semantic Web visualization; in particular, evaluation criteria must be defined in order to compare the various existing approaches. Moreover, scalability must be addressed, as most current visualization tools can only represent a limited volume of data.

To conclude we strongly believe in the potential of multi-disciplinary approaches in Web mining for supporting ontology management.

ACKNOWLEDGMENT

The authors want to thank Mr. Rausch, Mr. Hector, and Mr. Hoffmann from the French city of Metz for making their log files available to us. We also thank Mr. Mercier and Mr. Vialle for helping us to make contacts with the French city of Metz. The authors also want to thank Doru Tanasa for his support in the preprocessing step of the tourism logs, and Alex Thibau and Sophie Honnarat for their helpful support.

REFERENCES

Agirre, E., Ansa, O., Hovy, E., & Martinez, D. (2000). Enriching very large ontologies using the WWW. In *Proceedings of ECAI Workshop on Ontology Learning.*

Agrawal, R., & Srikant, R. (1995). Mining Sequential Patterns. In *Proceedings of the 11th International Conference on Data Engineering* (pp. 3-14).

ANSI/NISO. (1993). *Guidelines for the construction, format, and management of monolingual thesauri.* National Information Standards Organization.

Aussenac-Gilles, N., Biébow, B., & Szulman, S. (2002). Revisiting ontology design: A methodology based on corpus analysis. In *Proceedings of the 12th International Conference in Knowledge Engineering and Knowledge Management (EKAW),* Juan-Les-Pins, France.

AxIS. (2005). *2005 AxIS research project activity report.* Section 'Overall Objectives.' http://www.inria.fr/rapportsactivite/RA2005/axis/axis_tf.html

Mustapha, N., Aufaure, M-A., & Baazhaoui-Zghal, H. (2006). Towards an architecture of ontological components for the semantic web. In *Proceedings of Wism (Web Information Systems Modeling) Workshop, CAiSE 2006,* Luxembourg (pp. 22-35).

Berendt, B., Hotho, A., & Stumme. G. (2002). Towards Semantic Web mining. In *Proceedings of the First International Semantic Web Conference on the Semantic Web* (pp. 264-278). Springer.

Berendt, B., Hotho, A., & Stumme. G. (2005, September 15-16). Semantic Web mining and the representation, analysis, and evolution of Web space. In *Proceedings of RAWS'2005—Workshop on the Representation and Analysis of Web Space,* Prague-Tocna.

Bock, H.H. (1993). Classification and clustering: Problems for the future. In E. Diday, Y. Lechevallier, M. Schader, P. Bertrand, & B. Burtschy, (Eds.), *New approaches in classification and data analysis* (pp. 3-24). Springer, Heidelberg.

Bonchi, F., Giannotti, F., Gozzi, C., Manco, G., Nanni, M., Pedreschi, D., et al. (2001). Web log data warehousing and mining for intelligent web caching. *Data Knowledge Engineering, 39*(2), 165-189.

Castano, S., Ferrara, A., & Montanelli., S. (2006). A matchmaking-based ontology evolution methodology. In *Proceedings of the 3rd CAiSE INTEROP Workshop on Enterprise Modelling and Ontologies for Interoperability (EMOI-INTEROP 2006)*, Luxembourg.

Craven, M., DiPasquo, D., Freitag, D., McCallum, A., Mitchell, T., Nigam, K., et al. (2000). Learning to construct knowledge bases from the World Wide Web. *Artificial Intelligence, 118*(1-2), 69-113.

Davulcu, H., Vadrevu, S., & Nagarajan, S. (2003). OntoMiner: Bootstrapping and populating ontologies from domain specific websites. In *Proceedings of the First International Workshop on Semantic Web and Databases (SWDB 2003)*, Berlin.

Decker, S., Erdmann, M., Fensel, D., & Studer, R. (1999). Ontobroker: Ontology based access to distributed and semistructured information. *In Semantic Issues in Multimedia Systems, Proceedings of DS-8* (pp. 351-369). Boston: Kluwer Academic Publisher.

Deitel, A.C., Faron, C. & Dieng, R. (2001). Learning ontologies from RDF annotations. In *Proceedings of the IJCAI'01 Workshop on Ontology Learning*, Seattle, WA.

Diday, E. (1975). La méthode des nuées dynamiques. *Revue de Statistique Appliquée, 19*(2), 19-34.

Euzenat, J. (1995). Building consensual knowledge bases: Context and architecture. In *Proceedings of 2nd International Conference on Building and Sharing Very Large-Scale Knowledge Bases*. Enschede, Amsterdam: IOS Press.

Faatz, A., & Steinmetz, R. (2002). *Ontology enrichment with texts from the WWW*. Semantic Web Mining 2nd Workshop at ECML/PKDD-2002. Helsinki, Finland.

Flouris, G. (2006). *On belief change and ontology evolution*. Doctoral Dissertation, Department of Computer Science, University of Crete.

Flouris, G., & Plexousakis, D.G. (2006). Evolving ontology evolution, Invited Talk. In *Proceedings of the 32nd International Conference on Current Trends in Theory and Practice of Computer Science (SOFSEM 06)* (p. 7). Merin, Czech Republic.

Fu, Y., Sandhu, K., & Shih, M. (2000). A generalization-based approach to clustering of web usage sessions. In *Proceedings of the 1999 KDD Workshop on Web Mining* (Vol. 1836, pp. 21-38). San Diego, CA: Springer-Verlag.

Gerson, N., & Eick, S.G. (1995). Visualisation's new tack: Making sense of information. *IEEE Spectrum, 38-56*.

Gòmez-Pérez, A., & Rojas, M.D. (1999). Ontological reengineering and reuse. In D. Fensel & R. Studer (Ed.), *European Workshop on Knowledge Acquisition, Modeling and Management (EKAW). Lecture Notes in Artificial Intelligence LNAI 1621* (pp. 139-156). Springer-Verlag.

Gordon, A.D. (1981). *Classification: Methods for the exploratory analysis of multivariate data*. London: Chapman & Hall.

Govaert, G. (1977). Algorithme de classification d'un tableau de contingence. In *Proceedings of first international symposium on Data Analysis and Informatics* (pp. 487-500). INRIA, Versailles.

Govaert, G., & Nadif, M. (2003). Clustering with block mixture models. Pattern recognition. *Elservier Science Publishers, 36*, 463-473.

Gruber, T. (1993). Toward principles for the design of ontologies used for knowledge sharing. In N. Guarino & R. Poli, (Eds.), *International Journal of Human-Computer Studies, special issue on Formal Ontology in Conceptual Analysis and Knowledge Representation,* LADSEB-CNR Int. Rep. ACM.

Grüninger, M., & Fox, M.S. (1995). Methodology for the design and evaluation of ontologies. *IJCAI'95 Workshop on Basic Ontological Issues in Knowledge Sharing, Montreal,* Canada.

Guarino, N. (1998). Formal Ontology in Information Systems. Guarino (Ed.), *First International Conference on Formal Ontology in Information Systems* (pp. 3-15). Italy.

Jannink, J. (1999). Thesaurus entry extraction from an on-line dictionary. In *Proceedings of Fusion 99,* Sunnyvale CA.

Junker, M., Sintek, M., & Rinck, M. (1999). Learning for Text Categorization and Information Extraction with ILP. In J. Cussens (Eds.), *Proceedings of the 1st Workshop on Learning Language in Logic* (pp. 84-93). Bled: Slovenia.

Karoui, L., Aufaure, M.-A., & Bennacer, N. (2004). Ontology discovery from web pages: Application to tourism. *Workshop on Knowledge Discovery and Ontologies (KDO), co-located with ECML/ PKDD,* Pisa, Italy, pp. 115-120.

Kosala, R., & Blockeel, H. (2000). Web mining research: A survey. *SIGKDD Explorations: Newsletter of the ACM Special Interest Group on Knowledge Discovery and Data Mining, 2*(1), 1-5.

Le Grand, B., & Soto, M. (2005). Topic Maps, RDF Graphs and Ontologies Visualization. In V. Geromienko, & C. Chen (Eds.), *Visualizing the Semantic Web* (2nd ed). Springer.

Masseglia, F., Poncelet, P., & Cicchetti, R. (1999). An efficient algorithm for web usage mining. *Networking and Information Systems Journal (NIS), 2*(5-6), 571-603.

Masseglia, F., Tanasa, D., & Trousse, B. (2004). Web usage mining: Sequential pattern extraction with a very low support. *In Advanced Web Technologies and Applications: 6th Asia-Pacific Web Conference, APWeb 2004,* vol. 3007 (pp. 513-522). Hangzhou, China: Springer-Verlag.

Nakagawa, M., & Mobasher, B. (2003). Impact of site characteristics on recommendation models based on association rules and sequential patterns. In *Proceedings of the IJCAI'03 Workshop on Intelligent Techniques for Web Personalization,* Acapulco, Mexico.

Navigli, R., & Velardi, P. (2004). Learning domain ontologies from document warehouses and dedicated web sites. *Computational Linguistics, 30*(2), 151-179.

Noy, N.F., & Klein, M. (2004). Ontology evolution: Not the same as schema evolution. *Knowledge and Information Systems, 6*(4), 428-440.

Papatheodrou, C., Vassiliou, A., & Simon, B. (2002). C. Papatheodrou, Discovery of ontologies for learning resources using word-based clustering. In *Proceedings of ED MEDIA 2002,* Denver.

Rahm, E., & Bernstein, P. (2001). A survey of approaches to automatic schema matching, *The VLDB Journal,* 334-350.

Rubin, D.L., Hewett, M., Oliver, D.E., Klein, T.E., & Altman, R.B. (2002). Automatic data acquisition into ontologies from pharmacogenetics relational data sources using declarative object definitions and XML. In *Proceedings of the Pacific Symposium on Biology,* Lihue, HI.

Sanchez, D., & Moreno, A. (2004). Automatic generation of taxonomies from the WWW. In

Proceedings of the 5th International Conference on Practical Aspects of Knowledge Management (PAKM 2004). LNAI, Vol. 3336 (pp. 208-219). Vienna, Austria.

Sauberlich, F., & Huber, K.-P. (2001). A framework for web usage mining on anonymous logfile data. In Schwaiger M. & O. Opitz (Eds.), *Exploratory data analysis in empirical research* (pp. 309-318). Heidelberg: Springer-Verlag.

Spiliopoulou, M., Faulstich, L.C., & Winkler, K. (1999). A data miner analyzing the navigational behaviour of web users. In *Proceedings of the Workshop on Machine Learning in User Modeling of the ACAI'99 Int. Conf.*, Creta, Greece.

Spyropoulos, CD., Paliouras, G., & Karkaletsis, V. (2005, November 30- December 1). *BOEMIE: Bootstrapping ontology evolution with multimedia information extraction*. 2nd European Workshop on the integration of knowledge, Semantic and Digital Media Technologies, London.

Staab, S., Schnurr, H.-P., Studer, R., & Sure, Y. (2001). Knowledge processes and ontologies. *IEEE Intelligent Systems Special Issue on Knowledge Management, January/February, 16*(1).

Stojanovic, L., Stojanovic, N., & Volz, R. (2002). Migrating data-intensive web sites into the semantic web. In *Proceedings of the 17th ACM symposium on applied computing (SAC)* ACM Press.

Stumme, G., Hotho, A., & Berendt, B. (2006). Semantic Web mining: State of the art and future directions. *Journal of Web Semantics: Science, Services and Agents on the World Wide Web, 4*(2), 124-143.

Suryanto, H., & Compton, P. (2001). Discovery of ontologies from knowledge bases. In *Proceedings of the 1st International Conference on Knowledge Capture, the Association for Computing Machinery* (pp. 171-178). New York.

Tanasa, D. (2005). *Web usage mining: Contributions to intersites logs preprocessing and sequential pattern extraction with low support*. PhD thesis, University of Nice Sophia Antipolis.

Tanasa, D., & Trousse, B. (2004). Advanced data preprocessing for intersites Web usage mining. *IEEE Intelligent Systems, 19*(2) 59-65.

Trousse, B., Jaczynski, M. & Kanawati, R. (1999). Using user behavior similarity for recommandation computation: The broadway approach. In *Proceedings of 8th International Conference on Human Computer Interaction (HCI'99)* (pp. 85-89). Munich:Lawrence Erlbaum.

Verde, R., & Lechevallier, Y. (2003). Crossed Clustering method on Symbolic Data tables. In M. Vichi, P. Monari, S. Migneni, & A. Montanari, (Eds.), *New developments in classification, and data analysis* (pp. 87-96). Heidelberg: Springer-Verlag.

Volz, R., Oberle, D., Staab, S., & Studer, R. (2003). *OntoLiFT Prototype*. IST Project 2001-33052 WonderWeb Deliverable.

Yuefeng, L., & Ning, Z. (2006). Mining ontology for automatically acquiring web user information needs. *IEEE Trans. Knowl. Data Eng., 18*(4), 554-568.

Zhang, T., Ramakrishnan, R., & Livny, M. (1996). Birch: An efficient data clustering method for very large databases. In H.V.Jagadish, & I.S. Mumick (Ed.), *Proceedings of the 1996 ACM SIGMOD International Conference on Management of Data* (pp. 103-114). Montreal, Quebec, Canada: ACM Press.

Zhu, J., Hong, J., & Hughes, J.G. (2002). Using Markov Chains for link prediction in adaptive Web sites. *In Proceedings of Soft-Ware 2002: First International Conferance on Computing in an Imperfect World* (pp. 60-73). Belfast, UK.

ADDITIONAL READING

Garboni, C., Masseglia, F., & Trousse, B. (2006). A flexible structured-based representation for XML document mining. In *Advances in XML information retrieval and evaluation, 4th International Workshop of the Initiative for the Evaluation of XML Retrieval*, INEX 2005, Vol. 3977/2006:458-468 of LNCS. Springer Berlin / Heidelberg, Dagstuhl Cstle, Germany, 28 June.

Haase, P., & Stojanovic, L. (2005). Consistent evolution of OWL ontologies. In *Proceedings of the Second European Semantic Web Conference (ESWC 05)*, vol. 3532 of Lecture Notes in Computer Science, pp. 182-197.

Mikroyannidis, A., & Theodoulidis, B. (2006). Heraclitus II: A framework for ontology management and evolution. In *Proceedings of 2006 IEEE/WIC/ACM International Conference on Web Intelligence (WI'06)* (pp. 514-521).

Plessers, P., & De Troyer, O. (2006) Resolving inconsistencies in evolving ontologies. In Y. Sure & J. Domingue (Eds.), *Proceedings of the Third European Semantic Web Conference. ESWC 2006* (pp. 200-214).

Stojanovic, L., Maedche, A., Motik, B., & Stojanovic, N. (2004). User-driven ontology evolution management. In *Proceedings of the Thirteenth European Conference on Knowledge Engineering and Knowledge Management EKAW* (pp. 200-214). Springer Verlag.

Stojanovic, L. (2004). *Methods and tools for ontology evolution*. PhD Thesis, University of Karlsruhe, Germany.

Ee-Peng Lim and Aixin Sun (2005). Web mining: The ontology approach. In *Proceedings of the International Advanced Digital Library Conference (IADLC)*, Nagoya, Japan (invited paper).

Chapter IV
SOM–Based Clustering of Multilingual Documents Using an Ontology

Minh Hai Pham
Swiss Federal Institute of Technology, Switzerland

Delphine Bernhard
Laboratoire TIMC-IMAG, France

Gayo Diallo
Laboratoire TIMC-IMAG, France

Radja Messai
Laboratoire TIMC-IMAG, France

Michel Simonet
Laboratoire TIMC-IMAG, France

ABSTRACT

Clustering similar documents is a difficult task for text data mining. Difficulties stem especially from the way documents are translated into numerical vectors. In this chapter, we will present a method that uses Self Organizing Map (SOM) to cluster medical documents. The originality of the method is that it does not rely on the words shared by documents, but rather on concepts taken from an ontology. Our goal is to cluster various medical documents in thematically consistent groups (e.g., grouping all the documents related to cardiovascular diseases). Before applying the SOM algorithm, documents have to go through several preprocessing steps. First, textual data have to be extracted from the documents, which can be either in the PDF or HTML format. Documents are then indexed, using two kinds of indexing units: stems and concepts. After indexing, documents can be numerically represented by vectors whose dimensions correspond to indexing units. These vectors store the weight of the indexing unit within the document they represent. They are given as inputs to a SOM, which arranges the corresponding documents on a two-dimensional map. We have compared the results for two indexing schemes: stem-based indexing and conceptual indexing. We will show that using an ontology for document clustering has several advantages. It is possible to cluster documents written in several languages since concepts are language-independent. This is especially helpful in the medical domain where research articles are written in different languages. Another advantage is that the use of concepts helps reduce the size of the vectors, which, in turn, reduces processing time.

INTRODUCTION

In medicine, as in many other domains, text documents are not only numerous, but also written in many different languages. This can produce huge sets of multilingual medical documents that need to be exploited. There are many tools that can facilitate this exploitation. In general, searching for information is a very common task today for anyone who uses the Internet. Searches on the Internet are usually performed using some very popular and powerful search engines. However, results returned by these engines are presented as a very long list and the user still has to spend considerable time to verify if a result corresponds to her or his needs.

Document clustering is thus necessary to help cluster search results into groups of documents. Moreover, the groups must be labeled in order to help users choose the most suitable for their requirements. Among various clustering methods, Self-Organizing Map (Kohonen, 1982) seems to be the one that can best resolve this problem. On the one hand, it clusters documents in groups, on the other hand, it organizes groups on two-dimensional maps in such a way as to conserve the topology of the data structure. Moreover, Kohonen et al. (2000) proves that SOM can organize vast document collections according to textual similarities.

For clustering, documents have to be described by a set of features and values depending on the data representation model chosen. Some data representation models, such as word indexes are very common. However, the ontology-based method would appear to be appropriate for sets of multilingual documents. An ontology provides a mapping from terms to language-independent concepts. Furthermore, an ontology-based method can considerably reduce the dimensionality of input vectors that represent documents, since several terms may denote the same concept. This is extremely valuable because high dimensionality is a major problem in data mining in general.

Suppose that we have a corpus D of N documents and we want to cluster this set of documents into G groups of documents. Each document d_i, with $0 < i < N$ ($d_i \in D$) is represented by a list E of M semantic elements. M is the number of semantic elements in N documents. If the index j is the position of a semantic element in the list E then e_j, with $0 \leq j < M$ ($e_j \in E$) is the global frequency of this semantic element, i.e., its number of occurrences in N documents. The symbol $d_{i,j}$, with $0 \leq i < N$, $0 \leq j \leq M$ corresponds to the importance of the semantic element having index j in the document d_i. The group C_k, with $0 \leq k \leq G$ is a set of document indices that have been classified into this group. Note that, we use the concept "semantic element" to replace the concept "stem" or "term" or "concept" or "word category".

In this chapter, we will discuss in detail the SOM algorithm in the second section, "Self-Organizing Map," and the notion of ontology in the third section, "Ontology." The SOM-based method for clustering medical documents using an ontology is described in the "SOM-based Clustering of Multilingual Documents Using an Ontology" section. We will introduce the processing steps of our experiments and experimental results in the "Evaluation" section and our conclusion will be given in section six, "Conclusion."

SELF-ORGANIZING MAP (SOM)

Teuvo Kohonen first introduced SOM in 1982 (Kohonen, 1982). Until now, SOM has been broadly applied in many subdomains of computer science, e.g., image processing, data mining, and so forth. In the 90s, Kohonen and his colleagues, together with other independent research groups, were very successful in applying SOM to text data mining. Supervised by Kohonen, several projects of this type were carried out during this period. With the WEBSOM Project (Honkela et al., 1997), he and his colleagues proved that SOM could be used to cluster digital documents in an unsupervised way. Furthermore, it can help users to visualize groups of documents classified by SOM. In this section, we will describe the SOM method with the appropriate symbols and conventions.

Structure of a SOM

A self-organizing map is a type of neural network that has only one layer, called output layer. In this layer, neurons are organized according to a topology where a neuron may have 4, 6, 8, or more neighbors. During the learning process, a neuron's neighbors may influence the similarity between the documents belonging to this neuron and the documents belonging to its neighbors. In the maps shown in Figures 1 and 2, the dots on the Grid represent the neurons. In Figure 1, the neuron in the center of the circle has a maximum of four neighbors. Each neuron has two directions of neighbor relation so that it may have two neighbors in the vertical direction (one above and the other below) and two neighbors in the horizontal direction (one on the left and the other on the right). The neurons in the corners of the map have fewer neighbors (two neighbors); the other neurons along the edges of the map have three neighbors. Where a neuron has four neighbors, these neighbors make up a square. This type of topology is called square topology.

Hexagonal topology is another type of topology, as shown in Figure 2, where each neuron may have three directions of neighbor relation: west-east, southwest-northeast, and southeast-northwest so that a neuron has at most six neighbors.

A neuron on the map has the following characteristics:

- Its position on the map. This is important because it can determine the number of neighbors that it may have (Figures 1 and 2). In a two-dimensional map, the position is a combination of horizontal and vertical coordinates. For any one neuron, its position on the map is initialized during the construction of the map. This position is definitive.

Figure 1. A 5x5 SOM of square topology

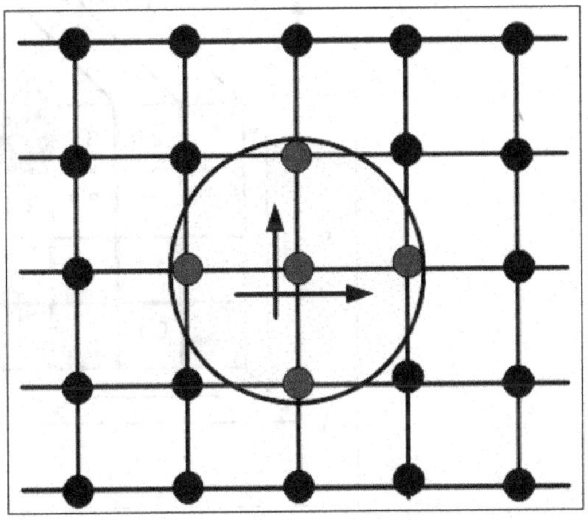

Figure 2. An 6x4 SOM of hexagonal topology

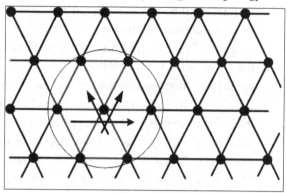

In accordance with the symbols and conventions described in the first section, the vector representing a neuron has M dimensions, which is the number of dimensions of input vectors. If the map has two dimensions, the number of neurons in each dimension is X and Y where $X.Y=G$ (G is the number of groups on the map). The neuron C_k, with $0 \leq k \leq G$ may be represented by indices x,y: $C_{x,y}$, with $0 \leq x < X$, $0 \leq y < Y$ where $k = x.X + y$. The neural vector corresponding to the neuron C_k or $C_{x,y}$ is c_k or $c_{x,y}$ (the c in lowercase). The jth component in the vector representing the kth neuron is then represented by c_{k_j} or $c_{x,y,j}$.

- A vector representing the neuron called neural vector. This vector has the same number of dimensions as the input vectors. After being trained (see the subsection "Learning Process" next) the components of this vector will best reflect the corresponding components of the input vectors belonging to this neuron. It means that a neuron represents a group of similar inputs. During the learning process, the components of a neural vector will change.

Learning Process

The goal of the learning process of the SOM is to gradually build up the neural vectors that best represent groups of inputs. Moreover, because of the particularity of the SOM algorithm a neural vector will be very similar to its neighbor vectors. Short distances in the data space express similarity. The learning process can be divided into five steps:

Figure 3. An example of a map of square topology. The neural vectors have M dimensions. The map has two dimensions with 6 horizontal neurons and 4 vertical ones. Each neuron has a different color. This means that neural vectors are different.

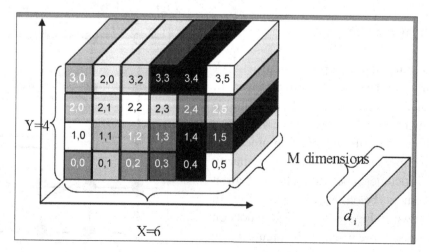

- **Step 1:** Initialization of neural vectors. There are many methods to do this task: random initialization, K-means based initialization, and so forth. Random initialization is the most widely used among these methods. Components of neural vectors will be assigned random numerical values.
- **Step 2:** For the tth iteration of the learning process, an input d_i is randomly chosen among N inputs.
- **Step 3:** Selection of the best matching neuron for the input d_i. A neuron is called best matching when the distance between the input d_i and the vector representing that neuron is at its minimum. This neuron is also called the winner for the input d_i at t^{th} iteration. We will use the term w_t to represent the winner vector at the moment t.
- **Step 4:** Determination of the winner's neighborhood and corresponding update of its neighbors.
- **Step 5:** If the end condition is not met, proceed to the next iteration ($t = t+1$) and repeat from Step 2.

We put particular emphasis on Step 4 due to its importance. Let us consider how the neural vector c_k is updated.

$$c_k(t+1) = c_k(t)+\gamma(t).h(c_k, w_t, t)(d_i-c_k(t)) \qquad (1)$$

In this formula, there are two distances that need to be calculated: ***local distance*** and ***data distance***. ***Local distance*** is the distance between two neurons on the map, which is usually a two-dimensional plane. As it has been explained in "The structure of a SOM" section, the position of a neuron never changes; therefore the distance between two neurons remains fixed. In (1), ***local distance*** is expressed by $\gamma(t).h(c_k, w_t, t)$ which is the multiplication of the learning rate $\gamma(t)$ by the neighborhood function $h(c_k, w_t, t)$. We can see that these two terms are time-dependent. The form of these two functions can be chosen in respect of the following rules:

The learning rate $\gamma(t)$ begins with a high value which then decreases as time increases. This gradual reduction guarantees the termination of the learning process in finite time. Moreover, initial values for each neural vector are far from optimal, so a "strong movement" towards optimal positions should be encouraged by setting a higher learning rate value. Over the course of time, this value becomes smaller so that the movement is lessened, which may prevent the neural vectors from stepping over the optimal positions. This

Figure 4. The form of a Mexican hat

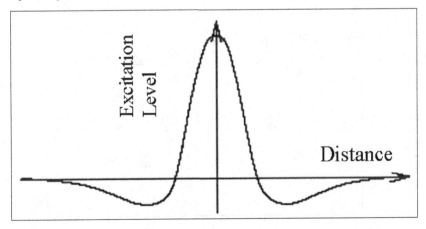

term does not directly concern either *local* or *data distance*.

The neighborhood function $h(c_k, w_p, t)$ starts with a high value which then decreases as time increases. The idea of this function stems from the fact that in the real neural system (in the brain of an animal), when a neuron is excited, other neurons around it will be excited too. They form the neighborhood of the central neuron, and around this neighborhood neurons are inhibited. This term depends strictly on the *local distance*. To represent this phenomenon, the neighborhood function should have the form of a Mexican hat, see Figure 4.

In general, there are many propositions for the formulaes of these two functions. Here we introduce the most widely used:

The learning rate $\gamma(t)$:

$\gamma(t) = \gamma(0).e^{-\frac{t}{\varepsilon}}$, where $\gamma(0)$ is the initial learning rate, ε is a predefined coefficient.

The neighborhood function $h(C_k, w_t, t)$:

$h(c_k, w_t, t) = e^{-\frac{\|c_k - w_t\|^2}{2.\sigma(t)^2}}$, where $\gamma(t) = \gamma(0).e^{-\frac{t}{\varepsilon}}$ with $\sigma(0)$ and ξ are predefined parameters.

The *data distance* in (1) is calculated by the term $(d_i - c_k(t))$ where d_i is an input vector (as we have seen, it will not change in the learning process) and $c_k(t)$ is the vector of the kth neuron at the tth iteration.

Classification

When the learning process is complete, the map can be used for classification. At this time, each neural vector has its own optimal position in the data space so that it can be the representative for a group of input vectors. The objective of classification is to map each input vector to its corresponding neural vector. For an input, we find its neuron by searching for the neural vector having the smallest distance to its input vector. Because there are fewer neurons than inputs, several inputs are mapped to the same neuron. These inputs form a group of inputs having the smallest distances to this neuron in comparison to the distances from other neurons.

When the mapping of all the inputs is completed, the kth neuron has a set C_k of indices i of inputs belonging to it and the neural vector c_k is

Figure 5. In this example, 13 input data (circles and triangles) are classified into two groups. The data space has two dimensions and after the learning process, two neurons (squares) have positions as shown in the graph. The line in the figure separates two groups.

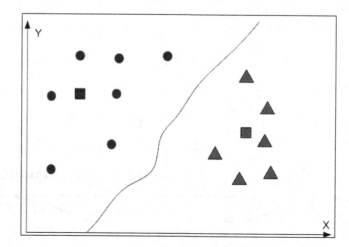

the center of gravity of these inputs in the data space (see Figure 5).

ONTOLOGY

What is an Ontology?

The term "ontology" was first used in philosophy to imply studies and discussions on existence. In computer science, this term refers to a specification of a conceptualization (Gruber, 1993) so that an ontology is a description (like a formal specification of a program) of the concepts and relationships that exist in a domain.

An ontology is usually defined as a hierarchy of concepts corresponding to the hierarchical data structure within a certain domain. This structure includes the inter-relationships between concepts, which can imply directed, acyclic, transitive and reflexive relations (Hotho et al., 2001). Concepts that are not domain-specific are described in a foundation ontology.

Let us consider the example of an ontology in the domain of "cancer". There are several types of cancer: breast cancer, lung cancer, stomach cancer, etc. We can say that breast cancer is a type of cancer, that is, "breast cancer" is a subconcept of the concept "cancer." We can also say that "cancer" is a subconcept of "tumor," since cancer is a malignant tumor.

Of course, the relationships between concepts in the ontological hierarchy of a given domain are based on their semantic relationships, which are specific to that domain.

Ontology for Document Representation: Related Work

In order to use ontologies in text clustering, two preprocessing steps are necessary. First, an ontology describing the target domain has to be built, using either text corpora or manual definitions or both. Text documents can be indexed through this structure in order to produce vectors representing them. These vectors will be used by a clustering method as inputs. To accomplish the first task, constructing the ontology, several tools may be used to determine the concepts and their relationships. For the second, an indexer is needed to produce characteristic vectors from documents.

Ontologies have not long been used to represent text documents. Most research in this direction has been done recently (after 2000). The first of the kind may be that of Hotho et al., (2001). Their approach, named concept selection and aggregation (COSA) uses a core ontology to, as the name suggests, restrict the set of relevant document features and automatically propose appropriate aggregations. The core ontology is defined as a sign system $O: = (L, F, C, H, ROOT)$ where:

Figure 6. A part of the hierarchical structure of the ontology in the domain of "cancer"

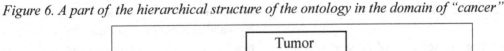
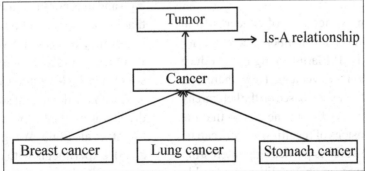

Figure 7. Application of ontology in document representation

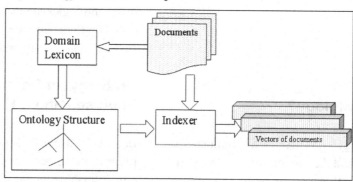

- L is a lexicon that contains a set of terms.
- C is a set of concepts.
- F is a reference function that links a set of terms (which is a subset of L) to the set of concepts they refer to.
- H is a heterarchy that contains relations between concepts. For example, $H(x,y)$ means that y is a subconcept of x.
- $ROOT$ is the top concept and belongs to the set C so that $H(ROOT,z)$ for all z belonging to C.

There are two steps in their approach: mapping terms to concepts and generating "abstract concepts." To map terms to concepts, they use an existing natural language processing tool that does following jobs:

- Identify and extract terms from text documents.
- Use its domain lexicon to map the terms extracted to domain dependent concepts.

This tool can extract a set of concepts from documents. However, the number of concepts for each document is still large enough to produce high dimensional input vectors. They, therefore, propose a heuristic method based on the heterarchy H that provides views from concepts so that the number of dimensions of resulting vectors can be reduced. This research is particularly interesting in that it helps lower dimensionality considerably without loss of information. The results obtained are very encouraging.

Following this proposition, research has been done in applying domain-specific ontologies to text clustering. For example, in (Smirnov et al., 2005) an ontology is used to cluster customers and requests in the area of customer service management. In Wang et al., (2005), the clustering task is based on an ontology in gene expression analysis. Bloehdorn et al., (2005) present the integrated framework OTTO (OnTology-based Text mining framewOrk), which uses text mining techniques and an ontology in order to improve the efficiency of both unsupervised and supervised text categorization (Bloehdorn et al., 2005). Each documents term vector is extended by new entries for ontological concepts appearing in the document set. Thus each document is represented by the concatenation of the term vector (based on the tf.idf measure) with the concept vector (concept frequency-based). In this approach the dimensionality of the document vector may be high and may contain duplicated features. A term that has a corresponding concept in the concept vector may be present twice.

Other works related to ontology-based feature selection which relies on set of ontologies associated with the document set have been reported in the literature (Gabrilovich & Markovitch, 2005; Litvak et al., 2005; Wang et al., 2003; Wu et al., 2003). Experiments with conceptual feature representations for supervised text categorization are presented in Wang et al. (2003). Gabrilovich and Markovich propose a framework and a collection of algorithms that perform feature generation based on very large scale repositories of human knowledge (Gabrilovich & Markovitch, 2005). The feature generator is based on the open directory project (ODP) categories called concepts. A hierarchical text classifier is induced that maps pieces of text onto relevant ODP concepts which serve as generated features. Each ODP node has a textual description and an URL which serves as training examples for learning the feature generator. Litvak et al. (2005) presents a methodology for the classification of multilingual Web documents using a domain ontology described in OWL (Litvak et al., 2005). A language independent key phrase extractor that integrates an ontology parser for each language is used.

Compared to other implicit knowledge representation mechanisms, an ontology presents several advantages (Wu et al., 2003): (1) it can be interpreted and edited by human beings, (2) noise and errors can be detected and refined, (3) it can be shared by various applications. The experimental results reported in Wang et al. (2003) show that the domain ontology effectively improves the accuracy of a KNN classifier. Moreover a "faster convergence of classification accuracy against the size of training set" is obtained. However, those results are obtained experimentally and should not be systematically generalized for other classifiers. Sebastiani, (1999) states that the experimental results of two classifiers can be compared if the experiments are performed on the same collection, with the same choice of training set and test set and finally with the same effectiveness measure. Moreover, even if the use of an ontology presents some advantages, building it is a difficult task. In medicine, substantial work has been done to develop standard medical terminologies and coding systems. Those standards may be exploited to build or to enrich ontologies (Simonet et al., 2005a).

SOM-BASED CLUSTERING OF MEDICAL DOCUMENTS USING AN ONTOLOGY

Document Representation Models for SOM

While preprocessing textual documents, there are two important questions that must be answered before clustering. First, how will a document be represented? Second, how will the importance of a semantic element be calculated? A semantic element can be a stem or a term or a concept or a word category (this depends on the representation model). Many methods can be used to represent a textual document. All these methods make use of a vector whose components describe the document's content. The vector space model (Salton et al., 1975) is the basis for this representation. One of the greatest challenges in data mining generally and clustering digital text documents by SOM in particular, is the large vector dimensionality during the processing of a huge set of documents. Each document contains a set of semantic elements and the number of dimensions of one document vector is different from that of another document. However, in order to compare documents, their vectors must have the same number of dimensions. A certain semantic element may appear in one document but may not in another. To solve this problem, a dictionary has to be built. This dictionary contains all the semantic elements found in the set of documents but none of them appears more than once in the dictionary. Based on the dictionary, a vector will be generated for each document. The vector generated has the same dimensionality as the dictionary. The importance of a semantic element within a document is based on its frequency of occurrence in that document. If an element is not present in the document, it will be weighted by a value of 0 (it means that this element has no importance at all in the document). At the end of this step, we have a set of vectors representing the documents (see Figure 5). There may be other preprocessing tasks such as the calculation of the global importance of the semantic element in the whole corpus and/or normalization to be completed before the set of vectors can be used as inputs for the clustering algorithm.

In a particular case where a semantic element is a term, the method used for calculating the global importance of terms can be *TF* or *TD.IDF* (Salton & Buckley, 1988):

- **TF**: Term Frequency, that is, the number of occurrences of the term in the document. The greater the *TF*, the more important the term is for the document. There are cases where a term has high *TF* value for all the documents in the document collection. It is clear that this term cannot help discriminate different groups of documents. For example, in a collection of medical documents, the word *"treatment"* will have a high *TF* value for all documents in this collection.

- **TF.IDF**: Term Frequency-Inverse Document Frequency. This method was proposed to overcome the disadvantage of the *TF* method.

$$fidf(i, j) = tf(i, j) * \log\left(\frac{N}{df(j)}\right)$$

Where *i* is the index of the current document, *j* is the index of the current term, *tf(i,j)* is the *TF* value of the term *j* in the document *i*, *df(j)* is the number of documents where the term *j* appears.

Some existing representation methods are very popular for use with SOM. In Honkela et al., (1997), Kohonen and his colleagues proposed, within the WEBSOM project, word category maps that can group words with similar contexts into a category. Instead of being represented by a vector of word occurrences, a document is characterized by a vector of word category occurrences, which has fewer dimensions. Two types of SOM have to be used in this approach: one for word categories and one for document clusters. Still within this project, random mapping is proposed to help considerably reduce the number of dimensions for a huge set of documents. At first, a document is fully represented by a vector of word occurrences. This vector is then multiplied by a matrix whose elements are randomly generated so that the resulting vector has lower dimensionality. Because the matrix is random, there is obviously reduced accuracy. Combination of word category maps and random mapping is also considered so

Figure 8. Representing each document as a vector of semantic elements. This vector is built based on the dictionary and the original document.

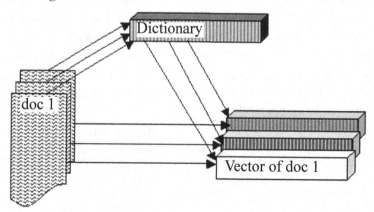

that first, documents are represented by vectors of word category maps then, random mapping is applied. However, the most frequently used method is full representation, that is, semantic elements are words that appear in the document collection. In some cases, stems are used instead of words. A stem is what is left from a word when all the suffixes have been stripped off. For example, the verb *laugh* has several inflected forms: *laugh, laughs, laughed, laughing,* which are all stemmed as *laugh.* For this reason, using stems can make document vectors more compact in size than those produced by using words.

Ontology-Based Document Representation Method

We have reviewed several methods for text representation, which are specific to SOM. Some of these are based on the full representation and then processed by mathematical transformations which make it impossible to explain the results obtained. Random mapping for example makes use of a random matrix so that resulting vectors are simply arrays of numbers having no meaning. If two documents fall into one group, the only thing we can say is that their correspondent vectors are similar: there is no conclusion concerning their content. Word category maps may be useful in this case. However, resulting vectors still have many dimensions. Furthermore, context is not sufficient to accurately group words that have the same meaning. Although full representation is widely used, it is a basic method for document representation. Vectors of words or stems represent documents, so the number of dimensions may be very large. This method, also known as the bag-of-words representation method, is not suitable when the document collection is exceptionally voluminous.

Even though results obtained by the preceding methods are encouraging, they have limitations that cannot be resolved especially in the medical domain where multilingual documents are abundant. For this reason, we use an ontology-based document representation method. As stated in the third section, the ontology must first be constructed. When an ontology is available, documents are indexed in order to be represented by vectors. Indexation process is performed on plain text documents.

The Ontology Model

Automatic characterization relies on the identification of terms in texts. The terminology in the ontology must offer a good coverage of the terms used in medical literature. Moreover, in order to manage the multilingual aspect of the ontology, each concept is expressed in several languages. Thus, a term enrichment process has to be performed on the ontology manually and/or automatically. The enrichment process may be based on domain corpora (Simonet et al., 2005b) or medical vocabularies such as UMLS (unified medical language system) metathesaurus[1].

Formaly an ontology O is the set (C, Rel, T, L) where:

- C is the set of concepts of the ontology.
- Rel is the Subconcept-Superconcept relationships (generally the subsumption relationship).
- T is the set of terms used to denote the concepts in the ontology.
- L is the set of languages used to denote the terms present in T.

For the experiments we have considered for each concept its French and English terms.

A cardiovascular ontology has been built up as part of the NOESIS project based on the MeSH (Medical Subject Headings) thesaurus[2] with enrichment from the UMLS metathesaurus. The ontology is still being enriched by vocabulary extracted from articles in the cardiovascular domain. This work is described in Simonet et al. (2005a).

We have also used an ontology for breast cancer (Messai et al., 2006). This ontology has been built manually using terms extracted from a corpus of selected documents. There are more than 1200 concepts in this ontology.

Document Preprocessing

Since an indexing process is performed on plain text inputs, documents in pdf or HTML format must first be converted.

Converting documents from pdf format to plain text format can naturally preserve the original text. However, in some cases, there may be some errors in conversion. These errors depend on the conversion module used. First, long words may be truncated at the end of a line. For example, "international" is a long word. It can be rewritten like "international" so that "inter-" is at the end of a line while "national" is at the beginning of the following line. When the text is converted, this word will be split into two different words. This happens very frequently in pdf documents so that several terms are not counted. Accordingly, the indexing process is not correctly done. Moreover, a document may contain several columns. While converting a document, columns in the resulting document (plain text format) may not appear in the right order. Since a term may contain several words spread over two columns it may occur that the word order within the term is not maintained. Another cause of error is that during conversion, words appearing in the header, the footer, or a legend are inserted between words of a term so that the term does not appear in the resulting document. It is important to note that errors during conversion have a negative impact on the quality of indexation.

Document Representation Process and Feature Selection

Document indexing is carried out so that vectors of concepts represent documents. The necessary steps are term extraction and concept extraction.

Concepts are not directly present in documents. They may be retrieved by locating the terms which represent the concepts in the ontology. A term is a word or an expression that has fixed meaning. A list of terms and corresponding frequencies is produced for each document. A concept may be denoted by several terms, possibly in several languages, so that its frequency in a document is computed as the summed frequencies of its denoting terms in the document (Diallo et al., 2006). Following this, the *CF-IDF* (Concept Frequency-Inversed Document Frequency) is used to measure the importance of concepts in documents. The *CF-IDF* method is an extension of the *TF-IDF* measure where *CF* is the sum of the *TF* for all the terms representing the concept. Instead of only using the concept frequency we use the *CF.IDF* measure because it makes it possible to weigh a concept's importance compared to the whole document collection.

All the concepts present in the ontology will not appear in the documents. For this reason, only concepts that have been used at least once to index the collection are considered as features. However, there may be some concepts that appear in every document of the collection and they are not useful in clustering documents. These concepts are excluded. The concepts obtained are included in a dictionary called the collection dictionary. Based on this dictionary, characteristic vectors are built for the documents.

When we have all characteristic vectors for every document, the vectors need to be normalized to eliminate the length effect. Then, they all have the same unit length. The similarity between two document vectors is measured by the cosine of the angle of those vectors in THE data space. Each document vector will be compared to A neural vector in the training process by the same method to choose the winner.

After the preprocessing task, we have a set of inputs, which are normalized document vectors. The inputs will be used in the training process of the SOM.

EVALUATION

In our experiments we have implemented and compared two feature selection modes: full representation (dictionary of stems) and ontology-based representation (dictionary of concepts). We have used the ontologies presented in the fourth section and two text corpora. For the second corpus, which concerns breast cancer, only the ontology-based method is used because the documents are in two languages.

Document Sources

We use two corpora in our experiments. One contains scientific articles in the cardiovascular domain and the other concerns articles on breast cancer. The former contains only articles in English and can be found and downloaded from the website http://www.biomedcentral.com, while the latter includes texts both in English and in French that have been downloaded from several sources.

The corpus on cardiovascular diseases contains 430 documents grouped in the following seven sections:

- Cardiovascular diabetology (41 documents)
- Cardiovascular ultrasound (44 documents)
- BMC cardiovascular disorders (94 documents)
- Current interventional cardiology reports (119 documents)
- Current controlled trials in cardiovascular medicine (120 documents)
- Thrombosis journal (25 documents)
- Nutrition journal (11 documents)

Sections for the documents have been chosen by the authors of the articles during submission and have been reviewed by the editors. According to the submission procedure, the classification of the documents in sections has been accomplished carefully. We have therefore chosen these sections as predefined groups of our experiments

These documents are in the pdf file format. The number of words in each document ranges from 1,200 to 8,000. The average number of words is more than 4,100. There may be from five to 15 pages for a document.

The corpus on breast cancer contains 440 documents in English and 574 in French. The collection contains documents in plain text or HTML format. Sources of documents are also very varied and there is no predefined group. The corpus was first used to extract concepts to build the ontology on breast cancer. For this reason, there are documents of many types: definitions, general information, current events, and scientific articles on breast cancer. Most of the documents are short.

Results

For the corpus on cardiovascular diseases, with seven predefined groups of documents, we have used a 7×7 square map, that is, 49 possible clusters on the SOM. The preclassification of documents into groups has been done manually. We will compare the clusters obtained by the SOM to these predefined clusters.

Suppose that we have documents from many predefined groups falling into one cluster of the SOM. We can then say that the main topic of this cluster is that of the predefined group having the most documents in the cluster. For example, if there are seven documents on two topics "Cardiovascular diabetology" (four documents) and "Cardiovascular ultrasound" (three documents), then the cluster is said to have the topic "Cardiovascular diabetology." We can say that there are four hit documents and three miss documents for the cluster. In (Kohonen, 1998), *all documents that represented a minority newsgroup at any Grid point were counted as classification errors* (p.68). In our experiments, newsgroups are replaced by predefined sections.

Table 1 presents the results of the experiments with the ontology. Note that in each cell of the table, there are the following values.

Total number of documents:Number of hits; Number of misses: (**Hits-Misses**).

We have the total sum of (Hits-Misses)=68 Table 2 presents the results of the experiments with full representation,

Using the same evaluation method we obtain the total sum of (Hits-Misses)= -3.

This result is much lower than the one produced by using the ontology. It means that by using the ontology to represent documents, we can obtain clusters that separate the document collection.

From the point of view of processing time, the number of vector dimensions for full representation is 25,762 and it took several days. With the ontology-based method, the number of vector dimensions is 4,315; the learning process is completed in several hours.

Table 1. Results of the experiment with concept-based representation

	0	1	2	3	4	5	6
0	43: 23; 20: +3	8:3; 5: -2	28:10; 18:-8	14:7; 7:0	24:16; 8:+8	4:4; 0:+4	5:2; 3:-1
1	4:3; 1:+2	5:3; 2:+1	3:2; 1:+1	18:5; 13:-8	1:1; 0:+1	4:4; 0:+4	0:0; 0:0
2	29:23; 6:+17	3:2; 1:+1	5:5; 0:+5	4:4; 0:+4	7:7; 0:+7	0:0; 0:0	11:5; 6:-1
3	6:3; 3:0	1:1; 0:+1	21:19; 2:+17	8:6; 2:+4	0:0; 0:0	10:8; 2:+6	3:2; 1:+1
4	26:9; 17:-8	8:5; 3:+2	7:6; 1:+5	3:1; 2:-1	14:7; 7:0	2:2; 0:+2	3:2; 1:+1
5	20:8; 12:-4	2:1; 1:0	2:1; 1:0	8:5; 3:+2	12:7; 5:+2	0:0; 0:0	11:6; 5: +1
6	5:2; 3:-1	1:1; 0:+1	8:4; 4:0	0:0; 0: 0	14:7; 7:0	8:5; 3:+2	7:2; 5:-3

Table 2. Results of the experiment with stem-based representation

	0	1	2	3	4	5	6
0	0:0; 0:0	0:0; 0:0	0:0; 0:0	0:0; 0:0	0:0; 0:0	0:0; 0:0	0:0; 0:0
1	0:0; 0:0	1:1; 0:+1	0:0; 0:0	0:0; 0:0	0:0; 0:0	0:0; 0:0	0:0; 0:0
2	0:0; 0:0	16:8; 8:0	10:5; 5:0	13:7; 6:+1	10:6; 4:+2	0:0; 0:0	0:0; 0:0
3	34:18; 16:+2	5:3; 2:+1	9:4; 5:-1	8:4; 4:0	8:4; 4:0	0:0; 0:0	0:0; 0:0
4	27:7; 20:-13	9:5; 4:+1	27:14; 13:+1	14:5; 9:-4	16:6; 10:-4	0:0; 0:0	0:0; 0:0
5	20:11; 9:+2	12:7; 5:+2	6:3; 3:0	5:5; 0:+5	18:12; 6:+6	4:2; 2:0	0:0; 0:0
6	58:23; 35:+12	12:6; 6:0	23:13; 10:+3	26:14; 12:+2	38:20; 18:+2	0:0; 0:0	0:0; 0:0

Moreover, SOM try to minimize the following objective function:

$$F = \sum_{i=1}^{N} \sum_{k=1}^{G} \left\| d_i - c_k \right\|^2$$

The smaller the value of F, the better the SOM can cluster inputs. In our experiments, this value with the full representation is 545.19 while with the ontology it is 508.57. This once again implies the better results with the use of the ontology-based document representation method. It means that by using an ontology, coordinates of centers are better distributed in the data space.

For the second corpus, which concerns breast cancer, it is more difficult to evaluate the results because it is in two languages and no predefined document cluster is available. In contrast to the corpus on cardiovascular diseases that contains scientific articles and is very specific, this second corpus contains both general information about breast cancer and specialized knowledge. What we expect when clustering this corpus is to examine the possibility of representing bilingual documents by concepts taken from an ontology.

We have taken two documents from the corpus, one in English, and the other in French. Their titles are similar: "What Are the Risk Factors for Breast Cancer?" and "Généralités et facteurs de risqué." However, they are clustered in two different groups. The former on risk factors for breast cancer for women is fairly general and synthetic. The latter is more specific and deals with research.

We have examined two other documents that are clustered in one group: "Does Weight Gain Increase Breast Cancer Risk?" and "Cancer et hormones: de l'espoir à la menace?" Surprisingly, the English document mentions "menopausal hormone therapy" as a treatment method and the French document confirms that using hormone can treat breast cancer. However, a document in French, titled "Dix kilos perdus et le risque de cancer du sein diminuerait," is not clustered in

that group although this document mentions the relationship between body weight and breast cancer as does the English document. This document is rewritten in French from the original document, "Intentional Weight Loss of 20 Pounds or More Linked to Decreased Cancer Risk," written in English. It is not simply a translation from English to French but these documents are still arranged in the same group because both express the same idea.

Evaluation in text clustering in general is a notorious problem. Evaluating the performance of the method in the experiment with the ontology on breast cancer is even more difficult. However, by manually browsing the results, we observe they are very encouraging.

CONCLUSION

In comparison to other document representation methods, the ontology-based method has the following advantages:

- It produces characteristic vectors of low dimensionality. The number of dimensions of these vectors is controllable. An ontology is domain-dependent so that not all the concepts appearing in a document are extracted. For this reason, unrelated concepts are not considered and this considerably reduces the number of vector dimensions. On the other hand, a concept may be represented by many terms so that the number of occurrences of that concept may be large. For some ontologies, based on concepts, views are built (see, Hotho et al., 2001). A view can contain several concepts that are related.

- It is an effective approach for clustering multilingual text documents. Terms are language dependent. But concepts are language independent. For this reason, a text document A in English can be represented by the same vector as the document B in French that is A's translation. In one language, a concept may also have many terms representing it. So, it is normal that the concept is represented by many terms in many languages. By using concepts, document indexing does not have to be based on one particular language.

- It may provide explanation. When two document vectors are arranged in one group, they must be very similar and thus share many concepts, which it is possible to list. However, when random mapping is applied, it is difficult to know why documents are considered as similar.

Inevitably, there are also some drawbacks to the ontology-based method. First, it is difficult to build and manage an ontology, especially since new concepts and terms constantly appear in specialized domains. Some terms may also be ambiguous and denote several concepts. Moreover, using an ontology for documents indexing is not an easy task. In our experiments, terms are extracted and then mapped to their correspondent concepts. In several cases, a longer term includes a shorter one. When such a case occurs, we extract the former and ignore the latter.

FUTURE RESEARCH DIRECTIONS

This chapter deals with two main research areas: clustering documents using SOM and characterizing the semantic contents of a document using an ontology.

Short-term research directions include applying other clustering and classification techniques to the same ontology-based indexing scheme, such as hierarchical clustering or text categorization using a naive Bayes classifier (Witschel and Biemann, 2006) or linear support vector machines (Hulth and Megyesi, 2006). Moreover, conceptual indexing could be complemented with relational information found in the ontology structure, especially hyper-/hyponymy relations.

The use of semantic relationships should lead to an improvement of the results.

Another possible research direction would be to investigate the use of multiple ontologies in the clustering task since a single ontology is not sufficient to support the task of document clustering in a distributed environment like the Semantic Web (Shadbolt & al., 2006). Further, in the context of ontology-based information integration (Wache & al., 2001), it would be interesting to analyse how clustering techniques, involving both schema and instances, may be used to automatically build the global ontology or to generate a mapping between global and local ontologies (Rahm and Bernstein, 2001; Castano & al., 2001).

A last research direction concerns the use of ontologies for information retrieval. An ontology can be used to semantically characterize both the documents and the queries (Mihalcea and Moldovan, 2000; Biemann, 2005). Henceforth, the documents to be retrieved do not have to share the same words with the query but rather the same concepts. Using ontologies for conceptual indexing and concept-based querying may therefore make it possible to overcome the drawbacks of current word-based information retrieval techniques (Muller & al., 2004).

REFERENCES

Bloehdorn, S., Cimiano, P., Hotho, S., & Staab, S. (2005). An ontology-based framwork for text mining. *LDV Forum: GLDV Journal for Computational Linguistics and Language Technology, 20*(1), 87-112.

Diallo, G., Simonet, M., & Simonet, A. (2006). An approach to automatic semantic annotation of biomedical texts. In *Proceedings of IEA/AIE'06, LNAI 4031* (pp. 1024-1033). Springer-Verlag.

Gabrilovich, E., & Markovitch, S. (2005, August). Feature generation for text categorization using world knowledge. In *Proceedings of the*

19ᵗʰ International Joint Conference in Artificial Intelligence (pp. 1048-1053).

Gruber, T. R. (1993). A translation approach to portable ontologies. *Knowledge Acquisition, 5*(2), 199-220.

Honkela, T., Kaski S., Lagus, K., & Kohonen, T. (1997, June). WEBSOM: Self-organizing maps of document collections. In *Proceedings of WSOM'97, Workshop on Self-Organizing Maps.* Helsinki University of Technology, Neural Networks Research Centre, Espoo, Finland.

Hotho, A., Maedche, A., & Staab, S. (2001, August). Ontology-based text clustering. In *Proceedings of the IJCAI-2001 Workshop of Text Learning, Beyond Supervision.* Seattle, USA.

Kohonen, T. (1982). Self-organized formation of topologically correct feature maps. *Biological Cybernetics, 43*, 59-69.

Kohonen, T. (1998). Self-organization of very large document collections: State of the art. In L. Niklasson, M. Bod, & T. Ziemke, (Eds.), *Proceedings of ICANN98, the 8ᵗʰ International Conference on Artificial Neural Networks* (Vol. 1, pp. 65-74). London: Springer.

Kohonen, T., Kaski, S., Lagus, K., Salojärvi, J., Honkela, J., Paatero, V., et al. (2000). Self organization of a massive document collection. *IEEE Transactions on Neural Networks, 11*(3) 574-585.

Litvak, M., Last, M., & Kisilevich, S. (2005, October). *Improving classification of multilingual Web documents using domain ontologies.* The Second International Workshop on Knowledge Discovery and Ontologies. Porto, Portugal.

Messai, R., Simonet, M., & Mousseau, M. (2006). A breast cancer terminology for lay people. *European Journal of Cancer EJC Supplements. 4*(2), 179-180.

Salton, G., Wong, A., & Yang, C. S. (1975). A vector space model for automatic indexing. *Communications of the ACM, 18*(11), 613-620.

Salton, G., & Buckley, C. (1988). Term-weighting approaches in automatic text retrieval. *Information Processing and Management, 24*, 513-523

Sebastiani, F. (1999). A tutorial on automated text categorization. In A. Amandi & Zunino (Eds.), *Proceedings of ASAI-99, 1ˢᵗ Argentinian Symposium on Artificial Intelligence* (pp 7-35). Buones Aires.

Simonet, M., Bernhard, D., Diallo, G., & Gedzelman, S. (2005a). *Building an ontology of cardiovascular diseases for concept-based information retrieval.* Computers in Cardiology, Lyon.

Simonet, M., Bernhard, D., Diallo, G., Gedzelman, S., Messai, R., & Patriarche, R. (2005b, December 14-16). An environment for ontology design and enrichment from texts. In *Proceedings of SWAP 2005, the 2ⁿᵈ Italian Semantic Web Workshop,* Trento, Italy, CEUR Workshop Proceedings, ISSN 1613-0073.

Smirnov, A., Pashkin, M., Chilov, N., Levashova, T., Krizhanovsky, A., & Kashevnik, A. (2005). Ontology-based users and requests clustering in customer service management system. In V. Gorodetsky, J. Liu, & V. Skormin (Ed.), *Autonomous intelligent systems: Agents and data mining.* AIS-ADM.

Wang, B.B., McKay, I., Abbass, H.A., & Barlow, M. (2003). A comparative study for domain ontology guided feature extraction. In *Proceedings of the 26ᵗʰ Australian Computer Science Conference (ACSC-2003)* (pp. 69-78). Adelaide, Australia. Australian Computer Society, Inc.

Wang, H., Azuaje, F., & Bodenreider, O. (2005). An ontology-driven clustering method for supporting gene expression analysis. In *Proceedings of the 18ᵗʰ IEEE Symposium on Computer-Based Medical Systems* (pp. 389-394).

Wu, S. H., Tsai, T. H., & Hsu, W. L. (2003). Text categorization using automatically acquired domain ontology. In *Proceedings of IRAL2003 Workshop on Information Retrieval with Asian Languages*, Sapporo, Japan.

ADDITIONAL READING

Biemann, C. (2005) *Semantic indexing with typed terms using rapid annotation in methods and applications of Semantic indexing*. Workshop at the 7th International Conference on Terminology and Knowledge Engineering. Copenhagen, Denmark.

Castano, S., De Antonellis, V., De Capitani, & di Vimercati, S. (2001). Global viewing of heterogeneous data sources. *IEEE Transactions on Knowledge and Data Engineering, 13*(2), 277-297.

Hulth, A., & Megyesi, B.B. (2006). A study on automatically extracted keywords in text categorization. In *Proceedings of the International Conference of the Association for Computational Linguistics* (pp. 537-544).

Maedche, A., & Zacharias, V. (2002) Clustering ontology-based metadata in the Semantic Web. In *Proceedings of the Joint Conferences 13th European Conference on Machine Learning (ECML'02) and 6th European Conference on Principles and Practice of Knowledge Discovery in Databases (PKDD'02), LNAI,* Finland, Helsinki. Springer.

Mihalcea, R., & Moldovan, D. (2000). Semantic indexing using WordNet senses. In *Proceedings of ACL Workshop on IR and NLP*, Hong Kong.

Muller, H.M., Kenny, E.E., & Sternberg, P.W. (2004). Textpresso: An ontology-based information retrieval and extraction system for biological literature. *PLoS Biol., 2(*11), E309.

Rahm, E., & Bernstein, P. A. (2001). A survey of approaches to automatic schema matching. *VLDB Journal, 10*(4), 334-350.

Shadbolt, N., Berneers-Lee, T., & Hall, W. (2006). The Semantic Web Revisited. *IEEE Intelligent Systems, 3*(2), 96-101.

Wache, H., Vogele, T., Visser, U., Stuckenschmidt, H., Schuster, G., Neumann, H., & Hubner, S. (2001). Ontology-based integration of information: A survey of existing approaches. In H. Stuckenschmidt (Ed.), *IJCAI-01 Workshop: Ontologies and Information Sharing* (pp. 108-117).

Witschel, H.F., & Biemann, C.(2006). Rigorous dimensionality reduction through linguistically motivated feature selection for text categorization. In S. Werner (Ed.), *Proceedings of the 15th NODALIDA Conference,* Joensuu 2005 (pp. 197-204).

ENDNOTES

[1]   Medical Subject Heading Browser http://www.nlm.nih.gov/mesh/MBrowser.html

[2]   The Unified Medical Language System. http://umlsks.nlm.nih.gov

Section II
Findings

Chapter V
Ontology–Based Interpretation and Validation of Mined Knowledge:
Normative and Cognitive Factors in Data Mining

Ana Isabel Canhoto
Henley Management College, UK

ABSTRACT

The use of automated systems to collect, process, and analyze vast amounts of data is now integral to the operations of many corporations and government agencies, in particular it has gained recognition as a strategic tool in the war on crime. Data mining, the technology behind such analysis, has its origins in quantitative sciences. Yet, analysts face important issues of a cognitive nature both in terms of the input for the data mining effort, and in terms of the analysis of the output. Domain knowledge and bias information influence, which patterns in the data are deemed as useful and, ultimately, valid. This chapter addresses the role of cognition and context in the interpretation and validation of mined knowledge. We propose the use of ontology charts and norm specifications to map how varying levels of access to information and exposure to specific social norms lead to divergent views of mined knowledge.

INTRODUCTION

Data mining has been described as a process where '*the interrogation of the data is done by the data mining algorithm rather than by the user. Data mining is a self organizing, data influenced (...) approach to data analysis. Simply put, what data mining does is sort through masses of data to uncover patterns and relationships, then build models to predict behaviour'* (Chan & Lewis, 2002). This description suggests that the use of data mining techniques tend to minimize the influence that analysts have in the process. Yet, as many practitioners would point out, the reality is very different: even though data mining is a largely quantitative and automated process, the analyst, and hence subjectivity, still plays a crucial role in several steps. Far from being a straightforward and objective process, data mining requires the use of *'intuition and creativity as well as statistical know-how, and you have to hope you have identified the right things to test'* (Humby et al., 2003).

This chapter looks at the role of the analyst in interpreting and validating the results of a data mining exercise. It suggests that, while the data mining community has long identified ways in which the analyst influences the data mining exercise, it has dedicated little attention, so far, to the understanding of the reasons why, and the mechanism how, this happens. As a result, the same literature has limited prescriptive and corrective value for subjectivity in data mining. We respond to the call for further research into the cognitive aspects of data mining (e.g., Chung & Gray, 1999; Kohavi et al., 2002; Pazzani, 2000), by proposing a framework to capture the cognitive and contextual elements shaping the process.

Nowadays, numerous organizations routinely capture and mine customer records to develop profiles of who their users are and what they do in order to inform future decision making. The areas of application range from improving service or performance, to analyzing and detecting terrorist activities (Hosein, 2005). Technologies, such as RFID and mobile technology, are likely to augment the mass of information that must be coped with, and accelerate the extension of profiling to ever more areas of social life. Therefore, the technical process of development of a profile—data mining—is a problem domain of central significance bound up in the growing debate on the role of profiling in the information society (Hildebrandt & Backhouse, 2005). This chapter contributes to an understanding of how the process, despite being highly automated, is still likely to be affected by cognitive and contextual elements, which may fundamentally affect the effectiveness of the exercise and its outcomes. In the next section, the author presents, in broad terms, the ongoing discussion regarding the nature of data mining, as well as to what extent the analyst may interfere in the process. Then, two theories that specifically deal with subjectivity in the interpretation and classification of various stimuli—classification theory and semiotics—are presented, compared, and contrasted. It is noted that these two theories complement each other in the sense that classification theory analyzes the cognitive process, whereas semiotics analyzes the contextual factors affecting that same process. Following from this, the author proposes a framework to capture the effect of affordances and social norms in shaping the cognitive process of the data mining analyst. The framework is applied to a short case study, and suggestions are given regarding areas for further research into the role of subjectivity in data mining.

BACKGROUND

The processing of data in a data mining exercise includes several steps ranging from data selection and preparation to the interpretation of the emerging results. The input to the data mining process is a collection of data objects organized in a database, and the actual data interrogation process will usually start with the specification of the problem domain and an understanding of the goals of the project. The following stage comprises an assessment of the existing knowledge, as well as of the data that needs to be collected. The target dataset resulting from this stage is treated and, later, interrogated in order to *dig pieces of knowledge from the database* (Bruha, 2000). The final stage consists of examining the outcomes of the data mining process, and interpreting and using the resulting information. At the end of the data mining process, the analyst has to judge whether the outcomes are possible, internally consistent, and plausible. The results typically raise further questions, sometimes in conflict with previously existing knowledge, often leading to the generation of new hypotheses and the start of a new data mining cycle.

Data mining researchers have long identified two means in which the user influences data mining. One way is *personal bias,* such as syntactic and support constraints introduced during the process about the search space, the rules to apply and, ultimately, which patterns in the data are deemed useful or interesting (Agrawal et al., 1993; Fayyad et al., 1996; Pazzani et al., 2001). Another factor is *domain knowledge*, which refers to the information available at the beginning of the data mining process and that impacts on the questions asked from the exercise, the selection of data and/or proxies for the exercise and, ultimately, acceptance of the mined output (Anand et al., 1995; Kohavi et al., 2002; Maojo, 2004). Furthermore, because data mining is an iterative process, with frequent feedback loops in which

information feeds back and influences prior steps in the process (Chung & Gray, 1999), the opportunities for users to influence the process are multiplied. Figure 1 illustrates how the analyst may interfere in the data mining process. The column on the left outlines the various stages of a data mining exercise. The column in the center provides examples of actions that the analyst may take, at each stage, and that impact on previous stages, for instance, in the final stage, the analyst examines the outcome of the data analysis. If the analyst is satisfied with the outcome, a particular action may be taken, for instance making an offer to a customer or reporting a suspected criminal to a law enforcement agency. If the analyst is dissatisfied with the outcome, he or she may move back to the previous stage in the process, and refine the query by changing a particular threshold, for instance. Finally, the column to the right provides examples of decisions that the analyst makes at each stage, and which impact on the result of that stage. For instance, in order to search through the data, the analyst needs to choose a model. Fayyad et al. (1996) noted that while researchers develop and advocate rather complex models, practitioners often use simple models that provide ease of interpretability. Such

Figure 1. Iterative and interactive nature of data mining

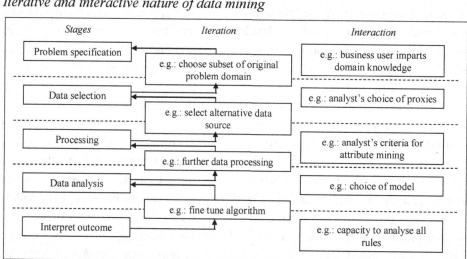

decision has a big impact on the data analysis stage because it determines both the robustness of the model and its interpretability.

In response to the call by Pazzani (2000), Chung and Grey (1999), and others for research into the cognitive aspects of data mining, the author reviews the conceptual understanding of these issues, in the classification theory literature. The next section examines how analysts' mental schemas are formed and what the impact is for action in organizations.

COGNITION AND CONTEXT

Researchers in organizational sciences provided significant evidence that mental schemas have strong effect on perceptual processes and action in organizations (Boland et al., 2001; Carson et al., 2003; Elsbach et al., 2005; Heracleous & Barrett, 2001). Researchers in the field of classification theory (Markman & Gentner, 2001; Mervis & Rosch, 1981; Rosch, 1975, 1978; Rosch & Mervis, 1975) concluded that individuals categorize on the basis of how close something is to the 'prototype' or ideal member of a category. What determines that a material or social object is classified as a member of a given category is not some quality of the object, instead it is the resemblance of the object to the prototype for that particular category. Consequently, research

into classification processes requires from the researcher a focus on the mental prototypes of the individual, rather than on the attributes of the objects. Prototypes consist of very persistent templates—the schemas—that structure cognition by identifying the prominent elements of a situation and by describing the causal relations between them (Elsbach et al., 2005; Fiske & Taylor, 1991; Markman & Gentner, 2001). Elsbach et al. (2005), building on the work of Fiske and Taylor (1991), identified several common forms of schemas, summarized in Figure 2.

The information stored in the schemas is a summary of the most typical features of members in a given category, and individuals classify new exemplars on the basis of their similarity to stored exemplars—for instance, the observation that among the category 'dogs known to have seriously injured or killed human beings' the pit bull breed is overrepresented, led several countries and municipalities to ban the ownership of pit bulls as pet dogs, even though not all pit bulls are dangerous and they can even be, according to some experts, extremely gentle (Gladwell, 2006). Once categories are established, individuals use them to infer features of a new situation following an inductive process—Canhoto and Backhouse (2005) report the case of a female personal assistant at Goldman Sachs, in London, who, in the spring of 2004, was convicted of stealing £4.3m from her bosses, through fraud and forgery, and

Figure 2. Typology of schemas

Form	Description
Person schema	Specific template about how people behave and think e.g., One's freshman chemistry professor
Role schema	General template about the behaviors of individuals occupying formal roles e.g., Police officers
Event schema	Abstract template about how sequences of common events proceed e.g., How a tropical storm progresses over time from a Level-1 tropical depression to a Level-5 hurricane
Rule schema	Concrete template about the relationship between certain types of actions, events or concepts e.g., How to ask a question in class

laundering the proceeds of her crime with the help of her mother and her husband. The case against the personal assistant took a long time to be investigated despite numerous alerts from several sources because, in the words of a financial investigator interviewed by the authors, the personal assistant *'did not fit the typical money launderer stereotype: man, white, 40 years old.'* Finally, it has also long been shown that category-consistent information is better recalled than category-inconsistent one, especially over extended periods of time (Dutton & Jackson, 1987). In summary, the cognitive representation built over time of an object, once it has been categorized, is an inaccurate, simplified picture that matches the category prototype more closely than did the original exemplar (Alba & Hasher, 1983; Dutton & Jackson, 1987). It is inaccurate in the sense that it does not represent all members of the category, and simplified because it tends to refer to category-consistent information, only.

Further studies focused on how individuals classify in the presence of incomplete or ambiguous stimuli. Researchers suggested that when information about a stimulus is incomplete, people tend to use general information about typical category membership to fill in for information not presented. If the information about a stimulus is ambiguous, then individuals tend to distort the information available toward conformity with unambiguous attributes of category members (Carmichael et al., 1932; Loftus, 1979). This is the case, for instance, of crime witnesses who sometimes report that a suspect acted in a particular way, or had a particular physical attribute, that does not correspond to the truth, but instead matches that witness's schema of the ethnicity, manners or *modus operandi* of a criminal. In cases where the individual is unable to confirm a categorization and has enough motivation and time, he or she may attempt to integrate the available information in a more piece meal fashion.

The rejection of a previously established schema, however, requires considerable effort from the individual (Gilbert, 1991).

It has also been noted that schemas have a transitory nature. That is, certain schemas fail to transfer across seemingly related situations, while others transfer when they should not—for instance, some students may excel at mathematics exercises in class, and yet struggle at applying the same mathematical concepts in nonclassroom concepts. This phenomenon is designated *situated cognition* (Cook & Brown, 1999; Elsbach et al., 2005; Lant, 2002; Lave & Wenger, 1991) and arises because the activity of categorizing is the product not only of one's mental schemas, but also of the relevant context, at a particular point in time. Individual cognition and context interact in a recursive process. While researchers in classification theory have recognized that the context affects cognition, research in this field evolved largely from laboratory studies of individuals, working independently of one another, and where the physical and social context was usually viewed as an extraneous factor to be controlled in the analysis, rather than embedded in it (Ashforth & Humphrey, 1997).

Individuals construct and work with computers, communication networks, and other artifacts within a particular organizational setting which, in turn, exists within a wider environmental context (Heeks, 2000). Hence, a framework is needed that brings together technology, individual cognitive processes, and context, in data mining. This chapter examines the data mining process as communication between three different analytical levels: (1) the technical level that captures and manipulates the data, (2) the individual level of human cognition in the process of giving meaning to the data provided by the technical level and acting upon this knowledge and (3) the contextual level of the organization where these agents participate. Looking at data mining as a communication issue facilitates the individual analysis of each element in the system, thus leading to an '*incremental understanding within the system*'(Smith et al., 2003). The framework proposed here to study analysts' decisions in the data mining process is grounded in the theory of semiotics.

Semiotics, the theory of signs, is a well developed body of communication theory that has been used to analyze a wide range of artifacts and social practices (Pagel & Westerfelhaus, 2005). It draws on different disciplines to explain not only what words mean, but also the process by which meanings are made. A sign is defined as '*everything that, on the grounds of a previously established social convention, can be taken as something standing for something else*' (Eco, 1976). For instance, a red rose is not only a flower, but also a symbol of love in Greek mythology, a symbol of martyrdom in Christian iconography and the logo for the UK's Labor party. The aforementioned definition, however, also suggests that the *something* is a sign only when it is recognized as so by an agent, that is, if the red rose is not taken to stand for love, martyrdom or a particular political orientation, by somebody, then the red rose is not a sign. From this distinction it emerges that a sign is a social object composed of three key components (Peirce, 1931-58): the *representamen,* or material form of the sign which '*may embody any meaning*' (2. 229); the *object,* or that for which the representamen stands for; and the *interpretant,* linking the representamen and the object together. The interpretant is embodied in the person involved in reading the representamen and to whom the signification makes sense. The sign exists in the intrinsic nature of the triadic correlation as a whole: *The sign is not a thing, rather it is a relation between three correlates* (Nake, 2002).

The process through which an agent attributes meaning to a sign is called *semiosis* (Morris, 1938/1970) and is influenced by the point of view of the agent and by the knowledge available (Liu, 2000). The fact that a sign requires a socially accepted convention in order to have meaning, and

that meaning is subject-dependent, implies that the meaning of a particular sign is not a logic immutable relation. Rather, meaning is constructed as a result of two fundamental factors: *affordances* and *norms.* The semiotic affordance is a natural extension of the theory of affordances developed by direct perception psychology (Gibson, 1979) and refers to the patterns of behavior made possible by some combined structure of organism and its environment—for example, a user and a web browser together afford surfing the Web (DeMoor, 2002). The semiotic norms are the social equivalent of the affordance in the sense that they provide the socially acceptable repertoire of behavior—for example, the Hippocratic ideals, the health service concern with affordable medicine, political principles of equitability, and practices of communication between medical hierarchies all guide the actions of members of a hospital (Liebenau & Harindranath, 2002). Of particular importance to the study of cognition in organizations is the taxonomy of norms originated in social psychology that distinguishes between perceptual, evaluative, cognitive and behavioral norms (DeMoor, 2002; Liu, 2000; Stamper et al., 2000). Perceptual norms refer to how employees receive signals from the environment, and the vocabularies that the employees refer to in order to label their perceptions. Evaluative norms embody the beliefs that affect the employees' expectations regarding the observed behavior pattern. Cognitive norms refer to how employees analyze the behaviors observed, and which patterns of cause and effect are imbued in the employees' classification process. Finally, behavioral norms dictate the appropriate actions that employees ought to take in the face of particular events. Perceptual norms are difficult to change and have profound effects on the organization. Evaluative norms vary between cultures, and tend to change slowly. Cognitive norms change alongside developments in the technology of products and processes, and with improving knowledge of the relevant social and economic environment. Behavioral norms change frequently, namely as a response to new laws or formal rules. Different organizations exhibit different combinations of these four kinds of norms (Stamper et al., 2000).

The semiotic distinction between *representamen* and *object* mirrors that made in classification theory between *object* and *prototype*. Thus, for the purpose of this chapter, we will regard the semiotic term representamen and the cognitive term object as interchangeable, as well as the pair of the semiotics term object and the cognitive term prototype. A second similarity between the semiotics and classification theory is that both theories consider that meaning is subjective and context dependent. Where these two theories differ is that classification theory looks at the mental processes of matching data object and prototypes, whereas semiotics looks at the external factors affecting this matching process. The differences between semiotics and classification theory reflect the different ontological positions from which each field looks at the same fundamental issue: that of making sense of particular facts or observations. In this sense, semiotics and classification theory complement each other.

In summary, meaning is created subjectively and socially, leading to subtle differences between groups of knowing agents. Data mining analysts develop differentiated perceptions because they have access to different information and/or are guided by different explicit and implicit norms. While affordances refer to the possible meanings of the sign, the norms refer to the accepted

meanings of the sign in a particular organizational context. Semiotics provides the tools to identify and model the affordances and the norms relevant to the interpretant and, therefore, fills in the contextual gap identified by researchers working on situated cognition. Similarly, classification theory enriches the understanding of the mental process of the interpretants, and the meaning-making mechanism.

FRAMEWORK

The theoretical framework here presented is based on semiotics enhanced with classification theory, and guides our understanding of how analysts make sense of the results of a data mining exercise. It is represented in Figure 3 and can be summarized as follows: the interpretation and validation of data mining results is a process of attributing meaning (*variable z*) to specific signs (*variable x*) through semiosis (*variable y*). Different analysts may reach diverse conclusions because they focus on distinct signs or as a result of differences in what the analysts are afforded to do (*variable y_1*) or the norms that guide the analysts' cognitive activity (*variable y_2*).

The *signs* are the knowledge objects available to or in the organization. Examples include identity data, such as the customer's date of birth, name, and address, as well as activity data such as the customer's spending patterns or product acquisition. The *affordances* are the possible actions

Figure 3. Research framework

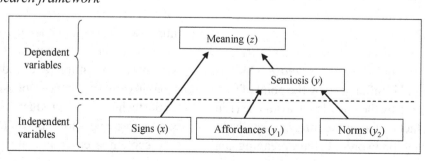

90

that the organization's employees and automated systems can perform, such as manipulation of data and dissemination of information. Finally, the *norms* are the range of socially accepted actions. Acceptance may stem from the perceptual, the evaluative, the cognitive, or the behavioral level. In summary, the framework proposed enables the analyst to detect the classifications emerging in the organization, as well as how such classifications are shaped by the attributes of the technical artifacts, the nature of the tasks or the existing explicit and implicit norms.

Semiotics also offers the tools to represent the organizational affordances and norms. In particular, semantic analysis enables the elicitation and specification of the elements that compose the information system, and the relations between them. The method specifically identifies the agents in the system and maps their roles, responsibilities and authority. The resulting semantic model, also called an *ontology chart*, represents the possible actions that the elements of an organization can perform. These actions, the affordances, are ontologically dependent on the agent performing them. The affordances are linked by lines if there is an ontological dependency, with the antecedents on the left and the dependents to the right. The meaning of a sign is treated as a relationship between the sign and the appropriate actions, as mapped in the charts (Stamper, 1996). The ontology chart highlights how affordances affect the meaning

of a particular sign. In the example provide in Figure 4, there is an agent 'person' who, as an employee of a particular organization, has particular duties—for instance, an employee located in the head office may have the duty to report a particular situation to the his or her supervisor whereas the employee based in the organization's branch may have the duty to keep confidentiality. The duty is ontologically dependent on the employment relationship between the agent and the organization, and the meaning of a particular situation will be different for different employees, who have different duties.

The second semiotic tool is norm analysis. It enables the researcher to capture the various perceptual, evaluative, cognitive or behavioral norms that condition and constraint the realization of the affordances. The norms can be specified in a generic form such as the one proposed by Liu and Dix (1997):

Whenever <condition>
If <state>
Then <agent>
Is <deontic operator (e.g., obliged, permitted, prohibited, ...>
To do <action>

The application of this framework is illustrated, next, with reference to a real data mining applica-

Figure 4. Ontology chart

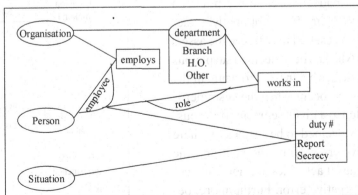

tion in a British financial institution, to be referred to as BFI. In order to protect the organization's security and operational interests, all names and figures have been disguised.

Application of Framework

The organization uses a neural network system whose algorithms process customer data on a daily basis in order to detected 'suspicious' transactions. Customers allocated to the 'suspicious' category are deemed undesirable for the organization because they are either engaged, or likely to be assisting, in various forms of financial crime, from fraud to tax evasion, money laundering, or even terrorist financing. Such customers may bring business to the organization in the short term, but are likely to cause losses in the medium to long term.

Monitoring at BFI, for the purpose of detecting financial crime, has two stages of decision making: in the first stage, the customers' banking transactions are monitored by the branch personnel and by an automated data mining system; if the automated system flags a certain customer or transaction as suspicious, an alert is raised and passed on to the financial crime analysts. Similarly, if the branch employee deems the observed pattern of behavior as suspicious, he or she raises an alert with the team of analysts. In the second stage, the analysts investigate the alert and, if they agree that the observed pattern of behavior is suspicious, a referral—the suspicious activity report (SAR)—is made to the country's financial intelligence unit (Figure 5). Additionally, under certain circumstances, BFI may freeze the assets of the customer who has been deemed suspicious and/or decline further business. Problems in the data mining process occur when the customer is wrongly allocated to a given segment. If the customer is wrongly deemed to be suspicious, there is a false positive error. If, on the contrary, the customer's wrongful activities are not detected, there is a false negative error. Furthermore, be-

cause the analyst will only process those cases for which an alert has been received, he or she can correct false positive errors, but not false negative ones.

The data mining algorithms are developed in extensive brainstorming sessions within the unit, as well as with other units of BFI and entities external to the organization, in order to gather the latest available information regarding the identity and the methods of financial criminals. Such models of who criminals are and what they do are then crystallized into rules. The automated system holds static data about the customer and the product, such as contact details or debit and credit cards associated with the account, as well as dynamic data about the transactions that took place in a given period. The system draws on data from three legacy systems, covering most, but not all, of BFI's products. There is a team of analysts that develop SQL rules to search through this data. These rules are the translation of a complex fuzzy concept—human behavior—to the structured machine code of the automated system. Or, as one designer put it:

Figure 5. Distributed financial crime detection process at BFI

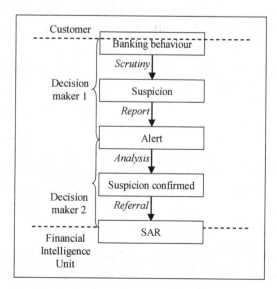

'They tell me in plain English what they want to see and I try and write it in the SQL system so that we can actually monitor it.'

The process consists of describing patterns of behavior that are deemed suspicious at decreasing levels of abstraction until specific unambiguous criteria are reached (Figure 6). It starts at a high level of abstraction, by determining what is understood as 'suspicious'—in this case, an action is deemed to be suspicious if it deviates from the usual pattern of transactions for a given customer. Given that there are different types of customers, the analysts then descends one level—and, thus, reduces abstraction—by focusing on one particular type of customer, for instance personal account holders as opposed to business account holders. It then follows that a given personal account holder will have different transaction patterns for the different products that he or she may have, leading the analyst to focus the definition a bit further, by limiting the analysis to, say, current accounts instead of savings accounts, or mortgage products. The process continuous in

several iterations, until the analyst eventually reaches the conclusion that the transaction pattern in a particular account, belonging to a particular customer, is suspicious. Along this process, the team attempts to connect otherwise disparate pieces of personal, product, and transaction data into a complex formula. At each step, the analyst makes a decision regarding the meaning of the transaction patterns, either deliberately or by default. And each decision on the meaning of the observed patterns of behavior is influenced by the relevant affordances and norms.

The process for developing the syntax varies with the type of semantic information available, in particular, whether analysts can draw on denotative information—that is, on facts about actions, payments or people—or, on the contrary, analysts use affective information such as interpretations, value judgments or intuition. When denotative information is available, the development of the SQL rules tends to follow a process of induction, where facts are observed, for instance financial products used, and conclusions drawn regarding which customer or product characteristics, and

Figure 6. Process of rule creation: Hypothetical example

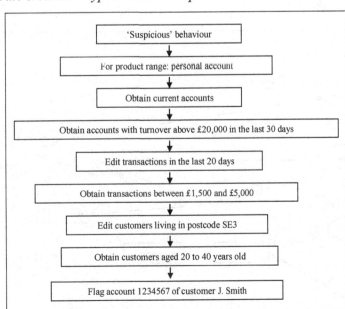

which patterns of transactions are applicable to other cases. For instance, intelligence that a terrorist group financed its activities by smuggling fuel across the border of two specific countries, prompted the team to develop rules for businesses with a SIC code[1] relating to fuel trading. However, in the case of predominantly affective descriptive information, the formulas are developed in a deductive approach: hypotheses about how such behavior would be reflected in transaction patterns are drawn and evaluated, and logical consequences assessed in terms of which data fields to monitor and how to assemble them in one formula. Still regarding the fuel smuggling case, the team made assumptions about the geographical location of such fuel stations, as well as volumes of transaction, for instance. The syntax development also draws on statistical observations such as that customers within a given age bracket are twice as likely to be flagged as suspicious, and market basket analysis, such as the observation that terrorist financers tend to live in a given postcode and be linked with a specific type of SIC code activity.

Having discussed the constituting elements of the data mining exercise, we now turn our attention to the affordances and how they affect the classification process. Starting with the data objects, and as previously mentioned, not all legacy systems feed into the data mining system. One example is the mortgage database that contains rich information collected for the purpose of risk underwriting, such as the professional occupation of the clients and their expected annual income or the portfolio of financial products held. However, for technical reasons, this database is not linked with the automated monitoring system. Additionally, the rules do not read text fields, such as notes from interviews between the customer and one of BFI's financial advisors, and only holds data for a limited period of time. Hence, the system is afforded a set of data that is a subset, only, from all the data available in the organization.

Furthermore, due to the system management team's position in the distributed monitoring process, and the nature of their tasks, the team is afforded a particular view of the customer.

Figure 7. System's affordances

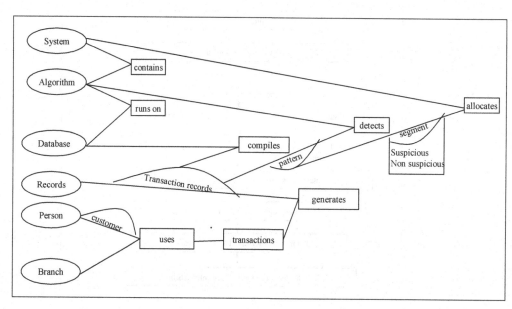

Namely, the team does not interact directly with the customer, and the system has access to hard data, only. Consequently, the algorithms can simply draw on transaction records stored in the database, as illustrated in Figure 7. Another defining characteristic of the system is that it can only run a limited number of rules at a time. As a result, when the team wants to monitor a new group of consumers or a particular SIC code, it needs to switch off another rule. In order to develop the rule, the team considers intelligence from a pool of external and internal sources, ranging from law enforcement agencies to other financial institutions or anecdotal reports in the press. Intelligence originating from law enforcement agencies is denotative but rare, whereas intelligence from other sources tends to be affective and very frequent.

We now examine the norms affecting the data mining process. The norms affect what data is considered for the exercise, from among all the data available. Indeed, not all the data available for the data mining process is utilized. Keeping updated data on all customers is costly for the organization and intrusive for the customer and, as a result, the team selects which data fields are particularly relevant for the exercise, and decide to update and use those fields only. For instance, static customer, data such as professional occupation or marital status, is usually considered of limited value and, hence, not used in the exercise. The norms also determine which data objects the team considers particularly insightful. For example, one of the date fields considered is 'account opening date.' Yet, the team feels that such date is not the most relevant to reflect the relationship between BFI and the customer and, consequently, the field actually holds the date that the customer first opened an account with BFI, rather than the date that the specific account was opened.

The norms also impact on what is deemed to be an effective rule. The knowledge that another financial institution, widely regarded as a leader in financial crime monitoring, was targeting certain geographical areas and SIC codes quickly prompted BFI to develop similar rules. In contrast, the fact that another organization was monitoring a given age group did not prompt BFI to develop a similar rule because it was felt that the two organizations faced different types of criminals. Having decided to develop a particular rule, the team has to decide between specific search paths (Figure 6) which, in turn, is deeply influenced by pragmatic judgements and not purely based on factual statements. This is not entirely the choice of BFI, however. Due to the secretive nature of the phenomenon being monitored, whose perpetrators usually take great care in disguising, most available knowledge about financial crime is, indeed, speculative. New formulas often derive from speculation, and the team is acutely aware of the nature of the process:

'We are not always going to get it right. We try. And I think that where we have learned the most is the cases where we get it wrong. We pull those cases and go through that... it is subjective, you know...'

The choice between alternative paths is also influenced by high level objectives such as the need to keep alerts within a limit that the analysts in stage two of process (Figure 5) can cope with, the team's goal regarding conversion of alerts into disclosures and the team's perception of the strategic interests of BFI. The following quote illustrates this fine balance[2]:

"We wrote a rule that says 'from our personal account customers, tell us which accounts are receiving in excess of £100,000 in a 30 day period.' Initially, that prompted many cases, and over time, we brought that Figure down to cases between £20,000 and £40,000 over 30 days. It is for large cash amounts coming in to all personal customer accounts. If [the account is being used] for business, they are probably trying to avoid charges. But, that could be an element of tax evasion,

which is an element of [financial crime]. We are not sure where the money is coming from, because [the account] is not flagged up as business. It is a good source of disclosures for us. The strike rate has gone up, which is good. That is what [the head of the team] wants to achieve. But it is also a good thing to identify those accounts that are being abused, because it is a loss of revenue for the group. (...) If we drilled it down a bit further we would hit huge volumes and we wouldn't be able to deal with that."

Finally, the norms impact on the attitude towards monitoring suspicious activity and the data mining system in particular. The members of the team reported that the automated system was perceived as an asset in the organization, an active contributor to the detection of potentially criminal transactions and, therefore, a key component of BFI's risk management strategy. Additionally, the team considers that the system enables BFI to detect suspicious activity that would not otherwise be noticed by branch or product staff:

'Technology changed our thinking enormously because, in 2002, which is only three years ago, we were purely reactive to a member of staff notifying us that they were suspicious.'

The popularity of the system has not always been this high, however. In an interview conducted just seven months earlier, the same team member described the system as a 'tick in the box' investment that did not add substantial value to BFI's ability to detect financial crime:

'It is a waste of money and time.'

IMPLICATIONS FOR PRACTICE

In summary, we note—and illustrate with reference to a real application—that what is ultimately interpreted as valid data for, and output from, the

data mining tool, in terms of detecting suspicious transaction activity, is not just a result of the data available, but also of the social context where the selection and the analysis of the data take place. Data mining practitioners ought to be aware that an automated data mining system exists first and foremost in an informal setting, where employees interact for the pursuit of diverse individual and organizational interests. The employees have their own perceptions, behaviors, beliefs, and values, and are influenced by the organization's culture and politics, as well as social norms. For instance, reward mechanisms and hierarchical structures influence which actions are monitored, and how analysts fine tune the rules. Some of the informal behavior in the organization have high regularity and have, thus, become formalized and officially documented in rules, procedures and other forms of bureaucracy. Social definitions of financial crime, like the social meaning of any other sign, are formalized via training manuals and policy documents, for instance. The technical solution is but the automation of the formal elements that have become so exactly specified that they can be executed by a computer. The particular data fields and thresholds are the translation into SQL of abstract definitions of customer behavior. The technical is embedded in the formal, which, in turn, exists in the relevant informal level. It is this embeddedness that led Bowker and Star (1994) to declare that software hides away *'arguments, decisions, uncertainties, and the processual nature of decision making.'*

Additionally, because data mining rules are social constructs, they are context specific and difficult to transfer across organizations. Organizations focus on developing and fine tuning models of the types of crimes that they consider that they are more exposed to. In the case of BFI, because it has branches in areas where terrorist cells are suspected of being active, considerable resources have been devoted to monitoring of terrorist financing activity. Other organizations may focus on different crimes or different customer characteristics, for instance age groups. The strategy of focusing on particular behaviors has been described by several members of the BFI team as *'working smarter,'* as it helps them to prioritize work and better manage limited resources. However, the reverse of the medal is that the organization runs the risk of focusing on forms of high volume criminal behavior, and overlook typologies that are less frequent, but more damaging for the organization, such as identity fraud or cyber crime. Practitioners can apply the framework proposed in their organizations by simply adjusting the terms and dependencies in the ontology charts, as well as the content of the norms. Practitioners, by auditing the data mining development processes in their organizations, using the proposed framework, will be in a better position to identify not only of the contextual limitation of the models being used, but also of the pragmatic implications of the choices made at each stage of the development and use of the data mining system.

Finally, data mining is not only subjective, but also the subjectivity is likely to persist. Legacy systems are extremely expensive and complex to replace and, on average, a financial services firm needs five years to renew a branch and other applications (Annesley, 2005). Moreover, limiting characteristics of the system, such as the number of rules that can search through the data at any one time, the number and type of fields feeding the system, or the inability to read text data are impossible to change unless the specific technical solution is replaced. Similarly, the study underlined the high prevalence of evaluative and perceptual norms which are, by default, extremely difficult to change. In order to change very stable norms, BFI needs to engage in a sustained communication effort, ideally engaging an opinion leader whose expertise and authority is recognized by the analysts. It has also been shown that denotative information is more suitable to change such perceptions than affect one. Yet, as

was mentioned, by and large, the vast majority of information available in the information, regarding the characteristics and transaction patterns of suspicious customers, is of an affective nature. Another form of shaping perceptual and evaluative norms is via formal assessment and reward mechanisms. However, given that employees are usually rewarded on short term commercial targets, rather than long term risk management ones, this is unlikely to become an actionable tool, at least for the organization as a whole. Data mining is a process of modeling a dynamic and extremely complex phenomenon—human behavior—using a relatively rigid tool—technology. Software codes and hardware choices are difficult to change, drastically reducing the ability of the data mining models to maintain its reliability through time. Some of the impacts of technology on organizations are opportunistic and unanticipated, requiring from the organization monitoring of emergent changes in ongoing practices (Orlikowski, 1996a, 1996b). Similarly, it is essential that organizations identify the sources of bias and correct them promptly, before the emerging categories become crystallized in the organization's data mining models. Additionally, it is critical for organizations to continuously reassess the content of their rules, question the value judgements shaping the emerging formulas, and evaluate the relevance of models in different periods and contexts.

The gap between information systems capabilities and organization's needs occurs, according to Liu, Sun et al. (2002), because the two are not treated as an integral unit. This is not because information systems researchers are insensitive to the need to handle both the technical and the social elements of a system. Rather, Eatock, Paul et al. (2002) argue, it is because neither clear guidance nor modeling techniques exist for the coordination of the two elements, and even those studies that explicitly target the integration of the social and the technical elements end up treating both elements separately. The framework proposed in this chapter may be located, exactly, at the junction between technical and social, providing both the underlying philosophy and the specific mode of analysis. It proposes guidelines and tools to identify divergent views of mined knowledge resulting from factors such as varying levels of access to information and existing social norms. The chapter contributes to the data mining literature by enhancing understanding of how users and context affect the results of classification process. Furthermore, we examined how the organization's employees construct images of their own consumers.

In addition to the practical contributions mentioned above, the study mentioned in this chapter also points towards a number of future research directions, as discussed in the last section. First, it was mentioned that there were other parties intervening in the monitoring process—for example, customer facing employees—but did not examine these employees' classification processes. Particular attention should be dedicated to the study of the impact of subjective signs such as the customer's physical appearance or manners towards the employee, as opposed to objective data such as transfers of money or SIC codes, and examine how such subjective signs cue perception and, ultimately, classification of consumers as 'suspicious.'

A second area of research should explore, in detail, the links between the several components of this distributed process. In a distributed decision making process, the employee who first encounters the problem makes a 'go' or 'pass' decision that, in fact, limits the strategic options available to the employee located next in the decision chain (Andersen, 2005), and tends to determine how the subsequent decision makers regard the situation under analysis (Ashforth & Humphrey, 1997). Data mining exists as component of this dynamic system.

There are also benefits to be drawn from research applying the framework presented in this

chapter to a large sample of analysts and models. The increased scale would enable researchers to model and measure relationships between the different framework variables which, in turn, would be greatly beneficial for instructional purposes.

Another interesting line of research could explore the effect of training, reward mechanisms, and others in shaping the norms affecting the mining of suspicious consumers. Such study would provide further insight into the situatedness of the analysts' cognitive processes.

Additionally, because the initiative to monitor suspicious consumers is partly driven by third parties, such as the regulator or the financial intelligence unit, who have very different objectives and characteristics, it would be interesting to investigate how the general model of suspicious behavior is built, and how that is reflected into the organization's data mining activities.

Finally, it would be extremely valuable to test the application of the framework in other industry scenarios. A similar framework has been applied in the field of homeland security. For instance, Desouza and Hensgen (2002) use a similar framework in the field of homeland security, to highlight the barriers to the collection of information and the interpretation of that information prior to the terrorist attacks of September 11, 2001. The authors report that data related to the attacks had been reported to various intelligence centers since the beginning of 2001. Yet, the lack of understanding of any relational basis for this data, the underestimating of the intended actions of the terrorists, and the pursuit of independent paths by the agencies involved seriously hindered the ability to develop a preemptive action plan. Other authors have applied similar frameworks to study the formation of legal obligations (e.g., Backhouse & Cheng, 2000) or the likelihood of occurrence of information systems' security breaches (e.g., Dhillon, 1995), for instance. However, in order to increase the relevance and impact for practitioners, further studies should be made of the contextual and cognition factors in data mining in other industries such as customer loyalty or risk scoring programs (Kamp et al., forthcoming).

CONCLUSION

This chapter set out to develop understanding of how technical, cognitive, and contextual factors impact on the process of interpretation and validation of mined knowledge. First, the chapter highlighted that the data mining literature tends to focus on the technical aspects of the data mining process and, as a result, it does not offer proper understanding of the reasons why, and the mechanism how, analysts interact and affect the exercise. Then, the chapter addressed the call for research into the cognitive aspects of data mining, and drew on the conceptual approach of classification theory to study how employees classify. Furthermore, the chapter noted that classification is made with reference to very stable prototypes of behavior, which are situated in context and time. It then looked at how context affects the cognitive process and the technical tool, through the lens of semiotics. The research framework proposed is based in three constructs—*sign*, *affordance* and *norms*—that were operationalised with the discussion of particular case study. Analysis of the case study data, and subsequent discussion, elucidated not only that data mining is subjective, but also that it is context specific and rigid. Finally, the chapter presented suggestions on how the organization can identify and attempt to correct the sources of biases. Above all, it was noted that data mining models, like mental schemas, are subject to situated cognition.

The framework proposed does not eliminate subjectivity; rather it acknowledges it, specifically. By understanding the sources of subjectivity, and how it impacts on the selection of the data and the interpretation of the mined results, data mining researchers can increase the prescriptive and corrective value of data mining. The ontology informing the data mining exercise is shaped by the affordances and the norms existing in the organization.

FUTURE RESEARCH DIRECTIONS

There are a number of promising research directions. First, it was mentioned that there were other parties intervening in the monitoring process —e.g., customer facing employees—but we did not examine these employees' classification processes. Particular attention should be dedicated to the study of the impact of subjective signs such as the customer's physical appearance or manners towards the employee, as opposed to objective data such as transfers of money or industry codes, and examine how such subjective signs cue perception and, ultimately, classification of consumers as 'suspicious'.

A second area of research should explore, in detail, the links between the several components of the distributed process. In a distributed decision making process, the employee who first encounters the problem makes a 'go' or 'pass' decision that, in fact, limits the strategic options available to the employee located next in the decision chain (Andersen, 2005), and tends to determine how the subsequent decision makers regard the situation under analysis (Ashforth & Humphrey, 1997). Data mining exists as component of this dynamic system.

There are also benefits to be drawn from research applying the framework presented in this chapter to a large sample of analysts and models. The increased scale would enable researchers to model and measure relationships between the different framework variables, which, in turn, would be greatly beneficial for instructional purposes.

Another interesting line of research could explore the effect of training, reward mechanism and others in shaping the norms affecting the mining of suspicious consumers. Such study would provide further insight into the *situatedness* of the analysts' cognitive processes.

Additionally, because the initiative to monitor suspicious consumers is partly driven by third parties who have very different objectives and characteristics, it would be interesting to investigate how the general model of suspicious behaviour is built, and how that is reflected into the organisation's data mining activities.

Finally, it would be extremely valuable to test the application of the framework in other industry scenarios. Desouza and Hensgen (2002) used a similar framework in the field of homeland security, to highlight the barriers to the collection of information and the interpretation of that information prior to the terrorist attacks of September 11th 2001. The authors reported that data related to the attacks had been reported to various intelligence centres since the beginning of 2001. Yet, the lack of understanding of any relational basis for this data, the underestimating of the intended actions of the terrorists and the pursuit of independent paths by the agencies involved seriously hindered the ability to develop a preemptive action plan. Other authors have applied similar frameworks to study the formation of legal obligations (e.g., (Backhouse & Cheng, 2000)) or the likelihood of occurrence of information systems' security breaches (e.g., (Dhillon, 1995)), for instance. However, in order to increase the relevance and impact for practitioners, further studies should focus on the contextual and cognition factors in data mining in other industries such as customer loyalty or risk scoring programmes (Kamp *et al.*, forthcoming).

REFERENCES

Agrawal, R., Imielinski, T., & Swami, A. (1993). Database mining: A performance perspective. *IEEE Transactions on Knowledge and Data Engineering, 5*(6), 914-925.

Alba, J.W., & Hasher, L. (1983). Is memory schematic? *Psychological Bulletin, 93*, 203-231.

Anand, S.S., Bell, D.A., & Hughes, J.G. (1995, November 29-December 02, 1995). *The role of domain knowledge in data mining.* Paper presented at the Conference on Information and Knowledge Management, Baltimore.

Andersen, T.J. (2005). The performance effect of computer-mediated communication and decentralized strategic decision making. *Journal of Business Research, 58*(8), 1059-1067.

Annesley, C. (2005). Banks' push to upgrade hampered by complexity of legacy systems. *Computer Weekly, 14.*

Ashforth, B.E., & Humphrey, R.H. (1997). The ubiquity and potency of labeling in organizations. *Organization Science, 8*(1), 43-58.

Backhouse, J., & Cheng, E.K. (2000). Signalling intentions and obliging behavior online: An application of semiotic and legal modeling in e-commerce. *Journal of End User Computing, 12*(2), 33-42.

Boland, R.J.J., Singh, J., Salipante, P., Aram, J., Fay, S.Y., & Kanawattanachai, P. (2001). Knowledge representations and knowledge transfer. *Academy of Management Journal, 44*, 393-417.

Bowker, G., & Star, S.L. (1994). Knowledge and infrastructure in international information management: Problems of classification and coding. In L. Bud-Frierman (Ed.), *Information acumen: The understanding and use of knowledge in modern business* (pp. 187-213). London: Routledge.

Bruha, I. (2000). From machine learning to knowledge discovery: Survey of preprocessing and postprocessing. *Intelligent Data Analysis, 4*, 363-374.

Canhoto, A.I., & Backhouse, J. (2005). Tracing the identity of a money launderer. In T. Nabeth (Ed.), *Fidis d2.2: Set of use case and scenarios.* Fontainebleau: Insead.

Carmichael, L., Hogan, H.P., & Walter, A.A. (1932). An experimental study on the effect of language on the reproduction of visually perceived form. *Journal of Experimental Psychology, 15*, 73-86.

Carson, S., Madhok, A., Varman, R., & John, G. (2003). Information processing moderators of the effectiveness of trust based governance in interfirm R&D collaboration. *Organization Science, 14*, 45-56.

Chan, C., & Lewis, B. (2002). A basic primer on data mining. *Information Systems Management, 19*(4), 56-60.

Chung, H.M., & Gray, P. (1999). Data mining. *Journal of Management Information Systems, 16*(1), 11-16.

Cook, S.D.N., & Brown, J.S. (1999). Bridging epistemologies: The generative dance between organizational knowledge and organizational knowing. *Organization Science, 10*(4), 381-400.

DeMoor, A. (2002). Language/action meets organizational semiotics: Situating conversations with norms. *Information Systems Frontiers, 4*(3), 257-272.

Desouza, K.C., & Hensgen, T. (2002). On information in organizations: An emergent information theory and semiotic framework. *Emergence, 4*(3), 95-114.

Dhillon, G.S. (1995). *Interpreting the management of information systems security*. London School of Economics.

Dutton, J.E., & Jackson, S.E. (1987). Categorizing strategic issues: Links to organizational action. *Academy of Management Review, 12*(1), 76-90.

Eatock, J., Paul, R.J., et al. (2002). Developing a theory to explain the insights gained concering information systems and business process behaviour: *The ASSESS-IT project. Information Systems Frontiers, 4*(3), 303-316.

Eco, U. (1976). *A theory of semiotics*. Bloomington, IN: Indiana University Press.

Elsbach, K.D., Barr, P.S., & Hargadon, A.B. (2005). Identifying situated cognition in organizations. *Organization Science, (16)*, 4.

Fayyad, U., Piatetsky-Shapiro, G., Smyth, P., & Uthurusamy, R. (Eds.). (1996). *Advances in knowledge discovery and data mining*. Cambridge, MA: AAAI / MIT Press.

Fiske, S. T., & Taylor, S. E. (1991). *Social cognition* (2nd ed.). New York: McGraw-Hill.

Gibson, J.J. (1979). *The ecological approach to visual perception*. Boston: Houghton Mifflin.

Gilbert, D.T. (1991). How mental systems believe. *American psychologist, 46*, 107-119.

Gladwell, M. (2006). Troublemakers. *The New Yorker.*

Heeks, R. (2000). Information technology, information systems and public sector accountability. In C. Avgerou & G. Walsham (Eds.), *Information technology in context* (pp. 201-220). Aldershot, Hampshire: Ashgate.

Heracleous, L., & Barrett, M. (2001). Organizational change as discourse: Communicative actions and deep structures in the context of information technology implementation. *Academy of Management Journal, 44*, 755-778.

Hildebrandt, M., & Backhouse, J. (2005). *D7.2: Descriptive analysis and inventory of profiling practices*. FIDIS Future of Identity in the Information Society.

Hosein, I. (2005). *Researching the ethics of knowledge management: The case of data-mining*. (Working paper). London School of Economics.

Humby, C., Hunt, T., & Phillips, T. (2003). *Scoring points: How tesco is winning customer loyalty*. London: Kogan Page.

Kamp, M., Korffer, B., & Meints, M. (forthcoming). Profiling of customers and consumers: Customer loyalty programs and scoring practices. In M. Hildebrandt & S. Gutwirth (Eds.), *Profiling the european citizen: Cross-disciplinary perspectives* (pp. 181-196). Spinger.

Kohavi, R., Rothleder, N.J., & Simoudis, E. (2002). Emerging trends in business analytics. *Communications of the ACM, 45*(8), 45-48.

Lant, T. (2002). Organizational cognition and interpretation. In J. A. C. Baum (Ed.), *Blackwell companion to organizations* (pp. 344-362). Malden: Blackwell Publishers.

Lave, J., & Wenger, E. (1991). *Situated learning: Legitimate peripheral participation*. Cambridge: Cambridge University Press.

Liebenau, J., & Harindranath, G. (2002). Organizational reconciliation and its implications for organizational decision support systems: A semiotic approach. *Decision Support Systems, 33*(4), 339-398.

Liu, K. (2000). *Semiotics in information systems engineering*. Cambridge: Cambridge University Press.

Liu, K., & Dix, A. (1997). *Norm governed agents in cscw*. Paper presented at the 1st International Workshop on Computational Semiotics, Paris.

Loftus, E. (1979). *Eyewitness testimony*. Cambridge, MA: Harvard University Press.

Maojo, V. (2004). *Domain specific particularities of data mining: Lessons learned*. Paper presented at the ISBMDA.

Markman, A.B., & Gentner, D. (2001). Thinking. *Annual Review of Psychology, 52*(1), 223-247.

Mervis, C.B., & Rosch, E. (1981). Categorization of natural objects. *Annual Review of Psychology, 32*, 89-115.

Morris, C.W. (1938/1970). *Foundations of the theory of signs*. Chicago University Press.

Nake, F. (2002). Data, information, and knowledge: A semiotic view of phenomena of organization. In E. Liu, R.J. Clarke, P.B. Andersen, R. Stamper, & E.S. Abou-Zeid (Eds.), *Organizational semitiocs: Evolving a science of information systems* (pp. 41-50). London: Kluwer Academic Publishers.

Orlikowski, W.J. (1996a). Evolving with notes: Organizational change around groupware technology. In C. Ciborra (Ed.), *Groupware and teamwork* (pp. 23-60). London: John Wiley & Sons.

Orlikowski, W.J. (1996b). Improving organizational transformation over time: A situated action perspective. *Information Systems Research, 7*(1), 63-92.

Pagel, S., & Westerfelhaus, R. (2005). Charting managerial reading preferences in relation to popular management theory books: A semiotic analysis. *Journal of Business Communication, 42*(4), 420-448.

Pazzani, M.J. (2000). Knowledge discovery from data? *IEEE Intelligent Systems & Their Applications, 15*(2), 10-13.

Pazzani, M.J., Mani, S., & Shankle, W.R. (2001). Acceptance by medical experts of rules generated by machine learning. *Methods of information in medicine, 40*(5), 380-385.

Peirce, C.S. (1931-58). *Collected writings*. Cambridge, MA: Harvard University Press.

Rosch, E. (1975). Cognitive reference points. *Cognitive Psychology, 1*, 532-547.

Rosch, E. (1978). Principles of categorization. In E. Rosch & B. Lloyd (Eds.), *Cognition and categorization* (pp. 27-47). Hillsdale, NJ: Erlbaum.

Rosch, E., & Mervis, C.B. (1975). Family resemblances: Studies in the internal structure of categories. *Cognitive Psychology, 7*, 573-605.

Smith, G., Blackman, D., & Good, B. (2003). Knowledge sharing and organizational learning: The impact of social architecture at ordnance survey. *Journal of Knowledge Management Practice, 4*(3), 18.

Stamper, R. (1996). Signs, information, norms and systems. In P. Holmqvist, P. B. Andersen, H. K. Klein, & R. Posner (Eds.), *Signs of work: Semiotics and information processing in organizations*: Walter de Gruyter.

Stamper, R., Liu, K., Hafkamp, M., & Ades, Y. (2000). Understanding the roles of signs and norms in organizations: A semiotic approach to information systems design. *Behaviour and Information Technology, 19*(1), 15-27.

FURTHER READINGS

On Profiling

Canhoto, A.I., & Backhouse, J. (2007). Profiling under conditions of ambiguity: An application in the financial services industry. *Journal of Retailing and Consumer Services* (forthcoming).

Hildebrandt, M., & Backhouse, J. (2005). *D7.2: Descriptive analysis and inventory of profiling practices.* FIDIS future of identity in the information society.

Kamp, M., Korffer, B., & Meints, M. (forthcoming). Profiling of customers and consumers: Customer loyalty programs and scoring practices. In M. Hildebrandt & S. Gutwirth (Eds.), *Profiling the European citizen: Cross-disciplinary perspectives* (pp. 181-196). Spinger.

On Data Mining

Agrawal, R., Imielinski, T., & Swami, A. (1993). Database mining: A performance perspective. *IEEE Transactions on Knowledge and Data Engineering, 5*(6), 914-925.

Anand, S.S., Bell, D.A., & Hughes, J.G. (1995, November 29-December 02, 1995). *The role of domain knowledge in data mining.* Paper presented at the Conference on Information and Knowledge Management, Baltimore.

Bruha, I. (2000). From machine learning to knowledge discovery: Survey of preprocessing and postprocessing. *Intelligent Data Analysis, 4*, 363-374.

Chan, C., & Lewis, B. (2002). A basic primer on data mining. *Information Systems Management, 19*(4), 56-60.

Chung, H.M., & Gray, P. (1999). Data mining. *Journal of Management Information Systems, 16*(1), 11-16.

Fayyad, U., Piatetsky-Shapiro, G., Smyth, P., & Uthurusamy, R. (Eds.). (1996). *Advances in knowledge discovery and data mining.* Cambridge, Massachussets. AAAI / MIT Press.

Kohavi, R., Rothleder, N.J., & Simoudis, E. (2002). Emerging trends in business analytics. *Communications of the ACM, 45*(8), 45-48.

Maojo, V. (2004). *Domain specific particularities of data mining: Lessons learned.* Paper presented at the ISBMDA.

Pazzani, M. J. (2000). Knowledge discovery from data? *IEEE Intelligent Systems & Their Applications, 15*(2), 10-13.

Pazzani, M.J., Mani, S., & Shankle, W.R. (2001). Acceptance by medical experts of rules generated by machine learning. *Methods of information in medicine, 40*(5), 380-385.

On Cognition and Sense-Making

Alba, J.W., & Hasher, L. (1983). Is memory schematic? *Psychological Bullentin, 93*, 203-231.

Ashforth, B.E., & Humphrey, R.H. (1997). The ubiquity and potency of labeling in organizations. *Organization Science, 8*(1), 43-58.

Carmichael, L., Hogan, H.P., & Walter, A.A. (1932). An experimental study on the effect of language on the reproduction of visually perceived form. *Journal of Experimental Psychology, 15,* 73-86.

Dutton, J.E., & Jackson, S.E. (1987). Categorizing strategic issues: Links to organizational action. *Academy of Management Review, 12*(1), 76-90.

Elsbach, K.D., Barr, P.S., & Hargadon, A.B. (2005). Identifying situated cognition in organizations. *Organization Science,* (16), 4.

Fiske, S.T., & Taylor, S.E. (1991). *Social cognition* (2nd ed.). New York: McGraw-Hill.

Gigerenzer, G., Todd, P.M., & A.R. Group (1999) *Simple heuristics that make us smart.* Oxford University Press, Oxford.

Gilbert, D.T. (1991). How mental systems believe. *American psychologist, 46,* 107-119.

Lant, T. (2002). Organizational cognition and interpretation. In J.A.C. Baum (Ed.), *Blackwell companion to organizations* (pp. 344-362). Malden: Blackwell Publishers.

Loftus, E. (1979). *Eyewitness testimony.* Cambridge, MA: Harvard University Press.

Markman, A.B., & Gentner, D. (2001). Thinking. *Annual Review of Psychology, 52*(1), 223-247.

Mervis, C.B., & Rosch, E. (1981). Categorization of natural objects. *Annual Review of Psychology, 32,* 89-115.

Rosch, E. (1975). Cognitive reference points. *Cognitive Psychology, 1,* 532-547.

Rosch, E. (1978). Principles of categorization. In E. Rosch & B. Lloyd (Eds.), *Cognition and categorization* (pp. 27-47). Hillsdale, NJ: Erlbaum.

Rosch, E., & Mervis, C.B. (1975). Family resemblances: Studies in the internal structure of categories. *Cognitive Psychology, 7,* 573-605.

On Semiotics

Andersen, P.B. (1990) *A theory of computer semiotics: Semiotic approaches construction and assessment of computer systems.* Cambridge University Press, Cambridge.

Ashforth, B.E., & Humphrey, R.H. (1997). The ubiquity and potency of labeling in organizations. *Organization Science, 8*(1), 43-58.

Backhouse, J., & Cheng, E.K. (2000). Signalling intentions and obliging behavior online: An application of semiotic and legal modeling in e-commerce. *Journal of End User Computing, 12*(2), 33-42.

Barley, S.R. (1983) Semiotics and the study of occupational and organizational cultures. *Administrative Science Quarterly, 28*(3), 393-413.

Barr, P., Biddle, R., & Noble, J. (2003) A semiotic model of user-interface metaphor. In *Proceedings of the 6th International Workshop on Organisational Semiotics,* Reading UK (pp. 11-12). Liu, Kecheng.

DeMoor, A. (2002). Language/action meets organisational semiotics: Situating conversations with norms. *Information Systems Frontiers, 4*(3), 257-272.

Desouza, K.C., & Hensgen, T. (2002). On information in organizations: An emergent information theory and semiotic framework. *Emergence, 4*(3), 95-114.

Desouza, K.C., & Hensgen, T. (2003) Semiotic Emergent framework to address the reality of cyberterrorism. *Technological forecasting and social change, 70,* 385-396.

Desouza, K.C., & Hensgen, T. (2005). *Managing information in complex organizations: Semiotics and signals.* M.E. Sharpe, London.

Dhillon, G.S. (1995). *Interpreting the management of information systems security.* London School of Economics, London.

Eco, U. (1976). *A theory of semiotics.* Bloomington, IN: Indiana University Press.

Hervey, S. (1982) *Semiotic Perspectives.* Allen and Unwin, London.

Heusden, B., & Jorna, R. (2001). Toward a semiotic theory of cognitive dynamics in organizations in information, organization and technology. In K. Liu, R.J. Clarke, P.B. Andersen, R. Stamper, & E.-S. Abou-Zeid (Eds.), *Studies in organisational semiotics* (pp. 83-113). Boston: Kluwer.

Liebenau, J., & Backhouse, J. (1990). *Understanding information: An introduction.* London: Macmillan.

Liebenau, J., & Harindranath, G. (2002). Organizational reconciliation and its implications for organizational decision support systems: A semiotic approach. *Decision Support Systems, 33*(4), 339-398.

Liu, K. (2000). *Semiotics in information systems engineering.* Cambridge: Cambridge University Press.

Liu, K., & Dix, A. (1997). *Norm governed agents in cscw.* Paper presented at the The First International Workshop on Computational Semiotics, Paris.

Martin, B., & Ringham, F. (2000) *Dictionary of Semiotics.* Cassell, London.

Nake, F. (2002). Data, information, and knowledge: A semiotic view of phenomena of organization. In K. Liu, R.J. Clarke, P.B. Andersen, R. Stamper, & E.-S. Abou-Zeid (Eds.), *Organizational semitiocs: Evolving a science of information systems* (pp. 41-50). London: Kluwer Academic Publishers.

Pagel, S., & Westerfelhaus, R. (2005). Charting managerial reading preferences in relation to popular management theory books: A semiotic analysis. *Journal of Business Communication, 42*(4), 420-448.

Peirce, C.S. (1931-58). *Collected writings.* Cambridge, MA: Harvard University Press.

Stamper, R. (1973) *Information in Business and Administrative Systems.* New York: John Wiley & Sons.

Stamper, R. (1996). Signs, information, norms and systems. In P. Holmqvist, P.B. Andersen, H.K. Klein, & R. Posner (Eds.), *Signs of work: Semiotics and information processing in organizations.* Walter de Gruyter.

Stamper, R., Liu, K., Hafkamp, M., & Ades, Y. (2000). Understanding the roles of signs and norms in organizations: A semiotic approach to information systems design. *Behaviour and Information Technology, 19*(1), 15-27.

ENDNOTES

[1] The Standard Industrial Classification codes are used to classify business establishments and other statistical units by the type of economic activities they are engaged in. Information on the origins, legal basis and other aspects of the UK's SIC system is available in http://www.statistics.gov.uk/methods_quality/sic/.

[2] Exact parameters and thresholds have been disguised

Chapter VI
Data Integration Through Protein Ontology

Amandeep S. Sidhu
University of Technology Sydney, Australia

Tharam S. Dillon
University of Technology Sydney, Australia

Elizabeth Chang
Curtin University of Technology, Perth

ABSTRACT

Traditional approaches to integrate protein data generally involved keyword searches, which immediately excludes unannotated or poorly annotated data. An alternative protein annotation approach is to rely on sequence identity, structural similarity, or functional identification. Some proteins have a high degree of sequence identity, structural similarity, or similarity in functions that are unique to members of that family alone. Consequently, this approach can not be generalized to integrate the protein data. Clearly, these traditional approaches have limitations in capturing and integrating data for protein annotation. For these reasons, we have adopted an alternative method that does not rely on keywords or similarity metrics, but instead uses ontology. In this chapter we discuss conceptual framework of protein ontology that has a hierarchical classification of concepts represented as classes, from general to specific; a list of attributes related to each concept, for each class; a set of relations between classes to link concepts in ontology in more complicated ways then implied by the hierarchy, to promote reuse of concepts in the ontology; and a set of algebraic operators for querying protein ontology instances.

INTRODUCTION

Since the first efforts of Maxam (Maxam & Gilbert, 1977) and Sanger (Sanger et al., 1977), the DNA sequence databases have been doubling in size every 18 months or so. This trend continues unabated. This forced the development of systems of software and mathematical techniques for managing and searching these collections. In the past decade, there has been an explosion in the amount of DNA sequence data available, due to very rapid progress of genome sequencing projects. There are three principal comprehensive databases of nucleic acid sequences in the world today.

- The European Molecular Biology Laboratory (EMBL) database is maintained at European Bioinformatics Institute in Cambridge, UK (Stoesser et al., 2003).
- GenBank is maintained at the National Center for Biotechnology Information in Maryland (Benson et al., 2000).
- The DNA Databank of Japan (DDBJ) is maintained at National Institute of Genetics in Mishima, Japan (Miyazaki et al., 2003).

These three databases share information and hence contain identical sets of sequences. The objective of these databases is to ensure that DNA sequence information is stored in a way that is publicly, and freely, accessible and that it can be retrieved and used by other researchers in the future.

Clearly, we have reached a point where computers are essential for the storage, retrieval, and analysis of biological sequence data. The sheer volume of data made it hard to find sequences of interest in each release of sequence databases. The data were distributed as collection of flat files, each of which contained some textual information (the annotation), such as organism name and keywords as well as the DNA sequence. The main way of searching for the sequence of interest was to use a string-matching program. This forced the development of relational database management systems in the main database centers but the databases continued to be delivered as flat files. One important system that is still in use, for browsing and searching the databases, was ACNUC (Gouy et al., 1985), from Manolo Gouy and colleagues in Lyon, France. This was developed in the mid-eighties and allowed fully relational searching and browsing of database annotation.

Another important type of biological data that is exponentially increasing is data of protein structures. Protein Data Bank (PDB) (Bernstein et al., 1977, Weissig & Bourne, 2002, Wesbrook et al., 2002) is a database of protein structures obtained from X-ray crystallography and NMR experiments. At the time of writing this chapter PDB contained over 35,000 structures. It consists of collections of fixed format records that describe the atomic coordinates, chemical and biochemical features, experimental details of structure determination, and some structural features, such as hydrogen bonds and secondary structure assignments. In recent years, dictionary based representations emerged to give data a consistent interface, making it easier to parse. A widely used dictionary-format is the macromolecular crystallographic information file (mmCIF).

The problem of managing biological macromolecular sequence data is as old as the data themselves. In 1998, a special issue of *Nucleic Acids Research* lists 64 different databanks covering diverse areas of biological research, and the nucleotide sequence data alone at over 1 billion bases. It is not only the flood and heterogeneity that make the issues of information representation, storage, structure, retrieval, and interpretation critical. There also has been a change in the user community. In the middle 1980s, fetching a biological entry on a mainframe computer was an adventurous step that only a few dared. At the end of the 1990s, thousands of researchers make use of biological databanks on a daily basis to answer queries, for example, to find sequences similar to a newly sequenced gene, or to retrieve bibliographic references, or to investigate fundamental problems of modern biology (Koonin & Galperin, 1997). New technologies, of which the World Wide Web (WWW) has been the most revolutionary in terms of impact on science, have made it possible to create a high density of links between databanks. Database systems today are facing the task of serving ever increasing amounts of data of ever growing complexity to a user community that is growing nearly as fast as the data, and is getting more and more demanding.

The exponential growth of experimental molecular biology in recent decades has been accompanied by a growth in the number and size of databases interpreting and describing the results of such experiments. While all of these databases strive for complete coverage within their chosen scope, the domain of interest for some users transcends individual resources. This may reflect the user's wish to combine different types of information, or inability of a single resource to fully contain the details of every relevant experiment. Additionally, large databases with broad domains tend to offer less detailed information than smaller more specialized resources with the result that data from many sources may need to be combined to provide a complete picture.

Much of the value of molecular biology resources is a part of an interconnected network of related databases. Many maintain cross-references to other databases, frequently through manual entries. These cross-references provide the basic platform for more advanced data integration strategies to address the problems, including: (a) establishment of identity of common concepts, (b) integration of data described in different formats, (c) the resolution of conflicts between different resources, (d) data synchronization, and (e) the presentation of a unified view. The resolution of specific conflicts and development of unified views rely on domain expertise and need the user community. However, some of the other issues can be addressed through generic approaches, such as standard identifiers, naming conventions,

controlled vocabularies, and adoption of standards for data representation and exchange.

In this chapter we will focus on protein data sources, and their data integration using protein ontology (PO) (Sidhu et al., 2006a). Section 2 discusses issues identified in biological data management. In Section 3 we provide a conceptual overview of protein ontology. Section 4 discusses interoperability of biological data sources. Section 5 concludes the chapter.

BIOLOGICAL DATA MANAGEMENT

Problems facing genomics and proteomics data are related to data semantics—the meaning of data represented in a data source—and the difference between semantics within a set of sources. The differences require addressing the issues of concept identification, data transformation, and concept overloading. Concept identification and resolution has two components: identifying when data contained in different data sources refer to same object and reconciling conflicting information found in these sources. Addressing these issues should begin by identifying which abstract concepts are represented in each data source. Once shared concepts have been identified, conflicting information can be easily located. As a simple example, two sources may have different values for an attribute that is supposed to be same. One of the wrinkles that genomics adds to the reconciliation process is that there may not be a right answer. Consider that a sequence representing the same gene should be identical in two different data sources. However, there may be legitimate differences between two sources, and these differences need to be preserved in the integrated view. This makes a seemingly simple query, "return the sequence associated with this protein," more complex than it first appears.

In the case where the differences are the result of alternative data formats, data transformations may be applied to map the data to a consistent format. Whereas mapping may be simple from technical prospective, determining what it is and when to apply it relies on the detailed representation of the concepts and appropriate domain knowledge. For example, the translation of a protein sequence from single-character representation to a three-character representation defines a corresponding mapping between the two representations. Not all transformations are easy to perform—and some may not be reversible. Furthermore, because of concept overloading, it is often difficult to determine whether or not two abstract concepts really have the same meanin—and to figure out what to do if they do not. For example, although two data sources may both represent genes as DNA sequences, one may only include sequences that are known to code for proteins. Whether or not this is important depends on a specific application and the semantics the unified view is supporting. The number of subtly distinct concepts used in genomics and proteomics and the use of the same name to refer to multiple variants makes overcoming these conflicts difficult.

Problem of Biological Data Integration

Unfortunately, the semantics of biological data are usually hard to define precisely because they are not explicitly stated but are implicitly included in the database design. The reason is simple: at a given time, within a single research community, common definitions of various terms are often well understood and have precise meaning. As a result, those within that community usually understand the semantics of the data source without needing to be explicitly defined. However, proteomics (much less all of biology or life science) is not a single, consistent scientific domain; it is composed of dozens of smaller, focused research communities. This would not be a significant issue if researchers only accessed data from within a single domain, but that is not usually the case. Typically, researchers require

integrated access to data from multiple domains, which requires resolving terms that have slightly different meanings across the communities. This is further complicated by the observations that the specific community whose terminology is being used by the data source is usually not explicitly identified and that the terminology evolves over time. For many of the larger, community data sources, the domain is obvious—the PDB handles protein structure information, the Swiss-Prot protein sequence database provides protein sequence information and useful annotation and so forth—but the terminology used may not be current and can reflect a combination of definitions from multiple domains.

Biology also demonstrates three challenges for data integration that are common in evolving scientific domains, but not typically found elsewhere. The first is the sheer number of available data sources and the inherent heterogeneity of their contents. Some of these sources contain data from a single lab or project, whereas others are the definitive repositories for very specific types of information (e.g., for a specific genetic mutation). Not only do these sources complicate the concept identification issue previously mentioned (because they use highly specialized data semantics), but they make it infeasible to incorporate all of them into a consistent repository. Second, the data formats and data access methods change regularly. These changes are an attempt to keep up with the scientific evolution occurring in the community at large. However, a change in a data source representation can have dramatic impact on systems that integrate that source, causing the integration to fail on the new format. Third, the data and related analysis are becoming increasingly complex. As the nature of genomics and proteomics research evolves from a predominantly wet-lab activity into knowledge-based analysis, the scientists' need to access the wide variety of available information increases dramatically. To address this need, information needs to be brought together from various heterogeneous data sources and presented to researchers in ways that allow them to answer their questions.

Biological Data Management and Knowledge Discovery

The field of bioinformatics plays an increasing role in the study of fundamental biological problems owing to the exponential explosion of sequence and structural information with time (Ohno-Machado et al., 2002). There are two major challenging areas in bioinformatics: (1) data management and (2) knowledge discovery.

After the completion of the Human Genome Project (HGP) (Collins et al., 2003), a new, post genomic era, is beginning to analyze and interpret the huge amount of genomic information. The Human Genome Project would have not been completed in advance without collaborative efforts carried out at research centers over the Internet. After completion of the HGP, genomic professionals face different problems related to topics such as discovering gene interactions, metabolic pathways, and protein structures that will need intensive computations and new informatics approaches. The greatest challenge facing the Genome to Life Program (Frazier et al., 2003a; Frazier et al., 2003b), and indeed all of biology, will be the capture, management, and analysis of the torrent of new data and information flooding over us in the next few decades. Many different types of data must be integrated into databases and metadata structures that will range well into petabyte scale—presenting huge analysis, data mining, and visualization challenges.

According to a survey, there were at least 335 data sources in 2002 (Baxevanis, 2002), the number climbed to 858 recently in 2006 (Galperin, 2006). The most popular resources including those concerned with protein sequences (SWISS-PROT, an annotated protein sequence database, and PIR—the protein Information Resource) and protein structure (PDB). The increasing volume and diversity of digital information related to bioinformatics has led to a growing problem that computational data management systems do not have, namely finding which information sources out of many candidate choices is more relevant and most accessible to answer a given user query (Liu et al., 2003). Moreover, there is rich domain information on how results for queries should be obtained and strong user preference for sources (for instance, one biologist may prefer SWISS-PROT to PDB for protein information due to its affiliation). The completeness (but not correctness) of results is negotiable in favor performance and timeliness.

A challenge to data management involves managing and integrating the existing biological databases. However, in some situations, a single database cannot provide answers to the complex problems of biologists. Integrating or assembling information from several databases to solve problems and discovering new knowledge are other major challenges in bioinformatics (Kuonen, 2003, Ng & Wong, 2004, Wong, 2000, Wong, 2002). The transformation of voluminous biological data into useful information and valuable knowledge is the challenge of knowledge discovery. Identification and interpretation of interesting patterns hidden in trillions of genetic and other biological data is a critical goal of bioinformatics. This goal covers identification of useful gene and protein structures from biological sequences, derivation of diagnostic knowledge from experimental data, and extraction of scientific information from the literature (Han & Kamber, 2001; Jagoto, 2000; Narayanan et al., 2002; Ng & Wong, 2004).

The existing research in bioinformatics is related to knowledge discovery, sequence analysis, and structure analysis. Sequence analysis is the discovery of functional and structural similarities and differences between multiple biological sequences. This can be done by comparing the new (unknown) sequence with well-studied and annotated (known) sequences. Scientists have found that two similar sequences possess the same functional role, regulatory or biochemical pathway, and protein structure. If two similar sequences are from different organisms, they are said to be homologous sequences. Finding homologous sequences is important in predicting the nature of a protein. Structure analysis is the study of proteins and their interactions. proteins are complex biological molecules composed of a chain of units, called amino acids, in a specific order. They are large molecules required for structure, function, and regulation of body's cells, tissues, and organs. Each protein has unique functions. The structures of proteins are hierarchical and consist of primary, secondary, and tertiary structures. In other words, at molecular level, proteins can be viewed as 3D structures. The understanding of protein structures and their functions leads to new approaches for diagnosis and treatment of diseases, and the discovery of new drugs. Current research on protein structural analysis involves comparison and prediction of protein structures. Due to the complexity and gigantic volume of biological data, the traditional computer science techniques and algorithms fail to solve the complex biological problems and discover new knowledge.

Need for Common Languages

Public databases distribute their contents as flat files, in some cases including indices for rapid data retrieval. In principle, all flat file formats are based on the organizational hierarchy of database, entry, and record. Entries are the fundamental entities of molecular databases, but in contrast to the situation in the living cell that they purport to describe, database entries store objects in the form of atomic, isolated, nonhierarchical structures. Different databases may describe different aspects of the same biological unit, for example the nucleic acid and amino acid sequences of a gene, and the relationship between them must be established by links that are not intrinsically part of the data archives themselves.

The development of individual databases has generated a large variety of formats in their implementations. There is consensus that a common language, or at least that mutual intelligibility, would be a good thing, but this goal has proved difficult to achieve. Attempts to unify data formats have included application of Backus–Naur based syntax (George et al., 1987), the development of an object-oriented database definition language (George et al., 1993) and the use of Abstract Syntax Notation 1 (ASN.1; Ohkawa et al., 1995; Ostell, 1990). None of these approaches has achieved the hoped-for degree of acceptance. Underlying the questions of mechanisms of intercommunication between databases of different structure and format is the need for common semantic standards and controlled vocabulary in annotations (see, for example, Pongor, 1988; Rawlings, 1988). This problem is especially acute in comparative genomics. From the technological point of view, intergenome comparisons are interdatabase comparisons, which means the databases to be compared have to speak the same language: keywords, information fields, weight factors, object catalogues, and so forth.

Perhaps the technical problems of standardization discussed in the preceding paragraphs could be addressed more easily in the context of a more general logical structure. As noted by Hafner & Fridman (1996), general biological data resources are databases rather than knowledge bases: they describe miscellaneous objects according to the database schema, but no representation of general concepts and their relationships is given. Schulze-Kremer (1998) addressed this problem by developing ontologies for knowledge sharing in molecular biology. He proposed to create a repository of terms and concepts relevant to molecular biology, hierarchically organized by means of 'is a subset of ' and 'is member of' operators.

PROTEIN ONTOLOGY FRAMEWORK

In this section we discuss conceptual framework of PO that has (1) a hierarchical classification of concepts represented as classes, from general to specific; (2) a list of attributes related to each concept, for each class; (3) a set of relations between classes to link concepts in ontology in more complicated ways then implied by the hierarchy, to promote reuse of concepts in the ontology; and (4) a set of algebraic operators for querying protein ontology instances.

Basically, ontology is the logical theory constituted by vocabulary and logical language. In domain of interest it formalizes signs describing things in the world, allowing a mapping from signs to things as exact as possible. A knowledge base may be defined on top of ontology describing particular circumstances. In context of this chapter, and biomedical domain in general, Figure 1 depicts the overall layered approach for generic protein ontology structure.

Three layers are distinguished here:

- Firstly, real-world data and information sources are considered—various proprietary biomedical data sources and scientific texts and literature.
- Secondly, data elements and models (both inherent data descriptors due to patterns

Figure 1. General protein ontology structure

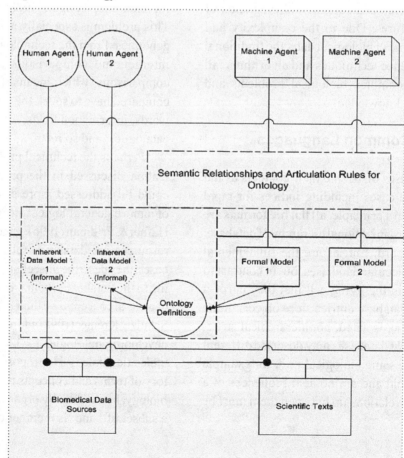

in data, and formal data models defined by scientists for specialized applications) describing syntactic structure of the protein ontology is exchanged.

- Thirdly, both human and machine agents that access and analyze the ontology are considered. Human agent interprets and analyzes ontology directly using their expertise. For machine agents to interpret and analyze ontology at same level as human agents the expertise is represented using semantic relationships and articulation rules in ontology framework.

Protein Ontology Hierarchy

Traditional approaches to integrate protein data generally involved keyword searches, which immediately excludes unannotated or poorly annotated data. It also excludes proteins annotated with synonyms unknown to the user. Of the protein data that is retrieved in this manner, some biological resources do not record information about the data source, so there is no evidence of the annotation. An alternative protein annotation approach is to rely on sequence identity, or structural similarity, or functional identification. The success of this method is dependent on the family the protein belongs to. Some proteins have high degree of sequence identity, or structural similarity, or similarity in functions that are unique to members of that family alone. Consequently, this approach can not be generalized to integrate the protein data. Clearly, these traditional approaches have limitations in capturing and integrating data for protein annotation. For these reasons, we have adopted an alternative method that does not rely on keywords or similarity metrics, but instead uses ontology. Protein ontology framework distinguishes three interlinked parts:

- Syntax deals with protein ontology concept definitions and relationships between concepts.

- Semantics analyzes the relationship between concepts and the real-world protein data they annotate. For this purpose semantic relationships not provided by representation language of protein ontology (OWL) are defined.
- Pragmatics goes beyond syntax and semantics and researches how ontology definitions are helpful in improving performance of formal and informal data models. Thus, it analyzes relationships between data models and specific machine agents through articulation rules.

Generic and Derived Concepts of PO

Protein ontology (Sidhu et al., 2006a; Sidhu et al., 2006b; Sidhu et al., 2005; and Sidhu et al, 2004a) provides a common structured vocabulary for this structured and unstructured information and provides researchers a medium to share knowledge in proteomics domain. PO provides description for protein domains that can be used to describe proteins in any organism. Protein ontology describes: (1) protein sequence and structure information, (2) protein folding process, (3) cellular functions of proteins, (4) molecular bindings internal and external to proteins and (5) Constraints affecting the final protein conformation. PO removes the constraints of potential interpretations of terms in various data sources and provides a structured vocabulary that unifies and integrates all data and knowledge sources for proteomics domain. There are seven concepts of PO, called **Generic Concepts**, that are used to define complex concepts in other PO concepts: *{Residue, Chain, Atom, Family, AtomicBind, Bind, and SiteGroup}*. These generic concepts are reused in defining complex PO concepts. We now briefly describe these generic concepts.

Details and properties of residues in a protein sequence are defined by instances of the *residue concept*. Instances of chains of residues are defined in the *chain concept*. All the three dimensional structure data of protein atoms is represented as instances of the *atom concept*. Defining chain, residue and atom as individual concepts has the benefit that any special properties or changes affecting a particular chain, residue and atom can be easily added. The *protein family concept* represents protein super family and family details of proteins. Data about binding atoms in chemical bonds like hydrogen bond, residue links, and salt bridges is entered into ontology as an instance of the *AtomicBind concept*. Similarly the data about binding residues in chemical bonds like disulphide bonds and CIS peptides is entered into ontology as an instance of the *bind concept*. All data related to site groups of the active binding sites of proteins is defined as instances of the *SiteGroup concept*. In PO the notions classification, reasoning, and con-

sistency are applied by defining new concepts from defined generic concepts. The concepts derived from generic concepts are placed precisely into class hierarchy of protein ontology to completely represent information defining a protein complex. The structure of PO provides the concepts necessary to describe individual proteins, but does not contain individual protein instances. Files using Web ontology language (OWL) format based on PO acts as instance store for the PO. The complete class hierarchy of PO is shown in Figure 2. More details about PO are available at the Web site: http://www.proteinontology.info/.

Our common conceptual model for the internal representation of PO is based on the work done by Gyssens et al. (1990). In its core, we represent protein ontology as a graph. Formally, an ontology

Figure 2. Class hierarchy of protein ontology

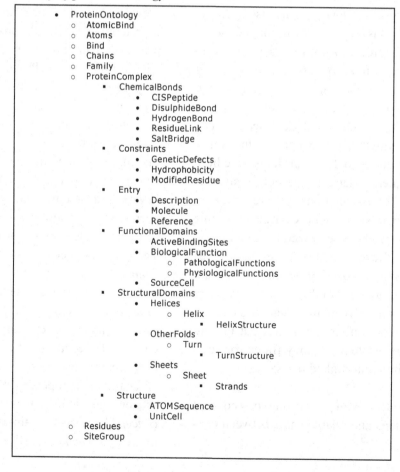

$O = (G, R)$ is represented as a directed labeled graph G and a set of rules R. The graph $G = (N, E)$ comprises a finite set of nodes N and a finite set of edges E. The label of a node is given by a non-null string. In the context of protein ontology, the label is often represents a concept defined in protein ontology. The label of an edge is the name of a semantic relationship among the concepts in protein ontology and can be null if the relationship is not known. The set of logical rules R, associated with protein ontology, are rules expressed in a logic-based language used to derive data from existing protein data sources.

INTEROPERABILTY OF BIOLOGICAL DATA

Biological data must be described in context rather than isolation (Karp, 1996). Hence, many databases provide multiple links to other resources, but efficient use of these links requires intelligent retrieval systems. Attempts have been made to create interdatabase links automatically, restricted to a few selected data resources, and with limited accuracy (Achard & Dessen, 1998). The user needs to be able to extract responses to a probe query from all possible sources, through a transparent and easy-to-use interface. The need for interoperability gave rise to the idea of an autonomous database federation (Robbins, 1994) through partial sharing of underlying database schema permitting cross-database queries, using, for example, SQL-based commercial database implementations. For example, attempts have been made to create a unified federated resource for microbiological information (Wertheim, 1995) suitable for intelligent interrogation. The prototype of such system is represented by the Ribosome Database Project (Maidak et al., 1996). An alternative approach is the concept of a warehouse, or a centralized data resource that manages a variety of data collections translated into a common format (Ritter, 1994).

Linking the community of databases through common semantics is impossible because of their extreme heterogeneity.

The recently emerged 'middleware' approach affords a chance to uncouple data access from data management and to allow for remote retrieval beyond the simple scripts fetching data from external databases. The most prominent industrial standard for a client-server based middleware is CORBA (common object request broker architecture; Ben-Natan, 1995) as defined by the Object Management Group (OMG). CORBA is a distributed object architecture that allows objects to communicate across networks through defined interfaces using the syntax of the interface definition language (IDL). The object management architecture of CORBA specifies an application-level communication infrastructure. Several CORBA-based applications have already appeared. Achard and Barillot (1997) suggest a set of interface definitions for molecular biology to access a simple, but realistic, data bank of sequence tag sites. The European Commission supports a project to provide CORBA access to a set of public databases (EMBL, SWISS-PROT, PIR, TRANSFAC, and several others). Stein et al. (1998) described an alternative approach to database interconnection. Their software system, Jade, establishes connection between the database servers and the application programs, and organizes data exchange through standardized relational tables and parameters. Information retrieved on the data server side is transformed into these tables with the help of a specialized application called Jade adapter. Jade currently supports the AceDB, although incorporation of other database systems is anticipated.

We need to resolve the heterogeneity among biological data sources and especially among protein data sources in this post genomic era to enable meaningful data exchange or interoperation among them. The two major sources of heterogeneity among the sources are as follows: first, different sources use different conceptual models and modeling languages to represent their data and metadata. Second, sources using the same conceptual model differ in their semantics. We use common PO format, which we have described in (Sidhu et al., 2006a) to resolve heterogeneity in protein data sources to some extent. The proposed system first converts data extracted from the external protein data sources to common PO format and then resolves the semantic heterogeneity among the protein data sources that we seek to articulate. Melnik (2000) has shown how to convert information sources and different classes of conceptual models into those using one common format. Information sources were, are, and will be modeled using different conceptual models. We do not foresee the creation of a de facto standard conceptual model that will be used by all protein data sources. On the other hand, we need use a common PO format for our internal representation of protein data. PO uses all relevant protein data sources to build the common format for presentation. The sources include new proteome information resources like PDB (Bernstein et al., 1977, Weissig & Bourne, 2002, Wesbrook et al., 2002), SCOP (Murzin et al., 1995), and RESID (Garavelli, 2003) as well as classical sources of information where information is maintained in a knowledge base of scientific text files like OMIM (McKusick, 1998) and from various published scientific literature in various journals.

Semantic Relationships in PO

Semantics in protein data is normally not interpreted by annotating systems, since they are not aware of the specific structural, chemical and cellular interactions of protein complexes. protein Ontology Framework provides specific set of rules to cover these application specific semantics. The rules use only the relationships whose semantics are predefined to establish correspondence among terms in PO. The set of relationships with predefined semantics is: {SubClassOf, PartOf,

AttributeOf, InstanceOf, and ValueOf}. The PO conceptual modeling encourages the use of strictly typed relations with precisely defined semantics. Some of these relationships (like SubClassOf, InstanceOf) are somewhat similar to those in RDF Schema but the set of relationships that have defined semantics in our conceptual PO model is small so as to maintain simplicity of the system. The following is a description of the set of predefined semantic relationships in our common PO conceptual model.

- **SubClassOf:** The relationship is used to indicate that one concept is a subclass of another concept, for instance: SourceCell SubClassOfFunctionalDomains. That is any instance of SouceCell class is also instance of FunctionalDomains class. All attributes of FunctionalDomains class (_FuncDomain_ Family, _FuncDomain_SuperFamily) are also the attributes of SourceCell class. The relationship SubClassOf is transitive.
- **AttrributeOf:** This relationship indicates that a concept is an attribute of another concept, for instance: _FuncDomain_Family AttributeOf Family. This relationship also referred as PropertyOf, has same semantics as in object-relational databases.
- **PartOf:** This relationship indicates that a concept is a part of another concept, for instance: Chain PartOf ATOMSequence indicates that chain describing various residue sequences in a protein is a part of definition of ATOMSequence for that protein.
- **InstanceOf:** This relationship indicates that an object is an instance of the class, for instance: ATOMSequenceInstance_10 InstanceOf ATOMSequence indicates that ATOMSequenceInstance_10 is an instance of class ATOMSequence.
- **ValueOf:** This relationship is used to indicate the value of an attribute of an object, for instance: "Homo Sapiens" ValueOf Organ-

ismScientific. The second concept, in turn has an edge, OrganismScientific AttributeOf Molecule, from the object it describes.

Sequences in PO

By itself semantic relationships described previously, does not impose order among the children of the node. In applications using protein sequences, the ability of expressing the order is paramount. Generally protein sequences are a collection of chains of sequence of residues, and that is the format protein sequences have been represented unit now using various data representations and data mining techniques for bioinformatics. When we are defining sequences for semantic heterogeneity of protein data sources using PO we are not only considering traditional representation of protein sequences but also link protein sequences to protein structure, by linking chains of residue sequences to atoms defining three-dimensional structure. In this section we will describe how we used a special semantic relationship like **sequence(s)** in protein ontology to describe complex concepts defining structure, structural folds and domains and chemical bonds describing protein complexes. PO defines these complex concepts as sequences of simpler generic concepts defined in PO. These simple concepts are sequences of object and data type properties defining them. The following sections provide a description of the set of sequences defined in PO conceptual framework.

Sequences defining PO structure concepts: Define a complex concept of ATOMSequence describing three dimensional structure of protein complex as a combination of simple concepts of Chains, Residues, and Atoms as: *ATOMSequence Sequence (Chains Sequence (Residues Sequence (Atoms)))*. Simple concepts defining ATOMSequence are defined as: *Chains Sequence (ChainID, ChainName, ChainProperty); Residues Sequence (ResidueID, ResidueName,*

ResidueProperty); and Atoms Sequence (AtomID, Atom, ATOMResSeqNum, X, Y, Z, Occupancy, TempratureFactor, Element).

Sequences defining PO structural domain concepts: Define three complex concepts that describe the structural folds and domains of helices, sheets and turns in a protein complex. Helices of a protein complex are defined using relationship of sequence as: *Helices Sequence (Helix Sequence (HelixStrucure))*. The concepts of helix and HelixStructure are defined as: *Helix Sequence (HelixID, HelixNumber, HelixClass, HelixLength); and HelixStructure Sequence (HelixChain, IntialResidue, IntialReqSeqNum, EndResidue, EndReqSeqNum)*. HelixChain, IntialResidue, and EndResidue are object properties of concepts chains, and residues that are already defined. Complex concepts of sheets and turns in a protein complex are defined as: *Sheets Sequence (Sheet Sequence (Strands))*; and *Turns Sequence (Turn Sequence (TurnStructure))*.

Sequences defining PO chemical bond concepts: Define complex concepts of DisulphideBond, CISPeptide, HydrogenBond, ResidueLink, and SaltBridge describing chemical bonds in a protein complex. Chemical bonds that have binding residue use the generic concept of bind while defining chemical bonds using sequence relationship, for instance: *DisulphideBond Sequence (Bind1, Bind2)*. Bind1 and Bind2 concepts are defined as: *Bind1 Sequence (BindChain1, BindResidue1, BindResSeqNum1) and Bind2 Sequence (BindChain2, BindResidue2, and BindResSeqNum2)*. Similarly the chemical bonds that have binding atoms use the generic concept of AtomicBind, for instance: *HydrogenBond Sequence (AtomicBindChain1, AtomicBindResidue1, AtomicBindResSeqNum1, AtomicBindAtom1, AtomicBindChain2, AtomicBindResidue2, AtomicBin-dResSeqNum2, and AtomicBindAtom2)*. BindChain, AtomicBindChain, BindResidue, AtomicBindResidue, and AtomicBindAtom are object properties of concepts chains, residues, and atoms that are already defined.

Logic Rules in PO

The key to scalability of PO conceptual model is the systematic and effective composition of data and information. In this section, we present PO ontology algebra that allows composition of multiple levels of information stored in the ontology for information retrieval. By retaining a log of composition process, we can also, with minimal adaptations, replay the composition whenever any of the underlying data sources that PO integrates change. The algebra has one unary operator: *Select*, and three binary operations: *Intersection*, *Union* and *Difference*.

Select Operator

The Select operator allows us to highlight and select portions of the PO that are relevant to query at hand. Given the PO structure and a concept to be selected, the select operator selects the sub tree rooted at that concept. Given the PO structure and a set of concepts, the select operator selects only those edges in the PO that connect nodes in a given set. Select operator is defined as:

$$OS = \sigma \; (NS, ES, RS) \; where$$
$$NS = Nodes \; (condition = true) \; and$$
$$ES = Edges \; (\forall \; N \in NS)$$

Intersection Operation

Intersection is the most important and interesting binary operation. Let $O1 = (N1, E1, R1)$, and $O2 = (N2, E2, R2)$ be the two parts of PO whose composition will provide answer to the query submitted by the user. Here N is the set of nodes or concepts of PO, E is the set of edges or the PO hierarchy, and R is set of semantic relationships.

The intersection of two parts of PO with respect to semantic relationships defined for PO (SR in Section 3.4) is: $OI \; (1, 2) = O1 \cap_{SR} O2 = (NI, EI, RI)$, where:

$NI = Nodes \; (SR \; (O1, O2))$,
$EI = Edges \; (E1, NI \cap N1) + Edges \; (E2, NI \cap N2) + Edges \; (SR \; (O1, O2))$, and
$RI = Relationships \; (O1, NI \cap N1) + Relationships \; (O2, NI \cap N2) + SR \; (O1, O2) - Edges \; (SR \; (O1, O2))$.

Note that SR is different from R as it does not include sequences. The nodes in the intersection ontology are those nodes that appear in the semantic relationships, SR. The edges in the intersection ontology are the edges among nodes that are either present in the source parts of the ontology or have been established as a semantic relationship, SR. Relationships in the intersection ontology are the relationships that have not been already been modeled as edges and those relationships present in source parts of the ontology that use only concepts that occur in intersection ontology.

Union Operation

The union of two parts of PO, $O1 = (N1, E1, R1)$, and $O2 = (N2, E2, R2)$ with respect to semantic relationships (SR) of PO (SR in Section 4.2) is expressed as:

$OI \; (1, 2) = O1 \cup_{SR} O2 = (NU, EU, RU)$, where,
$NU = N1 \cup N2 \cup NI \; (1, 2)$,
$EU = E1 \cup E2 \cup EI \; (1, 2)$, and
$RU = R1 \cup R2 \cup RI \; (1, 2)$, where,
$OI \; (1, 2) = O1 \cap_{SR} O2 = (NI \; (1, 2), EI \; (1, 2), RI \; (1, 2))$ is the intersection of two ontologies.

The union operation combines two parts of the ontology retaining only one copy of the concepts in the intersection.

Difference Operation

The difference of two parts of PO, O1 and O2, written as O1 – O2, includes portions of the first part that are not common to the second part. The difference can be rewritten as *O1 – (O1 $\cap_{SR}$ O2)*. The nodes, edges, and relationships that are not in intersection but are present in the first part comprise the difference. One of the objectives of computing the difference is to optimize the maintenance of PO. As the PO database is huge and so many people data to it, difference will suggest that data is not entered properly or there is change in underlying data sources that PO integrates. Change suggested by difference is forwarded to the administrator. If the change happens to be in difference between structures of parts considered, then it does not occur in intersection and is not related to any semantic relationships that establish bridged between the parts of the ontology. Therefore semantic relationships do not need to be changed. If the changes is because of changes happening to underlying data sources that PO integrates, then set of concepts and semantic relationships need to be checked for any changes required to remove the difference.

CONCLUSION

In this chapter we presented an overview of common conceptual representation of PO that is needed to resolve the heterogeneity among protein data sources to enable meaningful data exchange or interoperation among them. Next we discussed semantic relationships in protein data that interprets semantics that is normally not interpreted by annotating systems, since they are not aware of the specific structural, chemical, and cellular interactions of protein complexes. We also discussed sequence relationships that impose order among the children of the nodes. We also covered PO ontology algebra that allows composition of multiple levels of information stored in the ontol-ogy for information retrieval. The PO approach supports precise composition of information from multiple diverse sources providing semantic relationships between among such sources. This approach allows reliable exploitation of protein information sources without any imposition on sources themselves. PO algebra based on semantic relationships allows systematic composition, which unlike integration is more scalable.

REFERENCES

Achard, F., & Barillot, E. (1997). *Ubiquitous distributed objects with CORBA*. Pacific Symposium Biocomputing. London, World Scientific.

Achard, F., & Dessen, P. (1998). GenXref VI: Automatic generation of links between two heterogeneous databases. *Bioinformatics, 14*, 20-24.

Baxevanis, A. (2002). The molecular biology data collection: 2002 update. *Nucleic Acids Research, 30*, 1-12.

Ben-natan, R. (1995). *CORBA*. New York: McGraw Hill.

Benson, D., Karsch-mizrachi, I., Lipman, D., Ostell, J., Rapp, B., & Wheeler, D. (2000). GenBank. *Nucleic Acids Research, 28*, 8-15.

Bernstein, F.C., Koetzle, T.F., Williams, G.J., Meyer, E.F., Brice, M.D., Rodgers, J.R., et al. (1977). The protein data bank: A computer-based archival file for macromolecular structures. *Journal of Molecular Biology, 112*, 535-542.

Collins, F.S., Morgan, M., & Patrinos, A. (2003). The human genome project: Lessons from large-scale biology. *Science, 300*, 286-290.

Frazier, M.E., Johnson, G.M., Thomassen, D.G., Oliver, C.E., & Patrinos, A. (2003a). Realizing the potential of genome revolution: The genomes to life program. *Science, 300*, 290-293.

Frazier, M.E., Thomassen, D.G., Patrinos, A., Johnson, G.M., Oliver, C. E., & Uberbacher, E. (2003b). Setting up the pace of discovery: The genomes to life program. In *Proceedings of the 2ⁿᵈ IEEE Computer Society Bioinformatics Conference (CSB 2003)*. Stanford, CA: IEEE CS Press.

Galperin, M.Y. (2006). The molecular biology database collection: 2006 update. *Nucleic Acids Research, 34*, D3-D5.

Garavelli, J.S. (2003). The RESID database of protein modifications: 2003 developments. *Nucleic Acids Research, 31*, 499-501.

George, D.G., Mewes, H-W., & Kihara, H. (1987). A standardized format for sequence data exchange. *protein Seq. Data Anal., 1*, 27-29.

George, D. G., Orcutt, B.C., Mewes, H.-W., & Tsugita, A. (1993). An object-oriented sequence database definition language (sddl). *protein Seq. Data Anal., 5*, 357-399.

Gouy, M., Gautier, C., Attimonelli, M., Lanave, C., & Di Paola, G. (1985). ACNUC: A portable retrieval system for nucleic acid sequence databases: Logical and physical designs and usage. *Computer Applications in the Biosciences, 1*, 167-172.

Gyssens, M., Paredaens, P. & Gucht, D. (1990). A graph-oriented object database model. In *Proceedings of the 9ᵗʰ ACM SIGACT-SIGMOD-SIGART symposium on Principles of database systems*. Nashville, TN: ACM Press.

Hadzic, F., Dillon, T.S., Sidhu, A.S., Chang, E., & Tan, H. (2006). Mining substructures in protein data. *2006 IEEE Workshop on Data Mining in Bioinformatics (DMB 2006) in conjunction with 6ᵗʰ IEEE ICDM 2006*. Hong Kong:IEEE CS Press.

Hafner, C.D. & Fridman, N. (1996). Ontological foundations for biology knowledge models. In *Proceedings of the 4ᵗʰ International Conference on Intelligent Systems for Molecular Biology*. St. Louis: AAAI.

Han, J., & Kamber, M. (2001). *Data mining: Concepts and techniques*. San Francisco: Morgan Kaufmann.

Jagoto, A. (2000). *Data analysis and classification for bioinformatics*. CA: Bay Press.

Karp, P.D. (1996). A strategy for database interoperation. *Journal of Computational Biology, 2*, 573-583.

Koonin, E.V., & Galperin, M.Y. (1997). Prokaryotic genomes: the emerging paradigm of genome-based microbiology. *Current Opinions in Genetic Development, 7*, 757-763.

Kuonen, D. (2003). Challenges in bioinformatics for statistical data miners. *Bulletin of Swiss Statistical Society, 46*, 10-17.

Liu, L., Buttler, D.T.C., Han, W., Paques, H., Pu, C., & Rocco, D. (2003). BioSeek: Exploiting source-capability information for integrated access to multiple bioinformatics data sources. In *Proceedings of the 3ʳᵈ IEEE Symposium on Bioinformatics and Bioengineering (BIBE 2003)*. Bethesda, MD: IEEE CS Press.

Maidak, B.L., Olsen, G.J., Larsen, N., Overbeek, R., Mccaughey, M.J., & Woese, C.R. (1996). The ribosomal database project (RDP). *Nucleic Acids Research, 24*, 82-85.

Maxam, A.M., & Gilbert, W. (1977). A new method for sequencing DNA. In *Proceedings of National Academic of Science, 74* (pp. 560-564).

Mckusick, V.A. (1998). *Mendelian inheritance in man: A catalog of human genes and genetic disorders*. Baltimore: Johns Hopkins University Press.

Miyazaki, S., Sugawara, H., Gojobori, T., & Tateno, Y. (2003). DNA Databank of Japan (DDBJ). *Nucleic Acids Research, 31*, 13-16.

Murzin, A.G., Brenner, S.E., Hubbard, T., & Chothia, C. (1995). SCOP: A structural classification of proteins database for the investigation of sequences and structures. *Journal of Molecular Biology, 247*, 536-540.

Narayanan, A., Keedwell, E.C., & Olsson, B. (2002). Artificial intelligence techniques for bioinformatics. *Applied Bioinformatics, 1*, 191-222.

Ng, S.K., & Wong, L. (2004). Accomplishments and challenges in bioinformatics. *IT Professional, 6*, 44-50.

Ohkawa, H., Ostell, J., & Bryant, S. (1995). MMDB: An ASN.1 specification for macromolecular structure. In *Proceedings of the 3rd International Conference on Intelligent Systems for Molecular Biology.* Cambridge, UK: AAAI.

Ohno-machado, L., Vinterbo, S., & Weber, G. (2002). Classification of gene expression data using fuzzy logic. *Journal of Intelligent and Fuzzy Systems, 12*, 19-24.

Ostell, J. (1990). *GenInfo ASN.1 Syntax: Sequences.* NCBI Technical Report Series. National Library of Medicine, NIH.

Pongor, S. (1998) Novel databases for molecular biology. *Nature, 332*, 24-24.

Rawlings, C.J. (1998). Designing databases for molecular biology. *Nature, 334*, 447-447.

Ritter, O. (1994). The integrated genomic database. In S. Suhai (Ed.), *Computational methods in genome research.* New York: Plenum.

Robbins, R.J. (1994). Genome informatics I: community databases. *Journal of Computational Biology, 1*, 173-190.

Sanger, F., Nicklen, S., & Coulson, A.R. (1977). DNA sequencing with chain-terminating inhibitors. In *Proceedings of National Academic of Science, 74* (pp. 5463-5467).

Schulze-Kremer, S. (1998). Ontologies for molecular biology. Pacific Symposium of Biocomputing. In *Proceedings of the PSB 1998 Electronic,* Hawaii.

Sidhu, A.S., Dillon, T.S., & Chang, E. (2005). Ontological foundation for protein data models. In *Proceedings of the 1st IFIP WG 2.12 & WG 12.4 International Workshop on Web Semantics (SWWS 2005). In conjunction with On The Move Federated Conferences (OTM 2005).* Agia Napa, Cyprus: Springer

Sidhu, A.S., Dillon, T.S., & Chang, E. (2006a). protein ontology. In Z. Ma & J.Y. Chen (Eds.), *Database modeling in biology: Practices and challenges.* New York: Springer.

Sidhu, A.S., Dillon, T.S., & Chang, E. (2006b). Advances in protein ontology project. In *Proceedings of the 19th IEEE International Symposium on Computer-Based Medical Systems (CBMS 2006).* Salt Lake City, UT: IEEE CS Press.

Sidhu, A.S., Dillon, T.S., Sidhu, B.S., & Setiawan, H. (2004a). A unified representation of protein structure databases. In M.S. Reddy & S. Khanna (Eds.), *Biotechnological approaches for sustainable development.* India: Allied Publishers.

Sidhu, A.S., Dillon, T.S., Sidhu, B.S., & Setiawan, H. (2004b). An XML based Semantic protein map. In A., Zanasi, N.F.F. Ebecken, & C.A. Brebbia (Eds.), *5th International Conference on Data Mining, Text Mining and their Business Applications (Data Mining 2004).* Malaga, Spain: WIT Press.

Sidhu, A.S., Dillon, T.S., Setiawan, H., & Sidhu, B.S. (2004c). Comprehensive protein database representation. In A. Gramada & P.E. Bourne (Eds.), *8th International Conference on Research in Computational Molecular Biology 2004 (RECOMB 2004).* San Diego, CA: ACM Press.

Stein, L.D., Cartinhour, S., Thierry-mieg, D., & Thierry-Mieg, J. (1998). JADE: An approach for interconnecting bioinformatics databases. *Gene, 209,* 39-43.

Stoesser, G., Baker, W., Van Den Broek, A., Garcia-Pastor, M., Kanz, C., & Kulikova, T. (2003). The EMBL nucleotide sequence database: Major new developments. *Nucleic Acids Research, 31,* 17-22.

Weissig, H., & Bourne, P.E. (2002). Protein structure resources. *Biological Crystallography, D58,* 908-915.

Wertheim, M. (1995). Call to desegregate microbial databases. *Science, 269,* 1516.

Wesbrook, J., Feng, Z., Jain, S., Bhat, T.N., Thanki, N., Ravichandran, V., et al. (2002). The protein data bank: Unifying the archive. *Nucleic Acids Research, 30,* 245-248.

Wong, L. (2002). Technologies for integrating biological data. *Briefings in Bioinformatics, 3,* 389-404.

Wong, L. (2000). Kleisli, a functional query system. *Journal of Functional Programming, 10,* 19-56.

Zaki, M.J. (2005). Efficiently mining frequent trees in a forest: Algorithms and applications. *IEEE Transaction on Knowledge and Data Engineering, 17,* 1021-1035.

Chapter VII
TtoO:
Mining a Thesaurus and Texts to Build and Update a Domain Ontology

Josiane Mothe
Institut de Recherche en Informatique de Toulouse Université de Toulouse, France

Nathalie Hernandez
Institut de Recherche en Informatique de Toulouse Université de Toulouse, France

ABSTRACT

This chapter introduces a method re-using a thesaurus built for a given domain, in order to create new resources of a higher semantic level in the form of an ontology. Considering ontologies for data-mining tasks relies on the intuition that the meaning of textual information depends on the conceptual relations between the objects to which they refer rather than on the linguistic and statistical relations of their content. To put forward such advanced mechanisms, the first step is to build the ontologies. The originality of the method is that it is based both on the knowledge extracted from a thesaurus and on the knowledge semiautomatically extracted from a textual corpus. The whole process is semiautomated and experts' tasks are limited to validating certain steps. In parallel, we have developed mechanisms based on the obtained ontology to accomplish a science monitoring task. An example will be given.

INTRODUCTION

Scientific and technical data, whatever their types (textual, factual, formal, or nonformal), constitute strategic mines of information for decision makers in economic intelligence and science monitoring activities, and for researchers and engineers (e.g., for scientific and technological watch). However, in front of the growing mass of information, these activities require increasingly powerful systems offering greater possibilities for exploring and representing the collected information or extracted knowledge. Upstream, they must ensure search, selection and filtering of the electronic information available. Downstream, when communicating and restituting results, they must privilege ergonomics in presentation, exploration, navigation, and synthesis.

To be manipulated by advanced processes, textual document content has first to be represented synthetically. This process is known as indexing and consists in defining a set of terms or descriptors that best correspond to the text content. Descriptors can either be extracted from the document themselves or by considering external resources such as thesauri. In the first approach, which can be fully automatic and thus more appropriate for large volumes of electronic documents, the texts are analyzed and the most representative terms are extracted (Salton, 1971). These are the terms which constitute the indexing language. The automatic weighting of index terms (Robertson & Sparck-Jones, 1976), their stemming (Porter, 1981), the automatic query reformulation by relevance feedback (Harman, 1992) or per addition of co-occurring terms (Qiu & Frei, 1993) in information retrieval systems (IRS) are methods associated with automatic indexing and have been effective as attested by international evaluation campaigns, such as text retrieval conference (trec.nist.gov). One common point of all these approaches is that they make the assumption that the documents contain all the knowledge necessary for their indexing. On the other hand, thesauri are used to control the terminology representing the documents by translating the natural language of the documents into a stricter language (documentary language) (Chaumier, 1988). A thesaurus is based on a hierarchical structuring of one or more domains of knowledge in which terms of one or more natural languages are organized by relations between them, represented with conventional signs (AFNOR, 1987). With ISO 2788 and ANSI Z39, their contents can be standardized in terms of equivalence, hierarchical, and associative relations between lexemes. Indexing based

on a thesaurus is generally carried out manually by librarians who, starting from their expertise, choose the terms of the thesaurus constituting the index of each document read. In an IRS, the same thesaurus is then used to restrict the range of a query or, on the contrary, to extend it, according to the needs of the user and the contents of the collection. Other types of systems combine the use of a thesaurus with classification and navigation mechanisms. The Cat a Cone system (Hearst, 1997) or IRAIA system (Englmeier & Mothe, 2003) make use of the hierarchical structure of the thesaurus to allow the user to browse within this structure and thus to access the documents associated with the terms. Compared to automatic indexing, the thesaurus approach leads to more semantic indexing, as terms are considered within their context (meaning and related terms). However, using thesauri raises several problems: they are created manually and their construction requires considerable effort; their updating is necessary; their format is not standardized (ASCII files, HTML, data bases coexist); finally, thesauri have a weak degree of formalization since they are built to be used by domain experts and not by automatic processes. Various solutions to these issues have been proposed in the literature. Automatic thesauri construction can call upon techniques based on term correlation (Tudhope, 2001), document classification (Crouch & Yang, 1992), or natural language processing (Grefenstette, 1992). On the other hand, the standards under development within the framework of the W3C as SKOS Core (Miles et al., 2005) aim at making the thesaurus migrate towards resources that are more homogeneous and represented in a formal way by using OWL language (McGuiness & Harmelen, 2004) and making these resources available on the Semantic Web. However, thesauri represent a domain in terms of indexing categories and not in terms or meaning. They do not have a level of conceptual abstraction (Soergel et al., 2004), which plays a crucial role in man-machine communication. Ontologies make it possible to reconsider this problem since it is a "formal and explicit specification of a shared conceptualization" (Fensel, 1998). Automatic semantic indexing, starting from concepts rather than terms that are frequently ambiguous, then becomes possible (Aussenac & Mothe, 2004). However, the development of an ontology is costly as it requires many manual interventions. Indeed, ontology construction techniques in the literature generally do not base the development of ontologies on existing terminological representations of the field but on a reference corpus, which is analyzed (Aussenac et al., 2000).

In this chapter, we propose to present the method we have developed and implemented to re-use a thesaurus built for a given domain, in order to create new resources of a higher semantic level in the form of a domain ontology. The originality of the method is that it is based both on the knowledge extracted from a thesaurus and on the knowledge automatically extracted from a textual corpus. It thus takes advantage of the domain terms stated in the thesaurus. This method includes the incremental population and update of an ontology, by the mining of a new set of documents. The whole process is semiautomated and experts' tasks are limited to validating certain steps. In parallel, we have developed mechanisms based on the obtained ontology to accomplish a science monitoring task. We will give an example in order to illustrate the added value of using ontologies for data mining. This chapter is organized as follows: Section 2 presents the main differences between thesauri and ontologies. In Section 3, we review the literature related to ontology building and ontology integration for representing and accessing documents. Section 4 presents our method for building the ontology from the thesaurus. Section 5 explains how we propose to mine documents to update the ontology. Finally, in Section 6, we present our case study: building a lightweight ontology in astronomy by transforming the IAU thesaurus and developing a prototype enabling a science monitoring task on the domain.

THESAURI AND ONTOLOGIES

The main distinction between a thesaurus and an ontology is their degree of semantic engagement (Lassila & McGuiness, 2001). This degree corresponds to the level of formal specification restricting the interpretation of each concept, thus specifying their semantics.

Standardization of Thesauri Content

The ISO 2788 and ANSI Z39 (http://www.techstreet.com/cgi-bin/pdf/free/228866/z39-19a.pdf)

Figure 1. Relations between terms in a thesaurus

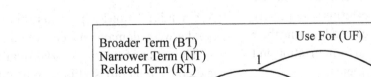
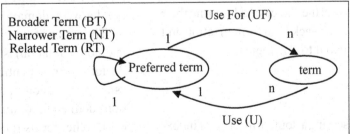

standards have proposed the guiding principles for building a thesaurus. It is a terminological resource in which terms are organized according to restricted relations (Foskett, 1980): equivalence (term$_i$ *"use for" referring* to term$_j$, *instead of* term$_j$ *"use"* term$_i$), hierarchical term1 (term$_k$ *"broader term" of* term$_l$, term$_l$ *"narrower term"* of term$_k$), and cross reference (term$_m$ *"related term" to* term$_n$). The relations present in a thesaurus meeting those standards are shown in Figure 1.

From the point of view of knowledge representation, thesauri have a low degree of formalization. The distinction between a unit of meaning (or concept) and its lexicon is not clearly established. Synonymy relations are defined between terms, but concepts are not identified. This can be explained by the initial use of thesauri, which was to express how a domain can be understood not in terms of meaning but in terms of terminology and categories to help the manual indexing of domain documents. Moreover, the semantics associated to a thesaurus are limited. Relations are vague and ambiguous. The semantic links between terms often reflect the planned use of the terms rather than their correct semantic relations. The relation *"broader term"* can, for example, include the relations « *is an instance of* », « *is a part of* » (Fischer, 1998). The associative relation «*related term*» is often difficult to exploit as it can connect terms suggesting different semantics (Tudhope et al., 2001). For example, in the BIT thesaurus (http://www.ilo.org/public/libdoc/ILO-Thesaurus/french/tr1740.htm) describing the world of work, the term « family » is related to the term « woman » and « leave of absence », the semantic relation between those pairs of terms is intuitively different. Because of the choices made during their elaboration, thesauri lack both formalization and coherence compared to ontologies.

Ontologies

Instead of representing a domain in terms of indexing categories, the aim of ontologies is to propose a sound base for communication between machines, but also between machines and humans. They consensually define the meaning of objects, firstly through symbols (words or phrases) that designate and characterize them, and secondly through a structured or formal representation of their role in the domain (Aussenac, 2004). Before presenting ontologies through their degree of formalization (lightweight and heavyweight ontologies), we define the three units of knowledge on which they rely: concept, relations, and axioms.

Concepts

A **concept** represents a material object, a notion, or an idea (Uschold & King, 1995). It is composed of three parts: one or several **terms**, a notion, and a set of objects. The notion corresponds to the concept's semantics and is defined through its relations to other concepts and its attributes. The set of objects corresponds to the objects defined by the concept and is called concept extension; objects are concept instances. The terms designate the concepts. They are also called concept **labels**. For example, the term « chair » references an artifact, piece of furniture on which one can sit and all objects having this definition. In order to identify a concept with no ambiguity, it is recommended to reference a concept with several terms that eliminate the problem of synonymy and to disambiguate the meanings of terms by comparing them to each other (Gomez-Perez et al., 1996).

Relations Between Concepts

A semantic relation R represents a kind of interaction between domain concepts c1, c2,... cn.

The notion of *subsumption* (also called *"is a"* or taxonomic relation) is a binary relation implying the following semantic engagement: a concept c1 *"subsumes"* a concept c2 if all the semantic relations defined for c1 are also semantic relations of c2, in other terms if concept c2 is more specific than concept c1.

« *Associative* » relations are interaction relations between two concepts that are not subsumption relations. This corresponds to the notion of role in description logics and makes it possible to characterize concepts. These relations are either relations between concepts or relations between a concept and a data type. The semantics associated to it are referenced by a label. Examples of associative relations are "*is a part of,*" "*is composed of,*" "*has a color*"... They can also be specified with logic properties associated to the relation such as transitivity.

Axioms

Axioms aim at representing in a logic language the description of concepts and their relations. They represent the intention of concepts and relations and the knowledge that does not have a terminological character. Their specification in an ontology can have different purposes: define the signature of a relation (domain and range of the relation), define restriction on values of a relation, define the logic property of a relation (transitivity, symmetry...). Through axioms both the consistency of the knowledge stated in the ontology is checked and new knowledge inferred.

Lightweight Ontologies vs. Heavyweight Ontologies

Lightweight ontologies are composed of two semiotic levels (Maedche & Staab, 2002). The lexical level (L) covers all the terms or labels defined to designate the concepts, enabling their detection within textual contents. The conceptual level defined in the structure (S) of the ontology represents the concepts and semantics defined from the conceptual relations that link them.

The structure of an ontology is a tuple $S := \{C, R, \leq_C, \sigma_R \}$ where:

- C, R are disjoint sets containing concepts and associative relations

- $\leq_C$: C x C is a partial order on C, it defines the hierarchy of concepts

  $\leq_C$ (c1, c2) meaning that c2 "is a" c1, it is called a taxonomic relation

- σ_R : R → C x C is the signature of an associative (or nontaxonomic) relation

  The lexicon of a lightweight ontology is a tuple L : $\{L^C, L^R, F, G\}$

- L^C, L^R are disjoint sets containing labels (or terms) referencing concepts and relations

- F, G are two relations called reference, they enable access to the concepts and relations designated by a term and vice versa.

- F →L^C for the concepts and G→L^R for the relations:

  ° For l∈ L^C, F(l)={c / c∈C}
  ° For c∈ C, F^{-1}(c)={l / l∈L^C}
  ° For l∈ L^R, G(l)={r/r∈R}
  ° For r∈ R, G-1(r)={l / l∈L^R}

Heavyweight ontologies are based on the same structure and lexicon as lightweight ontologies and also include a set of axioms. This kind of ontology considerably restricts the interpretation of concepts, thus limiting ambiguity. However, their construction is extremely time-consuming and thus they cover only precisely defined domains. For data representation and data mining, considering lightweight ontologies is the first step in integrating formal knowledge in systems. Lightweight ontologies can play the role formerly played by thesauri by defining an indexing language relying on a more formalized knowledge that can be exploited in the retrieval or mining process. Moreover, as described in the next section, lightweight ontologies are easier to construct.

RELATED WORK: ELABORATING ONTOLOGIES

Designing ontologies is a difficult task involving the development of elaborate processes that extract domain knowledge that can be manipulated by information systems and interpreted by humans. Two kinds of design exist: entirely manual design and design based on learning stages.

Several assumptions and methodologies have been defined to facilitate manual design. The assumptions rely on philosophical characteristics and follow collaborative modeling processes (Guarino et al., 1994). However, this approach is time consuming and causes maintenance and update problems (Ding, 2002). Over the last decade, ontology learning has emerged as a sub domain of knowledge engineering. Thanks to technological progress in the domain of information retrieval, automatic learning, and natural language processing, attempts are now being made to make the elaboration of ontologies semiautomatic. Ontology learning generally leads to the development of lightweight ontologies. In Maedche and Staab (2001), different types of approaches are distinguished in function of the resources used to support the elaboration: texts, dictionaries or thesauri, knowledge bases, semistructured schemas, and relational schemas. We have focused on approaches based on texts and thesauri as they offer, in our point of view, the possibility of taking advantage of existing resources and up-dating ontologies.

In order to transform a thesaurus into an ontology, existing approaches aim at capturing the informal semantics of the thesaurus manually (Wielinga et al., 2001), with syntactic patterns (Soergel et al., 2004), or with inferences (Hahn & Schulz, 2004). Considering the time it requires, an entire manual process is conceivable only in specific cases. A semiautomatic treatment appears more adapted. A first contribution by Soergel et al. (2004) aims at facilitating the transformation. However, the manual work required of the experts remains considerable as they have to analyze each pair of terms in order to extract patterns that explicit their semantic relations. Our contribution limits the manual work by defining syntactic patterns for generic concepts instead of

for each pair. Moreover, a drawback of the literature approaches is that the ontology is elaborated only according to the knowledge stated in the thesaurus. This knowledge does not necessarily reflect the evolution of knowledge in the domain considered. We thus propose to transform a thesaurus from the knowledge it contains, but also from information stated in a reference document corpus of the domain.

Concerning ontology elaboration from texts, different tools have been developed. Each presents different functionalities and has enabled the elaboration of various ontologies. Text-To-Onto, developed by the AIFB Institute of Karlsruhe University, is an application based on the extraction of knowledge from Web documents that considers the reuse of existing ontologies (Maedche & Staab, 2001). It is integrated in the KAON platform that performs the editing and maintenance of ontologies (Bozsak et al., 2002). OntoBuilder (Gal et al., 2004), developed by the Technion of Haifa, helps to construct ontologies from XML files guided by a refining stage done by the user.

The TERMINAE methodology (Aussenac et al., 2000) proposes an approach for selecting concepts and their relations in texts. It uses natural language processing tools to detect relevant terms from documents and their syntactic relations. Terms are then clustered according to their syntactic context, thus helping in the identification of concepts and relations between them. As presented in Section 4, our methodology extends TERMINAE by integrating terminological resources such as thesauri.

FROM A THESAURUS TO AN ONTOLOGY

General Framework

In order to specify the key points in the process of transforming a thesaurus into an ontology, we present our approach in the framework of the methodology TERMINAE (Aussenac et al., 2000). This methodology that is well known for ontology elaboration from texts involves five steps.

The aim of the *first step* is to specify the needs the ontology must satisfy. In the case of the transformation of a thesaurus into a lightweight domain ontology to represent and access documents, the needs identified are:

- Identifying domain terms and their lexical variants in order to detect them in documents.
- Grouping these terms as concepts in order to determine the objects and notions referenced in the documents.
- Structuring the concepts through taxonomic and associative relations in order to guarantee a good semantic indexation.
- Formalizing the ontology in a language understood by the systems so that they will be able to manipulate it.

The *second step* lies in the choice of reference corpus from which the ontology will be built. This choice is a deciding factor in the construction of ontologies. The corpus must describe the items of knowledge that will be integrated into the ontology. When a thesaurus is being transformed, the corpus must satisfy two conditions. Firstly, it must be possible to capture the implicit knowledge that is not formalized in the thesaurus. Secondly, the corpus must help the updating process through recent documents in the domain. In our approach, the corpus is extracted from existing corpuses and experts must guarantee that it covers the whole domain in a representative period. Abstracts of articles published in journals of the domain describe this type of information. Full articles may be used but the advantage of abstracts is that the information they contain is condensed.

The *third step* is that of the linguistic study of the corpus. The aim is to extract from the documents the representative domain terms and their relations (lexical and syntactic) using appropriate tools. At the end of this step, a set of terms, the relations between the terms and clusters are obtained. For the transformation of a thesaurus, this step integrates the knowledge represented in the thesaurus as the terms it contains are representative of the domain and may be grouped according to their relations. The linguistic study of the reference corpus is also necessary for the extraction of terms that are not present in the thesaurus and the relations between terms that are not explicated there. For this analysis, we used the syntactic analyzer Syntex (Bourigault & Fabre, 2000). It presents the advantage of being based on endogenous learning to carry out analysis on different domains. It extracts phrases from the documents and the context of their occurrence (the words they dominate and by which they are dominated). A method must be elaborated, however, to define the mechanisms to select the terms and their relations from the knowledge extracted from the thesaurus and the information extracted from the corpus. This is done by the method we propose.

The *fourth step* corresponds to the normalization of the results obtained by the previous step. Concepts and semantic relations are defined from the terms and lexical relations. At this stage, the thesaurus can be used to specify the concepts.

The *final step* concerns formalization: the semantic network defined in the previous step is translated into a formal language and in this case can be done using OWL. The advantage of this language is that it is composed of three sublanguages of an incremental level of formalization. The use of OWL-Lite gives a first formalization of the ontology, which can evolve.

To transform a thesaurus, the method we propose implements Steps 3, 4, and 5 of the methodology. Our implementation relies on three hypotheses based on the re-use of thesaurus relations:

- The preferred terms are the main terms in the domain and are clues for the constitution of terms designating domain concepts.
- The relations between terms and preferred terms are relations of synonymy between terms, they enable the grouping of terms as being the label of a particular concept.
- The relations between preferred terms are clues for the definition of relations between concepts.

Figure 2 schematizes the overall process. It is based on a mechanism, which can be decomposed into several phases described in the following section.

Defining Concepts and Their Labels

Concepts and concept labels are key elements of an ontology. This stage aims to extract from the thesaurus lexicon a conceptualization in order to define a first set of the ontology concepts. In order to do so, terms defined as "preferred terms" and the relations "use for" and "use" are analyzed. We consider these relations as synonym relations.

Term clusters are made from each preferred term and the set of terms they are linked to according to the relations UF and U. Rule R1 represents this process.

If t3 U t1 **then** t1 and t3 are grouped, with t1 preferred term.
If t1 UF t2 **then** t1 and t2 are grouped, with t1 preferred term

(R1)

The latter are then aggregated according to the transitive closure of the U and UF relations. If a preferred term has led to a first cluster and appears in another cluster, both clusters are grouped. The transitive closure consists in grouping terms by Rule R2.

If t1 UF t2 and t2 UF t3, **then** t1 UF t3 => t1, t2 and t3 are grouped,
with t1 as principal preferred term

Figure 2. Overall process

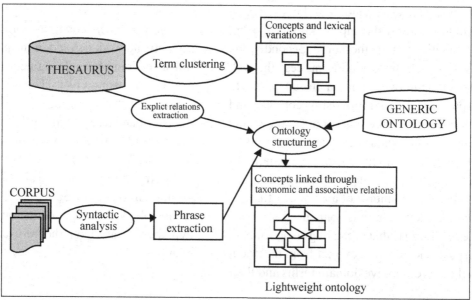

If t4 U t5 and t5 U t6 **then** t4 UP t6 => t4, t5 and t6 are grouped,
with t6 as principal preferred term

(R2)

Structuring These Concepts: Taxonomic Relations Extraction

Some taxonomic relations are directly extracted from the explicit relations of the thesaurus. A higher hierarchical level is added thanks to the analysis of syntactic labels and the creation of generic concepts. Figure 3 schematizes these mechanisms.

Extracting Explicit Taxonomic Relations

In order to extract taxonomic relations from the thesaurus, thesaurus « Broader Term » and « Narrower Term » relations are considered. These relations defined between terms, now concept labels, are used to define candidate taxonomic relations between the concepts whose labels are linked in the thesaurus (see R3). These relations have to be analyzed carefully as they can imply the « is part of » and « is an instance of » relations. Our work does not deal with the automatic disambiguation of these relations. Note that several domain thesauri

consider the « broader term » and « narrower term » in their strict meaning.

> **If** t1 « narrower term » t2 with t1 label of concept c1 and t2 label of concept c2
> **then** c2 « is a » c1
> **If** t3 « broader term » t4 with t3 label of concept c3 and t4 label of concept c4
> **then** c3 « is a » c4

(R3)

New Taxonomic Level: Generic Concepts

A drawback of thesauri is that their highest hierarchical level generally contains a huge number of terms (Soergel et al., 2004). These terms are the ones for which no « broader term » relations have been defined. This is explained by the fact that thesauri do not define generic categories enabling the classification of the domain terms. This drawback is also noticed in ontologies obtained by the transformation of thesauri, causing problems when the user chooses to explore the ontology from top to bottom. The first hierarchical level is vast, making the start of the browsing difficult. For example, the highest level of the transformation of

Figure 3. Taxonomic relations extraction process

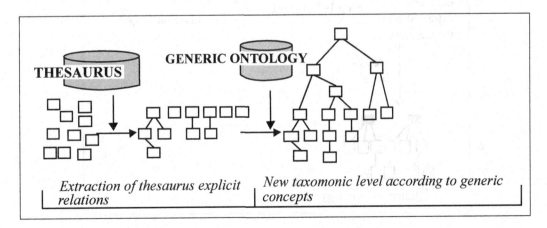

Extraction of thesaurus explicit relations

New taxomonic level according to generic concepts

the IAU thesaurus used to evaluate our approach contains more than 1100 concepts.

We thus propose to add a new hierarchical level to ease the browsing of the ontology. We propose the definition of generic concepts, which characterize top level concepts. A generic concept refers to a concept of the domain or a concept added to structure the ontology. In (Soergel et al., 2004), generic concepts are defined according to a categorization schema existing in the domain. This process cannot be applied to all domains, as they do not always exist. Moreover, it implies manual work by the expert who has to map the ontology concepts to the created generic concepts. We propose a new, more automatic approach. A generic ontology (such as WordNet (Miller, 1988) or DOLCE (Gangemi et al., 2002), is used to define generic concepts. First, the level 0 concepts of the built ontology are mapped to the concepts of the generic ontology. The generic concepts are then defined according to the most specific ancestors of those concepts in the generic ontology. Figure 4 schematizes the process.

Formula R4 synthesizes the entire process.

If $c \Leftrightarrow sw$ with $sw \in \{$ WordNet_concepts$\}$
then c « is a subconcept of » ta
with ta the most specific hypernomym of sw

(R4)

Generic Concepts Definition

We have developed a method to map the ontology concepts to concepts of WordNet. This resource is a lexical reference system whose construction was inspired by linguistic theories. It covers the general English language domain.

The labels of the top concepts in the ontology are used to select candidate concepts in WordNet. A disambiguation process is defined to disambiguate labels that refer to different WordNet concepts. This process relies on:

- The glossary provided by WordNet to describe in natural language the meaning of the concepts.

Figure 4. Adding an abstraction level to the ontology

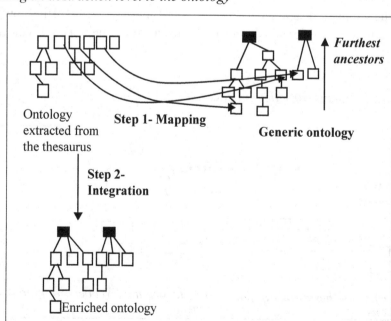

- The descendant concepts of each concept defined by the WordNet hyperonymy relation.
- The ancestor concepts of each concept defined by the WordNet hyponymy relation.

General terms referring to the considered domain treated by the ontology are first specified by experts. They are then looked for in the glossary associated to each candidate concept.

The following three propositions are successively applied:

- **Proposition 1:** If one of the terms is found in its glossary, the candidate concept is automatically chosen for the mapping. Otherwise, proposition 2 is applied.
- **Proposition 2:** The descendant concepts of the WordNet concept are compared to those of the ontology concept. If at least two of them share the same label, the concept in WordNet is chosen. Otherwise, proposition 3 is applied.
- **Proposition 3:** The ancestor concepts of a candidate concept are analyzed according to proposition 1. If the proposition is verified, the candidate concept is chosen for the mapping, if it is not the case, the concept is not disambiguated.

Concerning the identification of the generic concepts, the most specific ancestors of the mapped concepts are proposed to represent the generic concepts of the ontology. Examples of generic concepts extracted for the astronomy domain are:

- "instrumentation:" an artifact (or system of artifacts) that is instrumental in accomplishing some end.
- "phenomenon:" any state or process known through the senses rather than by intuition or reasoning

- "natural object:" an object occurring naturally; not made by man

The generic concepts are proposed to the domain experts who judge their relevance. They are integrated in the ontology by the following process.

Integrating Generic Concepts in The Ontology

In order to link the level 0 concepts of the current ontology to the generic concepts previously extracted, an « is a subclass » relation is defined between the level 0 concepts and the generic concepts extracted by the mapping.

Note that if for a given level 0 concept no generic concept has been extracted (no possible mapping in the generic ontology), the mapping to the generic concepts has to be done manually.

Structuring These Concepts: Associative Relations Extraction

The second stage in formalizing the ontology structure is to define the associative relations between concepts. This implies identifying a semantic relation between two concepts and labeling this relation. The process we propose relies on labeling the possible semantic relations that can be defined between pairs of generic concepts and using those labels to disambiguate the associative relations between concepts that can be extracted from the "related term" thesaurus relations.

Specifying Relations Between Generic Concepts

The specification of semantic relations between generic concepts is based on the proposition of relations associated to each pair of concepts by an automatic syntactic analysis of the reference corpus. These propositions form the basis of the manual definition of relations.

The context of the labels of each concept is extracted by the syntactic analysis of the reference corpus. By « context », we mean the phrase depending syntactically on each label (objects and subjects of verbs in which the labels appear). These contexts are then grouped according to the generic concepts they are linked with. The terms that occur frequently in the grouped contexts are retained to characterize the generic concept and are proposed as labels for the associative relations that the concepts linked to the generic concept may have. An example to illustrate this idea is *instrumentation* in the astronomy ontology. The terms occurring most frequently are the verbs « observe » and « measure » indicating that the astronomical instruments are used to observe and measure the other concepts of the domain.

Semantic relations are defined between each pair of generic concepts. A 2D matrix is built. This matrix contains, in lines and columns, all the different types of generic concepts identified manually based on the preceding propositions. Each cell contains the possible relations. An expert in the domain can thus identify the relations which link the pairs of generic concepts and add the labels he has chosen in the cell of the matrix. Figure 5 presents a sample of the matrix defined for our case study.

This mechanism is a first step in helping experts determine relation labels. Experts have to validate or reject the propositions made according to verbs extracted in the context. The large number of verbs leads to numerous propositions giving experts many labels to verify. This step of our methodology can be considered as the most time-consuming as far as the experts are concerned. More sophisticated analyses are currently being considered.

Disambiguating Thesaurus "Related Term" Relations

The vague thesaurus « *related term* » relations are first transcribed in the ontology. Two terms linked in the thesaurus will thus lead to an association between the concepts for which they are labels in the ontology. This association is then labeled, thanks to the relations identified in the matrix between the generic concepts associated with the concepts. For example, the relation identified between the generic concepts « instrumentation » and « natural object» being the relation « *observes* », the thesaurus « related term » relation between « coronagraph » and « *solar corona* » (concepts derived from these two generic concepts) is modified into the relation « *coronagraph* » « *observes* » « *solar corona* ». If several semantic relations are identified, the choice is left to the domain expert.

Rule (R5) specifies the process.

Let ta_1 and ta_2 be two generic concepts with $ta_1 \in C_{Onto}$ and $ta_2 \in C_{Onto}$

Figure 5. Sample of the matrix defining the possible labels of semantic relations between generic concepts

	Property	Phenomenon	Event	Science
Property	*Influences / Is influenced by Determined by / Determines Exclude Has part / Is part*	*Is a property of induces*	*Is a property of induces*	*Is studied by*
Insrumentation	*Makes Observes*	*Observes Measures*	*Observes Measures*	*Is Used to studied*

Let $r,r' \in R_{Onto}$ with $\sigma_{ROnto}: R_{Onto} \rightarrow C \times C$ and $r(ta_1,ta_2)$ with $G^{-1}(r)$ specified in the domain

If $r'(c_1,c_2)$ with $c_1 \in C_{Onto}$ and $c_2 \in C_{Onto}$ and c_1 « is subclass of » ta_1 and c_2 « is subclass od » ta_2 and $G^{-1}(r')$=« is linked to »

   then $G^{-1}(r') \in G^{-1}(r)$

$$(R5)$$

MINING A TEXTUAL CORPUS TO ENRICH THE ONTOLOGY

Documents from the reference corpus are used to update the knowledge represented in the ontology. This update leads first to the definition of new semantic relations between existing concepts (Section 1). We also propose to extract new terms that were not previously in the ontology lexicon (Section 2) and to situate them according to the existing knowledge (Section 5.3).

Detecting New Associative Relations Between Ontology Concepts

Contrary to approaches in the literature, which aim solely at transforming a thesaurus into an ontology through the knowledge represented in it, we aim at establishing new associative relations between concepts by analyzing the textual documents of the domain (cf Rule R6).

Using the previously established matrix, new relations can be found between the ontology concepts. For this, the syntactic context of the different concept labels is analyzed. The context is defined from the terms frequently co-occurring near the ontology concept labels.

When a concept label appears in the context of the label of another concept and the two concepts are not linked by a relation in the ontology, a relation is proposed. The label of this relation is established through the matrix defined above by considering the two generic concepts linked to the two concepts.

For example, in the context of the label « *luminosity* » referring to the concept of the same name, the label « *galaxy* » corresponding to the concept « *galaxy* » is found. As these concepts are of the types « *property* » and « *natural object* », the relation « has a » is proposed between « *galaxy* » and « *luminosity* » (cf Figure 5). As no relation has been previously established between the two concepts, the new relation is added to the ontology.

Let ta_1 and ta_2 be two abstract types with $ta_1 \in C_{Onto}$ and $ta_2 \in C_{Onto}$

Let $r,r' \in R_{Onto}$ with $\sigma_{ROnto}: R_{Onto} \rightarrow C \times C$ and $r(ta_1,ta_2)$ with $G^{-1}(r)$ specified in the domain

If $r'(c_1,c_2)$ is extracted by the corpus analysis with $c_1 \in C_{Onto}$ and $c_2 \in C_{Onto}$

   then $G^{-1}(r') \in G^{-1}(r)$ $$(R6)$$

Adding New Terms in The Ontology

In order to extract new domain terms, we consider two different weighting measures. The measures are complementary and aim at selecting from the set of terms extracted by the syntactic analyzer that are most relevant.

The first weighting measure is the overall occurrence frequency of a term in the corpus. The frequently used terms and thus the most general ones are extracted. The terms considered are noun phrases, stop words, such as articles or common verbs, will thus not be extracted. The formula used is the following:

$$globality(term,corpus)=\text{tf}_{term,corpus} \qquad (1)$$

where $\text{tf}_{term,corpus}$ represents the occurrence frequency of the term in the corpus.

The second weighting measure aims at extracting specific terms of the corpus. It relies on tf.idf that is used in information tetrieval to detect discriminating terms. It promotes terms appearing frequently in a document but rarely in the rest of the corpus. In order to apply this measure to term extraction, the measure is considered by the average td.idf obtained by each term on all the documents.

$$specificity(term, corpus)$$

$$= \underset{\{document_i\} \in corpus}{average} (tf_{term,document_i} \times idf_{term})$$

$$idf_{term} = \log(\frac{N}{f_{term}}) + 1 \qquad (2)$$

where $tf_{term,document}$ represents the occurrence frequency of a term in a document and f_{term} corresponds to the number of documents containing this term.

According to a threshold, the terms extracted by measures (1) and (2) are proposed to be added to the ontology lexicon (R7 and R8).

Figure 6. Frequent terms of the astronomy domain not stated in the ontology

```
column density
high resolution
globular cluster
white dwarf
binary system
soft X ray
power law
```

Figure 7. Specific terms of the astronomy domain not stated in the ontology extracted from the thesaurus

```
Yarkovsky force
Relativistic gravity
Suprathermal electron
Halpha knot
Penumbral wave
Mean free path
Integral magnitude
Mixing layer
stellar population
```

If $t \in L_{corpus}$ and globality(t)>threshold
    then $t \in L_{COnto}$ **(R7)**

If $t \in L_{corpus}$ and specificity (t)>threshold
    then $t \in L_{COnto}$ **(R8)**

Figures 6 and 7 provide example of terms extracted by the two measures.

Adding New Semantic Links Between Concepts

The new terms extracted by the previous measures have to be integrated in the ontology. The integration process we propose relies on the comparison of the words composing the extracted terms and the terms forming the concept labels in the ontology. More specifically, we consider for each extracted term the main word (i.e., the word on which the remaining words depend syntactically) and the remaining ones. For example, in a nominal phrase "column density" the main word is "density" as "column" is a noun complement.

Three different processes are applied.

If the main word and the rest of the term refer to two concept labels in the ontology, the corresponding concepts and their generic concepts are extracted. The new term is integrated in the ontology by the creation of an associative relation is then created between the two concepts. The relation is labeled on the basis of the relations defined between the two generic concepts. R9 expresses this process.

If only the main word corresponds to a concept label, the new term is proposed to be the label of a new concept that will be subsumed by the concept referenced by the main word. As the new term defines information on the main word, it specifies the meaning of the concept referenced by the main word. (cf Rule R10).

Let $t \in L_{corpus}$ to be added to L_{COnto}, $ta_1 \in C_{Onto}$ and $ta_2 \in C_{Onto}$

If $\text{main\_term}(t) \in L_{COnto}$ with $F(\text{main\_term}(t))$ « sub class of » ta_1 and $\text{remaining}(t) \in L_{Conto}$ with

$F^{-1}(\text{remaining}(t))$« sub class of » ta_2 and $r \in R_{Onto}$ with $\sigma_{ROnto}: R_{Onto} \rightarrow C \times C$ and $r(ta_1, ta_2)$ with $G^{-1}(r)$ specified in the domain **then** $r' \in R_{Onto}$ avec $G^{-1}(r') \in G^{-1}(r)$

(R9)

Extraction of concepts

Terms in the thesaurus	Concepts created	Concept validated
2957	2547	85%

Definition of the new abstract level in the ontology

Mapping of top level concepts to concepts of the generic ontology (WordNet)	
Top concepts that have candidate concepts in the generic ontology	72%
Top concepts for which the disambiguation process was successful	65%
Extraction of generic concepts	
Number of generic concepts extracted	19
Number of generic concepts validated	74%
Integration of generic concepts in the ontology	
Top level ontology concept correctly associated to a generic concept	89"%

Extraction of associative relations

Disambiguation of the associative relations extracted from the thesaurus "is related to" relation	
Number of relations evaluated	49
Correctly labeled relations	84%

Ontology update

Extraction of new associative relations between concepts	
Number of proposed relations	74
Validated relations	92%
Validated labels	87%
New terms extraction	
Percentage of correct global terms extracted	72%
Percentage of correct specific terms extracted	62%
New terms integration to the ontology	
Percentage of correct new concepts extracted	100%
Percentage of correct new relations extracted	62%
Validated labels	87%

Let $t \in L_{corpus}$ to be added to L_{COnto},

If main_term $(t) \in L_{COnto}$ and remaining(t) $\in L_{Conto}$

    then $t \in L_{COnto}$ with F(t)=c and c « subclass of » F(tmain_term(t))

$$\text{(R10)}$$

CASE STUDY: BUILDING AND USING AN ONTOLOGY IN THE ASTRONOMICAL FIELD

We have applied the proposed method to the transformation of a thesaurus into a lightweight ontology in the field of astronomy. The IAU thesaurus (http://www.mso.anu.edu.au/library/thesaurus/) was built to standardize the terminology of astronomy. Its use was to help librarians index and retrieve catalogues and scientific publications of the domain. Its building, requested by the International Union of Astronomy in 1984, was finished in 1995. Its transformation into an ontology has been done in the framework of the French project Data Mass in Astronomy (http://cdsweb.u-strasbg.fr/MDA/mda.html). We present in Section 6.1, the results obtained by applying the different rules presented in the article. In Section 6.2, we give an example of how the constructed ontology has been integrated to a science-monitoring task.

Evaluation of the Proposed Method

Two corpuses of the domain have been considered. The documents they contain are abstracts of articles published in the international journal Astronomy and Astrophysics (www.edpsciences.org/aa). The first corpus is composed of articles published in 1995. The use of this corpus aims at capturing the implicit knowledge of the domain not stated in the thesaurus when it was built. The second corpus contains articles published in 2002. This corpus has been chosen to enable the update of the domain knowledge from recent documents. Domain experts have validated that both corpuses

describe the knowledge to be represented in the ontology.

The protocol defined to evaluate the transformation relies on presenting the results obtained by the different rules to two astronomers who accept or reject the propositions.

We present here the most significant results.

The evaluation of our method in the field of astronomy has demonstrated its interest. The aim of our method is not to be automatic but to facilitate the creation of ontologies. Note that for each step the task of experts is to confirm or reject propositions and not to give results. For this, our method is efficient. The identification of domain concepts and their labels is highly relevant (85% of the concepts are validated). It leads to the definition of generic concepts that are mostly validated and facilitates their integration in the ontology. Associative relations extracted from the thesaurus are validated for 84%. Thanks to the mining of the reference corpus, relevant semantic relations between existing concepts are added and new terms integrated by means of the creation of new concepts or new relations.

Using Ontologies for a Science Monitoring Task

Ontologies are used for semantically indexing documents. This relies on the intuition that the meaning of textual information (and the words that compose the document) depends on the conceptual relations between the objects to which they refer rather than on the linguistic and statistical relations of their content (Haav & Lubi, 2001).

Semantic indexing is done in two steps: identifying document concepts within documents and weighting those concepts. The weighting process uses the relations between concepts identified in the documents according to the structure of the ontology. For more precise details, see (Hernandez et al., 2005).

Based on this semantic indexing, we propose to take the ontology into account to provide the user access to the information contained in a corpus. The interface is developed to support OWL ontology visualization. A snapshot is presented in Figure 8. With the interface, it is possible to visualize both the domain ontology linked to the content of documents and the specific metadata the user is looking for.

The user explores the corpus according to the specific theme of the domain (in our case astronomy).

Figure 8. Visualization through the astronomy ontology

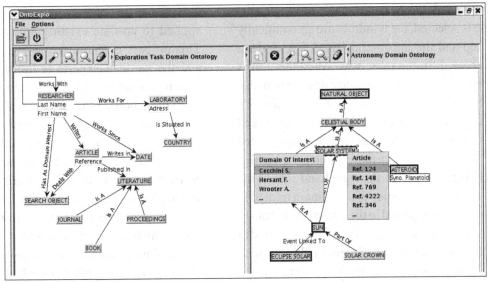

Figure 9. Visualization of the knowledge learnt for an article

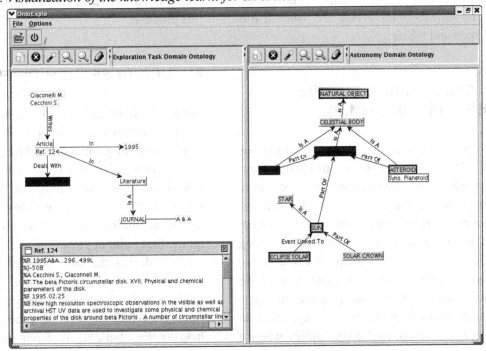

This possibility is illustrated in Figure 9. On the right hand side of the screen, the domain ontology is shown with its concepts and relations. The concepts present in the corpus are highlighted; they can be interpreted in their context as their relations to other concepts are represented. By clicking on a concept, the user can find the articles treating the theme and the researchers working on this theme. When a researcher working on the theme is selected, the windows are automatically updated and the information on this researcher is presented. In the same way, when the user is interested in accessing the article dealing with this subject, he selects it. The windows are updated: a pop-up window containing the article appears and the information linked to this article is represented as in Figure 8. The information known about this article is presented on the right hand side of the screen and all the themes of the domain treated in the article are presented in the astronomy ontology frame. The astronomy ontology concepts found in the document are presented in red on the left-hand side of the window (the article of reference 124 deals with comet and solar system). This makes it possible to evaluate rapidly if the document treats the themes in which the user is interested, who the authors of the article are, when it was published and where.

CONCLUSION AND FUTURE WORKS IN THE DOMAIN

The representation of textual contents is an issue to be addressed if systems are to handle documents efficiently. The assumption according to which documents contain all the information necessary to their representation is no longer enough. However, a more semantic indexing implies the use of terminological resources or domain knowledge. In this chapter, we have proposed a methodology that produces this type of linguistic resource in a formal way, based on ontologies. This methodology applies when a thesaurus and a textual corpus on the domain are available. The process is based on the following main steps: extraction of initial knowledge from the thesaurus itself (basically terms, concepts and taxonomic links) and enrichment of the resulting ontology based on text mining (disambiguation of existing relations between concepts, extraction of new terms, and new relations from texts). We, thus, define an incremental process that can be applied to up-date existing ontologies as well. This process is automated as much as possible and the work of experts is limited, consisting only in validating the results (generic concepts, relations labels). Indeed, our methodology and its implementation is less demanding with regard to experts' time (Soergel et al., 2004) (Wielinga et al, 2001). An important result is that relations between concepts are semiautomatically extracted and a label is associated to them.

This work is a contribution to the Semantic Web, which structures the web in a way that it is meaningful not only to computers but also to humans. (Lu et al., 2002) consider that one of the main challenges of developing the Semantic Web is through ontologies. To meet this challenge new methods and tools are needed in order to facilitate this process.

FUTURE RESEARCH DIRECTIONS

Mining for information on the Semantic Web refers to various points of views (Corby et al. 2004): that of designing ontologies which aim at representing a field of knowledge, that of semantically indexing resources according to these ontologies, finally, that of providing access to resources for a user or an engine. The work we present focuses on the first point of view.

Considering the same point of view, one of the challenges is the evolution of domains and related needs. Domain knowledge evolves with time. Now that methods have been defined to help ontology building, research should take into consideration how ontology can evolve. It implies populating existing ontologies with new instances that are extracted from recent domain resources, restructuring ontologies when new concepts are identified or when knowledge become obsolete. Ontology evolution is also linked to the knowledge needed by information systems to better interact with users. When applications are modified or when user's expertise of the application or the field changes, the ontology has to be restructured according to what is really useful. The PASCAL Ontology Learning Challenge aims at incouraging and evaluating work in such directions.

Semantic Web research incorporates a number of technologies and methodologies defined in different fields including artificial intelligence, ontology engineering, human language technology, machine learning, web services, databases, distributed systems, software engineering, human computer interaction and information systems. One of the challenges is to make these communities work together in order to integrate the advances in the different fields. Moreover, many application domains have been investigated (e-business, e-health, e-government, multimedia, e-learning, bio-pharmacy) but scalable applications is still a challenge when considering the 11.5 billion pages of indexable Web.

Another challenge is that ontologies are yet build in order to state the consensual knowledge of the domain. In order to be applied on large scale document repositories where many groups of users interact, processes should be developed to add descriptions to ontologies in order to define in which context and for whom the ontology is useful. This last point is part of the aims of the pragmatic web which is envisioned to be the new evolution of the Semantic Web.

REFERENCES

Aussenac-Gilles, N., Biébow, B., & Szulman, S. (2000). Revisiting ontology design: A method based on corpus analysis. In R. Dieng & O. Corby (Eds.), *Proceedings of the 12th European Knowledge Acquisition Workshop (EKAW'00)* (pp. 172-188).

Aussenac-Gilles, N., & Mothe, J. (2004). Ontologies as background knowledge to explore document collections. In *Proceedings of RIAO* (pp. 129-142)

Bozsak, E., Ehrig, M., Handschuh, S., Hotho, A., Maedche, A., Motik, B., et al. (2002). KAON: Towards a large scale Semantic Web. In *Proceedings of the 3rd International Conference on E-Commerce and Web Technologies* (Vol. 2455, pp. 304-313).

Bourigault, D., & Fabre, C. (2000). Approche linguistique pour l'analyse syntaxique de corpus, Cahiers de Grammaire, 25, Université Toulouse le Mirail (pp. 131-151).

Chaumier, J. (1988). *Le traitement linguistique de l'information*. Entreprise moderne d'éd.

Crouch, C.J., & Yang, B. (1992). Experiments in automatic statistical thesaurus construction. *Conference on Research and Development in Information Retrieval (SIGIR)* (pp. 77-88).

Ding, Y., & Foo, S. (2002). Ontology research and development: Part 1—A review of ontology generation. *Journal of Information Science, 28*(2).

Englmeier, K., & Mothe, J. (2003). IRAIA: A portal technology with a semantic layer coordinating multimedia retrieval and cross-owner content building. In *Proceedings of the International Conference on Cross Media Service Delivery, Cross-Media Service Delivery Series. The International Series in Engineering and Computer Science* (Vol. 740, pp. 181-192).

Fensel, S.B. (1998). Knowledge engineering: Principles and methods. *Data and Knowledge Engineering, 25*, 161-197.

Fischer, D.H. (1998). From thesauri towards ontologies? In W.M. Hadi, J. Maniez, & S. Pollitt (Eds.), *Structures and Relations in Knowledge Organization: Proceedings of the 5th International ISKO Conference* (pp. 18-30). Würzburg: Ergon.

Foskett, D.J. (1980). Thesaurus. In A. Kent & H. Lancour (Eds), *Encyclopedia of library and information science* (pp. 416-463).

Gal, A., Modica, G., & Jamil, H.M. (2004). OntoBuilder: Fully automatic extraction and consolidation of ontologies from Web sources. In *Proceedings of the 20th International Conference on Data Engineering.* IEEE Computer Society.

Gangemi, A., Guarino, N., Masolo, C., Oltramari, A., & Schneider, L. (2002). Sweetening ontologies with DOLCE. In *Proceedings of the International Conference on Knowledge Engineering and Knowledge Management* (pp. 166-181).

Gómez-Pérez, A., Fernandez, M., & de Vicente, A.J. (1996). Towards a method to conceptualize domain ontologies. In *Proceedings of the European Conference on Artificial Intelligence (ECAI'96)* (pp. 41-52).

Grefenstette, G. (1992). Use of syntactic context to produce term association lists for retrieval. In *Proceedings of the Conference on Research and Development in Information Retrieval (SIGIR)* (pp. 89-97).

Guarino, N., Carrara, M., & Giaretta, P. (1994). Formalizing ontological commitments. In *Proceedings of the AAAI Conference.*

Haav, H.M., & Lubi, T.L. (2001). A survey of concept-based information retrieval tools on the web. In *Proceedings of the 5th East-European Conference ADBIS* (Vol. 2, pp. 29-41).

Hahn, U., & Schulz, S. (2004) Building a very large ontology from medical thesauri. In S. Staab & R. Stuber (Eds.), *Handbook on ontologies* (pp. 133-150).

Harman, D. (1992). The DARPA TIPSTER project. *SIGIR Forum, 26*(2), 26-28.

Hearst, M.A. (1992). Automatic acquisition of hyponyms from large text corpora. In *Proceedings of the 14th International Conference on Computational Linguistics.*

Hernandez, N., Mothe, J., & Poulain, S. (2005). Accessing and mining scientific domains using ontologies: The OntoExplo System. In *Proceedings of the 28th Annual International ACM SIGIR* (pp. 607-608).

Lassila, O., & McGuiness, D. (2001). The role of frame-based representation on the Semantic Web. Rapport technique KSL-01-02, Knowledge Systems Laboratory, Stanford University.

Lu, S., Dong, M., & Fotouhi, F. (2002). The Semantic Web: Opportunities and challenges for next-generation Web applications. Retrieved from http://informationr.net/ir/7-4/paper134.html

Maedche, A., & Staab, S. (2001). Ontology learning for the Semantic Web. *IEEE Intelligent Systems, Special Issue on the Semantic Web, 16*(2).

McGuinness, D.L., van Harmelen F. (2004). OWL Web ontology language overview, W3C Recommendation. Retrieved February 10, 2004, from http://www.w3.org/TR/owl-features/

Miles, A., & Brichley, D. (2005). SKOS Core GuideW3C Working Draft. Retrieved May 10, 2005, from http://www.w3.org/TR/swbp-skos-core-guide/

Mills, D. (2006). *Semantic waves 2006.* Retrieved from http://www.ift.ulaval.ca/~kone/Cours/WS/WS-PlanCours2006.pdf

Miller, G.A. (1988). Nouns in WordNet. In C. Fellbaum (Ed.), *WordNet. An electronic lexical database* (pp. 23-46). MIT Press.

Porter, M. (1980). An algorithm for suffix. *Stripping Program, 14*(3), 130-137.

Qiu, Y., & Frei, H.P. (1993). Concept based query expension. *Conference on Research and Development in Information Retrieval (SIGIR),* (pp. 160-169).

Robertson, S., Sparck, E., & Jones, K. (1976). Relevance weighting of search terms. *Journal of the American Society for Information Sciences, 27*(3), 129-146.

Salton, G. (1971). *The smart retrieval system.* Englewood Cliffs, NJ: Prentice Hall.

Smith, M.K., Welty, C., & McGuinness, D.L. (2004). OWL Web ontology language guide. *W3C Recommendation.* Retrieved February 10, 2004, from http://www.w3.org/TR/owl-guide/

Soergel, D., Lauser, B., Liang, A., Fisseha, F., Keizer, J., & Katz, S. (2004). Reengineering thesauri for new applications: The AGROVOC example, *Journal of Digital Information, 4*(4).

Tudhope, D., Alani, H., & Jones, C. (2001). Augmenting thesaurus relationships: Possibilities for retrieval. *Journal of Digital Information, 1-8*(41).

Uschold, M., & King, M. (1995). Towards a methodology for building ontologies. In *Proceedings of the Workshop on Basic Ontological Issues in Knowledge Sharing at the International Joint Conference on Artificial Intelligence (IJCAI1995).*

Wielinga, B., Schreiber, G., Wielemaker, J., & Sandber, J.A.C. (2001). From thesaurus to ontology. In *Proceedings of the International Conference on Knowledge Capture.*

ADDITIONAL READING

Brewster C., Alani H., Dasmahapatra S., & Wilks Y. (2004). Data driven ontology evaluation. In *Proceedings of 4th International Conference on Language Resources and Evaluation.*

Chébotko A., Lu S., & Fotouhi F. (2006). *Challenges for information systems towards the Semantic Web.* SIGSEMIS Journal. Retrieved from http://www.sigsemis.org/?p=9

Chrisment C., Dousset B., & Dkaki T. (2007). Combining mining and visualization tools to discover the geographic structure of a domain. *Computers Environment and Urban Systems Journal,* to be published in 2007.

Corby, O., Dieng-Kuntz, R., & Faron-Zucker, C. (2004). Querying the Semantic Web with corese search engine. In *Proceedings of the European conference on artificial intelligence* (pp. 705-709).

Desmontils E., & Jaquin C.(2002). Indexing a Web site with a terminology oriented ontology. In I. Cruz, S. Decker, J. Euzenat, & D.L. McGuinness (Eds.), *The emerging Semantic Web* (pp. 181-197). IOS Press.

Englmeier, K., & Mothe, J. (2003). IRAIA: A portal technology with a semantic layer coordinating multimedia retrieval and cross-owner content building. In *Proceedings of the International Conference on Cross Media Service Delivery, Cross-Media Service Delivery Series.* In *Proceedings of the International Series in Engineering and Computer Science, 740* (pp. 181-192).

Guha, R.V., McCool, R., & Miller, E. (2003). Semantic search. In *Proceedings of the 12th International World Wide Web Conference* (pp. 700-709).

Hernandez, N., & Mothe, J. (2004). An approach to evaluate existing ontologies for indexing a document corpus. In *Proceedings of the Eleventh International Conference on Artificial Intelligence: Methodology, Systems, Applications (AIMSA) Semantic Web Challenges* (pp. 11-21).

Hernandez, N., Mothe, J., Chrisment, C., & Egret, D. (2007). Modeling context through domain ontologies. *Journal of Information Retrieval,* to be published in 2007.

Jarvelin, K., & Ingwersen, P. (2004) Information seeking research needs extensions towards tasks and technology. *Information Retrieval, 10*(1), 212.

Kiryakov, A., Popov, B., Terziev, I., Manov, D., & Ognyanoff, D. (2004). Semantic annotation, indexing, and retrieval. *Journal of Web Semantics, 2*(1).

Lozano-Tello, A., & Gómez-Pérez, A. (2004). ONTOMETRIC: A method to choose the appropriate ontology. *Journal of Database Management, 15*(2).

Mothe, J., Chrisment, C., Dousset, B., & Alaux, J. (2003). DocCube: Multidimensional visualisation and exploration of large document sets. *Journal of the American Society for Information Science and Technology, 54*(2), 650-659.

Shaban-Nejad, A., Baker, C. J. O., Haarslev, V., & Butler, G. (2005). *The FungalWeb ontology: Semantic Web challenges in bioinformatics and Genomics Semantic Web challenges.*

Studer, R., Benjamins, R., & Fensel, D. (1998). *Knowledge engineering: Principles and methods, data and knowledge engineering, 25*(1-2) 161-197.

Uschold M. (2003). Where are the semantics in the Semantic Web? *AI Magazine, 24*(3), 25-36.

Vallet, D., Fernández, M., & Castells, P. (2005). An ontology-based information retrieval model. In *Proceedings of the 2nd European Semantic Web Conference* (pp. 455-470).

Chapter VIII
Evaluating the Construction of Domain Ontologies for Recommender Systems Based on Texts

Stanley Loh
Catholic University of Pelotas and Lutheran University of Brazil, Brazil

Daniel Lichtnow
Catholic University of Pelotas, Brazil

Thyago Borges
Catholic University of Pelotas, Brazil

Gustavo Piltcher
Catholic University of Pelotas, Brazil

ABSTRACT

This chapter investigates different aspects in the construction of a domain ontology to a content-based recommender system. The recommender systems suggests textual electronic documents from a digital library, based on documents read by the users and based on textual messages posted in electronic discussions through a Web chat. The domain ontology is used to represent the user's interest and the content of the documents. In this context, the ontology is composed by a hierarchy of concepts and keywords. Each concept has a vector of keywords with weights associated. Keywords are used to identify the content of the texts (documents and messages), through the application of text mining techniques. The chapter discusses different approaches for constructing the domain ontology, including the use of text mining software tools for supervised learning, the interference of domain experts in the engineering process and the use of a normalization step.

INTRODUCTION

Recommender systems are an emerging technology recently used by marketing departments and vendors, that utilizes data mining and machine learning techniques to analyze behavior and preferences of users or customers and that suggests new offers.

A content-based recommender system utilizes the content of items to generate recommendations to users. Items may be products, services, objects, Websites, people, etc. According to Burke (2002), content-based recommendation is an evolution of information filtering research. In the content-based approach, the recommender system learns a profile of the user's interests based on the features present in objects associated to the user and recommends other items with similar features. When the content of an item matches the interest of a user, this item is recommended to that user.

Some works have reported improvements in retrieval tasks using ontologies. Gauch et al., (2003) argued that *"one increasingly popular way to structure information is through the use of ontologies, or graphs of concepts."* Labrou and Finin (1999) use categories from *Yahoo!* as an ontology to describe content and features of documents. Middleton et al., (2003) associate concepts from an ontology to users' profiles and to documents.

In a recommender system, an ontology may be used to identify and represent the content of the items and the interest (profile) of the users. For example, supermarkets can use ontologies to classify products in sections and brands and the interest of the user may be composed by sections and brands of the items bought by the user. Then a recommender system may suggest to the user other items with the same brand or within the same section.

In this work, we consider an ontology as a formal and explicit definition of concepts (classes or categories) and their attributes and relations (Noy & McGuinness, 2003). A domain ontology is a description of "things" that exist or can exist in a domain (Sowa, 2002) and contains the vocabulary related to the domain (Guarino, 1998).

When dealing with items that have textual descriptions, the ontology may manage keywords that are used to represent the content of the items or user's profile. Textual descriptions may appear as product information (i.e., marketing slogans, technical specifications) or as content of the item (i.e., textual documents, Websites, e-mail messages).

The process of constructing such a domain ontology is important to the recommender system generate better recommendations. There are many approaches for constructing ontologies. This chapter deals with the special case of creating domain ontologies based on keywords or textual characteristics. Ontological engineering techniques must consider the textual content of the items. For this purpose, text mining techniques may be used in a supervised learning process to automate part of the construction process, minimizing the charge on the engineer.

The chapter presents the approaches based on a real recommender system that suggests electronic documents from a digital library based on documents read by users and based on textual messages sent during electronic discussions in a Web chat.

GENERAL EXPLANATION OF THE RECOMMENDER SYSTEM

This section presents the recommender system used as case study. The goal of the system is to provide people with useful information during a collaboration session. To do that, the system analyzes textual messages sent by users when interacting in a private Web chat, identifies topics (subjects/themes/concepts) inside the messages and recommends items cataloged in a private digital library, previously classified in the same topics. Figure 1 presents the architecture of the system with its main components. The digital library contains electronic documents, Web links and bibliographic references.

According to the classification of Terveen and Hill (2001), the system is a *content-based recommender system* because the context of the messages is matched against the content of items in the database.

The chat works like traditional chats over the Web. The difference is that it is specially constructed for this system and it is not open to nonregistered users. Thus, users have to be authorized for using the system. There is no limit for the number of persons interacting at the same time. At the moment, only one chat channel is allowed. Thus a discussion session concerns all messages sent during a day. In the future, this restriction will be eliminated.

The text mining module analyzes each message posted to the chat (like a *sniffer*). The words present in the message are compared against terms present in a domain ontology. Generic terms like prepositions (called *stopwords*) will be discarded. Each message is compared online against all concepts in the ontology.

The text mining method employed in this work (a kind of classification task) was first presented in Loh et al.,(2000). Instead of using natural language processing (NLP) to analyze syntax and semantics, the method is based on probabilistic techniques: themes can be identified by cues. Using a *fuzzy* reasoning about the cues found in a text, it is possible to calculate the likelihood of a theme or subject being present in that text. The algorithm is based on Bayesian algorithms, since it uses a prototype-like vector to represent texts and concepts and the probability theory to treat uncertainty. The method evaluates the relationship between a text and a concept of the ontology using a similarity function that calculates the distance between the two vectors. The vectors representing texts and concepts are composed by a list of terms with a weight associated to each term. In the case of texts, the weight represents the relative frequency of the term in the text (number of

Figure 1. Architecture of the system

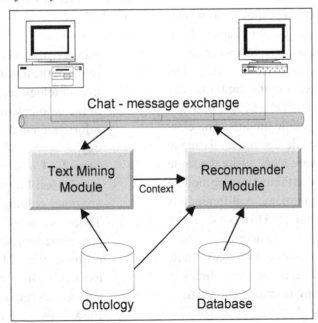

occurrences divided by the total number of terms in the text). And the weight in the concept vector represents the probability of the term being present in a text of that theme. The next section (the ontology) describes how concept weights are defined.

The text mining method compares the vector representing the text of a message against vectors representing concepts in the ontology. The method multiplies the weights of common terms (those present in both vectors). The overall sum of these products is the degree of relation between the text and the concept, meaning the relative probability of the concept presence in the text or that the text holds the concept with a specific degree of importance. The decision concerning if a concept is present or not depends then on the threshold used to cut off undesirable degrees. This threshold is dependent on the domain ontology used in the system and is previously set by experts after some initial evaluations.

After that, the text mining module passes the identified concepts to the recommender module, which looks in the digital library for items to suggest. The concepts identified in the messages represent users' interests and will be used to generate the recommendations.

The digital library is a repository of information sources, like electronic documents, links to Web page and bibliographic references, especially created for the recommendation system. The inclusion (upload) of items in the digital library is responsibility of authorized people and can be made offline in a specific module. The classification of the electronic documents is made automatically by software tools, using the same text mining method used in the text mining module and the same domain ontology. A difference is that a document may be related to more than one concept. A threshold is used to determine which concepts can be related to one document. Thus, the relation between concepts and documents in the digital library is many-to-many. The relationship degree is also stored.

The profile base contains identification of authorized users. Besides administrative data like name, institution, department, e-mail, and so forth, the profile base also stores the interest areas of each person, as well an associated degree, informing the user's knowledge level on the subject or how much is his/her competence in the area. The interest areas must exist in the ontology. The profile base also records the items accessed (uploaded, added, read, or downloaded) by the user or recommended to him/her. This information is useful to avoid recommending known items.

The recommender module suggests to the users that participate in the chat items from the digital library, according to the theme being discussed. Recommendations are particular of each user; thus, each user receives a different list of suggestions in the screen.

THE ENGINEERING PROCESS FOR CONSTRUCTING A DOMAIN ONTOLOGY

Noy and McGuinnes (2003) propose a methodology (set of ordered steps) for constructing ontologies:

- **Step 1—Determine the domain and the scope of the ontology:** To answer this question, ontology engineers must elicit the goal of the ontology, the intended users and the information that will be stored in the ontology.
- **Step 2—Consider the reuse of existing ontologies:** Engineers must verify if there are other ontologies for the same domain. There are many ontologies available in electronic formats that can be adapted. For example, there libraries of ontologies such as Ontolingua (www.ksl.stanford.edu/software/ontolingua) and the DAML ontology library (www.daml.org/ontologies). The

reuse minimizes the time and effort in the construction process and furthermore it gives quality to the final result since the existing ontologies must have been already tested.

- **Step 3—Identify the important terms of the ontology:** And identify concepts that these terms represent. Elements that compose the ontology must be specified as concepts and will be the base for the construction of the ontology.

- **Step 4—Define the classes and the hierarchy of classes:** This step may be performed following one of the approaches (Uschold & Gruninger, 1996):
    - **Top-down:** Starts with the definition of more general concepts and follows dividing these concepts in more specific ones.
    - **Bottom-up:** Starts with the definition of more specific classes and then groups classes to compose more general concepts.
    - **Hybrid:** A combination of the two approaches above; starts with the definition of the more important concepts; after that, general concepts are composed from grouping some of those and more specific concepts are created of the initial ones.

- **Step 5—Define the characteristics of the classes:** Classes alone are not very useful. It is necessary to find the characteristics of the classes. Characteristics may be terms identified in the Step 3 and not yet classified in one concept or may be associations between classes.

- **Step 6—Define the attributes of the characteristics:** This step must define attributes such as cardinality, type, domain, and so forth, to each characteristic defined early.

- **Step 7—Create instances:** The last step is to populate the ontology with instances for each class, including their attributes.

CHALLENGES FOR CONSTRUCTING A DOMAIN ONTOLOGY

The process of constructing an ontology consumes a lot of time and effort. One of the challenges for researchers is to develop tools to help this process, especially for minimizing the need for human work. Some works have investigated ways to construct ontologies in semiautomatic ways. The majority of them analyze text to discover concepts and relations for an ontology (as for example Kietz et al., 2000). Furthermore, the terms (words and expressions) are used as characteristics of the concepts.

For example, Saias (2003) enriches an initial ontology, developed by experts, with information extracted from texts selected about the domain. Syntactic information is used to discover classes (subjects, verbs, and complements in a sentence) and to infer relations among classes (syntactic relations).

Alani et al., (2002) complement an existing ontology with instances and new classes extracted from texts by syntactic analysis. New terms are added as characteristics of the classes by analyzing synonyms in the WordNet.

Lame (2003) also uses syntactic analysis to discover classes of the ontology. However, all terms are considered as potential classes, including adjectives and adverbs. Different terms are associated to the same class by analyzing the similarity between them, using statistical methods.

This chapter presents an engineering process for constructing domain ontologies. The focus of this work is on Steps 5 and 6 of the general methodology proposed by Noy and McGuinnes (2003). The goal is to find terms that represent classes/concepts of the ontology and the degree of importance of each term.

The process is based on statistics and probabilities; it does not use natural language processing, as syntactic or morphological analysis. The idea is to have a simple process for constructing ontologies, based on analysis of textual documents. The work compares a manual process (with help of software tools based on statistics of words) against a semiautomatic process (also based on statistics of words). In both cases, we consider that part of the ontology is previously created, that is, the concepts are defined the hierarchy of concepts is established.

The comparison is on defining terms to represent each concept and the weights of each term. In the manual process, humans considered experts in the domain define the terms and weights with help of software tools. In the semiautomatic process, terms and weights are defined under a supervised learning process, where experts select textual documents and a software selects terms and weights using the TFIDF method.

EXPERIMENTS AND EVALUATIONS

Some experiments were carried out to investigate different approaches to construct domain ontologies. The idea is to compare these approaches to determine good practices in this process.

Figure 2. Part of the hierarchy of concepts for all ontologies

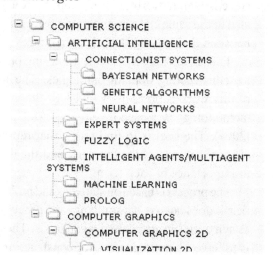

All the ontologies constructed for the experiments have the same internal structure: a hierarchy of concepts. Each concept is represented by a node in the hierarchy. The root (main) node is the own domain ontology. Nodes can have one or many child-nodes and only one parent node. Each concept has associated to it a list of terms and their respective weights. Weights are used to state the relative importance or the probability of the term for identifying the concept in a text. The relation between concepts and terms is many-to-many, that is, a term may be present in more than one concept and a concept may be described by many terms.

The hierarchy of concepts was constructed manually by experts for all approaches, that is, all ontologies constructed for the experiments have the same hierarchy of concepts. The difference relies on the way how the list of terms and weights were created in each approach.

The ontology was created for the domain of computer science, following the classification of computer science areas proposed by the ACM (Association for Computing Machinery). However, experts refined the hierarchy adding new child/leaf nodes for some concepts. The generated ontology has a total of 57 concepts and is different from the original ACM classification. Figure 2 shows part of the hierarchy of concepts constructed for the experiments.

The main investigation was to compare the intervention of humans in the elaboration of the lists of terms and weights for each concept and the use of software tools for automatically extracting terms and weights. Two ontologies were constructed under different conditions:

a. The first ontology (*manually constructed*) was elaborated by humans, considered experts in subareas of computer science (subareas correspond to concepts in the ontology).

b. The second ontology (*semiautomatic*) was constructed under a supervised learning process.

The Engineering Process for the Manually Constructed Ontology

For each concept present in the ontology, a list of terms and corresponding weights was created by experts in the concept. The elaboration of each list was performed independently of other concepts or lists.

The first step was to select documents about the considered concept (made by the own experts). For each concept, a set of 100 textual documents was selected from the Citeseer digital library (www.researchindex.org). Then a software tool was used to extract a centroid of the documents. A centroid is a list of the terms more frequent in the documents, disregarding stopwords. The weight associated to each term in the list was calculated as the average among the relative frequencies of the term in each document. The relative frequency of a term inside a document is the number of times that the term appears in the document divided by the total number of terms in that document.

After this step, experts refined the list of terms and weights, analyzing individually each list and using a software tool that identifies subjects in texts using a probabilistic method comparing documents and the ontology. Analyzing these results, experts could include new terms (for example, synonyms), exclude terms (for example, polysemic words or general terms that do not help in identifying a concept) or adjust the weight of the terms. Experts reduced the weight of the terms that appear in more than one concept or increased the weight of important terms.

Experts also analyzed terms that appeared in both parent and child concepts: the idea was to verify if the term was better suited for one of the concepts or if the weights should be adjusted according to some human criteria. For example, if the term was specific of the child concept, that is, it was a narrow term; the weight in the child concept should be greater than in the parent concept. Otherwise, if the term is more general but also can be used to determine a specific concept, the weight should be greater in the parent concept than in the child one.

The Engineering Process for the Semiautomatic Constructed Ontology

For each concept present in the ontology, a list of terms and corresponding weights was created by a software tool using the supervised learning approach (machine learning method). The TFIDF method—*term frequency and inverse document frequency* (Salton & McGill, 1983) was used to elaborate each list of terms and weights analyzing documents selected by experts.

The method used as learning examples the same sets of documents per concept used in the first ontology, that is, a set of 100 textual documents selected for each concept, extracted by experts from the Citeseer digital library (www. researchindex.org).

The TFIDF method increases the weight of terms that frequently appear in documents of the set and decreases the weight of terms that appear in more than one concept set. There was no human intervention after this step.

As we can see in Table 1, the TFIDF method resulted in eight times more terms than the manual process. The reason is that humans do not have patience to set and include a great volume of terms, thus limiting the number of terms to be used in each concept.

THE NORMALIZATION STEP

A special approach was investigated in the experiments. Since term weights in the different concepts could range in different scales, a normalization step was done in the two ontologies (manual and semiautomatic).

The reason is that some concepts could be identified more often than others if the weights of their terms were greater than the values in other concepts. As we can see in the Table 1, the greatest weight in the manually constructed ontology is quite different from the greatest weight in the semiautomatic ontology and so on with the smallest weights. In the normalization process, the limits were defined arbitrarily as: superior limit = 0.01; inferior limit = 0.000001. These values were chosen because the text mining method should not generate a degree greater than one. The inferior limit was defined to make a large range between the limits. All the weights in the original ontologies were transposed to the new scale preserving the proportion and the relations between a certain value and both superior and inferior limits.

EVALUATION OF THE ONTOLOGIES FOR INDEXING DOCUMENTS

Four ontologies were evaluated to compare the approaches for constructing ontologies. These four ontologies were described early and their

characteristics are presented in the Table 1. Ontologies were evaluated for finding concepts inside textual documents, using a Bayesian classification method. Thirty documents were selected from Citeseer (www.researchindex.org).

In a first round, thresholds were used to filter concepts to be considered and to eliminate weak concepts. Precision and recall of each ontology for identifying concepts was calculated. Experts judged each concept identified for each document and listed the concepts that should have been identified but were not. The precision (Pr) for each document was calculated as the number of concepts correctly identified divided by the total number of concepts identified. Recall (Rc) was evaluated as the number of concepts correctly identified divided by the number of concepts that should be identified. Precision and recall for each ontology were calculated as the average for all documents. F-measure (F-m) was used to determine the best performance considering both precision (Pr) and recall (Rc) and it was calculated as { (2 * Precision * Recall) / (Precision + Recall) } according to (Lewis, 1991). Different thresholds

Table 1. Some characteristics of each ontology

	Total of terms in the ontology	Greatest weight	Smallest weight
Manually constructed	3,689	0.033987	0.000001
Manually constructed with normalization	3,689	0.010000	0.000001
Semiautomatic	27,154	0.314645	0.000140
Semiautomatic with normalization	27,154	0.010000	0.000001

Table 2. Evaluation of each ontology over textual documents (first round)

Thresholds	0.0001	0.0001	0.0001	0.00005	0.00005	0.00005	0.00001	0.00001	0.00001
Ontologies	Pr	Rc	F-m	Pr	Rc	F-m	Pr	Rc	F-m
Manually constructed	100.0%	20.0%	33.3%	60.1%	40.7%	48.5%	33.4%	73.2%	45.9%
Manually constructed with normalization	47.4%	38.5%	42.5%	43.2%	49.8%	46.3%	30.2%	79.8%	43.8%
Semiautomatic	12.4%	25.1%	16.6%	10.1%	43.9%	16.5%	21.2%	77.3%	33.3%
Semiautomatic with normalization	47.5%	28.2%	35.4%	43.2%	65.3%	52.0%	20.2%	94.7%	33.3%

were tested assuming that a certain threshold can favor one ontology. Table 2 shows the results of the first round.

In a second round, the precision was calculated using the top N concepts identified in each document. In this case, we are assuming that there is not a best threshold or that it is not easy to determine the best one. In addition, it is possible to occur that one ontology has one best threshold and other ontology has an other best threshold. Thus, we evaluated the performance of the ontologies using the top N concepts in the ranking of concepts identified in the documents. The ranking is the ordered presentation of the concepts, from top to down, initiating with the concept with highest degree. We considered three kinds of rankings: top 3, top 5 and top 10. Table 3 shows the results of the second round.

Analyzing the results of the first round (Table 2), we can see that the best performance is of the *semiautomatic with normalization* ontology (at the threshold 0.00005, with 52% of F-measure).

If considering the performances in each threshold, we found that: (a) the *manually constructed* ontology achieves the best performance with the least threshold (0.00001) with 45.9% of F-measure, (b) the *semiautomatic with normalization* ontology wins at the intermediary threshold (0.00005) with 52% of F-measure and (c) the *manually constructed with normalization* ontology obtains the best F-measure (42.5%) in the highest threshold (0.0001). One conclusion is that we can not determine the best way to construct ontologies when using thresholds. In the same sense, we can not determine if there is a best threshold, maybe because each ontology may have its best threshold.

One interesting finding is that the best threshold in all ontologies was the intermediary one (0.00005), maybe because this threshold can equilibrate measures of precision and recall; has the highest threshold favors precision but loses recall and vice-versa for the smallest threshold.

Table 3. Evaluation of each ontology over textual documents (second round)

Top N	Top 3	Top 3	Top 3	Top 5	Top 5	Top 5	Top 10	Top 10	Top 10
Ontologies	Pr	Rc	F-m	Pr	Rc	F-m	Pr	Rc	F-m
Manually constructed	59.5%	47.8%	53.0%	47.1%	61.6%	53.4%	33.1%	81.1%	47.0%
Manually constructed with normalization	61.9%	37.9%	47.0%	43.4%	47.8%	45.5%	29.3%	80.5%	42.9%
Semiautomatic	33.3%	4.3%	7.6%	21.9%	8.9%	12.7%	13.9%	17.8%	15.6%
Semiautomatic with normalization	50.6%	22.3%	30.9%	40.0%	27.8%	32.8%	25.1%	47.3%	32.8%

Table 4. Average number of concepts identified in the first round

	0.0001	0.00005	0.00001
Manually constructed	1	1.5	8.3
Manually constructed with normalization	1.7	4.6	21.7
Semiautomatic	20.4	29.7	40.9
Semiautomatic with normalization	11.4	24.3	39.9

Table 4 presents the average number of concepts identified in the texts of the first round, by threshold. This table makes clear that thresholds may cause problems in evaluations. We can see that the same threshold range may bring a small number of concepts in some cases (*manually constructed* ontologies) and an excessive number of concepts in other cases (*semiautomatic* ontologies). Future work will try to investigate the use of different thresholds for different ontologies.

Analyzing the results of the second round (Table 3), we can see that the best performance for F-measure in all top N is due to the *manually constructed* ontology.

An interesting finding is that normalization improved the performance of the *semiautomatic* ontology in the three top N evaluations but reduced the values of F-measure of the *manually constructed* ontology in the three top N.

Analyzing the performance of the normalization step, we have the following:

- **Manual (thresholds):** Without normalization 2 × 1 with normalization.
- **Manual (top N):** Without normalization 3 × 0 with normalization.
- **Semiautomatic (thresholds):** Without normalization 0 × 2 with normalization (1 tie).
- **Semiautomatic (top N):** Without normalization 0 × 3 with normalization.

The final conclusion about the normalization step is that normalization should not be used in the manually constructed ontologies but it is useful in ontologies created by semiautomatic processes.

Comparing manually constructed ontologies to semiautomtic ones, we can see the following:

- **Without normalization (thresholds):** Manual 3 × 0 semiautomatic.
- **Without normalization (top N):** Manual 3 × 0 semiautomatic.

- **With normalization (thresholds):** Manual 2 × 1 semiautomatic.
- **With normalization (top N):** Manual 3 × 0 semiautomatic.

These results lead us to conclude that manually constructed ontologies are better than semiautomatic ones, at least when using the methods and steps described in this paper (and used in the experiments).

The best combination (*manually constructed* ontology without normalization) wins in four of the six evaluations (three with thresholds and three with top N) and its best performance in thresholds (48.5%) is only 9.3% minor than the best one (52%), while in top N this ontology achieves the best performance.

One interesting observation is that the *manually constructed ontology with normalization* does not achieve the best performance in none of the evaluations in both rounds. One reason may be that experts, when creating the term list for each concept, adjust the weights in a way that normalizes the scales for all concepts.

Analyzing the overall performances, we can say that the best one (53.4% of F-measure) is still far from the desired one. Future works must evaluate a better combination of human intervention and automated tools.

EVALUATIONS OF THE ONTOLOGIES ON CHAT MESSAGES

We carried out a final evaluation of the ontologies using them to identify concepts in chat messages. A discussion session, which occurred in a private chat of the recommender system, was used as a sample for this evaluation. Messages with more than two words were individually extracted from the session, resulting in 165 messages to be used in this experiment. Experts identified the correct concepts that should be identified. Again, precision, recall, and F-measure were use in the comparison. The evaluations were done using only the top N concepts identified by each ontology. Table 5 presents the results of this final round.

We can see that the *manually constructed* ontology was again the best one in all top N evaluations. The best performance of 67% was greater than the best performance among all ontologies on textual documents using thresholds (52%) and with top N concepts (53.4%).

Again, normalization was not useful with *manually constructed* ontologies and improves performance of the *semiautomatic* ontologies. And the *manually constructed* ontology wins the *semiautomatic* with and without normalization.

CONCLUDING REMARKS

This chapter presented an investigation on the construction of domain ontologies for content-based recommender systems. The work is focused on the step for defining characteristics for concepts present in a previous ontology. The goal was to compare manually constructed ontologies to semiautomatic constructed ontologies in a specific task for classifying texts (identifying themes in texts).

Experiments were carried out on textual documents and on textual messages of a chat. A normalization step was also investigated to minimize limits problems in term weights; the goal was to determine if normalization improves the ontology quality for identifying themes in texts. Precision, recall, and F-measure were used to compare the performances in all experiments.

The conclusion is that manually constructed ontologies achieve better results for identifying concepts in texts than semiautomatic ones, at least when using the methods and steps described in this chapter (and used in the experiments). Software tools are useful to help in identifying terms that can represent concepts in an ontology, but the final decision must be responsibility of humans. Furthermore, even with a smaller set of terms, the manually constructed ontologies achieved better performance than semiautomatic ones. Therefore, the hint is to use human interference in the process to get a more concise set of properties (minimizing processing efforts and resources) with a grant of superior quality.

Regarding the normalization step, we noted that normalization should not be used in the manually constructed ontologies, but it is useful in ontologies created by semiautomatic processes. The reason is that humans tend to normalize term weights (even intuitively) when creating the ontology.

The chapter showed that is feasible to use ontologies to mine textual messages in a chat in order to identify the content of the discussion. The result of this discovery process can be used by recommender systems suggest more precise items to users.

Table 5. Evaluation of each ontology on chat messages

Top N			Top 3				Top 5			Top 10	
Ontologies	Pr	Rc	F-m	Pr	Rc	F-m	Pr	Rc	F-m	Pr	Rc	F-m
Manually constructed	56.6%	81.9%	67.0%	46.6%	92.0%	61.9%	35.1%	97.1%	51.6%
Manually constructed with normalization	53.3%	76.4%	62.8%	41.1%	80.1%	54.4%	33.6%	84.0%	48.0%
Semiautomatic	18.5%	15.4%	16.8%	13.3%	19.0%	15.6%	7.2%	31.5%	11.8%
Semiautomatic with normalization	38.6%	64.2%	48.2%	22.1%	65.4%	33.0%	14.2%	79.1%	24.1%

FUTURE TRENDS

The chapter showed that semiautomatic construction of domain ontologies is feasible. However, the part that can be automated is the construction of the term list for each concept, under a supervised learning process, where experts select good documents to be used by the software tool.

The challenge is to create methods able to automatically identify the concepts and the relations between them (for example, the hierarchy). One direction of the researches is the use of clustering methods that automatically groups textual documents. The goal of the clustering process is to allocate in a same group (cluster) those documents with similar content and allocate in different clusters documents that are not similar. For more details about clustering, see (Jain et al., 1999).

We can assume that each cluster represents a different concept, since the documents inside the cluster are grouped for having similar content or because they are about the same subject. In this sense, after the clustering process, we can identify the term list analyzing the content of the documents inside the cluster (as in a supervised learning process). The problem is to determine the name of the concept.

Furthermore, it is possible to use a divisive clustering algorithm that results in a hierarchy of clusters, from one cluster in the top (with all elements) to the bottom level where there are many clusters as elements (each cluster with only one element). This hierarchical schema may be used as the hierarchy of concepts.

Another approach using clustering is to group not documents but words, in a way similar to latent semantic indexing (Deerwester et al., 1990). In this case, the clustering algorithm is used on data about similarities between words. Each resulting cluster may be considered a concept in the ontology and the respective set of words inside the cluster composes the characteristics of the concept (the term list and the weights).

ACKNOWLEDGMENT

This research is partially supported by CNPq, an entity of the Brazilian government for scientific and technological development (Project DIGITEX - Editoração, Indexação e Busca em Bibliotecas, grant number 550845/2005-4), and FAPERGS, Foundation for Supporting Research in Rio Grande do Sul state (Project Rec-Semântica - Plataforma de Recomendação e Consulta na Web Semântica Evolutiva, grant number 0408933).

FUTURE RESEARCH DIRECTIONS

Constructing ontologies is a challenging task and so much must yet to be done. One interesting direction is the use of computational intelligence to minimize human effort in this process. Techniques and tools from expert systems and knowledge acquisition areas can accelerate some parts of the process. Machine learning can help engineers to find initial structures and/or to complete the structures.

In special, the use of machine learning techniques over textual documents is a promising field. Organizations have lots of texts, but this kind of document has unstructured information. The acquisition of information from texts is still a challenge, even with text mining advances and the evolution in information retrieval techniques. Ontologies can support in acquiring information from texts but they can also benefit from this process. Words carry meaning and represent the real world; by analyzing words and their semantics, we can observe how people describe the world and thus how the world is composed or structured. For this reason, we must approximate our research to those concerning computational linguistics and knowledge representation.

REFERENCES

Alani, H., Kim, S., Millard, D.E., Weal, M.J., Hall, W., Lewis, P.H., et al. (2002). *Automatic ontology-based knowledge extraction and tailored biography generation from the Web*. Technical Report 02-049.

Burke, R. (2002). Hybrid recommender systems: Survey and experiments. *User Modeling and User-Adapted Interaction, 12*(4), 331-370.

Deerwester, S., et al. (1990). Indexing by latent semantic analysis. *Journal of the Society for Information Science, 41*(6).

Gauch, S., Chaffee, J., & Pretschner, A. (2003). Ontology-based personalized search and browsing. *Web Intelligence and Agent System, 1*(3-4), 219-234.

Guarino, N. (1998). Formal ontology and information systems. In *International Conference on Formal Ontologies in Information Systems FOIS'98*, Trento, Italy (pp. 3-15).

Jain, A.K., Murty, M.N., & Flynn, P.J. (1999). Data clustering: a review. *ACM Computing Surveys, 31*(3), 264-323.

Kietz, J.U., Maedche, A., & Volz, R. (2000). A method for semiautomatic ontology acquisition from a corporate intranet. In *Proceedings of EKAW-2000 Workshop Ontologies and Text*. Lecture Notes in Artificial Intelligence (LNAI). France: Springer-Verlag.

Labrou, Y., & Finin, T. (1999). Yahoo! as an ontology: Using Yahoo! categories to describe documents. In *8th International Conference on Knowledge and Information Management (CIKM-99* (pp.180-187). Kansas City, MO.

Lame, G. (2003). Using text analysis techniques to identify legal ontologies components. In *Workshop on Legal Ontologies of the International Conference on Artificial Intelligence and Law*.

Lewis, D.D. (1991). Evaluating text categorization. In *Proceedings of the Speech and Natural Language Workshop* (pp. 312-318).

Loh, S., Wives, L.K., & Oliveira, J.P.M. (2000). Concept-based knowledge discovery in texts extracted from the web. *ACM SIGKDD Explorations, 2*(1), 29-39.

Middleton, S.E., Shadbolt, N.R. & Roure, D.C.D. (2003). Capturing interest through inference and visualization: Ontological user profiling in recommender systems. In *International Conference on Knowledge Capture KCAP'03*, (pp. 62-69). New York: ACM Press.

Noy, F.N., & McGuinnes, D.L. (2003). *Ontology development 101: A guide to create your first ontology*. Retrieved 2003 from http://ksl.stanford.edu/people/dlm/papers/ontology-tutorial-noy-mcguinnes.doc

Saias, J. (2003). Uma metodologia para a construção automática de ontologias e a sua aplicação em sistemas de recuperação de informação (*A methodology for the automatic construction of ontologies and applications in information retrieval systems*). PhD thesis. University of Évora, Portugal (in Portuguese).

Salton, G., & McGill, M. (1983). *Introduction to modern information retrieval*. McGraw-Hill.

Sowa, J.F. (2000). *Knowledge representation: logical, philosophical, and computational foundations*. Pacific Grove, CA: Brooks/Cole Publishing.

Terveen, L., & Hill, W. (2001). Beyond recommender systems: helping people help each other. In J. Carroll (Ed.), *Human computer interaction in the new millennium*. Addison-Wesley.

Uschold, M., & Gruninger, M. (1996). Ontologies: Principles, methods and applications. *Knowledge Engineering Review, 11*(2).

ADDITIONAL READING

Baeza-Yates, R., & Ribeiro-Neto, B. (1999). *Modern information retrieval.* Harlow: ACM Press.

Balabanovic, M., & Shoham, Y. (1997). Fab: Content-based, collaborative recommendation. *Communications of the ACM, 40*(3), 66-72.

Chen, Z. (1993). Let documents talk to each other: A computer model for connection of short documents. *Journal of Documentation, 49*(1), 44-54.

Chen, H. (1994). The vocabulary problem in collaboration. *Computer, 27*(5), 2-10.

Chen, H., et al. (1994). Automatic concept classification of text from electronic meetings. *Communications of the ACM, 37*(10), 56-73.

Cowie, J., & Lehnert, W. (1996). Information extraction. *Communications of the ACM, 39*(1), 80-91.

Davies, R. (1989). The creation of new knowledge by information retrieval and classification. *Journal of Documentation, 45*(4), 273-301.

Resnick, P., & Varian, H. (1997). Recommender Systems. *Communications of the ACM, 40,* 56-58.

Sparck-Jones, K., & Willet, P. (Eds.). (1997). *Readings in information retrieval.* San Francisco: Morgan Kaufmann.

Swanson, D.R., & Smalheiser, N. R. (1997). An interactive system for finding complementary literatures: A stimulus to scientific discovery. *Artificial Intelligence, 91*(2), 183-203.

Tan, A-H. (1999). Text mining: The state of the art and the challenges. In *Pacific-Asia Workshop on Knowledge Discovery from Advanced Databases,* Beijing (LNCS v.1574, pp. 65-70). Springer-Verlag.

Willet, P. (1988). Recent trends in hierarchic document clustering: A critical review. *Information Processing and Management, 24*(5), 577-597.

Section III
Frameworks

Chapter IX
Enhancing the Process of Knowledge Discovery in Geographic Databases Using Geo-Ontologies

Vania Bogorny
Universidade Federal do Rio Grande do Sul (UFRGS), Brazil, and Transnational University of Limburg, Belgium

Paulo Martins Engel
Universidade Federal do Rio Grande do Sul (UFRGS), Brazil

Luis Otavio Alavares
Universidade Federal do Rio Grande do Sul (UFRGS), Brazil

ABSTRACT

This chapter introduces the problem of mining frequent geographic patterns and spatial association rules from geographic databases. In the geographic domain most discovered patterns are trivial, non-novel, and noninteresting, which simply represent natural geographic associations intrinsic to geographic data. A large amount of natural geographic associations are explicitly represented in geographic database schemas and geo-ontologies, which have not been used so far in frequent geographic pattern mining. Therefore, this chapter presents a novel approach to extract patterns from geographic databases using geo-ontologies as prior knowledge. The main goal of this chapter is to show how the large amount of knowledge represented in geo-ontologies can be used to avoid the extraction of patterns that are previously known as noninteresting.

INTRODUCTION

Knowledge discovery in databases (KDD) is the nontrivial process of identifying valid, novel, potentially useful and ultimately understandable patterns from data (Fayyad et al., 1996). In frequent pattern mining (FPM), which is the essential role in mining associations, one of the main problems is the large amount of generated patterns and rules. In geographic databases this problem increases significantly because most discovered patterns include well-known natural associations intrinsic to geographic data. While in transactional databases items are supposed to be independent from each other (e.g.,, milk, cereal, bread), independently of their meaning, in geographic databases a large amount of data are semantically dependent (e.g., island *within* water).

Geographic dependences are semantic constraints that must hold in geographic databases (GDB) to warrant the consistency of the data (e.g.,, island must be completely located inside a water body). They are part of the concept of geographic data and are explicitly represented in geo-ontologies. Without considering semantics of geographic data, the same geographic dependences explicitly represented in geo-ontologies and geographic database schemas are unnecessarily extracted by association rule mining algorithms and presented to the user.

Geographic dependences produce two main problems in the process of mining spatial association rules:

a. **Data preprocessing:** A large computational time is required to preprocess GDB to extract spatial relationships (e.g., *intersection* between districts and water bodies). The spatial join (Cartesian product) operation, required to extract spatial relationships, is the most expensive operation in databases and the processing bottleneck of spatial data analysis and knowledge discovery.

b. **Frequent pattern and association rule generation:** A large number of patterns and spatial association rules without novel, useful, and interesting knowledge is generated (e.g., *is_a(Island)* → *within (Water)*).

Aiming to improve geographic data preprocessing and eliminate well-known geographic dependences in geographic FPM in order to generate more interesting spatial association rules (SAR), this chapter presents a unified framework for FPM considering the semantics of geographic data, using geo-ontologies. While dozens of spatial and nonspatial FPM algorithms define syntactic constraints and different thresholds to reduce the number of patterns and association rules, we consider **semantic knowledge constraints** (Bogorny et al., 2005b), and eliminate the exact sets of geographic objects that produce well-known patterns (Bogorny et al., 2006b, 2006c).

The main objective of this chapter is to show the important role that ontologies can play in the knowledge discovery process using the FPM technique. The focus addresses the use of semantic knowledge stored in ontologies to reduce uninteresting patterns, but not to create ontologies for data mining.

The remainder of the chapter is organized as follows: Section 2 presents some background concepts about geographic data, spatial relationships, spatial integrity constraints, and geo-ontologies. Section 3 introduces the concepts of frequent patterns and spatial association rules, the problem generated by geographic dependences in both data preprocessing and spatial association rule mining, and what has been done so far to alleviate this problem. Section 4 presents a framework to improve geographic data preprocessing and spatial association rule mining using geo-ontologies. Experiments are presented to show the significant reduction in the number of frequent patterns and association rules. Section 5 presents future trends and Section 6 concludes the chapter.

BACKGROUND

Geographic data are real world entities, also called spatial features, which have a location on Earth's surface (Open GIS Consortium, 1999a). Spatial features (e.g., Brazil, Argentina) belong to a feature type (e.g., country), and have both nonspatial attributes (e.g., name, population) and spatial attributes (geographic coordinates *x,y*). The latter normally represent points, lines, polygons, or complex geometries.

In geographic databases, every different feature type is normally stored in a different database relation, since most geographic databases follow the relational approach (Shekhar & Chawla, 2003). Figure 1 shows an example of how geographic data can be stored in relational databases. There is a different relation for every different geographic object type (Shekhar & Chawla, 2003) street, water resource, and gas station, which can also be called as *spatial layers.*

The spatial attributes of geographic object types, represented by *shape* in Figure 1, have implicitly encoded spatial relationships (e.g., close, far, contains, intersects). Because of these relationships, real world entities can affect the behavior of other features in the neighborhood. This makes spatial relationships the main characteristic of geographic data to be considered for data mining, knowledge discovery (Ester et al., 2000; Lu et al., 1993), and the main characteristic, which separates spatial data mining from nonspatial data mining.

The process of extracting spatial relationships brings together many interesting and uninteresting spatial associations. Figure 2 shows an example where gas stations and industrial residues repositories may have any type of spatial relationship with water resources. Considering, for example, that water analysis showed high chemical pollution, the different spatial relationships among water resources, gas stations, and industrial residues repositories will be interesting for knowledge discovery. Notice in Figure 2 that there is NO standard pattern among the data.

Figure 3 shows two examples of spatial relationships that represent well-known geographic domain dependences. In Figure 3 (left), viaducts intersect streets, and bridges intersect both water resources and streets, since both bridges and viaducts have the semantics of connecting streets. In Figure 3 (right), gas stations intersect

Figure 1. Example of geographic data storage in relational databases

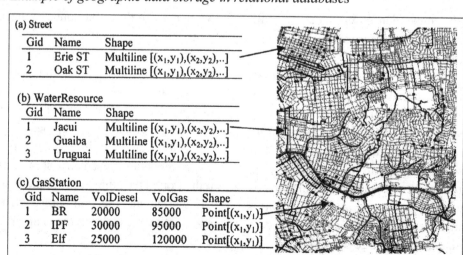

Figure 2. Examples of implicit spatial relationships

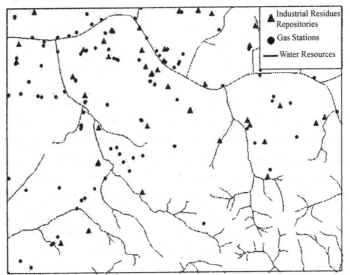

Figure 3. Examples of spatial relationships that produce well known geographic patterns in spatial data mining

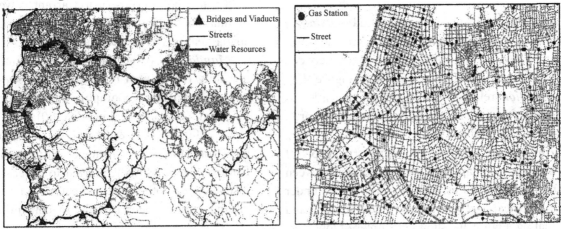

streets because they do only exist in areas with streets access.

The main difference between the examples shown in Figure 2 and Figure 3 is that in the former spatial relationships may hold or not, and may conduce to more interesting patterns. In the latter, under rare exceptions or some geographic location inconsistency, the spatial relationships hold for practical purposes in a 100% of the cases,

and will produce well known geographic domain patterns in the discovery process. If considered in association rule mining, well known spatial relationships will generate high confidence rules such as $is\_a(Viaduct) \rightarrow intersect(Street)(99\%)$ or $is\_a(GasStation) \rightarrow intersect(Street)(100\%)$. Although users might be interested in high confidence rules, not all strong **rules** necessarily hold considerable information. Moreover, the mixed presentation of thousands of interesting and uninteresting rules can discourage users from interpreting them in order to find novel and unexpected knowledge (Appice et al., 2005).

Patterns in the discovery process should be considered interesting when they represent *unknown* strong regularities, rare exceptions, or when they help to distinguish different groups of data. In geographic databases, however, there are a large number of patterns intrinsic to the data, which represent strong regularities, but do not add novel and useful knowledge to the discovery. They are mandatory spatial relationships which represent spatial integrity constraints that must hold in order to warrant the consistency of geographic data.

Spatial Relationships and Spatial Integrity Constraints

Spatial relationships can be classified as *distance, direction,* and *topological. Distance* relationships are based on the Euclidean distance between two spatial features, as shown in Figure 4(a). *Direction* relationships deal with the order as spatial features are located in space such as north, south, east, and so forth, as shown in Figure 4(b). *Topological* relationships describe concepts of adjacency, containment, and intersection between two spatial features, and remain invariant under topological transformations such as rotating and scaling. Figure 4(c) shows examples of topologi-

cal relationships, which will be the focus in this chapter.

Binary topological relationships are mutually exclusive, and there are many approaches in the literature to formally define a set of topological relationships among points, lines, and polygons (Clementini et al., 1993; Egenhofer & Franzosa, 1995). The Open GIS Consortium (OGC) (Open GIS Consortium, 2001), which is an organization dedicated to develop standards for spatial operations and spatial data interchange to provide interoperability between Geographic Information Systems (GIS), defines a standard set of topological operations: *disjoint, overlaps, touches, contains, within, crosses,* and *equals.*

Topological relationships can be *mandatory, prohibited,* or *possible.* Mandatory and prohibited spatial relationships represent spatial integrity constraints (Cockcroft, 1997; Serviane et al., 2000), and their purpose is to warrant as well as maintain both the quality and the consistency of spatial features in geographic databases.

Mandatory spatial integrity constraints are normally represented by cardinalities *one-one* and *one-many* in geographic data conceptual modeling (Bogorny & Lochpe, 2001; Serviane et al., 2000; Shekhar & Chawla, 2003) in order to warrant that every instance of a geographic feature type is spatially related to at least one instance of another spatial feature type (e.g., "island within water body"). In data mining,

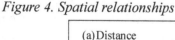

Figure 4. Spatial relationships

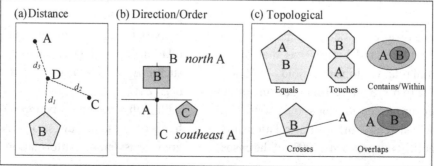

such constraints produce well-known patterns and high confidence rules because of the strong co-relation of the data.

While mandatory relationships must hold, *prohibited* relationships should not (e.g., "road cannot contain river").

Possible relationships, however, are usually not explicitly represented, since they can either exist or not (e.g., "roads cross water bodies," "counties contain factories"). *Possible* relationships may produce more interesting patterns, and are therefore the most relevant to find novel and useful knowledge in spatial data mining.

Mandatory constraints are well-known concepts to geographers and geographic database designers, and are normally explicitly represented in geographic database schemas (Bogorny et al.,

2006b, 2006c) and geo-ontologies (Bogorny et al., 2005b).

Geo-Ontologies and Spatial Integrity Constraints

Ontology is an explicit specification of a conceptualization (Gruber, 1993). More specifically ontology is a logic theory corresponding to the intentional meaning of a formal vocabulary, that is, an ontological commitment with a specific conceptualization of the world (Guarino, 1998). It is an agreement about the concepts meaning and structure for a specific domain. Each concept definition must be unique, clear, complete, and nonambiguous. The structure represents the properties of the concept, including a description, attributes, and relationships with other concepts.

Figure 5. Geo-ontology representation and OWL code

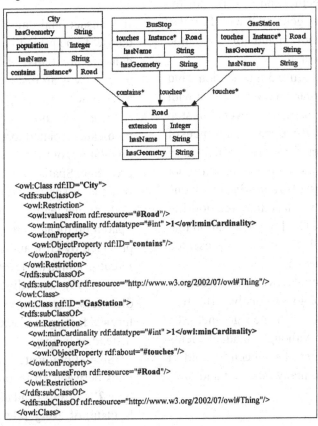

```
<owl:Class rdf:ID="City">
 <rdfs:subClassOf>
  <owl:Restriction>
   <owl:valuesFrom rdf:resource="#Road"/>
   <owl:minCardinality rdf:datatype="#int" >1</owl:minCardinality>
   <owl:onProperty>
    <owl:ObjectProperty rdf:ID="contains"/>
   </owl:onProperty>
  </owl:Restriction>
 </rdfs:subClassOf>
 <rdfs:subClassOf rdf:resource="http://www.w3.org/2002/07/owl#Thing"/>
</owl:Class>
<owl:Class rdf:ID="GasStation">
 <rdfs:subClassOf>
  <owl:Restriction>
   <owl:minCardinality rdf:datatype="#int" >1</owl:minCardinality>
   <owl:onProperty>
    <owl:ObjectProperty rdf:about="#touches"/>
   </owl:onProperty>
   <owl:valuesFrom rdf:resource="#Road"/>
  </owl:Restriction>
 </rdfs:subClassOf>
 <rdfs:subClassOf rdf:resource="http://www.w3.org/2002/07/owl#Thing"/>
</owl:Class>
```

Ontologies have been used recently in many and different fields in computer science, such as artificial intelligence, databases, conceptual modeling, semantics Web, and so forth. Therefore, a relevant number of ontologies has been proposed, and a number of models, languages, and tools was developed. Chaves et al. (2005a), besides defining a geo-ontology for administrative data for the country of Portugal, defines a metamodel, named GKB (geographic knowledge base), which is a starting point to define an ontology for geographic data.

In geo-ontologies, spatial integrity constraints are represented by properties of geographic data. They are specified as restriction properties given by a spatial relationship and both minimum and maximum cardinalities. For instance, a concept *island*, which is a piece of land surrounded by water, must have a mandatory *one-one* relationship with the concept *water*.

Figure 5 shows a small example of a geographic ontology with the specification of different topological relationships, generated with Protégé, in order to illustrate how mandatory semantic constraints are represented.

In the example in Figure 5, gas stations and bus stops must have a mandatory constraint with road because every gas station and every bus stop must topologically *touch* one or more instances of a road. Roads, however, do not necessarily have gas stations or bus stops, so their relationship is not represented. Cities must also *contain* at least one road, while roads have no mandatory relationship with city. Notice in the OWL representation that minimum cardinality 1 is explicitly represented and can be easily retrieved.

To evaluate the amount of well-known dependences in real geo-ontologies we analyzed the first geo-ontology of Portugal, named geo-net-pt01 (Chaves et al., 2005b). Although not all elements of the geographic domain have been defined in geo-net-pt01, there are many *one-one* and *one-many* dependences.

The repository of the geo-ontology stores three levels of information: geo-administrative, geo-physical, and network. The geo-administrative level stores administrative information about territorial division, and includes geographic feature types such as municipalities, streets, and so forth. The network level stores nonspatial data and relationships about the geo-administrative layer (e.g., population of a district). The geo-physical level stores feature types including continents, oceans, lakes, bays, water bodies, and so forth.

In geo-net-pt01, among 58 different spatial feature types, 55 *one-one* relationships were defined in the geo-administrative level.

The following section introduces the problem of mining geographic data with well-known dependences.

THE PROBLEM OF GEOGRAPHIC DEPENDENCES IN SPATIAL ASSOCIATION RULE MINING

In transactional data mining, every row in the dataset to be mined is usually a transaction and columns are items, while in spatial data mining, every row is an instance (e.g., Buenos Aires) of a reference object type (e.g., city), called *target feature type*, and columns are predicates. Every predicate is related to a nonspatial attribute (e.g., population) of the target feature type or a spatial predicate. Spatial predicate is a *relevant feature type* that is spatially related to specific instances of the target feature type (e.g., contains factory). Spatial predicates are extracted with operations provided by GIS, and can be represented at different granularity levels (Han & Fu, 1995; Lu, et al. 1993), according to the objective of the discovery. For example, chemical factory, metallurgical factory, and textile factory could be used instead of factory.

Spatial predicates are computed with spatial joins between all instances *t* of a target feature type *T* (e.g., city) and all instances *o* (e.g., Rio de la Plata) of every relevant feature type *O* (e.g., river) in a set of relevant feature types S (e.g., river, port, street, factory) that have any spatial relationship (e.g., touches, contains, close, far) with T. Being T a set of instances $T=\{t_1, t_2,...,t_n\}$, $S = \{ O_1, O_i,..., O_m\}$, and $O_i = \{ o_1, o_2,..., o_q\}$, the extraction of spatial predicates implies the comparison of every instance of T with every instance of O, for all $O \subset S$.

The spatial predicate computation is the first step for extracting association rules from geographic databases. An association rule consists of an implication of the form $X \rightarrow Y$, where X and Y are sets of items co-occurring in a given tuple (Agrawal, Imielinkski & Swami, 1993). *Spatial* association rules are defined in terms of spatial predicates, where at least one element in X or Y is a spatial predicate (Koperski, 1995). For example, *is_a(Slum)* ∧ *far_from(WaterNetwork)* → *disease=Hepatitis* is a spatial association rule.

We assume that $F= \{f_1, f_2, ...,f_k, ...,f_n\}$ is a set of nonspatial attributes (e.g., population) and spatial predicates (e.g., close_to(Water)) that characterize a reference feature type, and Ψ (dataset) is a set of instances of a reference feature type, where each instance is a row W such that $W \subseteq F$. There is exactly one tuple in the dataset to be mined for each instance of the reference feature type.

The support s of a predicate set X is the percentage of tuples in which the predicate set X occurs as a subset. The support of the rule $X \rightarrow Y$ is given as $s(X \cup Y)$.

The rule $X \rightarrow Y$ is valid in Ψ with confidence factor $0 \leq c \leq 1$, **if at least** c% of the instances in Ψ that satisfy X also satisfy Y. The notation $X \rightarrow Y(c)$ specifies that the rule $X \rightarrow Y$ has confidence factor of c. More precisely, the confidence factor is given as $s(X \cup Y)/s(X)$.

The general problem of mining *spatial* association rules can be decomposed in three main steps, where the first one is usually performed as a data preprocessing method:

a. **Extract spatial predicates:** A spatial predicate is a spatial relationship (e.g., distance, order, topological) between the reference feature type and a set of relevant feature types.

b. **Find all frequent patterns/predicates:** A set of predicates is a frequent pattern if its support is at least equal to a certain threshold, called minsup.

c. **Generate strong rules:** A rule is strong if it reaches minimum support and the confidence is at least equal to a certain threshold, called minconf.

Assertion 1 (Agrawal & Srikant, 1994): if a predicate set Z is a frequent pattern, then every subset of Z will also be frequent. If the set Z is infrequent, then every set that contains Z is infrequent too. All rules derived from Z satisfy the support constraint if Z satisfies the support constraints.

Well-known geographic dependences appear in the three steps of the spatial association rule mining process. In the first step (a) well-known geographic dependences may exist among T and any $O \subset S$. In the second (b) and third (c) steps, dependences exist among relevant feature types, that is, between pairs of $O \subset S$. In the following sections we describe the problem that such dependences generate in frequent geographic pattern mining and what has been done so far to reduce this problem.

Geographic Dependences Between the Target Feature Type and Relevant Feature Types

In data preprocessing, time and effort are required from the data mining user to extract spatial relationships and transform geographic data in a single table or single file, which is the input format required by most data mining algorithms. Even in multirelational data mining where geographic data are transformed to first-order logic, the process of extracting spatial relationships is required.

The problem of **which** spatial relationships should be considered for knowledge discovery has been addressed in earlier works. (Koperski & Han, 1995;Lu et al., 1993) presented a top-down progressive refinement method where spatial approximations are calculated in a first step, and in a second step, more precise spatial relationships are computed to the outcome of the first step. The method has been implemented in the module Geo-Associator of the GeoMiner system (Han, Koperski & Stefanvic, 1997), which is no longer available. Ester et al., (2000) proposed new operations such as graphs and paths to compute spatial neighborhoods. However, these operations are not implemented by most GIS, and to compute all relationships between all objects in the database in order to obtain the graphs and paths is computationally expensive for real databases. Appice et al., (2005) proposed an upgrade of Geo-Associator to first-order logic, and all spatial relationships are extracted. This process is computationally expensive and nontrivial in real databases. While the above approaches consider different spatial relationships and any geometric object type, a few approaches such as (Huang, Shekhar & Xiong, 2004; Yoo & Shekhar, 2006)

compute only distance relationships for point object types.

Table 1 shows an example of a spatial dataset at a high granularity level, where every row is a city and predicates refer to different geographic object types (port, water body, hospital, street, and factory) spatially related to city. Let us consider two geographic dependences: city and street, and port and water body, where the former is between the target feature type and a relevant feature type and the latter is among the two relevant feature types.

In the dataset shown in Table 1, the dependence between the target feature type city and the relevant feature type street is explicit, because every city has at least one street and the predicate **contains(Street)** has a 100% support. Predicates with 100% support appear in at least half of the total number of patterns and generate a large number of noninteresting association rules. For example, a rule such as **contains(factory)** $\rightarrow$ **contains(Street)** expresses that cities that contain factories do also contain streets. Although such a rule seems to be interesting, it can be considered obvious due the simple fact that **all** cities contain streets, having they factories, or not.

Table 1. Example of a preprocessed dataset in a high granularity level for mining frequent patterns and SAR

Tuple (city)	Spatial Predicates
1	contains(Port), contains(Hospital), contains(Street), contains(Factory), crosses(Water Body)
2	contains(Hospital), contains(Street), crosses(Water Body)
3	contains(Port), contains(Street), contains(Factory), crosses(Water Body)
4	contains(Port), contains(Hospital), contains(Street), crosses(Water Body)
5	contains(Port), contains(Hospital), contains(Street), contains(Factory), crosses(Water Body)
6	contains(Hospital), contains(Street), contains(Factory)

Table 2. Frequent patterns and rules with dependences

Min Sup %	Total FrequentSets/ Rules	Rules with Dependence / Rules without Dependence	FrequentSets with dependence / FrequentSets without dependence
20	31 / 180	130 / 50	16 / 15
50	25 / 96	72 / 24	13 / 12

Table 2 shows the result of a small experiment performed with Apriori (Agrawal & Srikant, 1994) over the dataset in Table 1. Considering 20% minimum support, 31 frequent sets and 180 rules were generated. Among the 31 frequent sets and the 180 rules, 16 frequent sets and 130 rules had the dependence **contains(Street)**. Notice that increasing minimum support to 50% does not warrant the elimination of the geographic dependence. Although the number of frequent sets is reduced to 25 and rules to 96, 13 frequent sets and 72 rules still have the dependence.

Geographic dependences besides generating a large number of well-known patterns and association rules, require unnecessary spatial joins. To illustrate the power that semantics may have in spatial join computation, let us consider a few examples, shown in Table 3. Without considering semantics, **all** topological relationships between two spatial feature types would be tested in order to verify which one holds. Considering semantics, the number of relationships to test reduces significantly. As shown in Table 3, the only topological relationship semantically consistent between gas

station and road should be **touches.** A city hall must be **within** a city, while a water body can be **disjoint, touch,** or **cross** a road.

Although the topological relationships shown in Table 3 are semantically possible, not all of them are interesting for knowledge discovery. So, if besides considering the semantics of spatial features we also consider spatial integrity constraints, it is possible to reduce still further the number of topological relationships and define which should be computed for knowledge discovery. Remembering that **mandatory** relationships produce well known patterns and that only **possible** relationships are interesting for knowledge discovery, Table 4 shows the topological relationships of the same objects in Table 3 that would be computed if semantics and integrity constraints were considered. The pairs gas station and road, bridge and water body, city hall and city, as well as treated water net and city have **mandatory** one-one or one-many constraints and no relationship is necessary for KDD.

Despite **mandatory** and **prohibited** constraints do not explicitly define the interesting spatial relationships to be extracted for knowledge

Table 3. Possible and mandatory topological relationships considering semantics of feature types

Topological Relationship / Semantic Combinations	Disjoint	Overlaps	Touches	Contains	Within	Crosses	Equals
Gas Station and Road			✓				
Bridge and Water Body						✓	
City Hall and City					✓		
Water Body and Road	✓		✓			✓	
Treated Water Net and City			✓		✓	✓	

Table 4. Possible topological relationships for knowledge discovery

Topological Relationship / Semantic Combinations	Disjoint	Overlaps	Touches	Contains	Within	Crosses	Equals
Gas Station and Road							
Bridge and Water Body							
City Hall and City							
Water Body and Road	✓		✓			✓	
Treated Water Net and City							

discovery, we are able to eliminate those which are either ***mandatory*** or ***prohibited,*** and specify those which are ***possible,*** as will be explained in Section 4.

Geographic Dependences Among Relevant Feature Types

To find ***frequent predicate sets*** and ***extract strong association rules,*** predicates are combined with each other for the different instances of the target feature type T, and not among T and O as explained in the previous section.

To illustrate the geographic dependence replication process in frequent geographic pattern mining, let us consider the frequent set generation introduced by (Agrawal & Srikant, 1994) for the Apriori algorithm. Apriori performs multiple passes over the dataset. In the first pass, the support of the individual elements is computed to determine k-predicate sets. In the subsequent passes, given k as the number of the current pass, the large sets L_{k-1} in the previous pass $(k-1)$ are grouped into sets C_k with k elements, which are called ***candidate sets***. The support of each candidate set is computed, and if it is equal or higher than minimum support, then this set is considered frequent/large. This process continues until the number of large sets is zero.

Geographic dependences appear the first time in frequent sets with 2 elements, where k=2. Table 5 shows the frequent sets extracted from the dataset in Table 1 with 50% minimum support, where k is the number of elements in the frequent sets. Notice that since the dependence has minimum support, that is, a frequent predicate set, this dependence is replicated to many frequent sets of size k>2 with predicates that reach minimum support, as shown in bold style in Table 5. Considering such a small example and high minimum support, one single geographic dependence participates in six frequent sets, which represents 30% of the frequent sets. Notice that the number of rules having a geographic dependence will be much larger than the frequent sets, mainly when the largest frequent set (with 4 elements) contains the dependence.

In Table 5, we can observe that the technique of generating ***closed frequent sets*** (Paskier et al., 1999; Zaki & Hsiao, 2002) would not eliminate geographic dependences, because both sets with 4 elements that contain the dependence are closed

Table 5. Large predicate sets with 50% minimum support

k	Frequent sets with support 50%
1	{contains(Port)}, {contains(Hospital)}, {contains(Street)}, {contains(Factory)}, {crosses(WaterBody)}
2	{contains(Port),contains(Hospital)}, {contains(Port),contains(Street)}, {contains(Port),contains(Factory)}, *{contains(Port),crosses(WaterBody)},* {contains(Hospital),contains(Street)}, {contains(Hospital),contains(Factory)}, {contains(Hospital),crosses(WaterBody)}, {contains(Street),contains(Factory)}, {contains(Street),crosses(WaterBody)}, {contains(Factory),crosses(WaterBody)}
3	{contains(Port),contains(Hospital),contains(Street)}, *{contains(Port),contains(Hospital),crosses(WaterBody)},* *{contains(Port),contains(Street),crosses(WaterBody)},* *{contains(Port),contains(Factory),crosses(WaterBody)},* {contains(Port),contains(Street),contains(Factory)}, {contains(Hospital),contains(Street),contains(Factory)} {contains(Hospital),contains(Street),crosses(WaterBody)}, {contains(Street),contains(Factory),crosses(WaterBody)}
4	*{contains(Port),contains(Hospital),contains(Street),crosses(WaterBody)}* *{contains(Port),contains(Street),contains(Factory),crosses(WaterBody)}*

frequent sets. The closed frequent set approach eliminates *redundant frequent sets*, but does not eliminate well known dependences if applied to the geographic domain.

In order to evaluate the amount of well-known rules generated with the dependence, let us observe Table 6, which shows a few examples of association rules generated with frequent predicate sets of size 2 {*Contains(Port),crosses(Water Body)*}, size 3 {*Contains(Port),contains(Hospital),cros ses(Water Body)*}, and size 4 {*Contains(Port), contains(Hospital), contains(Street),crosses(Water Body)*}. Rules 1 and 2 are generated from the set with two elements, and represent a single geographic dependence and its inverse. Rules 3, 4, 5, and 6 reproduce rules 1 and 2 with an additional element in the antecedent or the consequent of rule. The same happens with frequent sets that contain 4 elements. Rules 7, 8, and 9 are rules 1 and 2 with two additional elements that combined with the dependence reached minimum support.

Approaches that reduce the number of rules and eliminate redundant rules (Zaki, 2000) do not warrant the elimination of all association rules that contain geographic dependences.

Existing algorithms for mining frequent geographic patterns and generating strong spatial association rules do neither make use of semantic knowledge to specify which spatial relationships should be computed in data preprocessing, nor to reduce the number of well-known patterns. Koperski and Han (1995) reduces the number of rules using minimum support during the predicate generation. Clementini et al. (2000) presented a similar method for mining association rules from geographic objects with broad boundaries. Appice et al., (2005) reduces the number of rules with user specified *pattern constraints*, which require a lot of background knowledge from the data mining user. This method is inefficient since pattern constraints are applied in postprocessing steps, after both frequent sets and association rules have already been generated.

Because of the dependence replication process in both frequent sets and association rules, shown in Table 5 and Table 6 respectively, it might be difficult for the data mining user to analyze all rules to discover if they are really interesting or not. To help the data mining user, in the following section we present a framework to remove all well known geographic dependences, warranting that no association rules with such dependences will be generated.

Table 6. Examples of association rules with frequent sets of size 2, 3, and 4 having the geographic dependence

Set Size	Rule	Possible Rules
k=2	1	contains(Port) → crosses(Water Body)
k=2	2	crosses(Water Body) → contains(Port)
k=3	3	contains(Hospital) ^ contains(Port) → crosses(Water Body)
k=3	4	contains(Hospital) ^ crosses(Water Body) → contains(Port)
k=3	5	contains(Hospital) → contains(Port) ^ crosses(Water Body)
k=3	6	contains(Port) ^ crosses(Water Body) → contains(Hospital)
k=4	7	contains (Street) ^ *contains(Port)* → *crosses(Water Body)* ^ contains (Hospital)
k=4	8	contains (Street) → *contains(Port)* ^ *crosses(Water Body)* ^ intersects (Hospital)
k=4	9	contains (Street) ^ intersects (Hospital) → *contains(Port)* ^ *crosses (Water Body)*

A FRAMEWORK FOR GEOGRAPHIC DATA PREPROCESSING AND SPATIAL ASSOCIATION RULE MINING WITH ONTOLOGIES

Recently, in (Bogorny et al., 2005b, 2006a, 2006b, 2006c) we introduced the idea of using semantic knowledge for reducing spatial joins and well known patterns in SAR mining. In Bogorny et al., (2006a) we proposed to eliminate well-known patterns among the target feature type and relevant feature types with intelligent geographic data preprocessing. In data preprocessing, however, not all well-known dependences can be removed. Then, we presented a frequent pattern mining algorithm that uses semantic knowledge to eliminate dependences among relevant feature types during the frequent set generation (Bogorny et al., 2006b). In Bogorny et al. (2006c) we proposed an integrated framework, which eliminates geographic dependences completely in both data preprocessing and frequent pattern generation, using geographic database schemas as prior knowledge.

This section presents an interoperable framework for geographic data preprocessing and spatial association rule mining using geographic ontologies. Ontologies are used not only to eliminate well known dependences, but to verify which spatial relationships should be computed in the spatial predicate computation.

Figure 6 shows the framework that can be viewed in three levels: data repository, data preprocessing, and data mining. At the bottom are the geographic data repositories: the knowledge repository which stores geo-ontologies and geographic databases stored in GDBMS (geographic database management systems) constructed under OGC specifications. Following the OGC specifications (Open GIS Consortium, 1999b) makes our framework interoperable with all GDBMS constructed under OGC specifications (e.g., Oracle, PostGIS, MySQL, etc.).

At the center is the spatial data preparation level, which covers the *gap* between data mining tools and geographic databases. At this level, data and knowledge repositories are accessed through JDBC/ODBC connections and data are retrieved,

Figure 6. A framework for mining frequent geographic patterns using ontologies

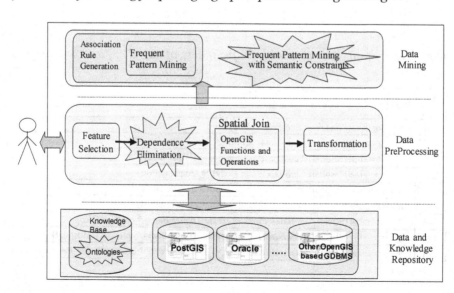

preprocessed, and transformed into the single table format. At this level, dependences among the target feature and relevant features are removed, as described in the next section.

On the top are the data mining toolkits or algorithms for mining frequent patterns and generating association rules. At this level, a new method for mining frequent geographic patterns is presented. Dependences among relevant feature types that can only be removed into the data mining algorithm are eliminated during the frequent set generation, as will be explained along with this section.

Data Preprocessing: Using Semantics to Eliminate Geographic Dependences Between the Target Feature Type and the Relevant Feature Types

There are four main steps to implement the tasks of geographic data preprocessing for association rule mining: *Feature Selection, Dependence Elimination, Spatial Join,* and *Transforma-*

tion. The *Feature Selection* step retrieves all relevant information from the database such that the user can choose the target feature type *T,* the target feature nonspatial attributes and the set *S* of relevant feature types that may have some influence on *T.* The feature types as well as their geometric attributes are retrieved through the OpenGIS database schema metadata, stored in the relation *geometry_columns* (see Bogorny et al., 2005a) for details.

The algorithm that implements the remaining data preprocessing steps is presented in Figure 7. The *Dependence Elimination* step searches the ontology φ and verifies the properties of *T.* If *T* has a mandatory dependence *M* with any *O* in *S,* then *O* is eliminated from the set *S* of relevant feature types. Notice that for each relevant feature type removed from the set *S,* no spatial join is required to extract spatial relationships. By consequence, no spatial association rule will be generated with this relevant feature type. If a prohibited relationship *P* is defined between *T* and *O* in the ontology φ, then the set of possible

Figure 7. Pseudo-code of the data preprocessing algorithm

```
Given:
       GDB, // geographic database
       φ, // geographic ontology
       T, // target feature type
       S, // set of relevant feature types O
       R; // set of all topological relationships
Variables:
       D; // relationships to compute for Data mining

Find: a dataset Ψ without geographic dependences between T and S;

Method:
Dependence_Elimination
Begin
       Ψ = T – geometry column;
       For (i=1; i=#O in S, i++) do
       Begin
              Find T in φ;
              If (T has a one-one or one-many property with Oᵢ in φ)
                     Remove Oᵢ from S;   // dependence elimination
              Else
                     If (T has prohibited properties P with Oᵢ in φ)
                            D = R – P; // possible relationships to compute
                     Else
                            D = R // all topological relationships
              Ψ = Ψ + Spatial_Join (D,T,Oᵢ);//computes spatial relationships D between T and O
       End;
End;
Transformation (Ψ) // transforms the resultant dataset into the data mining algorithm
              // format preserving the non-spatial attributes of T;
```

relationships to compute for data mining is given by $D_{(T,O)} = R - P_{(T,O)}$, where R is the set of all topological relationships $R = \{touches, contains, within, crosses, overlaps, equals, disjoint\}$. If there is no property of T in φ that relates T and O, then all relationships are computed.

The **Spatial Join** step computes the spatial relationships D between T and all remaining O in S. Spatial joins D to extract spatial predicates are performed on-the-fly with operations provided by the GIS.

The **Transformation** step transposes as well as discretizes the **Spatial Join** module output (Ψ) into the single table format understandable to association rule mining algorithms.

Frequent Pattern Generation: Using Semantics to Eliminate Geographic Dependences Among Relevant Features

Frequent pattern and association rule mining algorithms, under rare exceptions (Han, Pei & Yin, 2000) generate candidates and frequent sets. The candidate generation in spatial data mining is not a problem because the number of predicates is much smaller than the number of items in transactional databases (Shekhar & Chawla,

2003). Moreover, the computational cost relies on the spatial join computation.

Approaches that generate closed frequent sets do previously compute the frequent sets, and than verify if they are closed. Although they reduce the number of frequent sets, they do not warrant the elimination of well known geographic patterns. In SAR mining, it is more important to warrant that the results frequent sets are free of well-known dependences aiming to generate more interesting patterns, than to reduce the number of frequent sets. Apriori (Agrawal & Srikant, 1994) has been the basis for dozens of algorithms for mining spatial and nonspatial frequent sets, and association rules. We will illustrate the method of geographic dependence elimination during the frequent set generation using Apriori, as shown in Figure 8.

We propose to remove from the candidate sets all pairs of elements that have geographic dependences. As in Apriori, multiple passes are performed over the dataset. In the first pass, the support of the individual elements is computed to determine large-predicate sets. In the subsequent passes, given k as the number of the current pass, the large/frequent sets L_{k-1} in the previous pass (k-1) are grouped into sets C_k with k elements, which are called **candidate sets**. Then the support

Figure 8. Frequent set generation function

```
Given: φ, Ψ, minsup;
L₁ = {large 1-predicate sets};
For ( k = 2; L_{k-1} != ∅; k++ ) do  begin
    C_k = apriori_gen(L_{k-1}); // Generates new candidates
    If (k=2)
        Forall candidates c ∈ C₂ do
            If (feature types in pair c have any one-one or one-many relationship in φ)
                Remove the subset c from C₂;
    Forall rows w ∈ Ψ do begin
        C_w = subset(C_k, w); // Candidates contained in w
        Forall candidates c ∈ C_w do
            c.count++;
    End;
    L_k = {c ∈ C_k | c.count ≥ minsup};
End;
Answer = ∪_k L_k
```

Figure 9. Frequent sets generated with input space pruning

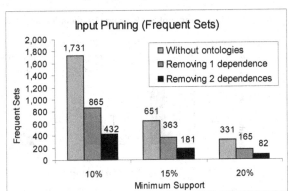

Figure 10. Spatial association rules with input space pruning and 70% minimum confidence

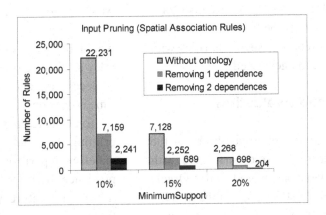

of each candidate set is computed, and if it is equal or higher than minimum support, then this set is considered frequent. This process continues until the number of frequent sets is zero.

Similarly to Srikant and Agrawal (1995), which eliminates in the second pass candidate sets that contain both parent and child specified in concept hierarchies, we eliminate all candidate sets which contain geographic dependences, but independently of any concept hierarchy.

The dependences are eliminated in an efficient way, when generating candidates with 2 elements, and before checking their frequency. If the pairs of predicates (e.g., *contains(Port), contains(Water Body)*) contain feature types (e.g., *Port, Water*

Body) that have a mandatory constraint in the ontology φ, then all pairs of predicates with a dependence in φ are removed from C_2.

According to Assertion 1, this step *warrants* that the pairs of geographic objects that have a mandatory constraint in the ontology φ will neither appear together in the frequent sets, nor in the spatial association rules. This makes the method effective independently of other thresholds, and clearly improves in efficiency, since less frequent sets will be generated.

The main strength of this method in our framework is its simplicity. This single, but very effective and efficient step, removes all well-known geographic dependences, and can

Figure 11. Frequent sets generated with frequent set pruning

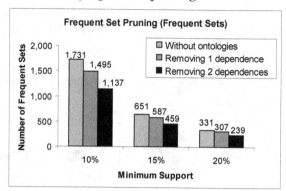

be implemented by any algorithm that generates frequent sets. Considering the example of frequent sets shown in Table 5, the dependence is eliminated when it appears at the first time, such that no larger frequent sets or association rules with the dependence will be generated.

Experiments and Evaluation

In order to evaluate the interoperability of the framework, experiments were performed with real geographic databases stored under Oracle 10g and PostGIS. Districts, a database table with 109 polygons and nonspatial attributes, such as population and sanitary condition, was defined as the target feature type *T*. Datasets with different relevant feature types (e.g., bus routes—4062 multilines, slums—513 polygons, water resources—1030 multilines, gas stations 450 points) were preprocessed and mined, using ontologies and without using ontologies.

Estimating the time reduction to compute spatial joins for mining frequent patterns is very difficult, since this step is completely data dependent. The computational time reduction to extract spatial joins depends on three main aspects: how many dependences (relevant feature types) are eliminated in data preprocessing; the geometry type of the relevant feature (point, line, or polygon); and the number of instances of the eliminated feature type (e.g., 60,000 rows). For

example, if a relevant feature type with 57 580 polygons is eliminated, spatial join computation would significantly decrease. If the eliminated feature type has 3062 points, time reduction would be less significant. However, for every relevant feature type eliminated, no spatial join is necessary, and this warrants preprocessing time reduction.

To evaluate the frequent pattern reduction by pruning the input space, Figure 9 describes an experiment performed with Apriori, where 2 dependences between the reference object type and the relevant feature types were eliminated. Notice that input space pruning reduces frequent patterns independently of minimum support. Considering *minsup* 10%, 15%, and 20%, the elimination of one single dependence pruned the frequent sets around 50%. The elimination of two dependences reduced the number of frequent sets in 75%. The rule reduction is still more significant, as can be observed in Figure 10, reaching around 70% when one dependence is removed and 90% when two dependences are eliminated, independently of minimum support.

Algorithms that generate closed frequent sets and eliminate nonredundant rules can reduce still further the number of both frequent sets and association rules if applied to the geographic domain using our method for pruning the input space.

Figure 11 shows the result of an experiment where two dependences among relevant feature

Figure 12. Frequent sets generated with input space and frequent set pruning

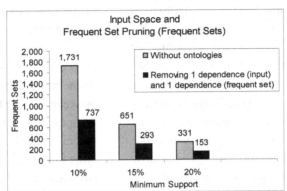

types were eliminated during the frequent set generation, but without input pruning. Notice that even using ontologies only in the frequent set generation we get a reduction on the number of frequent sets independently of minimum support. Moreover, the higher the number of dependences, the more significant is the reduction.

Figure 12 shows an experiment where dependences were eliminated in both input space (between the target feature and relevant features) and during the frequent set generation (among relevant features). The total number of frequent sets is reduced in more than 50% by removing one single dependence, independently of minimum support. Using ontologies we completely eliminate well known dependences, and very efficiently.

FUTURE TRENDS

Data mining techniques to extract knowledge from large spatial and nonspatial databases have mainly considered syntactic constraints and the data by itself, without considering semantics. The result is that the same geographic dependences that are well-known by GDB designers and explicitly represented in GDB schemas and geo-ontologies to warrant the consistency of the data, are extracted by data mining algorithms, which should discover only novel and useful patterns. When dealing with geographic data, which are semantically interdependent because of their nature, the meaning of data needs to be considered, at least to avoid the extraction of well known patterns.

There is an emerging necessity to consider semantic geographic domain knowledge in spatial data mining. The large amount of knowledge explicitly represented in geographic database schemas and spatio-temporal ontologies needs to be incorporated into data mining techniques, since they provide a valuable source of domain knowledge. How to use this knowledge in data mining systems and for which purposes are still open problems. In this chapter, we presented an efficient solution, addressing a small fraction of these problems. We used geo-ontologies in spatial association rule mining to reduce well-known patterns, but the use of ontologies in different data mining techniques such as clustering, classification, and outlier detection are still open problems. In clustering, for example, the use of semantics could either avoid the separation of geographic objects that have mandatory constraints or organize them into the same cluster without the need of computing their relationship. The use of prior knowledge to evaluate the interestingness of patterns extracted with the different data mining techniques still needs to be addressed.

The development of toolkits that integrate data mining techniques, geographic databases, and knowledge repositories is another need for practical applications. Although a large number of algorithms has been proposed, their implementation in toolkits with friendly graphical user interfaces that cover the whole KDD process is rare. The gap between data mining techniques and geographic databases is still a problem that makes geographic data preprocessing be the most effort and time consuming step for knowledge discovery in these databases.

CONCLUSION

This chapter presented an intelligent framework for geographic data preprocessing and SAR mining using geo-ontologies as prior knowledge. The knowledge refers to mandatory and prohibited semantic geographic constraints, which are explicitly represented in geo-ontologies because they are part of the concepts of geographic data. We showed that explicit mandatory relationships produce irrelevant patterns, and that prohibited relationships do not need to be computed, since they will never hold if the database is consistent. Possible implicit spatial relationships may lead to more interesting patterns and rules, and they can be inferred using geo-ontologies.

Experiments showed that independent of the number of elements, one dependence is enough to prune a large number of patterns and rules, and the higher the number of eliminated semantic constraints, the larger is the frequent pattern and rule reduction. We showed that well-known dependences can be partially eliminated with intelligent data preprocessing, independently of the algorithm to be used for frequent pattern mining. To completely eliminate geographic dependences we presented a pruning method that can be applied to any algorithm that generates frequent sets, including closed frequent sets. Algorithms for mining nonredundant association rules can reduce the number of rules further if applied to the geographic domain using our method to generate frequent sets.

Considering semantics in geographic data preprocessing and frequent pattern mining has three main advantages: spatial relationships between feature types with dependences are not computed; the number of both frequent sets and association rules is significantly reduced; and the most important, the generated frequent sets and rules are free of associations that are previously known as noninteresting.

The main contribution of the method presented in this chapter for mining spatial association rules is for the data mining user, which will analyze much less obvious rules. The method is effective independently of other thresholds, and warrants that geographic domain associations will not appear among the resultant set of rules.

ACKNOWLEDGMENT

The authors would like to thank both CAPES and CNPq, which partially provided the financial support for this research. To Procempa, for the geographic database and to Nodo XLDB da Linguateca of Universidade de Lisboa for the geographic ontology. Our special thanks for Mariusa Warpechowski and Daniela Leal Musa for the ontology modeling support, and for Sandro da Silva Camargo for the support with data mining algorithms.

REFERENCES

Agrawal, R., Imielinski, T., & Swami, A. (1993). Mining association rules between sets of items in large databases. In P. Buneman & S. Jajodia (Eds.), *ACM SIGMOD International Conference on Management of Data* (Vol. 20, pp. 207-216). New York: ACM Press.

Agrawal, R., & Srikant, R. (1994). Fast algorithms for mining association rules in large databases. In J.B. Bocca, M. Jarke, & C. Zaniolo (Eds.), *International Conference on Very Large Databases* (Vol. 20, pp. 487-499). San Francisco: Morgan Kaufmann Publishers.

Appice, A., Berardi, M., Ceci, M., & Malerba, D. (2005). Mining and filtering multilevel spatial association rules with ARES. In M. Hacid, N. V. Murray, Z. W. Ras, & S. Tsumoto (Eds.), *Foundations of Intelligent Systems, 15th International Symposium ISMIS. Vol. 3488* (pp. 342-353). Berlin: Springer.

Bogorny, V., & Iochpe, C. (2001). Extending the opengis model to support topological integrity constraints. In M. Mattoso & G. Xexéo (Eds.), *16th Brazilian Symposium in Databases* (pp. 25-39). Rio de Janeiro: COPPE/UFRJ.

Bogorny, V., Engel, P. M., & Alvares, L.O. (2005a). A reuse-based spatial data preparation framework for data mining. In J. Debenham & K. Zhang (Eds.), *15th International Conference on Software Engineering and Knowledge Engineering* (pp. 649-652). Taipei: Knowledge Systems Institute.

Bogorny, V., Engel, P. M., & Alvares, L.O. (2005b). Towards the reduction of spatial join for knowledge discovery in geographic databases using geo-ontologies and spatial integrity constraints. In M. Ackermann, B. Berendt, M. Grobelink, & V. Avatek (Eds.), *ECML/PKDD 2nd Workshop on Knowledge Discovery and Ontologies* (pp. 51-58). Porto.

Bogorny, V., Engel, P. M., & Alvares, L.O. (2006a). GeoARM: An interoperable framework to improve geographic data preprocessing and spatial association rule mining. In *Proceedings of the 18th International Conference on Software Engineering and Knowledge Engineering* (pp. 70-84). San Francisco: Knowledge Systems Institute.

Bogorny, V., Camargo, S., Engel, P., M., & Alvares, L.O. (2006b). Towards elimination of well known geographic domain patterns in spatial association rule mining. In *Proceedings of the 3rd IEEE International Conference on Intelligent Systems* (pp. 532-537). London: IEEE Computer Society.

Bogorny, V., Camargo, S., Engel, P., & Alvares, L. O. (2006c). Mining frequent geographic patterns with knowledge constraints. *In 14th ACM International Symposium on Advances in Geographic Information Systems.* Arlington, November (to appear).

Chaves, M. S., Silva, M. J., & Martins, B. (2005a). A geographic knowledge base for semantic web applications. In C. A. Heuser (Ed.), *20th Brazilian Symposium on Databases* (pp. 40-54). Uberlandia: UFU.

Chaves, M. S., Silva, M. J., & Martins, B. (2005b). *GKB—Geographic Knowledge Base.* (TR05-12). DI/FCUL.

Clementini, E., Di Felice, P., & Van Ostern, P. (1993). A small set of formal topological relationships for end-user interaction. In D.J. Abel & B.C. Ooi (Eds.), *Advances in Spatial Databases, 3rd International Symposium, 692* (pp. 277-295). Singapore: Springer.

Cockcroft, S. (1997). A Taxonomy of spatial data integrity constraints. *Geoinformatica, 1*(4), 327-343.

Clementini, E., Felice, Di, P., & Koperski, K. (2000). Mining multiple-level spatial association rules for objects with a broad boundary. *Data & Knowledge Engineering, 34*(3), 251-270.

Egenhofer, M., & Franzosa, R. (1995). On the equivalence of topological relations. *International Journal of Geographical Information Systems, 9*(2), 133-152.

Ester, M., Frommelt, A., Kriegel, H.-P., & Sander, J. (2000). Spatial data mining: Database primitives, algorithms and efficient DBMS support. *Journal of Data Mining and Knowledge Discovery, 4*(2-3), 193-216.

Fayyad, U., Piatetsky-Shapiro, G., & Smyth, P. (1996). From data mining to discovery knowledge in databases. *AI Magazine, 3*(17), 37-54.

Gruber, T. R. (1993). Towards principles for the design of ontologies used for knowledge sharing. Formal ontology in conceptual analysis and knowledge representation. *International Journal of Human-Computer Studies, 43,* 907-928.

Guarino, N. (1998). Formal ontology and information systems. In N. Guarino (Ed.), *International Conference on Formal Ontology in Information Systems* (pp. 3-15). Trento: IOS Press.

Han, J., & Fu, Y. (1995). Discovery of multiple-level association rules from large databases. In U. Dayal, P.M.D. Gray, & S. Nishio (Eds.), *International Conference on Very Large Data Bases* (pp. 420-431). Zurich: Morgan-Kaufmann.

Han, J., Koperski, K., & Stefanvic, N. (1997). GeoMiner: a system prototype for spatial data mining. In J. Peckham (Ed.), *ACMSIGMOD International Conference on Management of Data, 26* (pp. 553-556). Tucson: ACM Press.

Han, J., Pei J., & Yin, Y. (2000). Mining frequent patterns without candidate generation. In J.Chen, F. Naughton, & P.A. Bernstein (Eds.), *20th ACMSIGMOD International Conference on Management of Data* (pp. 1-12) Dallas: ACM.

Huang, Y., Shekhar, S., & Xiong, H. (2004). Discovering co-location patterns from spatial datasets: A general approach. *IEEE Transactions on Knowledge and Data Engineering, 16*(12), 1472-1485.

Koperski, K., & Han, J. (1995). Discovery of spatial association rules in geographic information databases. In M.J. Egenhofer, J.R. Herring (Eds.), *4th International Symposium on Large Geographical Databases, 951* (pp. 47-66). Portland: Springer.

Lu, W., Han, J., & Ooi, B. C. (1993). Discovery of general knowledge in large spatial databases. *In Far East Workshop on Geographic Information Systems* (pp. 275-289). Singapore.

Open Gis Consortium. (1999a). *Topic 5, the OpenGIS abstract specification—OpenGIS features—Version 4.* Retrieved August 20, 2005, from http://www.OpenGIS.org/techno/specs.htm

Open Gis Consortium. (1999b). *Open GIS Simple Features Specification For SQL.* Retrieved August 20, 2005, from http://www.opengeospatial.org/specs

Open Gis Consortium. (2001). *Feature Geometry.* Retrieved August 20, 2005, from http://www.opengeospatial.org/specs

Pasquier, N., Bastide, Y., Taouil, R., & Lakhal, L. (1999). In C. Beeri & P. Buneman (Eds.), *7th International Conference on Database Theory, 1540* (pp. 398-416). Jerusalem: Springer.

Servigne, S., Ubeda, T., Puricelli, A., & Laurini, R. (2000). A methodology for spatial consistency improvement of geographic databases. *Geoinformatica, 4*(1), 7-34.

Shekhar, S., & Chawla, S. (2003). *Spatial databases: a tour.* Upper Saddle, NJ: Prentice Hall.

Srikant, R. & Agrawal, R. (1995). Mining generalized association rules. In U. Dayal, P. M. D. Gray, S. Nishio (Eds.), *Proceedings of the 21st International Conference on Very Large Databases* (pp. 407-419). Zurich: Morgan Kaufmann.

Yoo, J. S., & Shekhar, S. (2006). A join-less approach for mining spatial co-location patterns. *IEEE Transactions on Knowledge and Data Engineering, 18*(10).

Zaki. M. (2000). Generating nonredundant association rules. In S.J. Simoff & O. R. Zaïane (Eds.), *Proceedings of the 6th ACMSIGKDD International Conference on Knowledge Discovery and Data Mining* (pp. 34-43) Boston: ACM Press.

Zaki., M., & Hsiao, C. (2002). CHARM: An efficient algorithm for closed itemset mining. In R.L. Grossman, J. Han, V. Kumar, H. Mannila, & R. Motwani (Eds.), *Proceeding of the 2nd SIAM International Conference on Data Mining* (pp. 457-473). Arlington: SIAM.

ADDITIONAL READING

Bernstein, A., Provost, Foster J., & Hill, S. (2005). Toward intelligent assistance for a data mining process: An ontology-based approach for cost-sensitive classification. *IEEE Transactions on Knowledge and. Data Engineering, 17*(4), 503-518.

Bogorny, V., Valiati, J.F., Camargo, S.S., Engel, P.M., Kuijpers, B., & Alvares, L.O. (2006). Mining maximal generalized frequent geographic patterns with knowledge constraints. *Sixth IEEE International Conference on Data Mining* (pp. 813-817). Hong Kong: IEEE Computer Society.

Bogorny, V. (2006). *Enhancing spatial association rule mining in geographic databases.* PhD Thesis. Porto Alegre, Brazil: Instituto de Informatica—UFRGS.

Chen, X., Zhou, X., Scherl, R.B., & Geller, J. (2003). Using an interest ontology for improved support in rule mining. In Y. Kambayashi, M. K. Mohania, & W. Wolfram (Eds), *Fifth International Conference on Data WareHouse and Knowledge Discovery* (pp. 320-329). Prague: Springer.

Farzanyar, Z., Kangavari, M., & Hashemi, S. (2006). A new algorithm for mining fuzzy association rules in the large databases based on ontology. *Workshops Proceedings of the 6th IEEE International Conference on Data Mining* (pp. 65-69). Hong Kong: IEEE Computer Society.

Jozefowska, J., Lawrynowicz, A., & Lukaszewski, T. (2006). Frequent pattern discovery from OWL DLP knowledge bases. In S. Staab & V. Sv (Eds). *International Conference on Managing Knowledge in a World of Networks* (pp. 287-302). Czech Republic: Springer.

Knowledge Discovery and Ontologies. (2004). *ECML/PKDD Workshop.* Retrieved February 12, 2006, from http://olp.dfki.de/pkdd04/cfp.htm

Knowledge Discovery and Ontologies. (2005). *ECML/PKDD Workshop.* Retrieved February 12, 2006, from http://webhosting.vse.cz/svatek/KDO05

Mennis, J., & Peuquet, D.J. (2003). The role of knowledge representation in geographic knowledge discovery: A case study. *Transactions in GIS, 7*(3), 371-391.

Singh, P., & Lee, Y. (2003). Context-based data mining using ontologies. In I. Song, S.W. Liddle, T. Wang Ling, & P. Scheuermann (Eds.), *International Conference on Conceptual Modeling* (pp. 405-418). Chicago: Springer.

Xu, W., & Huang, H. (2006). Research and application of spatio-temporal data mining based on ontology. *First International Conference on Innovative Computing, Infroumtion and Control,* (pp. 535-538). Los Alamitos: IEEE Computer Society.

Yu, S., Aufaure, M. Cullot, N., & Spaccapietra, S. (2003). Location-based spatial modelling using ontology. *Sixth AGILE Conference on Geographic Information Science.* Lyon, France.

Chapter X
Ontology–Based Construction of Grid Data Mining Workflows

Peter Brezany
University of Vienna, Austria

Ivan Janciak
University of Vienna, Austria

A Min Tjoa
Vienna University of Technology, Austria

ABSTRACT

This chapter introduces an ontology-based framework for automated construction of complex interactive data mining workflows as a means of improving productivity of Grid-enabled data exploration systems. The authors first characterize existing manual and automated workflow composition approaches and then present their solution called GridMiner Assistant (GMA), which addresses the whole life cycle of the knowledge discovery process. GMA is specified in the OWL language and is being developed around a novel data mining ontology, which is based on concepts of industry standards like the predictive model markup language, cross industry standard process for data mining, and Java data mining API. The ontology introduces basic data mining concepts like data mining elements, tasks, services, and so forth. In addition, conceptual and implementation architectures of the framework are presented and its application to an example taken from the medical domain is illustrated. The authors hope that the further research and development of this framework can lead to productivity improvements, which can have significant impact on many real-life spheres. For example, it can be a crucial factor in achievement of scientific discoveries, optimal treatment of patients, productive decision making, cutting costs, and so forth.

INTRODUCTION

Grid computing is emerging as a key enabling infrastructure for a wide range of disciplines in science and engineering. Some of the hot topics in current Grid research include the issues associated with data mining and other analytical processes performed on large-scale data repositories integrated into the Grid. These processes are not implemented as monolithic codes. Instead, the standalone processing phases, implemented as Grid services, are combined to process data and extract knowledge patterns in various ways. They can now be viewed as complex workflows, which are highly interactive and may involve several subprocesses, such as data cleaning, data integration, data selection, modeling (applying a data mining algorithm), and postprocessing the mining results (e.g., visualization). The targeted workflows are often large, both in terms of the number of tasks in a given workflow and in terms of the total execution time. There are many possible choices concerning each process's functionality and parameters as well as the ways a process is combined into the workflow but only some combinations are valid. Moreover, users need to discover Grid resources and analytical services manually and schedule these services directly on the Grid resources essentially composing detailed workflow descriptions by hand. At present, only such a "low-productivity" working model is available to the users of the first generation data mining Grids, like **GridMiner** (Brezany et al., 2004) (a system developed by our research group), DiscoveryNet (Sairafi et al., 2003), and so forth. Productivity improvements can have significant impact on many real-life spheres, for example, it can be a crucial factor in achievement of scientific discoveries, optimal treatment of patients, productive decision making, cutting costs, and so forth. There is a stringent need for automatic or semiautomatic support for constructing valid and efficient data mining workflows on the Grid,

and this (long-term) goal is associated with many research challenges.

The objective of this chapter is to present an ontology-based workflow construction framework reflecting the whole life cycle of the knowledge discovery process and explain the scientific rationale behind its design. We first introduce possible workflow composition approaches—we consider two main classes: (1) manual composition used by the current Grid data mining systems, for example, the GridMiner system, and (2) automated composition, which is addressed by our research and presented in this chapter. Then we relate these approaches to the work of others. The kernel part presents the whole framework built-up around a data mining ontology developed by us. This ontology is based on concepts reflecting the terms of several standards, namely, the predictive model markup language, cross industry process for data mining, and Java data mining API. The ontology is specified by means of OWL-S, a Web ontology language for services, and uses some concepts from Weka, a popular open source data mining toolkit. Further, conceptual and implementation architectures of the framework are discussed and illustrated by an application example taken from a medical domain. Based on the analysis of future and emerging trends and associated challenges, we discuss some future research directions followed by brief conclusions.

BACKGROUND

In the context of modern service-oriented Grid architectures, the data mining workflow can be seen as a collection of Grid services that are processed on distributed resources in a well-defined order to accomplish a larger and sophisticated data exploration goal. At the highest level, functions of Grid workflow management systems could be characterized into build-time functions and run-time functions. The build-time functions are concerned with defining and modeling workflow tasks and their dependencies while the run-time functions are concerned with managing the workflow execution and interactions with Grid resources for processing workflow applications. Users interact with workflow modeling tools to generate a workflow specification, which is submitted for execution to a run-time service called workflow enactment service, or *workflow engine*. Many languages, mostly based on XML, were defined for workflow description, like XLANG (Thatte, 2001), WSFL (Leymann, 2001), DSCL (Kickinger et al., 2003) and BPML (Arkin, 2002). Eventually the WSBPEL (Arkin et al., 2005) and BPEL4WS (BEA et al., 2003) specifications emerged as the de facto standard.

In our research, we consider two main workflow composition models: *manual* (implemented in the fully functional GridMiner prototype (Kickinger et al., 2003)) and *automated* (addressed in this chapter), as illustrated in Figure 1. Within manual composition, the user constructs the target workflow specification graphically in the workflow editor by means of the advanced graphical user interface. The graphical form is converted into a *workflow description* document, which is passed to the workflow engine. Based on the workflow description, the engine sequentially or in parallel calls the appropriate analytical services (database access, preprocessing, OLAP, classification, clustering, etc.). During the workflow execution, the user only has the ability to stop, inspect, resume, or cancel the execution. As a result, the user has limited abilities to interact with the workflow and influence the execution process. A similar approach was implemented in the DiscoveryNet (Sairafi et al., 2003) workflow management system.

The automated composition is based on an intensive support of five involved components: *workflow composer, resources monitoring, workflow engine, knowledge base*, and *reasoner*.

Figure 1. Workflow composition approaches

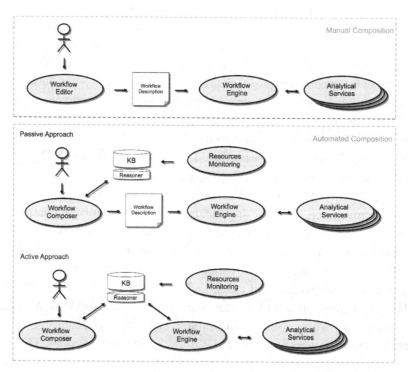

Workflow composer: Is a specialized tool, which interacts with a user during the workflow composition process. This chapter describes its functionality in detail.

Resources monitoring: Its main purpose is obtaining information concerning the utilization of system resources. Varieties of different systems exist for monitoring and managing distributed Grid-based resources and applications. For example, the monitoring and discovery system (MDS) is the information services component of the Globus Toolkit (Globus Alliance, 2005), which provides information about available resources on the Grid and their status. Moreover, MDS facilitates the discovery and characterization of resources and monitors services and computations. The information provided by resource monitoring can be continuously updated in the knowledge base (KB) to reflect the current status of the Grid resources.

Workflow engine: Is a runtime execution environment that performs the coordination of services as specified in the workflow description expressed in terms of a workflow language. The workflow engine is able to invoke and orchestrate the services and acts as their client, that is, listen to the notification messages, deliver outputs, and so forth.

Knowledge base (KB) and **reasoner:** A set of ontologies can be used for the specification of the KB structure, which is built-up using a set of instances of ontology classes and rules. The reasoner applies deductive reasoning about the stored knowledge in a logically consistent manner; it assures consistency of the ontology and answers given queries.

Due to different roles and behaviors of the presented components, we distinguish two modes of automated workflow composition: *passive* and *active*.

Passive Workflow Construction

The passive approach is based on the assumption that the *workflow composer* is able to compose a reasoning-based complete workflow description involving all possible scenarios of the workflow engine behavior and reflecting the status of the involved Grid resources and task parameters provided by the user at the workflow composition time. Although the KB is continuously modified by the user's entries and by information retrieved from the resource monitoring services, the composition of involved services is not updated during the workflow execution. Therefore, the composition does not reflect the 'state of the world,' which can be dynamically changed during the execution. It means that the workflow engine does not interact with the inference engine to reason about knowledge in the KB. Thus, the behavior of the engine (the decisions it takes) is steered by fixed condition statements as specified in the workflow document.

The essential tasks leading to a final outcome of the passive workflow composition approach can be summarized as follows:

1. The workflow composer constructs a complete workflow description based on the information collected in KB and presents it to the workflow engine in an appropriate workflow language.
2. The workflow engine executes each subsequent composition step as presented in the workflow description, which includes all possible scenarios of the engine behavior.

Active Workflow Construction

The active approach assumes a kind of intelligent behavior by the workflow engine supported by an inference engine and the related KB. Workflow composition is done in the same way as in the passive approach, but its usability is more efficient because it reflects a 'state of the world.' It means that the outputs and effects of the executed services are propagated to the KB together with changes of the involved Grid resources. Considering these changes, the workflow engine dynamically makes decisions about next execution steps. In this approach, no workflow document is needed because the workflow engine instructs itself using an inference engine which queries and updates the KB. The KB is queried each time the workflow engine needs information to invoke a consequent service, for example, it decides which concrete service should be executed, discovers the values of its input parameters in the KB, and so forth. The workflow engine also updates the KB when there is a new result returned from an analytical service that can be reused as input for the other services.

The essential tasks leading to a final outcome in active workflow composition approach can be summarized as follows:

1. The workflow composer constructs an abstract workflow description based on the information collected in the KB and propagates the workflow description back into the KB. The abstract workflow is not a detailed description of the particular steps in the workflow execution but instead a kind of path that leads to the demanded outcome.
2. The workflow engine executes each subsequent composition step as a result of its interaction with the KB reflecting its actual state. The workflow engine autonomously constructs directives for each service execution and adapts its behavior during the execution.

Related Work

A main focus of our work presented in this chapter is on the above mentioned passive approach of the automated workflow composition. This research was partially motivated by (Bernstein et al., 2001). They developed an intelligent discovery assistant

(IDA), which provides users (data miners) with (1) systematic enumerations of valid data mining processes according to the constraints imposed by the users' inputs, the data, and/or the data mining ontology in order that important and potentially fruitful options are not overlooked, and (2) effective rankings of these valid processes by different criteria (e.g., speed and accuracy) to facilitate the choice of data mining processes to execute. The IDA performs a search of the space of processes defined by the ontology. Hence, no standard language for ontology specification and appropriate reasoning mechanisms are used in their approach. Further, they do not consider any state-of-the-art workflow management framework and language.

Substantial work has already been done on automated composition of Web services using Semantic Web technologies. For example, Majithia et al., (2004) present a framework to facilitate automated service composition in service-oriented architectures (Tsalgatidou & Pilioura, 2002) using Semantic Web technologies. The main objective of the framework is to support the discovery, selection, and composition of semantically-described heterogeneous Web services. The framework supports mechanisms to allow users to elaborate workflows of two levels of granularity: abstract and concrete workflows. Abstract workflows specify the workflow without referring to any specific service implementation. Hence, services (and data sources) are referred to by their logical names. A concrete workflow specifies the actual names and network locations of the services participating in the workflow. These two level workflow granularities are also considered in our approach, as shown in an application example.

Challenges associated with Grid workflow planning based on artificial intelligence concepts and with generation of abstract and concrete workflows are addressed by (Deelman et al., 2003). However, they do not consider any service-oriented architecture. Workflow representation and enactment are also investigated by the NextGrid

Project (NextGrid Project, 2006). They proposed the OWL-WS (OWL for workflow and services) (Beco et al., 2006) ontology definition language. The myGrid project has developed the Taverna Workbench (Oinn et al., 2004) for the composition and execution of workflows for the life sciences community. The assisted composition approach of Sirin (Sirin et al., 2004) uses the richness of Semantic Web service descriptions and information from the compositional context to filter matching services and help select appropriate services.

UNDERLYING STANDARDS AND TECHNOLOGIES

CRoss Industry Standard Process for Data Mining

Cross industry standard process for data mining (CRISP-DM) (Chapman et al., 1999) is a data mining process model that describes commonly used approaches that expert data miners use to tackle problems of organizing phases in data mining projects. CRISP-DM does not describe a particular data mining technique; rather it focuses on the process of a data mining projects' life cycle. The CRISP-DM data mining methodology is described in terms of a hierarchical process model consisting of sets of tasks organized at four levels of abstraction: phase, generic task, specialized task, and process instance. At the top level, the life cycle of a data mining project is organized into six phases as depicted in Figure 2.

The sequence of the phases is not strict. Moving back and forth between different phases is always required. It depends on the outcome of each phase, which one, or which particular task of a phase has to be performed next. In this chapter, we focus our attention on the three phases of data mining projects' life cycle, namely: data understanding, data preparation, and modeling.

Figure 2. Phases of CRISP-DM reference model (Chapman et al., 1999)

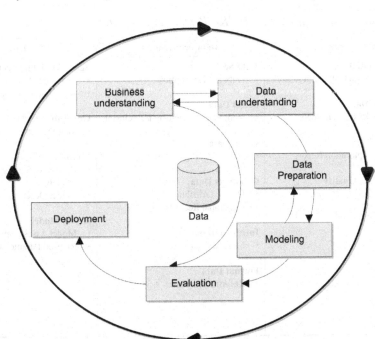

Data understanding: This phase starts with an initial data collection and proceeds with analytic activities in order to get familiar with the data, to identify data quality problems, to discover first insights into the data, or to detect interesting subsets to form hypotheses for hidden information.

Data preparation: This phase covers all activities to construct the final data set from the initial raw data. Data preparation tasks are likely to be performed multiple times and not in any prescribed order. The tasks include table, record, and attribute selection as well as transforming and cleaning data for the modeling phase.

Modeling: In this phase, various modeling techniques are selected and applied, and their parameters are calibrated to optimal values. Typically, there are several techniques for the same data mining problem type. Some techniques have specific requirements on the form of the data. Therefore, stepping back to the data preparation phase is often required.

The presented phases can be delimitated into a set of tasks defined by their outputs as presented in Table 1.

Predictive Model Markup Language

Predictive model markup language (PMML) (Data Mining Group, 2004) is an XML-based language that provides a way for applications to define statistical and data mining models and to share these models between PMML compliant applications. More precisely, the language's goal is to encapsulate a model in application and in a system independent fashion so that its producer and consumer can easily use it. Furthermore, the language can describe some of the operations required for cleaning and transforming input data prior to modeling. Since PMML version 3.1 is an XML based standard, its specification comes in the form of an XML schema that defines language primitives as follows:

Table 1. Generic tasks and outputs of the CRISP-DM reference model

Data Understanding	Data Preparation	Modeling
Collect Initial Data • Initial Data Collection Report **Describe Data** • Data Description Report **Explore Data** • Data Exploration Report **Verify Data Quality** • Data Quality Report	**Data Set** • Data Set Description **Select Data** • Rationale for Inclusion/ Exclusion **Clean Data** • Data Cleaning Report **Construct Data** • Derived Attributes • Generated Records **Integrate Data** • Merged Data **Format Data** • Reformatted Data	**Select Modeling Techniques** • Modeling Techniques • Modeling Assumption **Generate Text Design** • Text Design **Build Model** • Parameter Settings • Models • Model Description **Assess Model** • Model Assessment • Revised Parameter Settings

- **Data Dictionary:** It defines fields that are the inputs for models and specifies their types and value ranges. These definitions are assumed to be independent of specific data mining models. The values of a categorical field can be organized in a hierarchy as defined by the taxonomy element, and numeric fields can be specified by their intervals.

- **Mining schema:** The mining schema is a subset of fields as defined in the data dictionary. Each model contains one mining schema that lists fields as used in that model. The main purpose of the mining schema is to list fields, which a user has to provide in order to apply the model.

- **Transformations:** It contains descriptions of derived mining fields using the following transformations: normalization — mapping continuous or discrete values to numbers; discretization—mapping continuous values to discrete values; value mapping—mapping discrete values to discrete values; aggregation—summarizing or collecting groups of values, for example, compute averages; and functions—derive a value by applying a function to one or more parameters.

- **Model statistics:** It stores basic uni-variate statistics about the numerical attributes used in the model such as minimum, maximum, mean, standard deviation, median, and so forth.

- **Data mining model:** It contains specification of the actual parameters defining the statistical and data mining models. The latest PMML version addresses the following classes of models: association rules, decision trees, center-based clustering, distribution-based clustering, regression, general regression, neural networks, naive bayes, sequences, text, ruleset, and support vector machine.

The models presented in PMML can be additionally defined by a set of extensions that can increase the overall complexity of a mining model as follows:

- **Built-in functions:** PMML supports functions that can be used to perform preprocessing steps on the input data. A number of predefined built-in functions for simple arithmetic operations like sum, difference, product, division, square root, logarithm, and so forth, for numeric input fields, as well as functions for string handling such as trimming blanks or choosing substrings are provided.

- **Model composition:** Using simple models as transformations offers the possibility to combine multiple conventional models into a single new one by using individual models as building blocks. This can result in models being used in sequence, where the result of each model is the input to the next one. This approach, called 'model sequencing,' is not only useful for building more complex models but can also be applied to data preparation. Another approach, 'model selection,' is used when the result of a model can be used to select which model should be applied next.

- **Output:** It describes a set of result values that can be computed by the model. In particular, the output fields specify names, types and rules for selecting specific result features. The output section in the model specifies default names for columns in an output table that might be different from names used locally in the model. Furthermore, they describe how to compute the corresponding values.

- **Model verification:** A verification model provides a mechanism for attaching a sample data set with sample results so that a PMML consumer can verify that a model has been implemented correctly. This will make model exchange much more transparent for users and inform them in advance in case compatibility problems arise.

Weka Toolkit

Weka (Witten & Eibe, 2005) is a collection of machine learning algorithms, especially classifications, for data mining tasks. Moreover, Weka contains tools for data preprocessing, regression, clustering, association rules, and visualization. It is also well-suited for developing new machine learning schemes. The Weka's API is organized in a hierarchical structure, and the algorithms are delimited by their relevancy to the classes of data mining tasks as presented in Figure 3.

Java Data Mining Application Programming Interface

The Java data mining API (JDM) (Hornick et al., 2003) proposes a pure Java API for developing data mining applications. The idea is to have a common API for data mining that can be used by clients without users being aware or affected by the actual vendor implementations for data mining. A key JDM API benefit is that it abstracts out the physical components, tasks, and even algorithms of a data mining system into Java classes. It gives a very good basis for defining concrete data mining algorithms and describing their parameters and results. JDM does not define a large number of algorithms, but provides mechanisms to add

new ones, which helps in fine tuning the existing algorithms. Various data mining functions and techniques like statistical classification and association, regression analysis, data clustering, and attribute importance are covered by this standard.

Web Ontology Language for Services

Web ontology language for services (OWL-S) (Martin et al., 2004) consists of several interrelated OWL ontologies that provide a set of well defined terms for use in service applications. OWL-S leverages the rich expressive power of OWL together with its well-defined semantics to provide richer descriptions of Web services that include process preconditions and effects. This enables the encoding of service side-effects that are often important for automated selection and composition of Web services. OWL-S also provides means for the description of nonfunctional service constraints that are useful for automated Web service discovery or partnership bindings. OWL-S uses OWL to define a set of classes and their properties specific to the description of Web services. The class *Service* is at the top of this ontology (see Figure 4), which provides three essential types of knowledge about a service represented as classes: *ServiceProfile*, *ServiceGrounding* and *ServiceModel*.

Figure 3. Taxonomy of algorithms as presented in Weka API

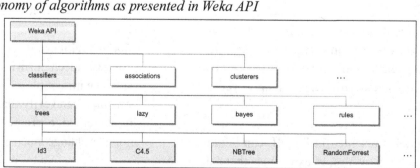

- The *ServiceProfile* describes "what the service does." The profile provides information about a service that can be used in the process of service discovery to determine whether the service meets one's needs.
- The *ServiceModel* informs "how to use the service." In more detail, the model gives information about the service itself and describes how to perform a specific task composed by subtasks involving certain conditions.
- The *ServiceGrounding* specifies the service-specific details of how to access the service, for example communication protocols, message formats, port numbers, and so forth. It is a kind of mapping from abstract activity description to its concrete implementation.

As we deal with the services composition, the aspects of *ServiceModel* and its main class *process*, including subclasses *AtomicProcess*,

Simple Process, and *Composite Process* and their properties are discussed here in more detail.

Atomic process: The atomic process specifies an action provided by the Web service that expects one message as an input and returns one message in response. It means that the atomic processes are directly invokable and have no other subprocesses to be executed in order to produce a result. By definition, for each atomic process there must be grounding provided, which is associated with a concrete service implementation.

Simple process: The simple process gives a higher abstraction level of the activity execution. It is not associated with groundings and is not directly invokable, but like the atomic process, it is conceived of having a single step execution.

Composite process: Web services composition is a task of combining and linking Web services to create new processes in order to add value to the

Figure 4. Selected classes and their relations in OWL-S ontology (Martin et al., 2004)

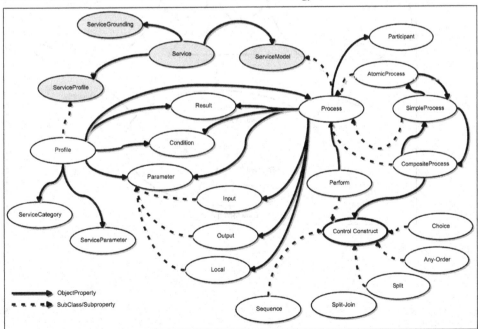

collection of services. In other words, it means that composition of several services can be viewed as one composite process with its defined inputs and outputs.

Moreover, OWL-S enables inclusion of some expressions to represent logical formulas in Semantic Web rule language (SWRL) (Horrocks et al., 2004). SWRL is a rule language that combines OWL with the rule markup language providing a rule language compatible with OWL. SWRL includes a high-level abstract syntax for Horn-like rules in OWL-DL and OWL-Lite, which are sublanguages of OWL. SWRL expressions may be used in OWL-S preconditions, process control conditions (such as if-then-else), and in effects expressions.

GRIDMINER ASSISTANT

Design Concepts

To achieve the goals presented in the Introduction section, we have designed a specialized tool—**GridMiner Assistant** (GMA)—that fulfils the role of the workflow composer shown in Figure 1. It is implemented as a Web application able to navigate a user in the phases of the knowledge discovery process (KDD) and construct a workflow consisting of a set of cooperating services aiming to realize concrete data mining objectives. The main goal of the GMA is to assist the user in the workflow composition process. The GMA provides support in choosing particular objectives of the knowledge discovery process and

Figure 5. Concept overview of the abstract data mining service

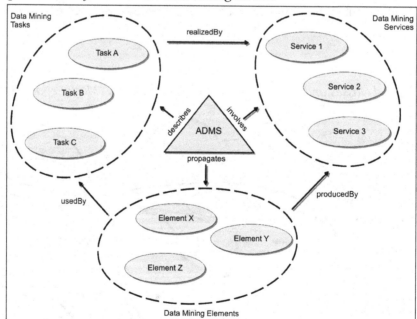

manage the entire process by which properties of data mining tasks are specified and results are presented. It can accurately select appropriate tasks and provide a detailed combination of services that can work together to create a complex workflow based on the selected outcome and its preferences. The GMA dynamically modifies the tasks composition depending on the entered values, defined process preconditions and effects, and existing description of services available in the KB. For this purpose we have designed a **data mining ontology** (DMO), which takes advantage of an explicit ontology of data mining techniques and standards (as presented in the above sections) using the OWL-S concepts to describe an abstract Semantic Web service for data mining and its main operations.

The service named **abstract data mining service** (ADMS) simplifies the architecture of the DMO as the realization of the OWL-S service with a detailed description of its *profile* and *model*. To clearly present the process of workflow composition using operations of the ADMS, we define three essential types of data mining components involved in the assisted workflow composition: DM-*elements, DM-tasks* and DM-*services,* as depicted in Figure 5. In order to design the ADMS, we consider a set of transactions representing its functionality described by DM-tasks. The DM-tasks can be seen as operations of the ADMS realized by concrete operations of involved DM-services using DM-elements as their inputs and outputs.

The following paragraphs introduce the data mining ontology, which is built through the description of the DM-tasks, DM-elements and involved DM-services. The ontology covers all phases of the knowledge discovery process and describes available data mining tasks, methods, algorithms, their inputs and results they produce. All these concepts are not strictly separated but are rather used in conjunction forming a consistent ontology.

Data Mining Elements

The DM-elements are represented by OWL classes together with variations of their representations in XML. It means that a concept described by an OWL class can have one or more related XML schemas that define its concrete representation in XML. The elements are propagated by the ADMS into the KB and can be used in any phase of data mining process. The instances of OWL classes and related XML elements are created and updated by the ADMS service operations as results of concrete services or user inputs. The elements can also determine the behavior of a workflow execution if used in SWRL rules and have an influence on preconditions or effects in the OWL-S processes. In the DMO, we distinguish two types of DM-elements: settings and results. The settings represent inputs for the DM-tasks, and on the other hand, the results represent outputs produced by these tasks. From the workflow execution point of view, there is no difference between inputs and outputs because it is obvious that an output from one process can be used, at the same time, as an input for another process. The main reason why we distinguish inputs and outputs as settings and results is to simplify the workflow composition process, to ease searching in the KB, and to exactly identify and select requested classes and their properties.

The **settings** are built through enumeration of properties of the data mining algorithms and characterization of their input parameters. Based on the concrete Java interfaces, as presented in the Weka API and JDM API, we constructed a set of OWL classes and their instances that handle input parameters of the algorithms and their default values (see Figure 6). The settings are also used to define different types of data sets that can be involved in the KDD process. Class *DataSet* and its derived subclasses collect all necessary information about the data set (file location, user name, SQL etc.) that can be represented by different data repositories such as a relational database, CSV, WebRowSet file, and so forth. Properties of the *DataSet* are usually specified by a user at the very beginning of the KDD process composition.

The following example shows a concrete instance of the OWL class *algorithm* keeping input parameters of an Apriory-type algorithm (Agrawal et al., 1994), which produces an association model. The example is presented in OWL abstract syntax (World Wide Web Consortium, 2004).

Class (Setting partial Element)
Class (Algorithm partial Element)
Class (Parameter partial Element)

ObjectProperty(hasParameter
domain(Setting)
  range(Parameter))

Individual(_algorithm_AprioryType_Setting
  annotation(rdfs:label "Apriori-type algorithm")
  type(Algorithm)
  value(hasParameter _number_of_rules)

  value(hasParameter _minimum_support)
  value(hasParameter _minimun_rule_confidence))

Individual(_number_of_rules
  annotation(rdfs:label "The required number of rules")
  type(Parameter)
  value(value "10"))

Individual(_minimum_support
  annotation(rdfs:label "The delta for minimum support")
  type(Parameter)
  value(value "0.05"))

Individual(_minimun_rule_confidence
  annotation(rdfs:label "The minimum confidence of a rule")
  type(Parameter)
  value(value "0.9"))

The **results** are built on taxonomy of data mining models and characterization of their main components as presented in the PMML specification, therefore, the terminology used for naming the result elements is tightly linked with the names of the elements in PMML. As a result, it is easy to map its concepts to the concrete XML representations as done in the PMML schema. Figure 7 depicts the basic classes and their relations used to describe the Result DM-elements in the DMO.

Figure 6. Basic setting classes used to describe input parameters

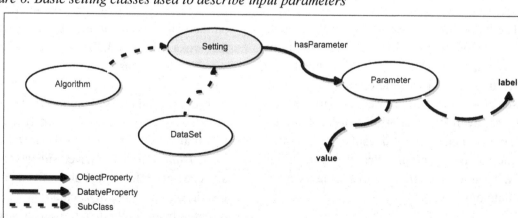

Figure 7. Basic classes used to describe Results in DMO

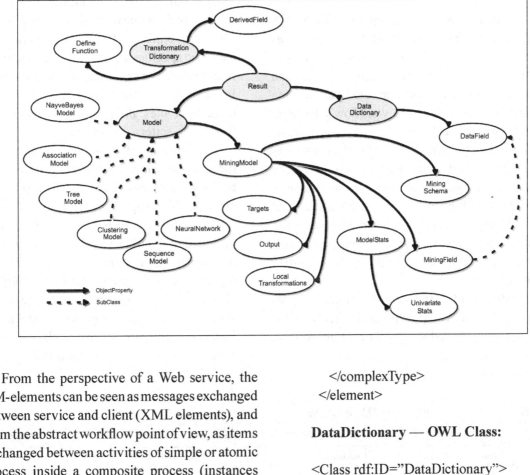

From the perspective of a Web service, the DM-elements can be seen as messages exchanged between service and client (XML elements), and from the abstract workflow point of view, as items exchanged between activities of simple or atomic process inside a composite process (instances of OWL classes). The following example shows how the PMML element DataDictionary, having subelements DataField and taxonomy, can be represented as *DataDictionary* class in the OWL.

DataDictionary — XML Schema:

```
<element name="DataDictionary">
  <complexType>
  <sequence>
          <element ref="DataField"
maxOccurs="unbounded" />
          <element ref="Taxonomy" minOccurs="0"
maxOccurs="unbounded" />
      </sequence>
          <attribute name="numberOfFields"
type="nonNegativeInteger" />
  </complexType>
</element>
```

DataDictionary — OWL Class:

```
<Class rdf:ID="DataDictionary">
  <Restriction>
      <onProperty rdf:resource="#hasDataFi
eld"/>
  </Restriction>
  <Restriction>
      <onProperty rdf:resource="#hasTaxono
my"/>
      <minCardinality rdf:datatype="#nonNeg
ativeInteger">0</minCardinality>
  </Restriction>
  <Restriction>
      <onProperty rdf:resource="#numberOf
Fields"/>
  </Restriction>
  </rdfs:subClassOf>
</Class>
```

Data Mining Tasks

The tasks are specialized operations of the ADMS organized in the phases of the KDD process as presented in the CRISP-DM reference model. The GMA composes these tasks into consistent and valid workflows to fulfill selected data mining objectives. The tasks are workflow's building blocks and are realized by concrete operations of involved DM-Services using DM-elements as their settings and results. Furthermore, GMA can automatically select and insert additional tasks into the workflow to assure validity and logical consistency of the data mining processes. We distinguish two types of DM-tasks that are forming the OWL-S *ServiceModel* of the ADMS—*setters* and *getters*.

Setters and getters give a functional description of the ADMS expressed in terms of the transformation produced by the abstract service.

Furthermore, the setters are used to specify the input parameters for data mining tasks, and the getters are designed to present results of concrete service operations. The setters interact with a user who specifies values of the input parameters represented as properties of the *settings* class, for example, location of data source, selection of target attributes, the number of clusters, and so forth. The setters do not return any results but usually have an effect on creating and updating the DM-elements. The setters are not realized by concrete operations of involved services but are used to compose compact workflows and assure interaction with the user. The getters are designed to describe actual data mining tasks at different levels of abstraction. Thus a getter can be represented by an instance of the *CompositeProcess* class as, for example, a sequence of several subtasks, or a getter can be directly defined as an instance of the *AtomicProcess* class realized by a concrete operation of a DM-service.

Table 2. DM-tasks and their DM-elements

	crisp-dm task	dmo dm-task	input	output
data understanding	collect initial data	setdataset	datasetsettings	dataset
	describe data	getdatadictionary	dataset	datadictionary
		settaxonomy	taxonomysettings	taxonomy
	explore data	getmodelstats	dataset	modelstats
	verify data quality			
data preparation	select data	setminingschema	miningschemasettings	miningschema
	clean data	gettransformation	definefunction	dataset
	construct data		derivedfield	dataset
	integrate data		mediationschema	dataset
	format data		miningschema	dataset
modeling	select modeling technique	setminingmodel	miningmodelsettings	miningmodel
	generate test design	settestset	datasetsettings	dataset
	build model	getclassificationmodel getassociationmodel getclusteringmodel getsequentialmodel getneuralnetworksmodel	mininingmodelsettings	model
	assess model	getmodelverification	mininingmodelsettings	model

Table 2 presents some of the setters and getters on the highest level of abstraction organized according to the phases of the CRISP-DM reference model and lists their input and output DM-elements.

The setters are designed to interact with the user, therefore, each *setter* has a related HTML input form used by the user to insert or select the input parameters' values of the examined DM-element. The GMA presents the form implemented as a dynamic Web page to the user, and based on his/her inputs, the GMA updates parameters of the DM-elements.

Data Mining Services

Realization of a particular DM-task is done by invoking concrete operations of involved DM-services described in OWL-S as an atomic, simple or composite process related to its *ServiceGrounding* (operators that can be executed)

as defined in the appropriate WSDL document. The operations produce DM-elements that can be reused by other operations in further steps of the workflow execution. Within our project, several data mining services were developed including decision tree, clustering, associations, sequences, and neural networks with detailed descriptions of their functionality in OWL-S.

Data Mining Ontology

Based on the concepts and principal classes in the preceding sections, we have constructed the final DMO as depicted in Figure 8. The DMO incorporates the presented OWL-S ontology and its classes describing DM-tasks and DM-services as well as *Result* and *Setting* classes, which describe the DM-elements. The ontology is also supplemented by a set of semantic rules that determine in detail particular relations between involved classes, but its presentation is out of the scope of this chapter.

Figure 8. Basic classes and their relations in DMO

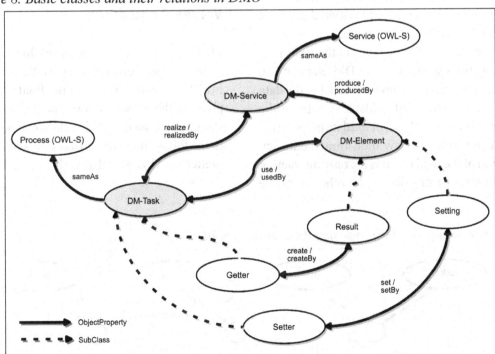

WORKFLOW CONSTRUCTION

In order to create the final workflow, the GMA follows a combination of the backward and forward chaining approaches. It means that the process begins with a user-based selection of a target task, which produces the desired data exploration output. Additional tasks are automatically inserted into a chain before the target task until a task without any or already satisfied preconditions is encountered (backward phase). Next, by insertion of additional tasks, this chain is automatically extended into a form in which all matching preconditions and inputs parameters are satisfied (forward chain). According to this, our approach to workflow construction is based on two phases as follows.

Tasks Composition

The aim of this phase is to create an abstract workflow consisting of a sequence of DM-tasks. Figure 9 presents an example of the abstract workflow composed of DM-tasks. 'Task D' is the initial task inserted into the workflow in the sense of the previously mentioned backward phase of the workflow composition, and the task's result, represented by a DM-element, is the final goal of the abstract workflow. The DM-element can be, for example, a decision tree model in the data mining phase, a list of all available statistics in the data understanding phase, or the data preparation phase can result in a new transformed data set. Selection of the final result is the only interaction with the user in this phase; the other steps are hidden. The composition then continues with an examination of preconditions and inputs of the target task 'Task D.' If the task has an input which does not exist (KB does not contain an instance of the required DM-element) or condition that has to be satisfied, then the KB is queried for such a task that can supply the required DM-elements or can satisfy these preconditions by its effects; the missing task can be 'Task C' in our case. The design of the ontology ensures that there is only one such task that can be selected and inserted into the workflow prior to the examined task. For example, if we want to obtain a list of statistics (getModelStats task) then there must be an existing DM-element DataSet. It means that a task which creates the DataSet element must anticipate the getModelStats task in the workflow composition (it can be the setDataSet task in our case). The newly added tasks are treated in the same way until a task without any preconditions or already satisfied preconditions is encountered, or a task without any input that is produced as result of another task is reached, which is 'Task A' in our example.

Values Acquisition

Figure 10 presents the same workflow but viewed from another perspective: now 'Task A' is the initial task and 'Task D' is the final one. In this phase of the workflow construction, the task parameters are set up. Their values can be obtained in the following ways: (a) as effects of DM-tasks (getters) or (b) entered directly by a user (setters).

Figure 9. Example of tasks composing the abstract workflow

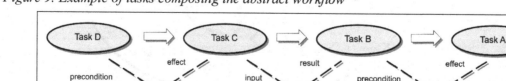

In other words, not all values of input parameters can be obtained automatically as results of previous operations and therefore must be supplied by a user. This phase of the values acquisition starts by tracing the abstract workflow from its beginning, 'Task A', and supplying the values by abstract interpretation of the partial workflow or providing them from a user. The user can enter the values directly by filling input fields offered by an appropriate graphical user interface or by selecting them from a list created as a result of a KB query, e.g., a list of data mining algorithms for a specific method is determined by available implementations of services able to perform the task. If the user selects a list item value that has influence on the precondition or effect that has to be satisfied in the next steps, then the KB is searched for such a task that can satisfy this request. The newly discovered tasks are inserted automatically into the workflow. It can be, for example, a case when the user wants to increase the quality of used data adding some transformation tasks, presenting the resulting model in different form, and so forth.

To illustrate the main features of the GMA and explain the phases of the tasks composition and values acquisition, we present a practical scenario addressing step-by-step construction of a simple workflow aiming at discovering of classification model for a given data set. This scenario is taken from a medical application dealing with patients suffering from serious traumatic brain injuries (TBI).

Workflow Construction Example

At the first clinical examination of a TBI patient (Brezany et al., 2003), it is very common to assign the patient into a category, which allows to define his/her next treatment and helps to predict the final outcome of the treatment. There are five categories of the final outcome defined by the Glasgow outcome scale (GOS): dead, vegetative, severely disabled, moderately disabled, and good recovery.

It is obvious that the outcome is influenced by several factors that are usually known and are often monitored and stored in a hospital data warehouse. For TBI patients, these factors are for example: injury severity score (ISS), abbreviated injury scale (AIS), Glasgow coma score (GCS), age, and so forth. It is evident that if we want to categorize the patient, then there must be a prior knowledge based on cases of other patients with the same type of injury. This knowledge can be mined from the historical data and represented as a classification model. The mined model is then used to assign the patient to the one of the outcome categories. In particular, the model can assign one of the values from the GOS to a concrete patient.

As we mentioned in the previous section, in the first phase, the composition of the abstract workflow proceeds by using the backward chaining approach starting with the task and then producing the demanded result. In our case, the classification model is represented by a decision

Figure 10. Example of values acquisition phase

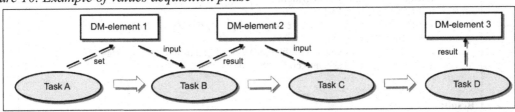

tree. Moreover, in this example, we assume that the data understanding phase of the KDD process was successfully finished, and we have all the necessary information about the data set to be mined. It means that appropriate records corresponding to the *DataSet* and *DataDictionary* DM-elements are already available in the KB, and the workflow can start with the data preprocessing task.

Phase 1: Tasks Composition

As we presented previously, the first step of the task composition is the interactive selection of the final model from a list of all available models.

The list can be obtained as a result of the following SPARQL (SPARQL, 2006) query returning a list of DM-tasks and models they produce. This query is issued by the GMA automatically. (See Box 1.)

Selection of the classification model gives us a direct link to the *getClassificationModel* DM-task that can be realized by a concrete service operation. Information about its input DM-elements and the corresponding DM-task producing them can be retrieved from the KB by submitting the following SPARQL query, which is also issued by the GMA automatically (see Box 2).

Box 1.

```
Query:

        PREFIX dmo: <http://dmo.gridminer.org/v1#>
        PREFIX rdfs: <http://www.w3.org/2000/01/rdf-schema#>
        PREFIX rdf:  <http://www.w3.org/1999/02/22-rdf-syntax-ns#>
        SELECT ?ModelName ?Task
        FROM      <http://www.gridminer.org/dmo/v1/dmo.owl>
        WHERE {
                    ?model rdf:type <#Model> .
                    ?model rdfs:label ?ModelName .
                    ?model dmo:createdBy ?Task
              }
        ORDER BY ?ModelName
```

Result:

ModelName T	ask
Association Model	getAssociationModel
Classification Model	getClassificationModel
Clustering Model	getClusteringModel
…	…

Box 2.

```
Query:
        PREFIX dmo: <http://dmo.gridminer.org/v1#>
        SELECT  ?Setting ?Task
        FROM      <http://www.gridminer.org/dmo/v1/dmo.owl>
        WHERE {
                    dmo:getClassificationModel dmo:hasSettings ?Setting .
                    ?Task dmo:create ?Setting
              }
```

Result:

Setting	Task
MiningModel	setMiningModel

Figure 11. Abstract workflow after the phase of tasks composition

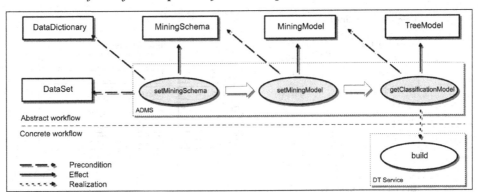

The discovered DM-task *setMiningModel* is inserted into the workflow prior to the *getClassificationModel* task, and its preconditions and inputs are examined. The only precondition of the *setMiningModel* task is the existence of the *MiningSchema* DM-element. This requirement can be satisfied by inserting the *setMiningSchema* task into the workflow, whose effect is the creation of the *MiningSchema* DM-element. The *setMiningSchema* task has two preconditions: the existence of the *DataSet* and *DataDictionary* DM-elements. Their corresponding records are already available in the KB, so no additional tasks are inserted into the abstract workflow. As the result, an abstract workflow consisting of three DM-tasks (see Figure 11) is created and is instanced as a new composite process of the ADMS in the KB. The figure also presents the DM-elements identified during the composition phase as preconditions of the involved tasks and a fragment of the concrete workflow.

Phase 2: Values Acquisition

The second phase of the workflow construction starts with the examination of the first DM-task in the abstract workflow (*setMiningSchema*). In this phase, the values of the DM-elements' properties, identified in the previous phase, are supplied by the user and additional DM-tasks are inserted as needed. The following paragraphs describe in more detail the steps of setting the DM-elements produced and used by the involved tasks.

setMiningSchema: This task can be seen as a simple data preprocessing step where data fields (attributes) used in the modeling phase can be selected and their usage types can be specified. The primary effect of this task is a new *MiningSchema* element instanced in the KB, keeping all the schema's parameters specified by the user. Moreover, the user can specify whether some preprocessing methods should be used to treat missing values and outliers of the numerical attributes. Selection of a preprocessing method requires an additional DM-task, which is able to perform the data transformations and produce a new data set that can be used in the next steps. If one of the transformation methods is selected then the KB is queried again for a task able to transform the data set. The *getTransformation* task has the ability to transform the selected data set, therefore, can be inserted into the abstract workflow in the next step.

As we presented in previous paragraphs, the *setters* are designed to interact with the user, therefore, each *setter* has a related HTML input form used by the user to insert or select the values of the examined DM-element input parameters. The GMA presents the form implemented as a

Figure 12. Input HTML form for the MiningSchema

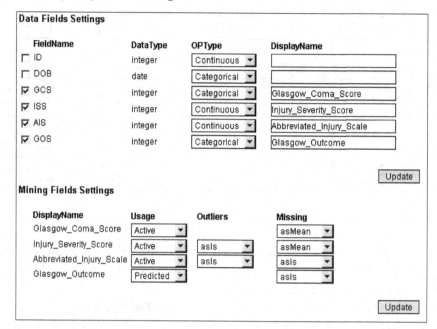

dynamic Web page to the user, and based on its inputs, the GMA updates values of the DM-elements' parameters.

Figure 12 presents the input form used by the GMA to construct the *MiningSchema* DM-element. In this form, there is one mandatory property for the classification task — 'target attribute.' It is one of the categorical *DataFields* from the *DataDictionary* element, which is the GOS in our case. Therefore, the 'target attribute' must be marked as 'predicted' in the *MiningSchema* DM-element. The effect of the *setMiningSchema* task is a newly created DM-element *Mining-Schema,* which describes mined fields and their transformations.

getTransformation: This task is inserted into the workflow right after the *setMiningSchema* task. It does not require interaction with the user because its input parameters are already specified in the *MiningSchema* created as the effect of the previous task. The task just examines the *MiningSchema* element and selects a concrete operation from

DM-Services available in the KB, which can satisfy the chosen data preprocessing objectives. The task can select operation 'transform' of the specialized *DataPreprocessing* service (DPP service) and insert it into the concrete workflow (see Figure 14).

setMiningModel: Specification of the properties of the selected model is the main purpose of this task. The GMA presents a list of all available data mining algorithms producing classification models and selects its input parameters. Based on the selected parameters, a new DM-element *MiningModel* describing model properties is created as an effect of this task. The following SPARQL query retrieves all parameters for the C4.5 classification algorithm (Quinlan, 1993) that is used to setup the *MiningModel* element in our example. (See Box 3.)

The GMA presents the results to the user in the HTML form presented in Figure 13, where the user specifies values of the input parameters

Box 3.

```
Query:

        PREFIX dmo: <http://dmo.gridminer.org/v1#>
        PREFIX rdfs:  <http://www.w3.org/2000/01/rdf-schema#>
        SELECT  ?ParameterName ?DefaultValue
        FROM        <http://www.gridminer.org/dmo/v1/dmo.owl>
        WHERE {
                        dmo:_algorithm_c4.5_Settings dmo:hasParameter ?Parameter .
                        ?Parameter rdfs:label ?ParameterName .
                        ?Parameter dmo:value ?DefaultValue
                }
        ORDER BY ?ParameterName
```

Figure 13. Input HTML form for the MiningModel

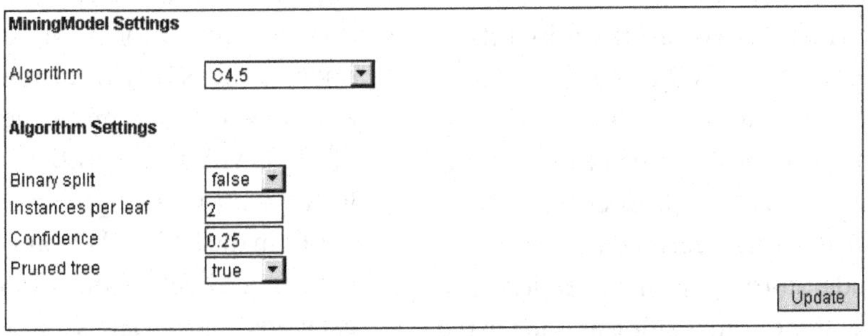

needed to build the classification model using the C4.5 algorithm.

getClassificationModel: This task examines the *MiningModel* element created in the previous task and identifies the appropriate operation that can build the classification model using *MiningModel* parameters. The task can be the operation 'build' implemented by the DecisionTree Service (DT Service), which returns the classification model represented by the PMML element TreeModel. Moreover, if parameter 'pruned tree' is marked as true (false by default) then the additional operation of the DT Service 'prune' is inserted into to the concrete workflow to assure that the discovered decision tree is modified using a pruning mechanism.

If all required parameters and preconditions of the tasks involved in the abstract workflow are satisfied then the GMA constructs a concrete workflow specification in the BPEL language and presents it to the workflow engine. The concrete workflow is a sequence of the real services and is related to the abstract DM-tasks as presented in Figure 14.

The final output returned from the workflow engine is a PMML document containing a TreeModel element that represents the demanded model that can be used to classify a particular patient into the GOS category.

The following BPEL document created in our scenario contains five variables representing the DM-elements used as inputs and outputs of the invoked operations. The variable DataSet is an

Figure 14. Abstract and concrete workflow after the phase of values acquisition

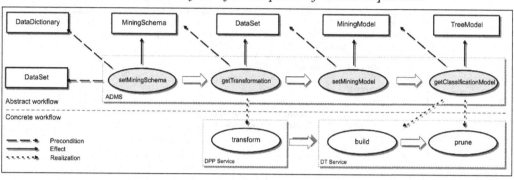

XML in WebRowSet format (RowSet Java object in XML format) storing all the initial data. TransformedDataset is a new WebRowSet created by the 'transform' operation, and TreeSettings is used as input for the 'build' and 'prune' operations. The variable TreeModel stores the PMML document with the full decision tree, and the PrunedTreeModel stores its pruned version. The BPEL flow reflects the composition as done in the concrete workflow consisting of three operations invoked in sequence. (See Box 4.)

SYSTEM PROTOTYPE

An overview of the first system prototype is shown in Figure 15. We use the OWL editor Protégé (Noy et al., 2001) to create and maintain the DMO, which is stored in the KB. To reason about knowledge in the KB, we use the Pellet reasoner (Sirin & Parsia, 2004), which is an open-source Java based OWL DL reasoner and provides a description logic interface (DIG) (Bechhofer et al., 2003). The GMA is implemented as a standalone Web application supported by the Jena Toolkit (McBride, 2003) and is able to interact with a user to assemble the required information. The GMA communicates over the DIG interface with the reasoner, which is able to answer a subset of RDQL queries (Seaborn, 2004). The GMA queries KB every time it needs to enumerate some

parameters or find a data mining task, algorithm, service, and so forth. Moreover, the GMA also updates the KB with instances of DMO classes and values of their properties. The final outcome of the GMA is a workflow document presented to the workflow engine Auriga (Brezany et al., 2006) in the BPEL4WS language. The GMA also acts as a client of the workflow engine, which executes appropriate services as described in the BPEL document and returns their outputs back to the GMA. A more detailed characterization of these major components follows.

Auriga WEEP workflow engine is an easy to execute and manage workflow enactment service for Grid and Web services. The core of the engine is implemented as a standalone application referred to as the Auriga WEEP Core, which orchestrates the services as specified in a BPEL. Auriga WEEP has also a specialized version, which is wrapped by a Grid service implementation focused on using the Globus 4 container as the running environment. The engine has a pluggable architecture, which allows additional Grid specific functionality to be used in the Auriga Core extensions.

- **Jena** is a Java framework for building Semantic Web applications. It provides a programming environment for RDF, RDFS, OWL and SPARQL and includes a rule-based inference engine.

Box 4.

```
Variables:

<variable name="DataSet" element="wrs:webRowSet"/>
<variable name="TransformedDataset" element="wrs:webRowSet "/>
<variable name="TreeModel" element="pmml:TreeModel"/>
<variable name="PrunedTreeModel" element="pmml:TreeModel"/>
<variable name="TreeSettings" element="dmo:Setting"/>

Sequence:

<sequence>
    < flow>
        <invoke partnerLink="DPPService" operation="transform"    inputVariable="DataSet"
        outputVariable="TransformedDataset" />

        <invoke partnerLink="DTService" operation="build"
        inputVariable="TreeSettings" outputVariable="TreeModel"/>

        <invoke partnerLink="DTService" operation="prune"
        inputVariable="TreeSettings"  outputVariable="PrunedTreeModel"/>
    </ flow>
</ sequence>
```

Figure 15. Overview of the prototype system

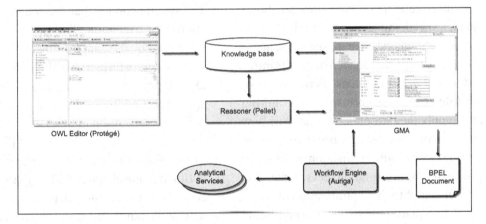

- **Pellet** provides functionalities to see the species validation, check consistency of ontologies, classify the taxonomy, check entailments and answer a subset of RDQL queries. Pellet is based on the tableaux algorithms developed for expressive Description Logics and supports the full expressivity of OWL DL.
- **Protégé** is an ontology editor and knowledge acquisition system. It implements a rich set of knowledge-modeling structures and ac-

tions that support the creation, visualization, and manipulation of ontologies in various representation formats including OWL.

FUTURE WORK

We envision the following key directions for future extension of the research presented in this chapter:

- **Active workflow engine:** This approach was already briefly discussed in the background section and sketched in Figure 1. In this case, the interaction mode between the user, workflow composer and the functionality of the composer basically remain the same as in the described passive approach. The functionality of the existing GridMiner workflow engine will be extended to be able to make dynamic decisions about the next workflow execution step based on the actual context of the knowledge base and the results of the reasoning. Moreover, the workflow composer can listen to the changes in the knowledge base and automatically interact with the user when some additional information or hints have to be supplied.

- **Workflow ranking:** The data mining ontology will be extended by estimations of each operation's effects on workflow attributes such as speed, model accuracy, etc. Due to the user's preferences (e.g., speed vs. accuracy) the composer can then better optimize individual selection steps, derive a set of workflows with the corresponding ranking and supply the best option to the workflow engine. In this process, information about the current Grid resource utilization provided by standard Grid information services can also be included into this optimization process.

- **Workflow planning:** We consider upgrading the intelligence of the workflow composer with the development of a supporting planning system which will be able to propose an abstract workflow from the specification of the goals and the initial state. We will exploit and adapt AI planning optimizations.

- **Support by autonomic computing:** We will investigate how the presented framework should be extended to be able to include some functionality of autonomic computing into the workflows composed. This involves in-vestigating workflow patterns, categorizing requirements and objectives, and designing corresponding rule templates.

CONCLUSION

The characteristics of data exploration in scientific environments impose unique requirements for workflow composition and execution systems. In this chapter, we addressed the issues of composing workflows with automated support developed on top of Semantic Web technologies and the work-flow management framework elaborated in our Grid data mining project. The kernel part of that support is a tool called the GridMiner workflow assistant (GMA), which helps the user interactively construct workflow description expressed in a standard workflow specification language. The specification is then passed to the workflow engine for execution. The GMA operations are controlled by the data mining ontology based on the concepts of PMML, JDM, WEKA and CRISP-DM. A practical example taken from a medical application addressing management of patients with traumatic brain injuries illustrates the use of the GMA. The results achieved will be extended in our future research whose key issues were outlined in the chapter. Although this research is conducted in the context of the GridMiner project, its results can be used in any system involving workflow construction activities.

FUTURE RESEARCH DIRECTIONS

In this section, we identify three future challenges and research problems in the ontology-based workflow construction and execution.

1. Extended Data Mining Ontology

Data mining as a scientific discipline is a huge domain which is still expanding. New approaches to data analyses, visualization techniques, or even new algorithms are continuously being developed. There are also plenty of real applications tailored to the application domain specifically for data mining tasks. Therefore, it is nearly impossible to completely describe this dynamic field of data mining with a static ontology. The ontology proposed in our chapter can only be used for a subset of the high number of data mining tasks. Hence we see new opportunities in extending the proposed data mining ontology with different, application domain specific, tasks that would better express the functionality of the constructed workflows.

2. Quality of Services and Workflows

Another issue that is not fully covered in the proposed ontology is the description of the quality of the involved data mining services. Especially in the Grid infrastructures, the properties of the involved resources (e.g., performance, price, bandwidth, etc.) play the crucial role in their discovery and right selection. So we see another opportunity in the detailed description of the data mining services' properties which can be done as a direct extension of the OLW-S language. Moreover, there can also be a detailed description of the composed workflows' quality which can be used for effective ranging of the entire workflows.

3. Autonomic Behavior of the Workflow Enactment Engine

Autonomic computing is one of the hottest topics in information technologies. Different areas in computer science, ranging from hardware to software implementation on the application level, try to apply some autonomic features (like, e.g., self-tuning, self-configuration, self-healing, etc.) to assure stability and availability of the system. The autonomic behavior of the Workflow Engine can ensure that the execution of the data mining workflows results in a required goal even in such a dynamic environment as the Grid where the Workflow Engine must react to the changes of the involved resources and adopt its behavior to new conditions and reflect the actual 'State of the Grid'.

REFERENCES

Agrawal, R., & Srikant, R. (1994). Fast algorithms for mining association rules in large databases. In *Proceedings of the International Conference on Very Large Databases* (pp. 478-499). Santiage, Chile: Morgan Kaufmann.

Antonioletti, M., Krause, A., Paton, N. W., Eisenberg, A., Laws, S., Malaika, S., et al. (2006). The WS-DAI family of specifications for web service data access and integration. *ACM SIGMOD Record, 35*(1), 48-55.

Arkin, A. (2002). *Business process modeling language* (BPML). Specification. BPMI.org.

Arkin, A., Askary, S., Bloch, B., Curbera, F., Goland, Y., Kartha, N., et al. (2005). *Web services business process execution language version* 2.0. wsbpel-specificationdraft-01, OASIS.

BEA, IBM, Microsoft, SAP, & Siebel. (2003). *Business process execution language for Web services*. Version 1.1. Specification. Retrieved May 15, 2006, from ftp://www6.software.ibm.com/software/developer/library/ws-bpel.pdf

Bechhofer, S., Moller, R., & Crowther, P. (2003). *The DIG description logic interface.* International Workshop on Description Logics, Rome, Italy.

Beco, S., Cantalupo, B., Matskanis, N., & Surridge M. (2006). *Putting semantics in Grid workflow management: The OWL-WS approach.* GGF16 Semantic Grid Workshop, Athens, Greece.

Bernstein, A., Hill, S., & Provost, F. (2001). An intelligent assistant for the knowledge discovery process. *In Proceedings of the IJCAI-01 Workshop on Wrappers for Performance Enhancement in KDD*. Seattle, WA: Morgan Kaufmann.

Brezany, P., Tjoa, A.M., Rusnak, M., & Janciak, I. (2003). Knowledge Grid support for treatment of traumatic brain injury victims. *International Conference on Computational Science and its Applications*. Montreal, Canada.

Brezany, P., Janciak, I., Woehrer, A., & Tjoa, A.M. (2004). *GridMiner: A Framework for knowledge discovery on the Grid - from a vision to design and implementation*. Cracow Grid Workshop, Cracow, Poland: Springer.

Brezany, P., Janciak, I., Kloner, C., & Petz, G. (2006). *Auriga — workflow engine for WS-I/WS-RF services*. Retrieved September 15, 2006, from http://www.Gridminer.org/auriga/

Bussler ,C., Davies, J., Dieter, F., & Studer , R. (2004). The Semantic Web: Research and applications. In *Proceedings of the 1st European Semantic Web Symposium, ESWS. Lecture Notes in Computer Science, 3053*. Springer.

Chapman, P., Clinton, J., Khabaza, T., Reinartz, T., & Wirth. R. (1999). *The CRISP-DM process model*. Technical report, CRISM-DM consortium. Retrieved May 15, 2006, from http://www.crisp-dm.org/CRISPWP-0800.pdf

Christensen, E., Curbera, F., Meredith, G., & Weerawarana, S. (2001). *Web Services Description Language* (WSDL) 1.1. Retrieved May 10, 2006, from http://www.w3.org/TR/wsdl

Data Mining Group. (2004). *Predictive model markup language*. Retrieved May 10, 2006, from http://www.dmg.org/

Deelman, E., Blythe, J., Gil, Y., & Kesselman, C. (2003). Workflow management in GriPhyN. *The Grid Resource Management*. The Netherlands: Kluwer.

Globus Alliance (2005). *Globus Toolkit 4*. http://www.globus.org

Globus Alliance, IBM, & HP (2004). *The WS-Resource framework*. Retrieved May 10, 2006, from http://www.globus.org/wsrf/

Hornick, F. M., et al. (2005). *Java data mining 2.0*. Retrieved June 20, 2006, from http://jcp.org/aboutJava/communityprocess/edr/jsr247/

Horrocks, I., Patel-Schneider, P. F., Boley, H., Tabet, S., Grosof, B., & Dean, M. (2004). *SWRL: A Semantic Web rule language combining OWL and RuleML*. W3C Member Submission. Retrieved May 10, 2006, from http://www.w3.org/Submission/2004/SUBM-SWRL-20040521

Kickinger, G., Hofer, J., Tjoa, A.M., & Brezany, P. (2003). Workflow mManagement in GridMiner. *The 3rd Cracow Grid Workshop*. Cracow, Poland: Springer.

Leymann, F. (2001). *Web services flow language (WSFL 1.0)*. Retrieved September 23, 2002, from www4.ibm.com/software/solutions/webservices/pdf/WSFL.pdf

Majithia, S., Walker, D. W., & Gray, W.A. (2004). *A framework for automated service composition in service-oriented architectures* (pp. 269-283). ESWS.

Martin, D., Paolucci, M., McIlraith, S., Burstein, M., McDermott, D., McGuinness, D., et al.(2004). Bringing semantics to Web services: The OWL-S approach. In *Proceedings of the 1st International Workshop on Semantic Web Services and Web Process Composition*. San Diego, California.

McBride, B. (2002). Jena: A Semantic Web toolkit. *IEEE Internet Computing*, November /December, 55-59.

Oinn, T. M., Addis, M., Ferris, J., Marvin, D., Senger, M., Greenwood, R. M., et al. (2004). Taverna: A tool for the composition and enactment of bioinformatics workflows. *Bioinformatics, 20*(17), 3045-3054.

Noy, N. F. , Sintek, M., Decker, S., Crubezy, M., Fergerson, R. W., & Musen, M.A. (2001). Creating Semantic Web contents with Protege-2000. *IEEE Intelligent Systems, 16*(2), 60-71.

Quinlan, R. (1993). *C4.5: Programs for machine learning.* San Mateo, CA: Morgan Kaufmann Publishers.

Sairafi, S., A., Emmanouil, F. S., Ghanem, M., Giannadakis, N., Guo, Y., Kalaitzopolous, D., et al. (2003). The design of discovery net: Towards open Grid services for knowledge discovery. *International Journal of High Performance Computing Applications, 17*(3).

Seaborne, A. (2004). *RDQL: A query language for RDF.* Retrieved May 10, 2006, from http://www. w3.org/Submission/RDQL/

Sirin, E., & Parsia, B. (2004). *Pellet: An OWL DL Reasoner, 3rd International Semantic Web Conference*, Hiroshima, Japan. Springer.

Sirin, E.B. Parsia, B., & Hendler, J. (2004). Filtering and selecting Semantic Web services with interactive composition techniques. *IEEE Intelligent Systems, 19*(4), 42-49.

SPARQL. Query Language for RDF, W3C Working Draft 4 October 2006. Retrieved October 8, 2006, from http://128.30.52.31/TR/rdf-sparql-query/

Thatte, S. (2001). *XLANG: Web services for business process design.* Microsoft Corporation, Initial Public Draft.

Tsalgatidou, A., & Pilioura, T. (2002). An overview of standards and related technology in web services. *Distributed and Parallel Databases. 12*(3).

Witten, I.H., & Eibe, F. (2005). *Data mining: Practical machine learning tools and techniques.* (2nd ed.). San Francisco: Morgan Kaufmann.

World Wide Web Consortium. (2004). *OWL Web ontology language semantics and abstract syntax.* W3C Recommendation 10 Feb, 2004.

ADDITIONAL READING

For more information on the topics covered in this chapter, see http://www.Gridminer.org and also the following references:

Alesso, P. H., & Smith, F. C. (2005). *Developing Semantic Web services.* A.K. Peterson Ltd.

Antoniou, G., & Harmelen, F. (2004). *A Semantic Web primer.* MIT Press.

Davies, J., Studer, R., & Warren P. (2006). *Semantic Web technologies: Trends and research in ontology-based systems.* John Wiley & Sons.

Davies, N. J., Fensel, D., & Harmelen, F. (2003). *Towards the Semantic Web: Ontology-driven knowledge management.* John Wiley & Sons.

Foster, I., & Kesselman, C. (1999). *The Grid: Blueprint for a new computing infrastructure.* Morgan Kaufmann.

Fox, G.C., Berman, F., & Hey, A.J.G. (2003). *Grid computing: Making the global infrastructure a reality.* John Wiley & Sons.

Han, J., & Kamber, M. (2000) *Data mining: Concepts and techniques.* Morgan Kaufmann.

Lacy, L.W. (2005). *Owl: Representing information using the Web ontology language.* Trafford Publishing.

Li, M., & Baker, M. (2005). *The Grid: Core technologies.* John Wiley & Sons.

Marinescu, D.C. (2002) *Internet-based workflow management: Toward a Semantic Web.* John Wiley & Sons.

Matjaz, B.J., Sarang, P.G., & Mathew, B. (2006). *Business process execution language for Web services* (2nd ed.). Packt Publishing.

Murch, R. (2004). *Autonomic computing.* Published by IBM Press.

Oberle, D. (2005). *The semantic management of middleware.* Springer.

Singh, M.P., & Huhns, M.N. (2006). *Service-oriented computing: Semantics, processes, agents.* John Wiley & Sons.

Sotomayor, B., & Childers, L. (2006). *Globus Toolkit 4: Programming Java services.* Morgan Kaufmann.

Stojanovic, Z., & Dahanayake. A. (2005). *Service oriented software system engineering: Challenges and practices.* Idea Group Inc.

Taylor, I. J., Deelman E., Gannon, D. B., & Shields, M. (2007). *Workflows for e-science.* Springer.

Zhong, N., Liu, J., & Yao, Y. (2003). *Web intelligence.* Springer.

Zhu, X., & Davidson, I. (2007). *Knowledge discovery and data mining: Challenges and realities.* Idea Group Inc.

Zhuge, H. (2004). *The knowledge Grid.* World Scientific.

Chapter XI
Ontology–Based Data Warehousing and Mining Approaches in Petroleum Industries

Shastri L. Nimmagadda
Kuwait Gulf Oil Company, Kuwait

Heinz Dreher
Curtin University of Technology, Australia

ABSTRACT

Several issues of database organization of petroleum industries have been highlighted. Complex geo-spatial heterogeneous data structures complicate the accessibility and presentation of data in petroleum industries. Objectives of the current research are to integrate the data from different sources and connect them intelligently. Data warehousing approach supported by ontology, has been described for effective data mining of petroleum data sources. Petroleum ontology framework, narrating the conceptualization of petroleum ontology and methodological architectural views, has been described. Ontology-based data warehousing with fine-grained multidimensional data structures, facilitate to mining and visualization of data patterns, trends, and correlations, hidden under massive volumes of data. Data structural designs and implementations deduced, through ontology supportive data warehousing approaches, will enable the researchers in commercial organizations, such as, the one of Western Australian petroleum indus-tries, for knowledge mapping and thus interpret knowledge models for making million dollar financial decisions.

OVERVIEW

Data in major commercial petroleum industries are complex in nature and often poorly organized and duplicated, and exist in different formats. Business, in these companies, is operated both in space and time. Due to the diverse nature of business products and operations in different geographic locations, these industries demand more accurate and precise information and data. Businesses operating in multiclient or multiuser environments with redundant data are prone to carry information with several ambiguities and anomalies.

With the widespread use of databases and explosive growth in their sizes, petroleum businesses face a problem of information overload. Effectively utilizing these massive volumes of data is becoming a major challenge for this type of industry. Data searching becomes tedious when specific queries are made, due to the piling up of volumes of data and information accumulated in several places, such as Websites and Web servers. In order to compete and increase profitability in world markets, it is vital for fast growing businesses to carry out mapping and integration of multioperational data structures. This can deliver accurate and precise information, which is crucial for elegant and economic decision support. Information in the form of knowledge or intelligence extracted from business data always adds value to the quality of decision-making. For the purpose of building knowledge from petroleum business data, an ontology approach that supports data warehousing, combined with data mining and visualization techniques, is a significant breakthrough. This chapter addresses issues of importing/exporting data from Web resources or data from offline sources, their logical and physical storage, and accessing, interpreting, and presenting the explored information.

Sedimentary basins, which are known to bear oil and natural gas deposits, may consist of several petroleum systems. We examine these systems as synonymous with other information systems. Ontology is proposed for simplifying the complexity of petroleum exploration and production data of different petroleum systems. This has prompted the development of various conceptual models and translating them into logical data models by a multidimensional data mapping approach.

These logical data models will be converted into implementation models, using a contemporary DBMS (for example, Oracle), such as warehouse approach, proposed by us. Specific requests will be made with queries for locating a specific piece of data or information from these warehouses. Simple mining algorithms will be developed and used for extracting patterns, correlations and trends from petroleum data. These patterns and trends are interpreted for a meaningful geological knowledge.

INTRODUCTION

Large amounts of petroleum operational data are routinely collected and stored in the archives of many organizations. Much of the data archived for informational, as well as audit purposes, are still under-utilized or many personnel do not know what to do with them. However, by analyzing the petroleum data of one basin, it would be possible to discover exploration, drilling, and production patterns of other basins and use these patterns for future planning of various classes of drillable exploratory or development wells. Such an approach was not feasible until recently due to limitations in both hardware and software. In the recent past (Pujari, 2002) there has been a tremendous improvement in hardware—several (gigabytes) GB of main memory, multi terabytes of disk space with multi GHz of processing speed on a PC. Thus, computer programs, which sift massive amounts of operational data recognize data patterns and provide hints to formulate hypotheses for tactical and strategic decision-making, can now be executed in a reasonable time. This has opened up a productive area of research to formulate appropriate algorithms for mining archival data to devise and test hypotheses. In this project, an array of ideas from computer science, information technology, statistics and management science are being applied for organizing these heterogeneous petroleum exploration and production data for effective data mining and data visualization.

Several data mining tools are available to analyze, hypothesize, and discover relations among various data items, stored in data warehouses. So far, these tools have been successfully applied in many finance and marketing companies. However, these technologies are still under-utilized in the petroleum industries; for example, a typical user forms a hypothesis about a relationship between data entities and verifies it or rejects it with a series of queries against the data. The petroleum business analyst might hypothesize about an oil-bearing sedimentary basin: whether the possibility of exploring oil or gas can be investigated; where favorable structural settings and other oil-play factors exist. Data mining could be employed to test such hypotheses in different basins of similar oil plays. Similarly, knowing that multipay horizons

Figure 1. Western Australian maps: (a) surveys, wells, permits and oil fields and (b) oil and gas fields associated with structures

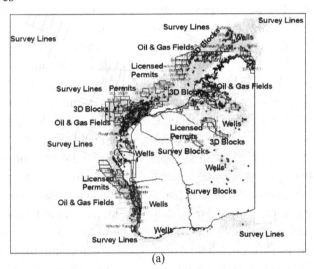

(a)

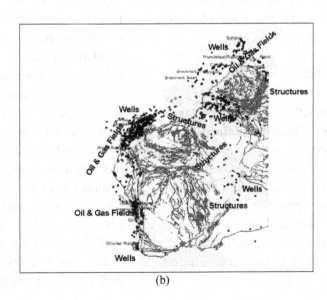

(b)

of a particular geological formation belonging to particular geological age are producing oil from a drilled-well of a particular basin, what are the chances of producing oil from similar pay horizons, from the wells of other adjacent basins?

In our proposed case scenarios, for example, several oil, gas, and condensate fields are situated in a number of Western Australian basins. Wells, located on these petroleum prospects, are drilled based on the analysis of variety of surveys (geological, geophysical, and geochemical) and well-log data (petro-physical in nature). Their life span ranges between 5-15 or even more than 20 years in productive basins. Some wells cease to produce petroleum after a few days. Many wells are abandoned and/or suspended, due to the nonexistence of hydrocarbons and the poor commercial viability of some oil fields. Such actions result from poor knowledge and understanding of petroleum systems and interpretation of such ambiguous petroleum-plays. There could be multipay horizons in many wells in different basins. Oil-pay horizons interpreted in certain drilled wells in a basin may eventually be present in other wells of other basins. Petroleum-plays in such situations are complex to narrate. Quality of oil-play factors of a prospect in one basin may be poor, but it may be better in other basins. Analysis of petroleum system and its associated oil-play factors is crucial to realization of the full potential of petroleum prospects.

Problem Definition

In spite of major breakthroughs and advances in resources technologies, identification and the precise description of petroleum systems that narrate oil play factors remain unresolved issues of basins around the globe, including Western Australian basins. Numerous exploration and discovery findings and their associated articles have been published in journals. These published records cover different petroleum systems describing oil-

plays and represent a huge range of exploration and development findings of many basins.

Two major issues are adversely affecting the efficiency and advancement of petroleum business data research and petroleum exploration. These issues are (1) effective access to distributed unstructured information (both Web and off-line sources) and (2) lack of an existing infrastructure to support just-in-time (JIT) precise and accurate information access, and its retrieval. If the operational data are not appropriately integrated, information that is shared by various operational units may lead to failure of crucial operational activities. We attempt to use a systematic shared ontology, supporting data warehouse modeling, and data mining research to organize and store valuable petroleum industries data. Most of the published results are available on the Web through journal databases and resources databases in several formats and on software platforms, and thus amenable to this approach. Historical data are also available in hard copies. For example, historical exploration and production data (see Figure 1) in Canning, Carnarvon, Bonaparte, Browse, Officer, Eucla and Perth basins are available in different media and at times, these valuable data are not simply retrievable for computer analysis.

Understanding the prospect of a basin is a significant problem. Data integration and information sharing among different fields or prospects of different basins are key issues of the present problem definition. Little attention has been given to integrating and organizing these historical data. Ontologies for structuring data warehouses and techniques for mining the warehoused data are needed for solving problems associated with data integration and information sharing. To date, there has been no systematic investigation of these data volumes using the proposed, focused technologies. Meticulous analysis of oil-plays of different petroleum systems of different fields associated with different basins is a much-needed research. Even without additional surveys or exploratory drilling, many more prospects can be explored or discovered by data mining of warehoused existing exploration and production data. Unorganized volumes of massive stores of oil and gas business data hide undiscovered (unknown knowledge or intelligence) data patterns. Interpreting the patterns, correlations and trends among exploration, drilling and production data as well as their oil-play factors into meaningful scientific geological and petroleum business information, is the goal of our current research.

The cost of drilling a well varies from five to ten million dollars. Two key data structural scenarios are considered to improve the economics of petroleum reservoirs both at exploration and development stages involving (1) oil-play factors (reservoir, structure, source-maturity, seal, migration, timing of petroleum generation) have a major role in ascertaining efficiency of different petroleum systems of Western Australian oil-bearing sedimentary basins narrating their potentiality (Figure 2a). (2) Exploration, drilling, production, and marketing data entities of Western Australian petroleum industry situation are considered for understanding the exploration and production system (which is again an information system) of each basin (Figure 2b).

Related Work

Research articles on ontology, data warehousing, and data mining have been examined for their feasibility and applicability to oil and gas company operations. (Guan & Zhu, 2004; O'Leary, 2000; Uschold, 1998) discuss concepts of ontology, and principles of conceptual modeling and ontology acquisition. Hadzic and Chang, (2005) (Jasper & Uschold, 1999; Shanks et al., 2003; Shanks et al., 2004) demonstrate ontology modeling, its validation, semantic conceptualization in various industry applications. Concepts of data warehousing, data modeling procedures for data warehouse design, and their applications in oil and gas industry scenarios are critically examined in (Gornik, 2000; Hoffer et al., 2005; Nimmagadda

et al., 2005b; Nimmagadda & Rudra, 2005c; Nimmagadda & Rudra, 2005d; Rudra & Nimmagadda, 2005; Nimmagadda & Dreher, 2006). They investigate issues of database structuring methodologies and multidimensionality and granularity of data structures in oil and gas exploration business applications. (Nimmagadda et al., 2005a) examine issues of ontology modeling approach in mapping complex oil and gas business data entities, described at various operational unit levels of a petroleum company. Pujari, (2002) and (Dunham, 2003) provide comprehensive insights of data mining technologies with different computing algorithms and applications of various company situations. Biswas et al., (1995), (Cheung et al., 2000; Guha et al., 1999; Huang, 1997; Matsuzawa & Fukuda, 2000; Ng & Han, 1994; Pei et al., 2000; Ramkumar & Swami, 1998; Yao & Zhong, 2000; Yun & Chen, 2000; Zhong et al., 1996) describe several data mining techniques such as clustering, associative rule mining and in constructing classifiers using decision tree structures. Often petroleum data are represented in spatio-temporal forms. Miller & Han, (2001), (Ott & Swiaczny, 2001; Zhou et al., 1996) illustrate use of spatio-temporal datasets and organize them in a warehouse environment and explore these data using data mining procedures.

Longley et al., (2001) illustrate the 21st century's frontier areas of petroleum prospects in Australian sedimentary basins. Telford et al., (1998) investigate critically the significance of geological, geophysical, and geochemical exploration and prospecting for petroleum deposits in different geological environments. They also significantly investigate types of oil-play and their analysis. Huston et al., (2003) and Gilbert et al., (2004) discuss several burning issues of exploring and exploiting prospective reservoirs using data integration techniques. Several issues on reservoir, structural, and strati-structural plays under different geological settings have been described. Dodds and Fletcher, (2004) describe issues of risks involved in drilling in explored, under-explored and detailed exploration areas. Hori and Ohashi, (2005) and Erdman and Rudi, (2001) demonstrate the use of XML technologies for preparing and delivering the explored data through Internet. Weimer and Davis, (1995) discuss different petroleum systems of the USA, Middle-East, Russia, and South America narrating stratigraphic and structural plays. Johnston, (2004) discusses issues of time-lapse 4-D technology that help minimize drilling dry holes and reservoir model uncertainty. Aside from brief discussions on ontology issues in oil companies (Meersman, 2004), there is no concrete literature available on ontology application in oil and gas industries as on today.

Major Issues of Petroleum Industries

Fast tracking and developing infrastructure for accessing accurate and precise petroleum data from multiple sources, the first author, with his vast work experience and knowledge of major oil companies and discussions with national and international operators in Western Australia and abroad, has identified the following major issues to be resolved:

- **Petroleum data management:**
    - Massive storage devices are needed to store volumes of data (of the order of 10 GB for each basin) to describe the number of petroleum systems in several basins. Data pertaining to a range of factors across several basins amount to several gigabytes in size; these factors include reservoir, structure, seal, source, migration, and deposition timing. The petroleum data include surveys, wells, permits, and production data. Large upstream integrated petroleum companies (exploration, drilling, production, and marketing) are unable to manage multifaceted data comprising of heterogeneous data structures (relational, hierarchical, and networking) with complex data types, such as spatio-temporal forms.
    - Handling numerous entities (of the order of 500) and attributes (of the order of 1000), mapping and modeling hundreds of tables is a tedious process.
    - Data integration (sometimes among 10-15 operational centers) of enormous amount of multidisciplinary data is a serious business in large oil and gas companies. Sharing of data in a multiclient environment must be a prerequisite for carrying out the successful exploration and production business.
    - Managing large volumes of databases in petroleum industries is one of the major issues today. As business grows, data volumes associated with petroleum industries get accumulated in unmanageable way, especially in the knowledge domain.
- **Petroleum data mining and knowledge building:**
    - Knowledge-building from these massive data structures is an intricate issue. With increasing volumes of periodic data, there is difficulty in understanding or retrieving knowledge. At times, many operational units are forced to integrate and share volumes of multidisciplinary data without prior knowledge of a petroleum system in a basin. In other words, expensive field operations (e.g., drilling, oil field monitoring, production casing) are carried out in many basins without prior knowledge or outcome of operations.
    - More petroleum resources can be explored and exploited based on existing exploration and production data.
    - Inconsistency among petroleum metadata and basin characteristics affects the economics involved in planning and developing drilling programs. Unknown

Figure 2. (a) Classifying the similarity of oil-play data properties for constructing a petroleum system; Figure 2. (b) classifying petroleum exploration and production attributes for constructing E&P systems

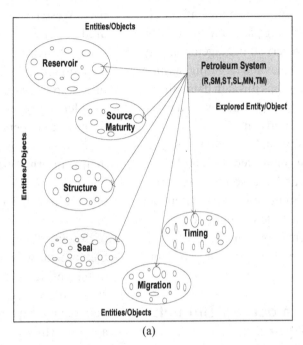

(a)

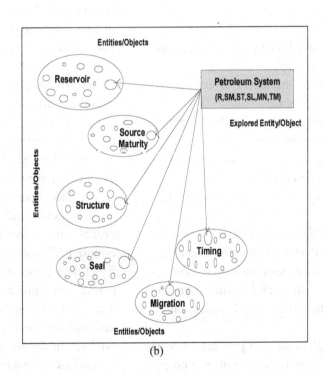

(b)

relationships among the hydrocarbon accumulations, formation (sequences of geological unit) pressures and their economic significance may affect pre and post drilling plans and their costs. Improved reservoir management, may reduce dry holes and targeting optimal well completions through data mining of reservoir and production data in the temporal dimension.

° Applicability and feasibility of data warehouse supported by ontological modeling, and a combined application of data mining and visualization can have a tremendous impact on petroleum system knowledge discovery that changes the economics of petroleum business.

Conceptual Data Modeling Through an Ontological Approach

The following steps are needed:

1. Acquire data attributed to the development of petroleum system.
2. Identify entities, attributes of exploration and production data.
3. Build relationships among entities with their common attributes.
4. Structure and de-structure complex relationships among data entities.
5. Acquire surveys, wells, permits and production data.
6. Represent all the entities in to relational, hierarchical and networked data structures.
7. Collect reservoir, structure, seal, source-maturity, migration and timing data and generate conceptual models using ontology.
8. Integrate exploration and production costs data and developing relationships with petroleum systems data.

Nimmagadda et al. (2005a) demonstrate ontology application in petroleum industry that evaluates the inventory of the petroleum reserves in the Western Australian producing basins. Hundreds of entities and their attributes associated with petroleum systems and their elements are well organized ontologically and semantically in a warehousing approach, so that basin and petroleum system knowledge is well understood for managing petroleum reserve inventories.

Ontology provides basic knowledge and semantic information for designing the data warehouse in petroleum exploration and production in oil-play knowledge domains. Database designers may use conceptual modeling to design hundreds of fact and dimension tables using relational and hierarchical structures. Unless the true meaning of the entities and their relationships are understood, the conceptual model, representing the petroleum company's data and the business rules applied, while mapping the entities and relationships, is incomplete, thus making its design more inconsistent. Inconsistencies or errors that occur during database design are expensive to fix at later stages of warehouse development. A commitment to ontology will help ensure consistency. Data warehouse maintenance and administration are other issues to be judged while developing an ontology or conceptual model. This plays a role in gaining a holistic understanding of petroleum company data. Models that use relationships and associations or properties of geological, geophysical and geo-chemical entities (Figure 2) that affect oil-play factors and characterize data integration process, may also undermine the data warehouse maintainer's ability to understand the complexity of data structures. They may complicate the maintenance process and become error prone if data structural inconsistencies are not rectified and true meaning of resources data entities has not been understood.

End users of a data warehouse may also employ conceptual models to help formulate the queries or updates of databases. If semantics of petroleum data and the relationships among their entities are not understood, users may not have realized the significance of the role of ontology in warehouse data model design. Ontologies and the semantics of petroleum data are very complex and one should try to model the full range of semantics and all possible conceptual model scenarios that will arise during the design of logical data schemas at later stages.

Key entities are considered for understanding the relationships among surveys, wells, permits, and production operational activities (Figure 3). Based on the operational activities, the hierarchical structural data view has been described. Exploration is a key, subject-oriented, and generalized super-type entity, from which other specialized entities such as onshore, offshore and geological, geophysical, and geo-chemical entities can also be derived for building future data relationships. The present study embodies the scenarios for applying ontology and achieving the purpose of oil and gas industry data integration, as discussed in the following sections.

Figure 3. Conceptual modeling of surveys, wells and permits entities showing known and unknown relationships

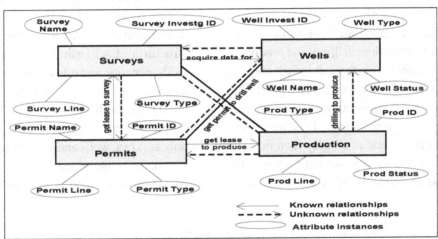

Figure 4. Conceptual modeling of oil-play entities showing known and unknown relationships

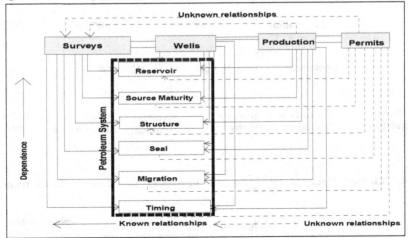

Similar to multidimensional schemas, object-oriented data schemas can also be constructed using petroleum ontology. In general, in multidimensional schemas, relationships among the common attributes are de-normalized, so that the final data views become finer for effective data mining. Here, data relevant to activities such as exploration, drilling and production have been organized in their corresponding data structures, thus emerging a metadata model that comprise of various data structures of different operational activities. Figure 4 represents a conceptual modeling of oil-play entities and performance indicators of petroleum systems.

A petroleum ontology is described in a warehousing environment that consist of all semantics, concepts of entities, attributes, properties, and associations among attributes, entities, and constraints. Exploration, drilling, and production databases possess multifaceted information. In exploration, the meaning of surveys (geological, geophysical and geo-chemical, Figure 5), wells and permits entities is translated and interpreted in other domains such as oil-play factors, reservoir, source maturity, seal, structure, migration, timing, and so forth. At times, there are direct

relationships among entities and in other cases, new relationships are created which may have been unknown (see Figures 3 and 4). Benefits of our proposed warehousing approach include knowledge reuse, improved maintainability, and long-term knowledge retention. An exploration ontology is a description and integration of the oil and gas company's exploration data. It is a specification of concepts to be used for expressing knowledge, including types and classes of entities, the kinds of attributes and properties they can have, the relationships and functions they can perform and constraints that they can hold. The IS-A skeleton of a typical ontology of oil and gas company with tree shaped hierarchical structures, is represented in Figures 5 and 6.

As shown in Figure 6, basin ontology is demonstrated with its hierarchical location data structuring. Each basin consists of several surveys, wells, permits, and other geographical data, such as river channels, geo-morphology in land and coastal areas, lineation features, hard and soft rock areas. In the context of petroleum provinces, only surveys, wells and permits have been shown Figure 3. As mentioned earlier, each petroleum province (region) consists of a sedimentary basin,

Figure 5. Demonstrating the oil and gas company's hierarchical ontology

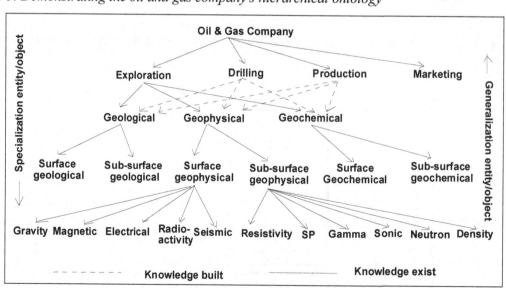

survey lines may be falling both in dip and strike direction of this region and each survey, may again be possessing hundreds of survey points such as CDP (common depth point) or CMP (common mid point). These points may be in 2D or 3D dimensions as depicted in Figure 6.

An ontology carries sufficient and useful information from its structuring. The ontology definition provider is responsible for defining a suitable ontology representation, which may save time and cost in capturing the data and information content from other multiple entities. Ontologists and RDBMS designers communicate with each other, and interact with existing database structures and integrate them with our proposed ontological structures from various data sources. Data may also have been captured from lateral (horizontal) or longitudinal (vertical) data sources, having several dimensions for the purpose of integrating data and extracting meaningful data or information. As shown in Figures 5 and 6, given two different ontological structures, with existing and built-up relationships, one can look for similarity of ontology and for exchange of common information or data into other structures. After an operational unit receives ontological data structures and transmits this to other applications, programming logic (such as our data warehouse) will enable communication among common structural entities. As revealed

in Figure 7, an application process integrates the incoming ontology into its own ontology. First, it will check the petroleum ontology database for similarities to establish the relationships that can map between two ontologies. If some dimensions or facts of the relationships contradict each other, the part in contradiction will be rejected or placed into other future ontology integration processes. As demonstrated in Figure 6, the application finds that S22 and T11 are common in their properties or characteristics, so T11 is merged with S22 in the resultant integrated structural ontology. During the ontology mapping process, if a parent ontology finds a common child ontology, then they are merged and integrated; accordingly the petroleum database ontology is updated after each and every integration and merging process.

For example, for the purpose of data integration, ontology structures of navigational, surveys and well-data need to be merged into one single metadata structure. This substantiates the view described in Figure 7. Other issues of ontology structuring involved in connecting different specialized entities of super-type entities are:

- **Ontology as specification:** Ontology in a given domain, such as exploration, drilling, or production, is created and used as a basis for specification and development of data warehouse schemas or UML models for

Figure 6. Demonstrating the basin (location hierarchy) ontology

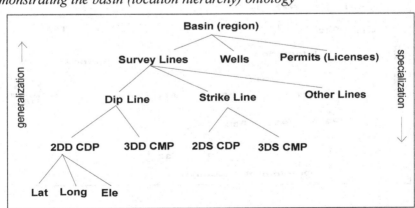

surveys (within the generalized entity of exploration) entity. Benefits of this approach include documentation, maintenance, reliability, and knowledge (re) use.

- **Common access to information:** Information is required by one or more persons (geologists, geophysicists, and reservoir engineers in our application) or computing applications (seismic workstation, ZMAP, LASLOG, GIS, or remote sensing), but is expressed using unfamiliar vocabulary, or in an inaccessible format. Ontology facilitates rendering of information intelligible by providing a shared understanding of the terms, or by mapping between sets of terms. Benefits of this approach include interoperability, and more effective use and reuse of knowledge resources in other applications.
- **Ontology-based search:** Ontology is used for searching an information repository for desired resources. The chief benefit of this approach is faster access to important information resources, which leads to more effective use and reuse of knowledge resources.

Ontology Application Framework

A comprehensive framework for understanding and classifying ontology application in software engineering has been discussed in (Jasper & Uschold, 1999). Figure 8 shows a flow chart of the application process, narrating ontology at application design and development levels. Petroleum data are represented in either relational or hierarchical structures. Constructing the ontology structure is a bonus for relational database application, since all the relationships and properties among entities described in ontology come to play a similar role as in relational data structure design. As depicted in Figure 8, an ontological view of the heterogeneous data, describing semantic information, rules/axioms is addressed. Further, the data undergo rigorous mapping and modeling in warehouse structuring, representing multidimensional views. These contain new structural data consisting of subject-oriented, integrated, time-variant, nonvolatile collections of data (Hoffer et al., 2005) used in support of management decision-making processes and extracting business intelligence in the data mining stage.

Figure 7. Process of integrating parent ontology with its similar property child ontology

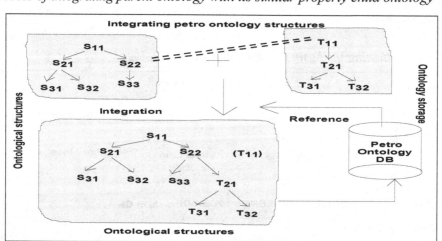

Figure 8 is a proposed architecture. Ontologically structured data are warehoused through logical multidimensional structures. These structures are similar to star, snowflake and fact constellation schemas (Hoffer et al., 2005), which are deployed for constructing multidimensional logical data models. These models are implemented in a warehousing environment, storing them for future data mining purposes. Mined data will be analyzed for data patterns at later stages.

In this research, our work is limited to describing ontology and its implication in a warehouse design. The proposed ontology framework (as illustrated in Figure 8) will provide integration of heterogeneous data, captured from various operational units for ontological structuring, including semantics and business rules applied during ontological mapping. The actual mechanism involving the ontologist, application developer, and user is described in the following section.

Ontology: A Composite Framework

Essentially, ontologies are used to improve communication between either computers or humans involved in developing ontologies. An ontologist develops several semantic database structures that are in agreement with petroleum data application developers' needs. As demonstrated in Figure 9, operational petroleum data have to be understood in terms of the true meaning of entities and their relationships participating either in the relational and or hierarchical database mapping and modeling process. Ontologist and application developers conform in reading/writing the data. Ontologically processed petroleum data are fed to the applications involved in data warehousing and data mining of resources data as shown in Figure 10.

For the sake of simplicity, we describe key ontological structures in a standard syntax. Similar syntax can be written for other structural models as well.

Knowledge-base structural models: A model structure Z for L (logic) is a 5-tuple <Pos, Expl, Dri, Prod, Mkt>. Here $S = U\{(Pos, Expl) R1\}$ and $U\{(Expl, Dri) R2\}$ are domains of Z structure, and consists of the union of two mutually disjoint sets (Pos, Expl), R1 and (Expl, Dri), R2. (Pos, Expl) is a set of individual entities of S and R is a set of relationships between (Pos, Expl) and (Expl,

Figure 8. Petroleum ontology framework

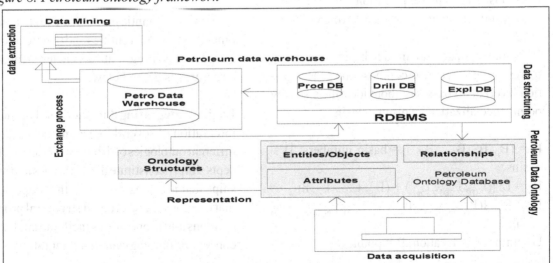

Figure 9. Conceptualization of petroleum ontology

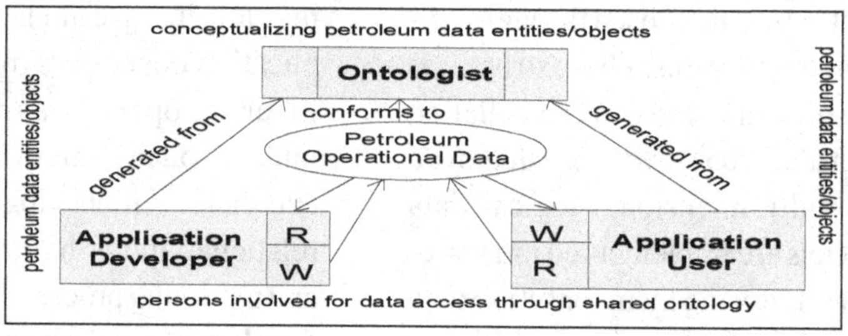

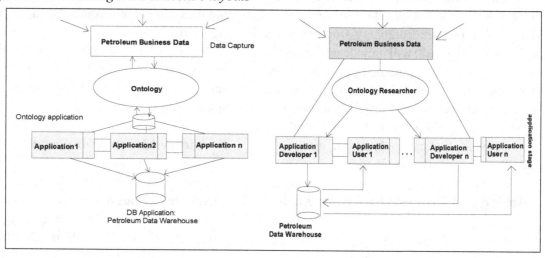

Figure 10. Methodological architecture layouts

Dri) entities. R is partitioned in different ways as designer wanted it as R1 and R2, since the prior entity combinations are logically related. Here Pos = position; Expl = exploration; Dri = drilling; Prod=production; and Mkt=marketing entities.

Another structural model basin_line_point representing a region (R) composite (at generalization level) of all basins is about locating a survey point (specialization level) in a basin.

$R = (B_1, B_2, B_3 ... B_i)$; i = basin numbers; B = basins

$B_m = U \{(L_{1D}, L_{2D}...L_{mD}) + (L_{1S}, L_{2S}...L_{mS})\}$;

$L_{m.n} = U \{(P_{m, (n,n+1,n+2)} P_{m, (n+3,n+4,n+5)} P_{m, (n+6,n+7,n+8)} ...)\}$;

U= union; L = location; P = point;

m = number of survey lines;

n = number of survey points on each survey line

Similar semantic models can be structured for other Prod and Mkt entities and their relationships. Purpose of writing syntax for heterogeneous data structures is given below:

Logic of integrating data models: The intelligent integration of several logical models is based on different ontologies of different concepts. The concepts simply constitute the properties and relationships that are constituents of the propositions of that ontology. Fine-grained structural properties, relations and propositions facilitate analyzing the concept of ontology and its integration.

Process of integration: The main part of the framework represents a set of ontology applications for building an integrated metadata model. The application implies the process of translating an ontological model to an implementation data model. As stated earlier, data warehouses and data marts are used in a wide range of applications (Hoffer et al., 2005). Business executives in oil and gas industry use the data warehouses and data marts, to perform data analysis and make strategic decisions, such as well planning and budgetary proposals for exploration and production. Generating reports and answering predefined queries are key uses of current data warehouse. In order to perform multidimensional data analysis, such as OLAP and slice and dice operations, issues of warehouse architecture designs affecting data integration process (Figure 11) have been addressed.

Model Implementation

Conceptualized and logically designed petroleum data are physically stored in a modern database program (such as Oracle) for implementation. Extracting user-defined business data views from warehouses and interpreting them for business intelligence are important issues for successful implementation of this methodology. Implementa-

tion of ontology-based data warehouse approach for mining of petroleum data is vital for knowledge building from petroleum systems of basins and effective reservoir management. Measuring the reservoir and production property attributes through periodic dimension has immense impact on reduction of economic resources while carrying out expensive drilling operations.

The implementation of an ontology approach is to validate petroleum resources data and for finer search of petroleum data from large online or offline warehouses and or information repositories for desired resources (e.g., documents interpreting well-data of a particular field and a particular basin, oil play analysis of a field, resources data of other basins worldwide and viewed as Web documents, names of surveys conducted while drilling of wells). The ontology approach instigates improving data mining precision as well as reducing the overall amount of time spent searching for data. Conceptual or ontological models also support data delivery technologies that include agents for searching the data, data delivery agents (Erdmann & Rudi, 2001) using metadata languages and knowledge representation tools. Users trigger warehouse access to a piece of petroleum data of a drilled well, ontology identifies the description of that data view and search-engine acts to locate the

Figure 11. Data integration process and warehousing of petroleum data

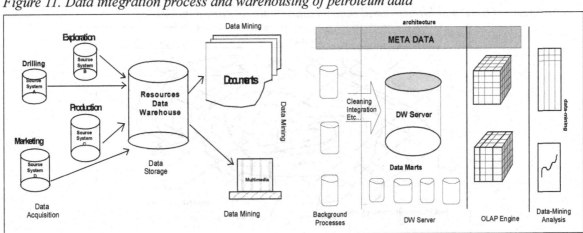

data from that data warehouse as demonstrated in the next section.

Authors attempt to implement a key data structure model as described in (Nimmagadda et al., 2006). Metadata of the current data structure has been used for extracting data views. One of such database view is processed and generated through mapping algorithms and it is represented as shown in Figure 12. As demonstrated in Figure 12, multidimensional objects have been extracted from a warehouse and mapped into an integrated data object structure (OLAP model). This is a combined view of several subclasses with their associated attributes, such as *reservoir* thickness, *oil-water contact* (OWC, an attribute derived from composite data structure, such as *Navig_Seismic_VSP_WellLog_Reservoir,* (Nimmagadda et al., 2006)), and *net oil pay* thickness. In other words, all the subclass objects data such as *points, seismic lines,* and *regions* have been uploaded and integrated to a single object data model, linking all their respective attributes from multiple object classes. One can interpret this model with an inference that all the ingredients of *oil play,* such as, *structure* and *reservoir* are present in a hydrocarbon province. An explorer can conclude the model implementation, "H" location as shown in Figure 12, as the best drillable exploratory location, which minimizes the risk

of *exploration* and also optimize the economics involved in future well-drilling plans.

The Significance of Ontology-Based Data Warehousing and Mining Approaches

Implemented models and their evaluation in petroleum industries are expected to deliver the following products:

- Integrated petroleum pay-horizon (a producing geological unit) data models consisting of different geological formations of different wells in different basins.
- Association rule mining among petroleum-play (Figure 13) factors; to establish joining among petroleum systems of different basins that can steer at planning and development stages.
- Construction of decision trees; computing classifiers; determining the accuracy of classifiers among sets of oil-play factors (Figure 13) including surveys, wells, permits and production data items.
- Petroleum data clustering—for better understanding of petroleum systems and their connectivity.

Figure 12. OLAP multidimensional objects data implementation model

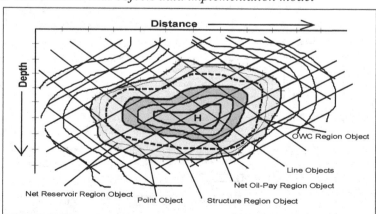

- Economic measures in the pre and postdrilling plans.
- Multidimensional data models and views representing data cubes for implementing in other applications.

Construction of composite syntax, integration modeling, understanding ontology, and presenting its semantic content, play key roles in ontology modeling of petroleum industry data. Ontology data integration is a key significant issue addressed in chapter and a gateway for building the logical metadata models. Exploring for semantics of an up-stream and integrated oil and gas company is often a more complex and tedious process. But, an ontology supportive data warehouse approach can simplify the logical data structuring as well as future data mining strategies, in particular while clustering of attributed data as extracted and interpreted from large volume of multivariate attributes of petroleum data sources. Implications of the ontology approach are discussed in the following sections.

Validating Ontology for Petroleum Business Data Warehousing Approach

Fundamentally, ontology in the context of petroleum business data is communicating through different wells, surveys, petroleum permits and oil-play entities (and or objects) intelligently, to achieve interoperability or to improve the process of data mining. The following scheme is adapted (Uschold, 1998) for qualifying the ontology approach for petroleum business industry:

- **Communication:** Ambiguity is minimized in identifying the entities and connecting them through their attributes and relationships, thus facilitating communication among entities more effectively for logical and implementation data modeling.
- **Interoperability:** Ontology is used as a semantic interchange interface to the logical and implementation modeling. It is achieved by translating different conceptual knowledge-domain models to the database logical

Figure 13. Data mining: (a) partitioning before swapping; (b) clustering of oil-play data properties after swapping

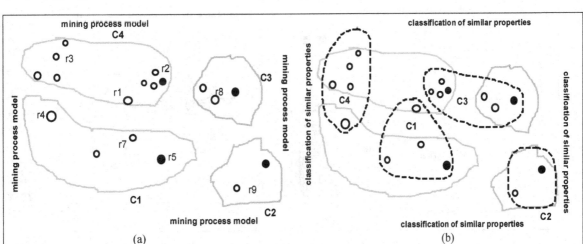

schemas and or combination of schemas in complex petroleum business situations (Figure 14).

Oil-field data objects are reused and interconnected (interoperability) among multiple petroleum fields (Figure 14), so that knowledge built from data warehouse integration process, is reused and interpreted for drillable exploratory or development well plans. As demonstrated in an OLAP model in Figure 12. "H" is an appropriate place to drill a well for exploring and exploiting for oil and gas. This is a successful data implementation model in a petroleum industry. Exploration managers are responsible for providing the valued processed exploration information, so that critical decisions made in planning new exploratory or development wells in the frontier oil bearing sedimentary basins are accurate and precise. Figure14 exhibits the interoperability of petroleum data objects among basins, when data objects are conceptualized and integrated using petroleum ontology (Nimmagadda et al., 2005a; Nimmagadda et al., 2006).

Petroleum Ontology System Design Benefits

- **Reusability:** Same entities (or if objects interpreted in classes) and their relationships are used in different domain applications and or modeling languages. Entities described in data structures in a basin can be reused in other basins. Even structures used in one basin can be used in other basins elsewhere.
- **Search:** Searching or viewing a piece of basin data from the warehoused metadata through data mining.
- **Reliability:** Ontology approach makes the petroleum business data more reliable, because of interoperability and automation of consistency in data structures.
- **Specification:** The ontology can assist the process of identifying requirements and defining specifications for data warehousing.
- **Maintenance:** Documenting ontology of petroleum business data is of immense help to reduce the operation and maintenance costs.

Figure 14. Interoperability of data objects among petro-fields

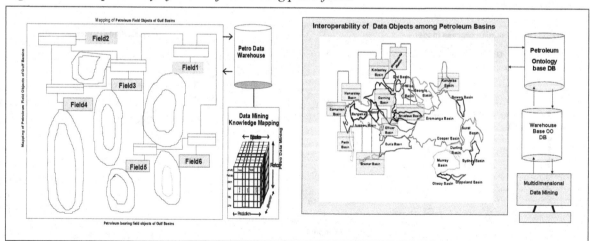

- **Knowledge acquisition:** Speed and reliability of ontology supportive data warehouse will facilitate the data-mining task much easier and faster in building intelligence from petroleum business data.

Nimmagadda et al. (2005a) address issues of evolving ontology application for effective design of data warehousing and data mining for petroleum industries with a focus on ontology acquisition and understanding. Hierarchical structural data content (as is the nature of petroleum organization structure) facilitates the evolutionary process of ontology application in petroleum data warehouse design and development. A finer hierarchical data structure (described at its atomic level) that carries knowledge and information exchange through ontological structuring process has definite edge to data mining application. Ontology knowledge building process also assists in understanding the integration of the fine-grained relational data structure of petroleum industry. Data delivery agents (such as XML and HTML) that respond to easy distribution of fine-grained meaningful structural content and semantics, appear to be essential knowledge base data distribution tools, also aiding software developers to distribute oil and gas business data in several geographic locations. Petroleum data ontology discussed in this paper can facilitate query formulation with several merits such as:

- Sharpen user requests by query expansion while understanding the finer specialized hierarchical structures.
- Widen query scopes of petroleum data contexts in accordance with generalized coarser hierarchical structures.
- Minimizing the ambiguity of user requests by finding the contexts relevant to the requests.
- Reformulate queries within the same contexts or by one chosen context to contexts of alternate ontologies that may be fitting for better actual queries of users' requests.

Exploration and interpretation of queries or views are accessed from the ontology-based warehouse in a manner to develop and predict the future petroleum reserves in, for example, the Western Australian resources industry. This approach will facilitate establishing the unexplored and unexploited petroleum inventory in any world-wide basin.

The following significant issues will be resolved by the proposed research methodologies:

- Companies handling multifaceted petroleum data need data integration and information sharing among various operational units—ontology-based data warehousing and data mining technologies will satisfy these needs.
- A common ontological framework will assist to understand and perceive petroleum industry's complex data entities and attributes—facilitate to structure these data into simpler conceptual models.
- Past experience (Nimmagadda & Rudra, 2004d) suggests that multidimensional logical data models, such as star, snowflake, and fact constellation schemas are ideally suited for designing data warehouse for oil and gas industries.
- Warehouse data models possess flexibility—accommodating future changes in complex company situations.
- Petroleum data considered here are of both technical and business in nature; focused on building knowledge on petroleum systems of different basins of Western Australia, with an intention to minimize the risk of well planning and also to make sound economic decision while drilling a prospect (for example data on formation pressures and reservoir qualities with depth will dramatically change economic situation of drilling an expensive well).
- Faster operational and user response times—minimizing operational exploration costs.

- Frequently, drilled wells *'go sick,'* which undergo for capital work-over jobs. Present study will improve the health and economics of a drilled well.
- From oil and gas industry point of view, many more oil fields can be discovered or explored by exploiting the existing exploration and production data of petroleum systems in Western Australia—supported by ontology, data warehouse and data mining technologies.
- Petroleum data have the following significant additional dimensions:
  1. Longitudinal (time-variant historical data, say 60 years of exploration and production data).
  2. Lateral (data from several sedimentary basins, each of around 5000 sq km in area).

The additional dimensions depicted in the data warehouse schemas will enhance the scope of data mining of petroleum data. So far, nobody has investigated these data volumes in terms of ontology, data warehousing and data mining, especially the exploration and production data associated with period dimension. Time series data, represented in 4D time-lapse domain can significantly minimize expensive well drilling plans. These technologies provide immense future scope in both private and public sectors of petroleum industries. There is an opportunity to extend and apply these proposed technologies in overseas basins.

Ontologies have become very common on the World Wide Web (WWW). Future work is aimed to develop a WWW consortium of petroleum resources description framework (PRDF), a language for encoding knowledge on Web pages to make it understandable to electronic agents searching for information. Ontologies of the petroleum systems range from large taxonomies categorizing petroleum systems of North West Shelf (NWS) to categorizations of basins, fields, and their features and properties. Many areas now develop standardized ontologies that domain experts can use to share and annotate information in their domain fields.

FUTURE DIRECTIONS OF RESEARCH

With the growing demand and need to store volume of resources data more intelligently, ontology based warehousing approach handles applications ranging across resources industries, computing industries to geographic information systems, and especially datasets that carry multidimensions with a key temporal dimension. The present chapter provides an immense future scope, particularly realizing the complexity and heterogeneity of resources business operations. Future research is warranted in building ontology-based metadata that can cater for multidisciplinary datasets from different operational units of integrated operational companies (such as BP, Shell, ChevronTexaco, ExxonMobil, ONGC, TATA Industries). These multinational companies manage several contractors and subcontractors, who handle hundreds of day-to-day business operations, costing millions of dollars.

Resources data are often heterogeneous and modeling such data is of enormous value to these industries. Exploration is one of the key (entity/object) business operations of oil and gas producing industries. Similar subtype class-objects can be interpreted from other business entities, such as drilling, production and marketing operations. Ontology based warehouse modeling application has already been demonstrated in resources industry scenarios facilitating efficient data-mining and knowledge-mapping applications. These technologies have great future scope in industry-automation and data-engineering. Our future research studies include mapping and modeling natural datasets for earthquake-prediction analysis, weather-forecast and climate-change studies.

Mapping and modeling data warehouses in longitudinal and cross-sectional research domains (Neuman, 1999 pp. 30-31) are very effective for modeling knowledge in multidimensions. Multiple dimensions depicted in the data warehouse schemas, enhance the scope of data mining of heterogeneous data sources. So far, nobody has investigated these data volumes in terms of ontology, data warehousing and data mining, especially technical and commercial data (such as resources data, active and dynamic *exploration* and *production* super entities) associated with time dimension. Time series data represented in 4D time-lapse (Dodds and Fletcher 2004) domain (spatio-temporal) can significantly minimize the risk in the making of crucial technical and financial decisions in resources industries. These technologies can return huge dividends to both private and public sectors of petroleum industries in Australia and other developing industrial countries.

Keeping in view the recent popularity of ontologies on WWW, future work is aimed to develop a WWW consortium of petroleum resources description framework (PRDF), a language for encoding knowledge on web pages, to make it understandable to electronic agents searching for information. For example, ontologies of the petroleum systems range, from large taxonomies categorizing petroleum systems of NWS (North West Shelf, a group of Western Australian producing basins) to classification of basins, fields, besides grouping their geological and reservoir attribute properties. Multidisciplines now develop standardized ontologies that domain experts can use to share and annotate information in their domain fields.

What these industries have in common is the need to analyze extremely large datasets, produced and collected by a diverse range of methods, to understand particular phenomena, such as earthquake-prediction and climate-change-global warming analysis. As in the scientific field, an effective means with which to analyze these data is to use, visualization to summarize the data and interpret data correlations, trends and patterns.

REFERENCES

Biswas, G., Weinberg, J., & Li, C. (1995). ITER-ATE: A conceptual clustering method for knowledge discovery in databases. *Artificial Intelligence in the Petroleum Industry* (pp. 111-139). Paris.

Cheung, D.W., Wang, L., Yiu, S.M., & Zhou, B. (2000). Density based mining of quantitative association rules. *PAKDD, LNAI, Vol. 1805* (pp. 257-268).

Dodds, K., & Fletcher, A. (2004). Interval probability process mapping as a tool for drilling decisions analysis: The R&D perspective. *The Leading Edge, 23*(6), 558-564.

Dunham, H.M. (2003). *Data mining, introductory and advanced topics*. Prentice Hall.

Erdmann, M., & Rudi, S. (2001). How to structure and access XML documents with ontology. *IEEE Data & Knowledge Engineering, 36,* 317-335.

Gilbert, R., Liu, Y., & Abriel, W. (2004). Reservoir modeling: integrating various data at appropriate scales. *The Leading Edge, 23*(8), 784-788.

Gornik, D. (2000). *Data modeling for data warehouses*. A rational software white paper. Rational E-development Company.

Guan, S., & Zhu, F. (2004). Ontology acquisition and exchange of evolutionary product-brokering agents. *Journal of Research and Practice in Information Technology, 36*(1), 35-45.

Guha, S., Rastogi, R., & Shim, K. (1999b). CURE: An efficient algorithm for clustering large databases. In *Proceedings of ACM-SIGMOD International Conference on Management of Data.*

Hadzic, M., & Chang, E. (2005). Ontology-based support for human disease study. In *Proceedings of the 38th Hawaii International Conference on System Sciences.*

Hoffer, J.A, Presscot, M.B., & McFadden, F.R. (2005). *Modern database management* (6th ed.). Prentice Hall.

Hori, M., & Ohashi, M. (2005). Applying XML web services into health care management. In *Proceedings of the 38th Hawaii International Conference on System Sciences.*

Huang, Z. (1997). A fast clustering algorithm to cluster very large categorical data sets in data mining. In *Proceedings of SIGMOD Workshop on Research Issues on Data Mining and Knowledge Discovery.*

Huston, D.C., Hunter, H., & Johnson, E. (2003). Geostatistical integration of velocity cube and log data to constrain 3D gravity modeling, Deepwater Gulf of Mexico. *The Leading Edge, 23*(4), 842-846.

Jasper, R., & Uschold, M. (1999). A framework for understanding and classifying ontology applications. In *Proceedings of the IJCAI-99 ontology workshop* (pp. 1-20).

Johnston, D.H. (2004). 4D-gives reservoir surveillance. *AAPG Explorer, 25*(12), 28-30.

Longley, I.M., Bradshaw, M.T., & Hebberger, J. (2001). Australian petroleum provinces of the 21st century. In M.W. Downey, J.C. Threet, & W.A. Morgan (Eds.), *Petroleum provinces of the 21st century, AAPG Memoir, 74,* 287-317.

Marakas, M.G. (2003). *Modern data warehousing, mining, and visualization core concepts.* Prentice Hall.

Matsuzawa, H., & Fukuda, T. (2000). Mining structured association patterns from databases. *PAKDD, LNAI 1805,* 233-244.

Mattison, R. (1996). *Data warehousing strategies, technologies and techniques.* Mc-Graw Hill.

Meersman, R.A. (2004). Foundations, implementations and applications of Web semantics. Parts 1, 2, 3, lectures at School of Information Systems.

Miller, H.J., & Han, J. (2001). Fundamentals of spatial data warehousing for geographic knowledge discovery. *Geographic Data Mining and Knowledge Discovery,* 51-72.

Nimmagadda, S.L., & Rudra, A. (2004c). Applicability of data warehousing and data mining technologies in the Australian resources industry. In *Proceedings of the 7th International Conference on IT,* Hyderabad, India.

Nimmagadda, S.L., & Rudra, A. (2004d). Data sources and requirement analysis for multidimensional database modeling: An Australian Resources Industry scenario. In *Proceedings of the 7th International Conference on IT,* Hyderabad, India.

Nimmagadda, S.L., Dreher, H., & Rudra, A. (2005a, August). Ontology of Western Australian petroleum exploration data for effective data warehouse design and data mining. In *Proceedings of the 3rd International IEEE Conference on Industry Informatics,* Perth, Australia.

Nimmagadda, S.L., Dreher, H., & Rudra, A. (2005b, August). Data warehouse structuring methodologies for efficient mining of Western Australian petroleum data sources. In *Proceedings of the 3rd international IEEE conference on Industry Informatics,* Perth, Australia

Nimmagadda, S.L., & Dreher, H. (2006, August). *Mapping and modeling of oil and gas relational data objects for warehouse development and efficient data mining.* Paper presented in the 4th International Conference in IEEE Industry Informatics, Singapore.

Nimmagadda, S.L., Dreher, H., & Rudra, A. (2006, August). *Mapping of oil and gas exploration business data entities for effective operational management*. Paper presented in the 4th International Conference in IEEE Industry Informatics, Singapore.

Ng, R.T., & Han, J. (1994). Efficient and effective clustering methods for spatial data mining. In *Proceedings of International Conference on Very Large Databases (VLDB'94)* (pp. 144-155). Santiago, Chile .

O'Leary, D.E. (2000). Different firms, different ontologies, and no one best ontology. *IEEE Intelligent Systems, 72-78.*

Ott, T., & Swiaczny, F. (2001). Time-integrative geographic information systems. *Management and analysis of spatio-temporal data*. Springer.

Pei, J., Han, J., Mortazavi-asl, B., & Zhu, H. (2000). Mining access patterns efficiently from web logs. *PAKDD, LNAI, 1805,* 396-407.

Pujari, A.K. (2002). *Data mining techniques.* India: University Press Pty Limited.

Ramkumar, G.D., & Swami, A. (1998). Clustering data without distance functions. *Bulletin of IEEE Computer Society Technical Committee on Data Engineering.*

Rudra, A., & Nimmagadda, S.L. (2005). Roles of multidimensionality and granularity in data mining of warehoused Australian resources data. In *IEEE Proceedings of the 38th Hawaii International Conference on Information System Sciences.*

Roiger, J.R., & Geatz, M.W. (2003). *Data mining, A tutorial — Based primer.* Addison Wesley.

Shanks, G., Tansley, E., & Weber, R. (2003). Using ontology to validate conceptual models. *Communications of the ACM, 46*(10), 85-89.

Shanks, G., Tansley, E., & Weber, R. (2004). Representing composites in conceptual modelling. *Communications of the ACM, 47*(7), 77-80.

Telford, W.M., Geldart, L.P., & Sheriff, R.E. (1998). *Applied geophysics* (2nd ed.) (pp. 100-350 and 600-750).

Uschold, M. (1998). Knowledge level modeling: Concepts and terminology. *Knowledge Engineering Review, 13*(1).

Weimer, P., & Davis, T.L. (1995). Applications of 3D-seismic data to exploration and production, *AAPG studies in geology, No.42, and SEG Geophysical Developments series, No.5.*

Yao, Y.Y., & Zhong, N. (2000). On association, similarity and dependency attributes. *PAKDD, LNAI, 1805,* 138-141.

Yun, C.H., & Chen, M.S. (2000). Mining Web transaction patterns in an electronic commerce environment. *PAKDD, LNAI, 1805,* 216-219.

Zhong, T., Raghu, R., & Livny, M. (1996). An efficient data clustering method for very large databases. In *Proceedings of ACM SIGMOD International Conference on Management of Data.*

Zhou, S., Zhou, A., Cao, J., Wen, J., Fan, Y., & Hu, Y. (1996). *Combining sampling technique with DBSCAN algorithm for clustering large spatial databases*. Springer.

FURTHER READING, SUPPORTING THE CHAPTER

Journals

Coburn, T.C., Yarus, J.M., & Stark, P.H. (2000). A conversation with petroleum information, GIS in Petroleum Exploration and Development, AAPG. *Computer Applications in Geology, 4,* 49-60.

Gilbert, R., Liu, Y., & Abriel, W. (2004). Reservoir modeling: Integrating various data at appropriate scales. *The Leading Edge, 23*(8), 784-788.

Gornik, D. (2000). *Data modeling for data warehouses.* A rational software white paper, Rational E-development Company.

Han, J., Kmber, M., & Tung, A.K.H. (2001). Spatial clustering methods in data mining: A survey. In H. Miller & J. Han (Eds.), *Geographic data mining and knowledge discovery.*

Jukic, N., & Lang, C. (2004). Using offshore resources to develop and support data warehousing applications. *Business Intelligence Journal,* 6-14.

Miller, H.J., & Han, J. (2001). Fundamentals of spatial data warehousing for geographic knowledge discovery. *Geographic data mining and knowledge discovery,* 51-72.

Neuman, W.L. (1999). *Social research methods, qualitative and quantitative approaches* (4th ed.). Allyn and Bacon Publishers.

Rajugan, R., Chang, E., Dillon, T.S., & Wouters, C. (2006). Subontology's and ontology views: A theoretical perspective. *International Journal of Metadata, Semantics and Ontologies (IJMSO).*

Chapters in Books

Hadzic, F., Dillon, T.S., Tan, H., Chang, E., & Feng, L. (2006). Mining frequent patterns using self-organizing map. In D. Taniar (Eds.), *Research and trends in data mining technologies and applications: Advances in data warehousing and mining.* Hershey, PA: Idea Group Inc.

Sidhu, A.S., Dillon, S., & Chang, E. (2007). Data integration through protein ontology. In H.O. Nigro, S.G. Císaro, & D. Xodo (Eds.), *Data mining with ontologies: Implementations, findings and frameworks.* Hershey, PA: Idea Group Inc.

Sidhu, A.S., Dillon, T.S., et al. (2006). Ontology for data integration in protein informatics. In Z. Ma & J.Y. Chen (Eds.), *Database modelling in biology: Practices and challenges.*

Conferences

Barrasa, J., Corcho, Ó., & Gómez-Pérez, A. (2004). R_2O, An extensible and semantically based database-to-ontology mapping language. In C. Bussler, V. Tannen, & I. Fundulaki (Eds.), *Semantic Web and Databases, Second International Workshop, SWDB 2004.* Toronto, Canada.

Bizer, C. (2003). D2R MAP: A database to RDF mapping language. In *Proceedings of the 12th International World Wide Web,* Budapest, Hungary. ACM.

Borst, W. (1997). *Construction of engineering ontologies.* PhD thesis, University of Twente, Enschede.

Bruijn, J., Mart´ın-Recuerda, F., Manov, D., & Ehrig, M. (2004). *The state-of-the-art survey on ontology merging and aligning.* Digital Enterprise Research Institute, University of Innsbruck, EU-IST Integrated Project (IP) IST-2003-506826 SEKT: Semantically Enabled Knowledge Technologies.

Fernandez, M., Gomez-Perez, A., & Juristo, N. (1997). METHONTOLOGY: From ontological art towards ontological engineering. *AAAI97 Spring Symposium Series on Ontological Engineering,* AAAI, Stanford (pp. 33-40).

Gomez-Perez, A., Fernandez-Lopez, M., & Corcho, O. (2004). *Ontological engineering: With examples from the areas of knowledge management, e-commerce and the Semantic Web.* London: Springer-Verlag.

Gómez-Pérez, A., Manzano-Macho, D., Alfonseca, E., Núñez, R., Blacoe, I., Staab, S., Corcho, O., Ding, Y., Paralic, J., & Troncy, R. (2003). *A survey of ontology learning methods and techniques.* OntoWeb Consortium.

Gruber, T.R. (1993). A translation approach to portable ontology specifications. *Knowledge Acquisition, 5*(2), 199-220.

Jarrar, M., & Meersman, R. (2002). Formal ontology engineering in the DOGMA approach. In R. Meersman & Z. Tari (Eds.), *On the Move to Meaningful Internet Systems 2002: CoopIS, DOA, and ODBASE; Confederated International Conferences CoopIS, DOA, and ODBASE 2002* (pp. 1238 -1254). Springer Verlag.

Kashyap, V. (1999). Design and creation of ontologies for environmental information retrieval. *Twelfth Workshop on Knowledge Acquisition, Modelling and Management*. MCC and Telcordia Technologies, Inc. Voyager Inn, Banff, Alberta, Canada.

Meersman, R. (1999) Semantic ontology tools in information system design. *ISMIS 99, Eleventh International Symposium on Methodologies for Intelligent Systems, Foundations of Intelligent Systems* (pp. 30-45). Berlin, Warsaw, Poland: Springer-Verlag.

Meersman, R. (2001). Ontologies and databases: More than a fleeting resemblance. In A. d'Atri & M. Missikoff (Eds.), *OES/SEO Workshop Rome*. Luiss, Rome.

Noy, N.F., & Musen, M.A. (1999). SMART: Automated support for ontology merging and alignment. In *Proceedings of the Twelfth Workshop on Knowledge Acquisition, Modeling and Management*, Banff, Canada.

Noy, N.F., & Musen, M.A. (2000). PROMPT: Algorithm and tool for automated ontology merging and alignment. *AAAI-2000*. Austin, Texas: MIT Press/AAAI Press.

Racer (2006). *The first ontology reasoner*. Retrieved September 9, 2006, from http://www.sts.tu-harburg.de/~r.f.moeller/racer/

Rajugan, R., Chang, E., & Dillon, TS. (2006). Ontology views: A theoretical perspective. In *Proceedings of the 2nd IFIP WG 2.12 & WG 12.4 International Workshop on Web Semantics (SWWS) in Conjunction with OTM 2006*, Montpellier, France (pp. 1814-1824).

Stanford Medical Informatics. (2006). *Protégé*, Stanford Medical Informatics. Retrieved June 9, 2006, from http://protege.stanford.edu

SUOWG (2003). *Suggested Upper Merged Ontology*. IEEE Standard Upper Ontology working group. Retrieved October 3, 2006, from http://suo.ieee.org/

Swartout, B., Patil, R., Knight, K., & Russ, T. (1996). Toward distributed use of large-scale ontologies. *KAW96, the Tenth Knowledge Acquisition Workshop* (pp. 32.1-32.19). GB R & MM A, SRDG Publications, University of Calgary, Banff, Canada.

Uschold, M., & Gruninger, M., (1996). Ontologies: Principles, methods and applications. *Knowledge Engineering Review, 11*(2), 93-155.

Wongthongtham, P., Chang, E., & Dillon, T.S. (2006, Oct 29-Nov 3). Software design process ontology development. In *Proceedings of the 2nd IFIP WG 2.12 & WG 12.4 International Workshop on Web Semantics (SWWS) in conjunction with OTM 2006*, France (pp. 1806-1813).

W3C. (2006a). *Ontology Web Language*, WC3. Retrieved September 5, 2006, from http://www.w3.org/2004/OWL/

W3C. (2006b). *RDF*. Retrieved June 2006, from http://www.w3.org/RDF/

GLOSSARY

Basin: A depression in the crust of the Earth, caused by plate tectonic activity and subsidence, in which sediments accumulate. Sedimentary basins vary from bowl-shaped to elongated troughs.

Exploration: The initial phase in petroleum operations that includes generation of a prospect or play or both, and drilling of an exploration well.

Oil-Play: Reservoir, structure, seal, migration, source and timing factors, playing a role for building a constructive (productive) petroleum system.

Chapter XII
A Framework for Integrating Ontologies and Pattern-Bases

Evangelos Kotsifakos
University of Piraeus, Greece

Gerasimos Marketos
University of Piraeus, Greece

Yannis Theodoridis
University of Piraeus, Greece

ABSTRACT

Pattern base management systems (PBMS) have been introduced as an effective way to manage the high volume of patterns available nowadays. PBMS provide pattern management functionality in the same way where a database management system provides data management functionality. However, not all the extracted patterns are interesting; some are trivial and insignificant because they do not make sense according to the domain knowledge. Thus, in order to automate the pattern evaluation process, we need to incorporate the domain knowledge in it. We propose the integration of PBMS and ontologies as a solution to the need of many scientific fields for efficient extraction of useful information from large databases and the exploitation of knowledge. In this chapter, we describe the potentiality of this integration and the issues that should be considered introducing an XML-based PBMS. We use a case study of data mining over scientific (seismological) data to illustrate the proposed PBMS and ontology integrated environment.

INTRODUCTION

In the *knowledge discovery from data* (KDD) process, data mining techniques are used to find patterns from a large collection of data (see data mining step in Figure 1). The role of the domain experts in this process is crucial. Their knowledge is used in early stages to prepare data (i.e., to decide for the data cleaning and preparation) and to choose the appropriate parameters for the data mining algorithms. Their contribution is also necessary for the evaluation and interpretation of the extracted patterns that lead to the generation of knowledge (Fayyad, Piatetsky-Shapiro, & Smyth, 1996).

In essence, extracted patterns are used from domain experts to explore new relations on data, evaluate theories on the field of interest, and discover unknown and hidden knowledge that will lead to new experiments and theories. However, some of the extracted patterns are considered trivial and some others insignificant, according to the domain knowledge. To evaluate extracted patterns experts have defined a lot of different, either objective or subjective interestingness measures based mostly on statistical properties of the patterns. Nevertheless, analyzing and assessing the usefulness of discovered patterns is a laborious task and is considered a hard problem (Piatetsky-Shapiro, 2000).

Two important issues are raised. The first refers to the *manipulation and management of the patterns in a unified way*, either they have been evaluated or not. Currently, the majority of the available data mining tools support the visualization of patterns, and in the best case storage in relational tables. Combined with the characterization of patterns as complex, compact, and rich in semantics representation of data (Rizzi et al., 2003), this issue raises the challenge for pattern management. In this context, we propose an XML-based pattern base management system (PBMS) for representing, storing, querying, indexing, and updating patterns. This system is

data mining engine independent, supporting interoperability and exchange of patterns between different pattern bases.

The second issue is related to the *incorporation of the existing domain knowledge in the data mining process*, and especially in the pattern evaluation phase. Several statistical and interestingness measures have been proposed for the evaluation of patterns (Freitas, 1999; Piatetsky-Shapiro, 1991; Piatetsky-Shapiro, & Matheus, 1994; Silberschatz & Tuzhilin, 1996). These measures are applied either before or during the data mining process. In the first case, they are used to reduce the number of patterns that will be extracted and to speed up the data mining process. While in the evaluation phase, they are used to clean up the patterns considered insignificant.

Nevertheless, no such measure for pattern evaluation is efficient enough as the domain expertise itself. Domain experts can better evaluate the patterns and decide whether they are trivial or not. It is the user who will distinguish interesting rare occurrences of patterns from statistical noise using his/her background knowledge (Pohle, 2003). In order to automate the pattern evaluation process, we need to incorporate the domain knowledge in it. It is generally acceptable that domain knowledge can be represented efficiently using ontologies (Pohle, 2003). An *ontology* is a specification of a conceptualization, a description of the concepts and relationships that can exist for an agent or a community of agents (Gruber, 1993).

We argue that domain knowledge expressed with ontologies could function as a filter in the

Figure 1. The KDD process

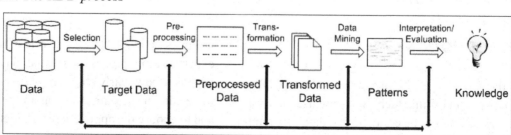

evaluation phase of the KDD process. Patterns extracted from data mining algorithms would be first evaluated with respect to the ontology. Patterns that contradict knowledge widely accepted according to the ontology provided (hereafter, called "*noisy*") will be marked as possibly invalid. Whereas, acceptable patterns will be further evaluated by the domain expert and, if recognized as useful knowledge, the ontology could be updated to incorporate these new patterns (of course, domain experts might reconsider the ontology by adding/removing relations, associations, etc.). In this case, priority is given to patterns considered interesting, at the same time not conflicting with well established beliefs. This approach could reduce the cost in terms of running time of the data mining algorithm and the effort of the domain expert to evaluate the discovered patterns. Note that "noisy" patterns are marked as invalid and are not being discarded unless a user wishes so. Thus, the danger to drop really useful knowledge is quite limited.

Towards the purpose of incorporating the domain knowledge in the evaluation phase of the knowledge discovery process, we propose the integration of the PBMS with ontologies that describe the field of interest. In the following sections, we will analyze each issue separately and we will discuss the various challenges and problems that have to be faced considering a real case study from the seismology domain.

The outline of this chapter is as follows: the related work on pattern management and data mining using ontologies is presented in Section 2. Section 3 discusses the need for pattern evaluation using domain knowledge through a case scenario and the ontology for that scenario. The proposed ontology-enhanced PBMS along with a preliminary validation study are presented in Sections 4 and 5, respectively. Section 6 summarizes the conclusions and gives hints for future work.

RELATED WORK

In the following paragraphs, we review the background literature in the areas of pattern management and ontology-aware data mining.

Pattern Management

Domain experts are interested in patterns extracted from large datasets. Patterns are of great importance because unlike the original data, they are compact and they represent knowledge hidden in data. Therefore, patterns should be stored, queried, compared, and combined with previously extracted patterns in an efficient and unified way. As more and more patterns are available, there is an emerging need for a pattern base management system nowadays. Few efforts have been made to store and manage patterns, including predictive model markup language (PMML, 2006), common warehouse model (CWM, 2001), ISO SQL/MM (2001), JAVA data mining API (JDM, 2003). Most deal with pattern storage and using relational tables or XML documents. PMML is the most popular approach, as it represents patterns (data mining models) in a unified way. A review of these approaches in relation to pattern management can be found in (Catania & Maddalena, 2006). These approaches deal with common data mining patterns and do not provide pattern management functionalities.

Two research projects (funded by the European community) have dealt with the pattern management problem in a more general way, namely consortium on discovering knowledge with inductive queries (CINQ, 2001) and patterns for next-generation database systems (PANDA, 2001). CINQ is based on the inductive database approach and assumes that patterns and data are stored in the same database, while PANDA assumes that patterns are stored in a different database than raw data, the pattern base. Recently, a prototype PBMS that was based on the PANDA pattern model, called PSYCHO, has been presented (Catania, Maddalena & Mazza, 2005). PSYCHO manages different types of patterns in a unified way and it is developed with specific tools over the object-relational Oracle DBMS.

PSYCHO architecture is shown in Figure 2. The system is composed of three distinct layers. The physical layer contains both the *Pattern Base* that stores patterns and the *Data Source* that stores raw data from which patterns have been extracted. The middle layer, called *PBMS Engine*, supports functionalities for pattern manipulation and retrieval (pattern storage and querying). The external layer corresponds to a set of user interfaces (a shell and a GUI) from which the user can send requests to the engine and import/export data in other formats.

Our proposed ontology-enhanced PBMS, which will be presented in the following paragraphs, is independent from the data mining engine and uses XML to store patterns in the pattern base. In addition to the pattern management operations, it provides pattern filtering functionalities using ontologies to automate the pattern evaluation step.

The efficient management of patterns extracted using data mining techniques as well as user-defined patterns is very important for domain experts in evaluating patterns. Patterns can be stored and retrieved as well as compared to find similarities between them. Further analysis of the pattern base management systems is beyond the main scope of this chapter (more information about PBMSs can be found in PBMS, 2006).

Data Mining Using Domain Knowledge

Until recently, although the importance of knowledge management was widely known, limited research has been devoted to intelligent pattern analysis and the accumulation of discovered knowledge with prior knowledge (Pohle, 2003). Regarding the use of domain knowledge in the data mining process, only a few related approaches can be found. Domain knowledge can be applied in the data mining process in three different ways. In the preprocessing step (to prepare the data to be mined), during the data mining process (data mining algorithm is using the domain knowledge to decide about the next step), or after the data

Figure 2. PSYCHO architecture

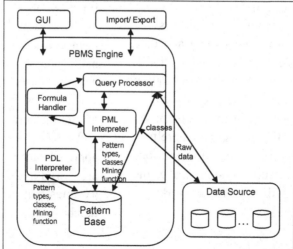

mining process (to evaluate the extracted patterns).

Consider the first way Chen, Zhou, Scherl, and Geller (2003) propose using an ontology as a concept hierarchy to prepare demographic data for association rule mining. In some tuples of the demographic database there are values from a lower level of the hierarchy while in other tuples, in the same column, there are values from higher levels of the hierarchy (for example the value "basketball" and the value "recreation sports" that are found at different levels in an interests hierarchy). By replacing the values of lower level with values at a higher level (raising), the authors show that the rule support is increasing and thus, more rules can be found.

Several papers can be found about how some interestingness measures (either objective or subjective) are used to evaluate extracted patterns. Objective interestingness measures are based in statistical functions. In Piatetsky-Shapiro (2000), basic principles of objective rule interestingness measures are defined, while in Freitas (1999), a comparison of objective interestingness criteria can be found. In contrast with objective interestingness measures, subjective measures try to take into account individual conditions of the human analyst. A general discussion can be found in Silberschatz and Tuzhilin, (1996), while Piatetsky-Shapiro and Matheus, (1994) and Padmanabhan and Tuzhilin, (1998) attempt to address this problem. All these approaches provide a way to evaluate patterns but do not make use of the domain knowledge.

There are also few attempts using domain knowledge to improve evaluation of extracted patterns. Domain knowledge in the form of concept hierarchies can be used to improve Web mining results (Pohle & Spiliopoulou, 2002), while an interestingness analysis system that requires the user to express various types of existing knowledge in terms of a proprietary specification language is presented in (Liu et al., 2000). These approaches use domain knowledge, but their disadvantage is

that they require the user to previously provide his/her knowledge in a specified and narrow form, according to the application each time.

In order to incorporate domain knowledge in data mining and to allow conceptual model sharing in domains, the use of ontologies is necessary (Maedche et al., 2003). An application of using ontologies before, during and after the data mining process is the one presented by Hotho et al. (2002), in which authors use ontologies and information extraction technologies to improve text mining algorithms and pattern interpretation.

Our system uses ontologies to improve the pattern evaluation step and querying the pattern base. During the evaluation step, the system based on the provided ontology and parameters that have been defined from the domain expert, filters the patterns and marks as "noisy" patterns that contradict to domain knowledge. Domain expert can then discard or further evaluate them. The system will also use the filtering mechanism to prevent a naïve user to query the pattern base for "noisy" patterns.

PROBLEM DESCRIPTION

Various examples indicating the need for integration of domain knowledge and data mining can be found, however, dealing with scientific data is more efficient mainly because domain experts in these areas know their data in intimate detail (Fayyad, Haussler, & Stolorz, 1996). In this section, we present a real case study of mining seismological data to illustrate the use of a PBMS and ontologies in an integrated environment for pattern management and evaluation.

A Case Scenario from the Seismological Domain

Let us consider a seismological database containing historical data about earthquake events (Theodoridis, Marketos, & Kalogeras, 2004). Such a database would include information about the event (magnitude, latitude/longitude coordinates, timestamp, and depth), the geographical position of both the earthquake epicenter and the affected sites that partitions world in disjoint polygons, as well as details about the fault(s) related with the event. Additionally, our database includes demographical and other information about the administrative partitions of countries, details about the geological morphology of the areas of various countries and macro-seismic information (intensity, etc.) (Theodoridis et al., 2004).

Seismologists use the database to store the data, a data warehouse to aggregate and analyze them, a knowledge base to store documents collected by various sources, and a tool to define ontologies to represent the domain area. Furthermore, they are interested in discovering hidden knowledge. Patterns produced by the KDD process are evaluated and stored in a PBMS. Obviously, if the "islands of information" are not integrated under a single tool then the maximum value of the stored information could not be utilized. The researcher is interested in posing a number of questions, perhaps having no idea about which tool to use to get the answers. Some query examples are:

- **Query 1:** Find the average magnitude and the max depth for the earthquakes happened in the North Adriatic Sea (or in a particular geographical area) between 1994-2004.
- **Query 2:** Is there any information about the earthquake maximum recorded intensity when I know that the depth of the epicenter is over 60 km and the geology of the site is characterized as rocky?
- **Query 3:** Find similarities in shock sequences (a main shock that follows preshocks and is followed by intensive aftershocks) happened in Greece during 2004.

Query 1 can be easily answered by a data-warehouse using the average and the max function on the appropriate earthquake data. Query 2 can also be easily answered using a decision tree. In case such a decision tree model (pattern) has not been already stored in the PBMS, then an appropriate classification algorithm can be applied on the data. Query 3 is more challenging since it requires the incorporation of more advanced domain knowledge: (a) the specification of the similarity measure, and (b) the definition of the shock sequence by the domain expert.

It is clear that Query 3 requires a lot of preprocessing work to be done by the seismologist in collaboration with a database analyst. Hierarchies and rules about seismological concepts and data have to be defined before a data mining algorithm is applied. Furthermore, even when patterns are produced and stored in the PBMS some more postprocessing work (similar to the preprocessing step) has to be done in order to extract the appropriate information. The seismologist may have already represented the required knowledge using ontologies, their integration into the PBMS could resolve the above problems.

On the other hand, other queries, such as:

- **Query 4:** Find any relation between earthquake magnitude and average temperature of the area around the epicenter during a related time period.
- **Query 5:** Find any relation between earthquake magnitude and season of the year.

can also be posed by a naïve (i.e., nonexpert) user and answered applying data mining tasks while semantically unacceptable (for example, seismologists do not recognize any relation between either earthquake magnitude and surface temperature or earthquake magnitude and season of the year). Although, the data mining engine could return results regarding these relations, a domain expert would definitely discard them.

Nevertheless, such a filtering is nowadays done manually at a postprocessing step. Exactly this is the contribution of the integrated ontology-enabled PBMS we propose: to filter out "noisy" patterns efficiently (i.e., online without the need of postprocessing) and effectively (i.e., with a quality guaranteed by the ontology-filter).

Domain Knowledge Using Ontologies

One of the challenges in incorporating prior knowledge in the knowledge discovery process is the representation of the domain knowledge. Ontologies are useful in providing the formalization of the description of a domain. They are considered as the explicit specification of a conceptualization (Guarino & Giaretta, 1995). Using ontologies, hierarchies of concepts, constraints, and axioms can be defined. In other words, ontologies provide a domain vocabulary capturing a shared understanding of terms.

To represent the seismological domain, we choose the suggested upper merged ontology (IEEE Standard Upper Ontology) (Niles & Pease, 2001), the mid-level ontology (Niles & Terry, 2004) and, finally, an ontology for representing geographical information all available at (SUMO). An upper ontology is limited to concepts that are meta, generic, abstract, or philosophical, and hence are general enough to address (at a high level) a broad range of domain areas. Concepts specific to particular domains are not included in an upper ontology, but such an ontology does

provide a structure upon which ontologies for specific domains (e.g., medicine, finance, engineering, etc.) can be constructed. A mid-level ontology is intended to act as a bridge between the high-level abstractions of the SUMO and the low-level detail of the domain ontologies which in our case is the geography ontology. The following schema is based on the above ontologies (Figure 3).

Obviously, Figure 3 does not represent the "universe of discourse," but is a part of the geography ontology related to seismology. It is clear that using ontologies, horizontal relationships between concepts can be defined (Pohle, 2003). For instance, in the domain of seismology there is such a relationship between seismology and geology (faults). This is important as the patterns that are stored for each domain in the PBMS, can be combined offering more complete querying and visualization capabilities to the user.

INTEGRATION OF ONTOLOGIES IN THE KDD EVALUATION PHASE

The system we propose provides both naïve users and domain experts' functionalities for efficient pattern management and pattern evaluation using an ontology discarding the nonuseful patterns and thus improving the performance of the data

Figure 3. A subset of the SUMO for seismology

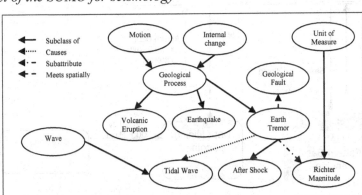

mining tasks and the query answering over the pattern base. The system is able to evaluate patterns before, during and after the data mining process, as well as every time a user poses a query to the pattern base. The system architecture is depicted in Figure 4.

Independent from data mining engine, the PBMS stores the extracted patterns in an XML pattern base. We choose XML for pattern storage as it performs better than relational and object-relational models (Kotsifakos, Ntoutsi, & Theodoridis, 2005). The pattern model used is the theoretical model defined in PANDA project (Rizzi et al., 2003) enhanced to support pattern temporal validation and semantically related pattern classes. Our extended model defines four logical concepts: *pattern type*, *pattern*, *class*, and *superclass*.

More specifically, each *pattern type* contains metadata information about:

- The data mining algorithm applied to extract the patterns it represents and its parameters.
- The date and time of the data mining process.
- The validity period.
- The data source.
- The mapping function.
- Information about the structure and the measures of the patterns it represents.

Patterns are instances of pattern types. In our XML architecture, pattern types are the XML Schema for a pattern (XML document). The pattern document contains metadata about the data mining process as well as the patterns extracted by that process. For example, an association rule pattern instance and its pattern type are shown in Figure 5 and Figure 6, respectively.

Apart from the *pattern type* and *pattern* concepts, *class* is defined as a set of semantically

Figure 4. The proposed ontology-enhanced PBMS architecture

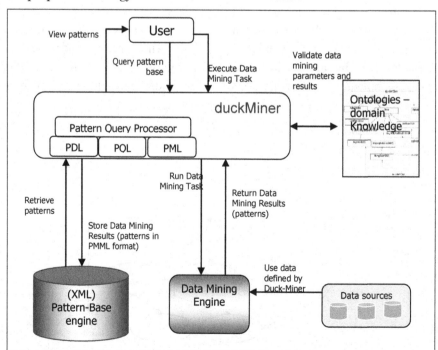

related patterns of the same pattern type. A class is defined by the user to group patterns that have a common meaning and belong to a specific pattern type. Each pattern may belong to more than one class. For example a user could define a class containing association rules related to seismic activity in the summer of 2003. This class would contain a lot of patterns that may belong to different association rule mining result sets but it will have the same meaning for the user. Figure 7 illustrates the pattern base logical model.

Furthermore, the concept of *superclass,* is defined as a set of classes with different pattern types. Thus, patterns belonging to different pattern types can be grouped together. For instance, a user might want to group all association rules related

Figure 5. Association rule patterns, XML example

```
<pt_assocRule xmlns:xsi="http://www.w3.org/2001/XMLSchema-instance" name="assocRule"
pt_descr="association rules" pt_id="1" xsi:noNamespaceSchemaLocation="pt_assocRule.xsd">
<        pt_metadata>
              <algorithm>apriori</algorithm>
<        parameters>min_support=0.1,min_conf=0.4,rules=10</parameters>
<            source>select * from earthquakes</source>
<            date>2006/04/12 13:03:34</date>
<            validity>2006/06/12 13:03:34</validity>
<            mapping_function>{{'depth', 'magnitude', 'season'} ⊆ transaction}
</mapping_function></pt_metadata>
<        patterns>
<                pattern p_id="1">
                     <structure>
<                          body>
                                  <attrib>depth</attrib>
                                  <attrib_value>0-1</attrib_value>
<                          /body>
<                          head>
                                  <attrib>magnitude</attrib>
                                  <attrib_value>(3,4]</attrib_value>
<                          /head>
                     </structure>
                     <measures>
<                          measure_name>support</measure_name>
<                          measure_value>0.18</measure_value>
<                          measure_name>confidence</measure_name>
<                          measure_value>0.67</measure_value>
                     </measures>
<              /pattern>
<              pattern p_id="2">
                     <structure>
<                          body>
                                  <attrib>season</attrib>
                                  <attrib_value>Autumn</attrib_value>
<                          /body>
<                          head>
                                  <attrib>magnitude</attrib>
                                  <attrib_value>(3-4]</attrib_value>
<                          /head>
                     </structure>
                     <measures>
<                          measure_name>support</measure_name>
<                          measure_value>0.18</measure_value>
<                          measure_name>confidence</measure_name>
<                          measure_value>0.58</measure_value>
                     </measures>
<              /pattern> </patterns> </pt_assocRule>
```

Figure 6. Pattern type association rule XSD diagram

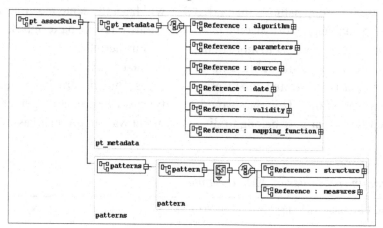

to seismic activity in the summer of 2003 and the clusters of faults that gave earthquakes of magnitude M>3 during the same time period. The link between the two types would be the magnitude of earthquakes. In other words, we are interested in studying the relation between earthquakes and geological faults, thus the grouping of classes of different pattern types is necessary.

Ontologies are stored in external files and are written in OWL (Horrocks & Patel-Schneider, 2003). Regarding association rule mining, a general rule that can be used to evaluate patterns with ontologies, is that patterns should associate attributes that belong to the same class or to subclasses of the same class. Reasonably, association of attributes belonging in different classes (in the ontology-hierarchy graph) or in classes that are several nodes away in the ontology diagram

might result in false associations of irrelevant (according to domain knowledge) attributes. Edge-distance and other approaches have been already proposed for searching semantic similarity between objects in an ontology. Such measures can be used to assess the relation between two attributes. This implies that the user can select the level of relevance between the attributes, defining the maximum distance that a class can have from another in the ontology graph.

The task of defining the rules that will be used to filter the patterns to be extracted involves the study of the ontology as well as the study of the pattern type and the results that users anticipate. Ontology components are classes, attributes, and relations between them. Classes have subclasses and each class may have a number of attributes.

Figure 7. Pattern base logical model

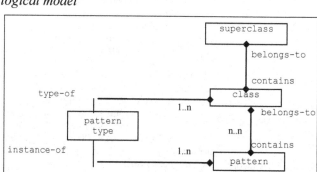

Figure 8. Class and Superclass relation

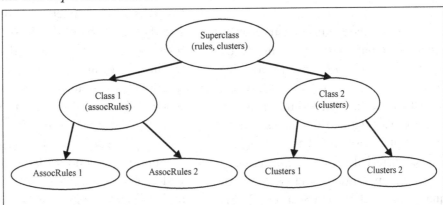

Usually classes for related concepts, belong to the same parent class while not related concepts are under different classes. The whole class and subclass diagram define a kind of hierarchy with various levels of detail. For example, classes "VolcanicEruption" and "Earhtremor" (Figure 3) lie at the same level, while their subclasses, "volcanicGasRelease" and "AfterShock," lie at lower level.

As each pattern has a different structure, filters for every pattern type have to be defined. Specifically for the association rule pattern type, we define the association rule filter. Each part of the rule contains attributes (depth, magnitude, etc.) that are related in the relational model, but also related in some way in the ontology. Thus, we can define for each rule a distance metric between the main earthquake class (*earth tremor*) and the nodes of the attributes contained in the rule. The shorter this distance is, the more the attributes are semantically related. In fact, we can define two approaches to measure this distance: in the so-called "*risky*" approach, we consider the maximum distance between the nodes of the attributes and the main earthquake class, whereas in the "*not risky*," we consider the minimum distance between them. Obviously, the attributes of the earthquake class have distance=0 and thus there are not included in this calculation.

A user selects the level of semantic relevance by specifying the maximum distance of the nodes from the main earthquake class. For instance, one may be interested in finding relationships not just between the attributes on an earthquake but also between them and geological faults. Thus, the level of semantic relevance has to be increased so as to include the appropriate node.

With the previously described process, a subgraph of the ontology that contains the attributes under consideration is constructed. Attributes of the produced rules are validated against this ontology subgraph. If all are included in the subgraph then the association rule that contains them is considered as semantically valid. Otherwise, if some of the attributes are not in the subgraph, the rules containing them are marked as "noisy." Note that the system does not reject "noisy" rules (although there is such an option) as they might contain previously unknown knowledge about the relations of some attributes, and thus domain expert's attention is required. Some rules can lead to new interesting relations and domain experts might reconsider the ontology.

Since the ontology represents the domain of interest, it has to be well-designed. In this way, pattern evaluation can be more accurate and may give useful results to domain experts.

PRELIMINARY VALIDATION STUDY

In this section, we use the example from seismology domain and the ontology defined in section *domain knowledge with ontologies* to describe system functionality. The system performs a validation test before the data mining process, checking if the user defined parameters make sense. For example, a user could ask the system to perform the Apriori algorithm to find associations between the "magnitude" and the "date" of an earthquake. As mentioned in Section 3.2, this association is not acceptable by the seismology domain and thus the system will suggest the user to change the parameters. If the user does not specify the attributes that he/she wants to search for associations, the system will perform the data mining algorithm using all attributes but, when generating the frequent itemsets, it will discard itemsets that contain values from attributes not related in the ontology. In this way, the time consuming phase of frequent itemset generation will be improved and no irrelative association rules will be generated. Of course, this is not always desirable as some interesting rules might not be generated. In this case the user should decide for

Table 1. Association rules extracted from seismological data

id	Association Rule	Conf.	Supp.
1	intensity≥5 → distance≤80	74%	19%
2	weekDay=Tuesday, 11≤depth≤20 → season=Summer	71%	10%
3	weekDay=Tuesday → season=Summer	71%	17%
4	weekDay=Monday → season=Spring	68%	10%
5	season=Summer → 11≤depth≤20	65%	21%
6	weekDay=Saturday → 21≤depth≤50	62%	12%
7	depth≥50 → season=Spring	60%	11%
8	distance≥150 → intensity≤3	59%	15%
9	weekDay=Tuesday, season=Summer → 11≤depth≤20	57%	10%
10	weekDay=Tuesday → 11≤depth≤20	57%	14%
11	11≤depth≤20 → season=Summer	57%	21%
12	season=Autumn → 11≤depth≤20	55%	14%
13	season=Summer → weekDay=Tuesday	54%	17%
14	intensity≤3 → distance≥150	54%	15%
15	distance≤80 → intensity≥5	52%	19%
16	distance≥150 → 1000<population≤4000	48%	13%
17	3<intensity≤4 → 80<distance<150	48%	15%
18	season=Summer, 11≤depth≤20 → weekDay=Tuesday	48%	10%
19	weekDay=Tuesday → 1000<population≤4000	46%	11%
20	season=Spring → 21≤depth≤50	46%	14%
21	intensity≤3 → 1000<population≤4000	46%	13%
22	21≤depth≤50 → season=Spring	45%	14%
23	500<population≤1000 → distance≤80	43%	11%
24	season=Spring → 1000<population≤4000	43%	13%
25	80<distance<150 → 1000<population≤4000	43%	15%

these rules. So, it is given as option to the user either to enable the system to automatically discard them or just to mark the "noisy" ones for further evaluation. In the latter case, the user decides which rules are interesting and should be stored to the pattern base.

Another case is when a user is posing a query to the pattern base to retrieve patterns for example, "fetch association rule patterns that contain both 'season and 'depth' attributes and the support of the rule is greater than 0.3." Such rules are not valid according to the domain knowledge and thus, the system notifies the user that it is rather impossible to find rules like those in the pattern base.

In our first experiments, we ran the Apriori data mining algorithm implemented in WEKA (Witten & Frank, 2005) to extract some association rules using real macroseismic data collected by the Greek Institute of Geodynamics (Seismo-Surfer). Attributes such as earthquake depth, intensity, site, date, and season of the year are some of the attributes of the table that contains 10336 tuples for the earthquake events during the 20th century. Table 1 lists 25 out of 70 rules extracted by Apriori confidence threshold = 30% and support threshold = 10% are listed in Table 1.

Out of these 25 rules, the domain expert marked only five rules (ids 1, 8, 14, 15, 17) as interesting

and all others as "noisy" because they describe a correlation between attributes/classes that is meaningless in the domain of seismology. The system needs a threshold parameter to be defined in order to mark some rules as "noisy." This threshold is the maximum path distance from the main "earth tremor" node/class. When this threshold is defined, the system retrieves the subgraph of the ontology defined by the "earth tremor" node and all the nodes with path distance less or equal to the threshold. Every rule that has attributes belonging to that subgraph, will be considered interesting while all others will be marked as "noisy."

Trying to detect a reasonable threshold in order for the system to retrieve the rules that will match the expert's evaluation, we varied threshold value from 1 to 5 and computed the rules marked as "noisy" by the system. This is illustrated in Figure 9.

According to this experiment we conclude that with threshold 3, the system matches expert choices. As such, this threshold can be used by the user for the next running of Apriori or can even be stored as metadata for the specific dataset and KDD process for future data mining.

With this procedure, we can measure the percentage of the rules that will be marked as "noisy" by the system and by the expert, but we

Figure 9. Threshold and rules rejected by the system and the seismologist

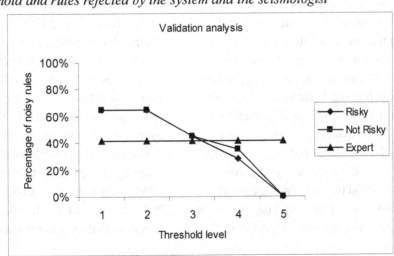

do not know if these are the same rules that is, if the rules marked by the system are the same with the rules marked by the domain expert (precision). While in our particular experiment we had a perfect match, it is not sure that we will have a perfect match each time.

CONCLUSION AND FUTURE WORK

In this chapter, we proposed a framework consisting of a PBMS that uses ontologies to improve data mining tasks, to evaluate extracted patterns and to improve querying over pattern base. The PBMS interacts with the data mining engine to discover patterns and stores them in XML format according to the presented pattern model in the pattern base. Users can pose queries over the pattern base and the data sources. Ontology is used to evaluate the patterns extracted from the data mining process, and to validate the queries the user is posing.

The main idea is that the system is independent from the data mining engine and the ontology. So, according to the application domain, the pattern types and the ontology have to be defined. The PBMS has also the proper design for defining complex patterns and for comparing patterns using similarity measures based on the structure and the measure component of the patterns.

The proposed framework provides domain experts with a powerful tool that can help them to better manage and evaluate the patterns extracted from data mining algorithms. We aim in improving and enhancing the KDD process. Domain knowledge and knowledge representation techniques can help both in reducing the required time to run a data mining algorithm and in evaluating the extracted patterns. It is clear though, that due to the complexity of ontologies and the lack of standards on ontology creation, this incorporation is not an easy task. We have listed the theoretical and technical problems that should be faced.

Both PBMS and ontologies are areas of recent research and their applications could be many. Apart from geosciences, every field that has a well defined ontology can use the integrated framework to improve the KDD process. For example in the domain of B2B marketplaces, finding associations between products is more efficient when using the hierarchies defined in the product ontology. Although there is not currently universally accepted product ontology, efforts are made to integrate different product ontologies (Omelayenko, 2000) towards this end.

In order to be able to use ontologies in KDD process and to have the results available to domain experts, ontologies have to be defined in a common way. There are a lot of efforts for ontology matching (Doan et al., 2003) and ontology integration (Cui et al., 2002; Pinto & Martins, 2001), and this illustrates the need for an ontology creation standard. In this way, exchange and comparison of ontologies describing different domains could be possible. Until now, only several domain specific ontologies and tools have been developed.

Integrating ontologies to the data mining process is not an easy task and a lot of issues have to be addressed. Things are complicated due to the fact that scientists and companies create ontologies according to their needs instead of adopting a universal ontology. There is a large number of ontology languages most of them designed for the semantic web like RDF (Beckett, 2004), SHOE (Luke & Heflin, 2000), DAML, DAML+OIL (Harmelen, Patel-Schneider, & Horrocks, 2001), OWL (McGuinness, & Harmelen, 2005). New ontologies are constructed for various fields and applications without centralized guidance and common agreement. This is getting even more complex as recent studies have indicated semantic and syntactic conflicts between these languages, especially between DAML+OIL and OWL (Horrocks & Patel-Schneider, 2003; Patel-Schneiderand & Fensel, 2002). Therefore, building a system that uses ontologies in the data mining process requires choosing a specific ontology language to support.

Another important theoretical issue concerns the evaluation of various pattern types using ontologies. It is very hard to define general rules that apply to all pattern types. The most popular pattern types from data mining field are association rules, clusters, decision trees, neural networks, and time series. We have defined filters for association rule mining but depending on the application filters for each pattern type separately have to be defined in order to build a system to support the majority of pattern types. Furthermore, we investigate the precision issue regarding the patterns that system marks as "noisy."

Our framework is currently under development. Extended experiments and expert evaluation of the results on real case studies with association rule and decision tree mining are to be conducted. Early results have been positively evaluated by seismologists. Future work includes defining filters for decision trees and clusters patterns for seismological data as well as applying the framework to other domains.

ACKNOWLEDGMENT

Research supported by the General Secretariat for Research and Technology of the Greek Ministry of Development under a PENED'2003 grant.

FUTURE RESEARCH DIRECTIONS

Ontology-assisted pattern management is an emerging research field that finds a wide area of applications. Market basket analysis is one of the most popular data mining applications. In this application, data mining algorithms are used to discover associations between products in order to (a) assist decisions on the management and promotion of products offered and (b) make recommendations to customers with respect to products others than those already bought. Clearly, when dealing with a large market, finding associations between products may be problematic if different product categories are involved (say, electronics and food). Using product hierarchies could result in more focused associations but an ontology that would filter the data mining results would give more accurate and sophisticated results / suggestions.

Constrained clustering is another application of ontology-filtered data mining. Constraints are commonly defined as must-link and cannot-link relations between data in order to optimize the creation of consistent clusters. These constraints could be implemented through a domain ontology to enable the must-link and cannot-link relations. In general, data mining algorithms have to be modified in order to involve an ontology filtering mechanism to evaluate the generated patterns of various types.

Last but not least, the flow of data coming from low-cost modern sensing technologies and wireless telecommunication devices (mobile and ubiquitous communications) enables novel research fields related with the management of time- and space-related data. Traditional knowledge discovery techniques are extended in order to implement appropriate analytics so as to transform raw data into useful knowledge. Consequently, pattern management technology should be adapted to satisfy the new requirement: management of patterns produced by spatio-temporal algorithms. Due to the new kind of data, the role of ontologies in the evaluation phase of KDD should be revisited.

Considering the applications described above, the integration of pattern management and ontologies is a promising field of applications, raising a lot of research issues that have to be addressed.

REFERENCES

Beckett, D. (2004). *RDF/XML Syntax Specification (Revised), W3C Recommendation.* http://www.w3.org/TR/rdf-syntax-grammar/

Catania, B., & Maddalena, A. (2006). Pattern Management: Practice and challenges. In J. Darmont & O. Boussaid (Eds.), *Processing and managing complex data for decision support.* Idea Group Publishing.

Catania B., Maddalena, A., & Mazza, M. (2005). PSYCHO: A prototype system for pattern management. In *Proceedings of the International Conference on Very Large Data Bases 2005.*

Chen X., Zhou, X., Scherl, R., & Geller, J. (2003). *Using an interest ontology for improved support in rule mining.* In DaWaK 2003 (pp. 320-329).

CINQ (Consortium on Discovering Knowledge with Inductive Queries). (2001). http://www.cinq-project.org

Cui, Z., Jones, D., & O'Brien, P. (2002). Semantic B2B Integration: Issues in Ontology-based Approaches. *ACM SIGMOD Record archive SPECIAL ISSUE: Data management issues in electronic commerce table of contents, 31*(1), 43-48.

CWM (Common Warehouse Model) (2001). homepage. http://www.omg.org/cwm

Doan, A., Madhavan, J., Domingos, P., & Halevy, A. (2003). Ontology matching: A machine learning Approach. In S. Staab & R. Studer (Eds), *Handbook on ontologies in information systems.* Springer-Velag.

Fayyad, U.M., Piatetsky-Shapiro, G., & Smyth, P. (1996). From data mining to knowledge discovery, an overview. In U. Fayyad, G. Piatetsky-Shapiro, P. Smyth, & R. Uthurusamy (Eds.), *Advances in knowledge discovery and data mining* (pp. 1-30). Menlo Park, CA: AAAI/MIT Press.

Fayyad, U., Haussler, D., & Stolorz, P. (1996). Mining scientific data. *Communications of the ACM, 39*(11), 51-57.

Freitas, A.A. (1999). On rule interestingness measures. *Knowledge-Based Systems, 12*(5-6), 309-315.

Gruber, T.R. (1993). A translation approach to portable ontologies. *Knowledge Acquisition, 5*(2), 199-220.

Guarino, N., & Giaretta, P. (1995). Ontologies and knowledge bases: Towards a terminological clarification. In N. Mars (Ed.), *Towards very large knowledge bases: Knowledge building and knowledge sharing* (pp. 25-32). Amsterdam: IOS Press.

Harmelen, F.V., Patel-Schneider, P.F., & Horrocks, I. (2001). *Reference Description of the DAML+ OIL Ontology Markup Langauge.* Retrieved from http://www.daml.org/2001/03/daml+oil-index.html

Horrocks, I., & Patel-Schneider, P.F. (2003). Three theses of representation in the Semantic Qeb. In *Proceedings of the Twelfth International Conference on World Wide Web.*

Hotho, A., Maedche, A., Staab, S., & Zacharias, V. (2002, April 26-27). On knowledgeable unsupervised text mining. In *Proceedings of the DaimlerChrysler Workshop on Text Mining,* Ulm.

ISO SQL/MM Part 6 (2001). http://www.sql-99.org/SC32/WG4/Progression_Documents/FCD/fcd-datamining-2001-05.pdf

Kotsifakos, E., Ntoutsi, I., & Theodoridis, Y. (2005). Database support for data mining patterns. In *Proceedings of PCI'05* (pp. 14-24). Springer Verlag.

Liu, B., Hsu, W., Chen, S., & Ma, Y. (2000). Analyzing the subjective interestingness of association rules. *IEEE Intelligent Systems, 15*(5), 47-55.

Luke, S., & Heflin, J. (2000). *SHOE 1.01 Proposed Specification, SHOE Project.* Retrieved from http://www.cs.umd.edu/projects/plus/SHOE/spec. htm

Maedche, A., Motik, B., Stojanovic, L., Studer, R., & Volz, R. (2003). Ontologies for enterprise knowledge management. *IEEE Intelligent Systems, 18*(2), 26-33.

McGuinness, D.L., & Harmelen, F.V. (2005). *OWL Web ontology language overview.* Retrieved Feburary 2005, from http://www.w3.org/TR/owl-features/

Niles, I., & Pease, A. (2001). Toward a Standard Upper Ontology. In *Proceedings of the 2nd International Conference on Formal Ontology in Information Systems (FOIS2001).*

Niles, I., & Terry, A. (2004). The MILO: A general-purpose, mid-level ontology. In *2004 International Conference on Information and Knowledge Engineering (IKE'04).*

Omelayenko, B. (2000). Integration of product ontologies for B2B marketplaces: A preview. *ACM SIGecom Exchanges, 2*(1), 19-25.

Padmanabhan, B., & Tuzhilin, A. (1998). A belief-driven method for discovering unexpected patterns. In *Proceedings of the International Conference on Knowledge Discovery and Data Mining* (pp. 94-100).

PANDA (Patterns for Next-generation Database Systems). (2001). *Project homepage.* http://dke. cti.gr/panda

Patel-Schneiderand, P.F., & Fensel, D. (2002). Layering the Semantic Web: Problems and directions. In *Proceedings of the 1st International Semantic Web Conference.* Springer.

Piatetsky-Shapiro, G. (1991). Discovery, analysis, and presentation of strong rules. In G. Piatetsky-Shapiro & W.J. Frawley (Eds.), *Knowledge discovery in databases* (pp. 229-248). Cambridge, MA: AAAI/MIT Press.

Piatetsky-Shapiro, G. (2000). Knowledge discovery in databases: 10 years after. *SIGKDD Explorations, 1*(2), 59-61.

Piatetsky-Shapiro, G. & Matheus, C.J. (1994). The interestingness of deviations. In *Proceedings of KDD-94: AAAI-94 Knowledge Discovery in Databases Workshop* (pp. 25-36). AAAI Press.

Pinto, H.S., & Martins, J.P. (2001) A methodology for ontology integration. In *Proceedings of the 1st International conference on Knowledge Captur.* (pp. 131-138).

Pohle, C., & Spiliopoulou, M. (2002). Building and exploiting ad hoc concept hierarchies for web log analysis. In Y. Kambayashi, W. Winiwarter, & M. Arikawa (Eds.), *Proceedings of the 4th International Conference on Data Warehousing and Knowledge Discovery, DaWaK 2002, Vol. 2454 of Lecture Notes in Computer Science* (pp. 83-93). Aix en Provence, France: Springer-Verlag.

Pohle, C. (2003) *Integrating and updating domain knowledge with data mining.* VLDB PhD Workshop.

Rizzi, S., Bertino, E., Catania, B., Golfarelli, M., Halkidi, M., Terrovitis, M., et al. (2003). Towards a logical model for patterns. In *Proceedings of ER'03 Conference.*

Seismo-Surfer. *A WebGIS application for integrating, visualizing and analyzing seismic data.* http://www.seismo.gr

Silberschatz, A. & Tuzhilin, A. (1996). What makes patterns interesting. In knowledge discovery systems. *IEEE Transactions on Knowledge and Data Engineering, 8*(6), 970-974.

Theodoridis, Y., Marketos, G., & Kalogeras, I.S. (2004). Collecting and mining seismic data in Greek territory: The seismo-surfer tool. In

Proceedings of the 7ᵗʰ Panhellenic Geographical Conference of the Hellenic Geographical Association (HGA'04), Mytilene, Lesvos, Greece.

Witten, I.H., & Frank, E. (2005). *Data Mining: Practical machine learning tools and techniques*, (2ⁿᵈ ed.). San Francisco: Morgan Kaufmann.

ADDITIONAL READING

Batagelj, V., & Ferligoj, A. (1998). *Constrained clustering problems*. IFCS'98, Rome.

Bradley, P.S., Bennett, K.P., & Demiriz, A. (2000). *Constrained k-means clustering (Technical Report MSR-TR-2000-65)*. Microsoft Research, Redmond.

Charest, M., Delisle, S., Cervantes, O., & Shen, Y. (2006, Oct). Invited Paper: Intelligent data mining assistance via cbr and ontologies. *In Proceedings of the 17ᵗʰ International Conference on Database and Expert Systems Applications* (pp. 593-597).

Chen, A., & McLeod, D. (2005, May 25-28). Semantics-based similarity decisions for ontologies. In *Proceedings of the 7ᵗʰ International Conference on Enterprise Information Systems*, Miami.

Choi, N., Song, I.Y., & Han, H. (2006). A survey on ontology mapping. *ACM SIGMOD Record archive 35*(3), 34-41.

Cody, W.F., Kreulen, J.T., Krishna, V., & Spangler, W.S. (2002). The integration of business intelligence and knowledge management. *IBM Systems Journal*.

Fensel, D. (2001). *Ontologies: Silver bullet for knowledge management and electronic commerce* (1ˢᵗ ed.). Springer.

Fonseca, F., Davis, C., & Camara, G. (2003). Bridging ontologies and conceptual schemas in geographic information integration. *Geoinformatica, 7*(4), 355-378.

Fu, Y., & Han, J. (1995, Dec). Metarule-guided mining of association rules in relational databases. In *Proceedings of KDOOD*, Singapore (pp. 39-46).

Ganti V., Gehrke, J., Ramakrishnan, R., & Loh, W. (1999). A framework for measuring changes in data characteristics. In *Proceedings of PODS'99*, Philadelphia.

Gordon, A.D. (1973). Classification in the presence of constraints. *Biometrics, 29*, 821-827.

Gordon, A.D. (1996). A survey of constrained classification. *Computational Statistics & Data Analysis, 21*(1), 17-29.

Han, J. (1995). Mining knowledge at multiple concept levels. *In Proceedings of CIKM*, Maryland (pp. 19-24).

Han, J., & Fu, Y. (1996). Exploration of the power of attribute-oriented induction in data mining. In U.M. Fayyad, G. Piatetsky-Shapiro, P. Smyth, & R. Uthurusamy (Eds.), *Advances in knowledge discovery and data mining* (pp. 399-421). AAAI/MIT Press.

Jurisica, I., Mylopoulos, J., & Yu, E. (2004). Ontologies for knowledge management: An information systems perspective. *Knowledge and Information Systems, 6*(4), 380-401.

Li, T., Zhu, S., & Ogihara, M. (2003). A new distributed data mining model based on similarity. In *Proceedings of ACM-SAC'03*.

Parekh, V., Gwo, J.P., & Finin, T. (2004). Ontology based semantic metadata for geoscience data. In *Proceedings of the International Conference of Information and Knowledge Engineering*.

Parthasarathy, S., & Ogihara, M. (2000). Clustering distributed homogeneous datasets. In *Proceedings of PKDD'00*, Lyon, France.

Philips, J., & Buchanan, B.G. (2001). Ontology-guided knowledge discovery in databases. In

Proceedings of the 1st International Conference on Knowledge Capture (pp. 123-130). Victoria, British Columbia, Canada.

Wagstaff K., Cardie C., Rogers S., & Schroedl S. (2001). Constrained K-means clustering with background knowledge. In *Proceedings of the Eighteenth International Conference on Machine Learning* (pp. 577-584). Williams College, MA: Morgan Kaufmann.

Wang, X., Chan, C.W., & Hamilton, H.J. (2002). Design of knowledge-based systems with the ontology-domain-system approach. In *Proceedings of the 14th International Conference on Software Engineering and Knowledge Engineering* (pp. 233-236).

Compilation of References

Achard, F., & Barillot, E. (1997). *Ubiquitous distributed objects with CORBA*. Pacific Symposium Biocomputing. London, World Scientific.

Achard, F., & Dessen, P. (1998). GenXref VI: Automatic generation of links between two heterogeneous databases. *Bioinformatics, 14*, 20-24.

Agirre, E., Ansa, O., Hovy, E., & Martinez, D. (2000). Enriching very large ontologies using the WWW. In *Proceedings of ECAI Workshop on Ontology Learning*.

Agrawal, R., & Srikant, R. (1994). Fast algorithms for mining association rules in large databases. In J.B. Bocca, M. Jarke, & C. Zaniolo (Eds.), *International Conference on Very Large Databases* (Vol. 20, pp. 487-499). San Francisco: Morgan Kaufmann Publishers.

Agrawal, R., & Srikant, R. (1995). Mining Sequential Patterns. In *Proceedings of the 11th International Conference on Data Engineering* (pp. 3-14).

Agrawal, R., Imielinski, T., & Swami, A. (1993). Database mining: A performance perspective. *IEEE Transactions on Knowledge and Data Engineering, 5*(6), 914-925.

Agrawal, R., Imielinski, T., & Swami, A. (1993). Mining association rules between sets of items in large databases. In P. Buneman & S. Jajodia (Eds.), *ACM SIGMOD International Conference on Management of Data* (Vol. 20, pp. 207-216). New York: ACM Press.

Alani, H., Kim, S., Millard, D.E., Weal, M.J., Hall, W., Lewis, P.H., et al. (2002). *Automatic ontology-based knowledge extraction and tailored biography generation from the Web*. Technical Report 02-049.

Alba, J.W., & Hasher, L. (1983). Is memory schematic? *Psychological Bulletin, 93*, 203-231.

Anand, S.S., Bell, D.A., & Hughes, J.G. (1995, November 29-December 02, 1995). *The role of domain knowledge in data mining*. Paper presented at the Conference on Information and Knowledge Management, Baltimore.

Andersen, T.J. (2005). The performance effect of computer-mediated communication and decentralized strategic decision making. *Journal of Business Research, 58*(8), 1059-1067.

Annesley, C. (2005). Banks' push to upgrade hampered by complexity of legacy systems. *Computer Weekly, 14*.

ANSI/NISO. (1993). *Guidelines for the construction, format, and management of monolingual thesauri*. National Information Standards Organization.

Antonioletti, M., Krause, A., Paton, N. W., Eisenberg, A., Laws, S., Malaika, S., et al. (2006). The WS-DAI family of specifications for web service data access and integration. *ACM SIGMOD Record, 35*(1), 48-55.

Appice, A., Berardi, M., Ceci, M., & Malerba, D. (2005). Mining and filtering multilevel spatial association rules with ARES. In M. Hacid, N. V. Murray, Z. W. Ras, & S. Tsumoto (Eds.), *Foundations of Intelligent Systems, 15th International Symposium ISMIS. Vol. 3488* (pp. 342-353). Berlin: Springer.

Apte, C., Damerau, F., & Weiss, S.M. (1994). Automated learning of decision rules for text categorization. *ACM Transactions on Information Systems, 12*(3), 233-251.

Arkin, A. (2002). *Business process modeling language* (BPML). Specification. BPMI.org.

Arkin, A., Askary, S., Bloch, B., Curbera, F., Goland, Y., Kartha, N., et al. (2005). *Web services business process execution language version* 2.0. wsbpel-specificationdraft-01, OASIS.

Arnoux, M., Lechevallier, Y., Tanasa, D., Trousse, B., & Verde, R. (2003). Automatic clustering for the Web usage mining. In D. Petcu, D. Zaharie, V. Negru, & T. Jebeleanu (Ed.). *Proceedings of the 5th International Workshop on Symbolic and Numeric Algorithms for Scientific Computing (SYNASC03)* (pp. 54-66). Editura Mirton, Timisoara.

Ashforth, B.E., & Humphrey, R.H. (1997). The ubiquity and potency of labeling in organizations. *Organization Science, 8*(1), 43-58.

Aussenac-Gilles, N., & Mothe, J. (2004). Ontologies as background knowledge to explore document collections. In *Proceedings of RIAO* (pp. 129-142)

Aussenac-Gilles, N., Biébow, B., & Szulman, S. (2000). Revisiting ontology design: A method based on corpus analysis. In R. Dieng & O. Corby (Eds.), *Proceedings of the 12th European Knowledge Acquisition Workshop (EKAW'00)* (pp. 172-188).

Aussenac-Gilles, N., Biébow, B., & Szulman, S. (2002). Revisiting ontology design: A methodology based on corpus analysis. In *Proceedings of the 12th International Conference in Knowledge Engineering and Knowledge Management (EKAW),* Juan-Les-Pins, France.

AxIS. (2005). *2005 AxIS research project activity report.* Section 'Overall Objectives.' http://www.inria.fr/rapportsactivite/RA2005/axis/axis_tf.html

Backhouse, J., & Cheng, E.K. (2000). Signalling intentions and obliging behavior online: An application of semiotic and legal modeling in e-commerce. *Journal of End User Computing, 12*(2), 33-42.

Barzilay, R., & Elhadad, M. (1997). *Lexical chains for text summarization.* Master's thesis, Ben-Gurion University.

Baxevanis, A. (2002). The molecular biology data collection: 2002 update. *Nucleic Acids Research, 30,* 1-12.

BEA, IBM, Microsoft, SAP, & Siebel. (2003). *Business process execution language for Web services.* Version 1.1. Specification. Retrieved May 15, 2006, from ftp://www6.software.ibm.com/software/developer/library/ws-bpel.pdf

Bechhofer, S., Moller, R., & Crowther, P. (2003). *The DIG description logic interface.* International Workshop on Description Logics, Rome, Italy.

Beckett, D. (2004). *RDF/XML Syntax Specification (Revised), W3C Recommendation.* http://www.w3.org/TR/rdf-syntax-grammar/

Beco, S., Cantalupo, B., Matskanis, N., & Surridge M. (2006). *Putting semantics in Grid workflow management: The OWL-WS approach.* GGF16 Semantic Grid Workshop, Athens, Greece.

Ben-natan, R. (1995). *CORBA.* New York: McGraw Hill.

Benson, D., Karsch-mizrachi, I., Lipman, D., Ostell, J., Rapp, B., & Wheeler, D. (2000). GenBank. *Nucleic Acids Research, 28,* 8-15.

Berendt, B., Hotho, A., & Stumme. G. (2002). Towards Semantic Web mining. In *Proceedings of the First International Semantic Web Conference on the Semantic Web* (pp. 264-278). Springer.

Berendt, B., Hotho, A., & Stumme. G. (2005, September 15-16). Semantic Web mining and the representation, analysis, and evolution of Web space. In *Proceedings of RAWS'2005 — Workshop on the Representation and Analysis of Web Space,* Prague-Tocna.

Bernstein, A., Hill, S., & Provost, F. (2001). An intelligent assistant for the knowledge discovery process. *In Proceedings of the IJCAI-01 Workshop on Wrappers for Performance Enhancement in KDD.* Seattle, WA: Morgan Kaufmann.

Bernstein, F.C., Koetzle, T.F., Williams, G.J., Meyer, E.F., Brice, M.D., Rodgers, J.R., et al. (1977). The protein data bank: A computer-based archival file for macromolecular structures. *Journal of Molecular Biology, 112,* 535-542.

Berzal, F., Blanco, I., Sanchez, D., & Vila, M.-A. (2001). Measuring the accuracy and interest of association rules: A new framework. *Intelligent Data Analysis, 6*(3), 221-235.

Biswas, G., Weinberg, J., & Li, C. (1995). ITERATE: A conceptual clustering method for knowledge discovery in databases. *Artificial Intelligence in the Petroleum Industry* (pp. 111-139). Paris.

Bloehdorn, S., Cimiano, P., Hotho, S., & Staab, S. (2005). An ontology-based framework for text mining. *LDV Forum: GLDV Journal for Computational Linguistics and Language Technology, 20*(1), 87-112.

Bock, H.H. (1993). Classification and clustering: Problems for the future. In E. Diday, Y. Lechevallier, M. Schader, P. Bertrand, & B. Burtschy, (Eds.), *New approaches in classification and data analysis* (pp. 3-24). Springer, Heidelberg.

Bogorny, V., & Iochpe, C. (2001). Extending the opengis model to support topological integrity constraints. In M. Mattoso & G. Xexéo (Eds.), *16th Brazilian Symposium in Databases* (pp. 25-39). Rio de Janeiro: COPPE/UFRJ.

Bogorny, V., Camargo, S., Engel, P., & Alvares, L. O. (2006c). Mining frequent geographic patterns with knowledge constraints. *In 14th ACM International Symposium on Advances in Geographic Information Systems.* Arlington, November (to appear).

Bogorny, V., Camargo, S., Engel, P., M., & Alvares, L.O. (2006b). Towards elimination of well known geographic domain patterns in spatial association rule mining. In *Proceedings of the 3rd IEEE International Conference on Intelligent Systems* (pp. 532-537). London: IEEE Computer Society.

Bogorny, V., Engel, P. M., & Alvares, L.O. (2005a). A reuse-based spatial data preparation framework for data mining. In J. Debenham & K. Zhang (Eds.), *15th International Conference on Software Engineering and Knowledge Engineering* (pp. 649-652). Taipei: Knowledge Systems Institute.

Bogorny, V., Engel, P. M., & Alvares, L.O. (2005b). Towards the reduction of spatial join for knowledge discovery in geographic databases using geo-ontologies and spatial integrity constraints. In M. Ackermann, B. Berendt, M. Grobelink, & V. Avatek (Eds.), *ECML/PKDD 2nd Workshop on Knowledge Discovery and Ontologies* (pp. 51-58). Porto.

Bogorny, V., Engel, P. M., & Alvares, L.O. (2006a). Geo-ARM: An interoperable framework to improve geographic data preprocessing and spatial association rule mining. In *Proceedings of the 18th International Conference on Software Engineering and Knowledge Engineering* (pp. 70-84). San Francisco: Knowledge Systems Institute.

Boland, R.J.J., Singh, J., Salipante, P., Aram, J., Fay, S.Y., & Kanawattanachai, P. (2001). Knowledge representations and knowledge transfer. *Academy of Management Journal, 44*, 393-417.

Bonchi, F., Giannotti, F., Gozzi, C., Manco, G., Nanni, M., Pedreschi, D., et al. (2001). Web log data warehousing and mining for intelligent web caching. *Data Knowledge Engineering, 39*(2), 165-189.

Bourigault, D., & Fabre, C. (2000). Approche linguistique pour l'analyse syntaxique de corpus, Cahiers de Grammaire, 25, Université Toulouse le Mirail (pp. 131-151).

Bowker, G., & Star, S.L. (1994). Knowledge and infrastructure in international information management: Problems of classification and coding. In L. Bud-Frierman (Ed.), *Information acumen: The understanding and use of knowledge in modern business* (pp. 187-213). London: Routledge.

Boyapati, V. (2002). Improving text classification using unlabeled data. In *Proceedings of the ACM Special Interest Group in Information Retrieval (SIGIR) Conference* (pp. 11-15).

Bozsak, E., Ehrig, M., Handschuh, S., Hotho, A., Maedche, A., Motik, B., et al. (2002). KAON: Towards a large scale Semantic Web. In *Proceedings of the 3rd International Conference on E-Commerce and Web Technologies* (Vol. 2455, pp. 304-313).

Brezany, P., Tjoa, A.M., Rusnak, M., & Janciak, I. (2003). Knowledge Grid support for treatment of traumatic brain injury victims. *International Conference on Computational Science and its Applications.* Montreal, Canada.

Brezany, P., Janciak, I., Kloner, C., & Petz, G. (2006). *Auriga — workflow engine for WS-I/WS-RF services.* Retrieved September 15, 2006, from http://www.Gridminer.org/auriga/

Brezany, P., Janciak, I., Woehrer, A., & Tjoa, A.M. (2004). *GridMiner: A Framework for knowledge discovery on the*

Grid - from a vision to design and implementation. Cracow Grid Workshop, Cracow, Poland: Springer.

Broader, A.Z., Glassman, S.C., Manasse, M., & Zweig, G. (1997). Syntactic clustering of the web. In *Proceedings of the 6th International World Wide Wweb (WWW) Conference* (pp.1157-1166).

Bruha, I. (2000). From machine learning to knowledge discovery: Survey of preprocessing and postprocessing. *Intelligent Data Analysis, 4*, 363-374.

Bunge, M. (1977). *Treatise on Basic Philosophy. Ontology I. The Furniture of the World.Vol. 3*, Boston: Reidel.

Burke, R. (2002). Hybrid recommender systems: Survey and experiments. *User Modeling and User-Adapted Interaction, 12*(4), 331-370.

Bussler ,C., Davies, J., Dieter, F., & Studer , R. (2004). The Semantic Web: Research and applications. In *Proceedings of the 1st European Semantic Web Symposium, ESWS. Lecture Notes in Computer Science, 3053.* Springer.

Cai, C.H., Fu, A.W., Cheng, C.H., & Kwong, W.W. (1998). Mining association rules with weighted items. In *Proceedings of 1998 Internatinal Database Engineering and Applications Symposium,* (pp. 68-77).

Canhoto, A.I., & Backhouse, J. (2005). Tracing the identity of a money launderer. In T. Nabeth (Ed.), *Fidis d2.2: Set of use case and scenarios.* Fontainebleau: Insead.

Carmichael, L., Hogan, H.P., & Walter, A.A. (1932). An experimental study on the effect of language on the reproduction of visually perceived form. *Journal of Experimental Psychology, 15*, 73-86.

Carson, S., Madhok, A., Varman, R., & John, G. (2003). Information processing moderators of the effectiveness of trust based governance in interfirm R&D collaboration. *Organization Science, 14*, 45-56.

Castano, S., Ferrara, A., & Montanelli., S. (2006). A matchmaking-based ontology evolution methodology. In *Proceedings of the 3rd CAiSE INTEROP Workshop on Enterprise Modelling and Ontologies for Interoperability (EMOI - INTEROP 2006),* Luxembourg.

Catania B., Maddalena, A., & Mazza, M. (2005). PSYCHO: A prototype system for pattern management. In *Proceedings of the International Conference on Very Large Data Bases 2005.*

Catania, B., & Maddalena, A. (2006). Pattern Management: Practice and challenges. In J. Darmont & O. Boussaid (Eds.), *Processing and managing complex data for decision support.* Idea Group Publishing.

Chakrabarti, S., Dom, B., & Indyk, P. (1998b). Enhanced hypertext categorization using hyperlinks. In *Proceedings of the ACM's Special Interest Group on Data on Data Management (SIGMOD) Conference.*

Chakrabarti, S., Dom, B., Agraval, R., & Raghavan, P. (1998a). Scalable feature selection, classification and signature generation for organizing large text databases into hierarchical topic taxonomies. *Very Large DataBases (VLDB) Journal, 7*, 163-178.

Chan, C., & Lewis, B. (2002). A basic primer on data mining. *Information Systems Management, 19*(4), 56-60.

Chapman, P., Clinton, J., Khabaza, T., Reinartz, T., & Wirth. R. (1999). *The CRISP-DM process model.* Technical report, CRISM-DM consortium. Retrieved May 15, 2006, from http://www.crisp-dm.org/CRISPWP-0800.pdf

Chaumier, J. (1988). *Le traitement linguistique de l'information.* Entreprise moderne d'éd.

Chaves, M. S., Silva, M. J., & Martins, B. (2005a). A geographic knowledge base for semantic web applications. In C. A. Heuser (Ed.), *20th Brazilian Symposium on Databases* (pp. 40-54). Uberlandia: UFU.

Chaves, M. S., Silva, M. J., & Martins, B. (2005b). *GKB— Geographic Knowledge Base.* (TR05-12). DI/FCUL.

Chen, H., & Dumais, S. (2000). Bringing order to the web: Automatically categorizing search results. In *Proceedings of the SIGCHI Conference on Human Factors in Computing Systems* (pp. 145-152).

Chen, X., Zhou, X., Scherl, R., & Geller, J. (2003). Using an interest ontology for improved support in rule mining. In *Proceedings of the 5th International Conference on Data*

Warehousing and Knowledge Discovery ser. *Lecture Notes in Computer Science,* Vol. 2738 (pp. 320-329). New York: Springer Verlag.

Cheung, D.W., Wang, L., Yiu, S.M., & Zhou, B. (2000). Density based mining of quantitative association rules. *PAKDD, LNAI, Vol. 1805* (pp. 257-268).

Christensen, E., Curbera, F., Meredith, G., & Weerawarana, S. (2001). *Web Services Description Language* (WSDL) 1.1. Retrieved May 10, 2006, from http://www.w3.org/TR/wsdl

Christianini, N., & Shawe-Taylor, J. (2000). *An introduction to support vector machines.* Cambridge University Press.

Chung, H.M., & Gray, P. (1999). Data mining. *Journal of Management Information Systems, 16*(1), 11-16.

CINQ (Consortium on Discovering Knowledge with Inductive Queries). (2001). http://www.cinq-project.org

Clementini, E., Di Felice, P., & Van Ostern, P. (1993). A small set of formal topological relationships for end-user interaction. In D.J. Abel & B.C. Ooi (Eds.), *Advances in Spatial Databases, 3rd International Symposium, 692* (pp. 277-295). Singapore: Springer.

Clementini, E., Felice, Di, P., & Koperski, K. (2000). Mining multiple-level spatial association rules for objects with a broad boundary. *Data & Knowledge Engineering, 34*(3), 251-270.

Cockcroft, S. (1997). A Taxonomy of spatial data integrity constraints. *Geoinformatica, 1*(4), 327-343.

Collins, F.S., Morgan, M., & Patrinos, A. (2003). The human genome project: Lessons from large-scale biology. *Science, 300,* 286-290.

Cook, S.D.N., & Brown, J.S. (1999). Bridging epistemologies: The generative dance between organizational knowledge and organizational knowing. *Organization Science, 10*(4), 381-400.

Craven, M., DiPasquo, D., Freitag, D., McCallum, A., Mitchell, T., Nigam, K., et al. (2000). Learning to construct knowledge bases from the World Wide Web. *Artificial Intelligence, 118*(1-2), 69-113.

Crouch, C.J., & Yang, B. (1992). Experiments in automatic statistical thesaurus construction. *Conference on Research and Development in Information Retrieval (SIGIR)* (pp. 77-88).

Cui, Z., Jones, D., & O'Brien, P. (2002). Semantic B2B Integration: Issues in Ontology-based Approaches. *ACM SIGMOD Record archive SPECIAL ISSUE: Data management issues in electronic commerce table of contents, 31*(1), 43-48.

CWM (Common Warehouse Model) (2001). homepage. http://www.omg.org/cwm

Data Mining Group. (2004). *Predictive model markup language.* Retrieved May 10, 2006, from http://www.dmg.org/

Davulcu, H., Vadrevu, S., & Nagarajan, S. (2003). OntoMiner: Bootstrapping and populating ontologies from domain specific websites. In *Proceedings of the First International Workshop on Semantic Web and Databases (SWDB 2003),* Berlin.

Decker, S., Erdmann, M., Fensel, D., & Studer, R. (1999). Ontobroker: Ontology based access to distributed and semi-structured information. *In Semantic Issues in Multimedia Systems, Proceedings of DS-8* (pp. 351-369). Boston: Kluwer Academic Publisher.

Deelman, E., Blythe, J., Gil, Y., & Kesselman, C. (2003). Workflow management in GriPhyN. *The Grid Resource Management.* The Netherlands: Kluwer.

Deerwester, S., et al. (1990). Indexing by latent semantic analysis. *Journal of the Society for Information Science, 41*(6).

Deitel, A.C., Faron, C. & Dieng, R. (2001). Learning ontologies from RDF annotations. In *Proceedings of the IJCAI'01 Workshop on Ontology Learning,* Seattle, WA.

DeMoor, A. (2002). Language/action meets organizational semiotics: Situating conversations with norms. *Information Systems Frontiers, 4*(3), 257-272.

Desouza, K.C., & Hensgen, T. (2002). On information in organizations: An emergent information theory and semiotic framework. *Emergence, 4*(3), 95-114.

Dhillon, G.S. (1995). *Interpreting the management of information systems security.* London School of Economics.

Diallo, G., Simonet, M., & Simonet, A. (2006). An approach to automatic semantic annotation of biomedical texts. In *Proceedings of IEA/AIE'06, LNAI 4031* (pp. 1024-1033). Springer-Verlag.

Diday, E. (1975). La méthode des nuées dynamiques. *Revue de Statistique Appliquée, 19*(2), 19-34.

Ding, Y., & Foo, S. (2002). Ontology research and development: Part 1—A review of ontology generation. *Journal of Information Science, 28*(2).

Doan, A., Madhavan, J., Domingos, P., & Halevy, A. (2003). Ontology matching: A machine learning Approach. In S. Staab & R. Studer (Eds), *Handbook on ontologies in information systems.* Springer-Velag.

Dodds, K., & Fletcher, A. (2004). Interval probability process mapping as a tool for drilling decisions analysis: The R&D perspective. *The Leading Edge, 23*(6), 558-564.

Duda, R.O., & Hart, P.E. (1973). *Pattern classification and sense analysis.* Wiley & Sons.

Dunham, H.M. (2003). *Data mining, introductory and advanced topics.* Prentice Hall.

Dutton, J.E., & Jackson, S.E. (1987). Categorizing strategic issues: Links to organizational action. *Academy of Management Review, 12*(1), 76-90.

Eatock, J., Paul, R.J., et al. (2002). Developing a theory to explain the insights gained concering information systems and business process behaviour: *The ASSESS-IT project. Information Systems Frontiers, 4*(3), 303-316.

Eco, U. (1976). *A theory of semiotics.* Bloomington, IN: Indiana University Press.

Egenhofer, M., & Franzosa, R. (1995). On the equivalence of topological relations. *International Journal of Geographical Information Systems, 9*(2), 133-152.

Elfeky, M.G., Saad, A.A., & Fouad, S.A. (2001). ODMQL: Object data mining query language. In *Proceedings of the 2000 International Symposium on Objects and Databases* (pp. 128-140). New York: Springer Verlag.

Elsbach, K.D., Barr, P.S., & Hargadon, A.B. (2005). Identifying situated cognition in organizations. *Organization Science, (16), 4.*

Englmeier, K., & Mothe, J. (2003). IRAIA: A portal technology with a semantic layer coordinating multimedia retrieval and cross-owner content building. In *Proceedings of the International Conference on Cross Media Service Delivery, Cross-Media Service Delivery Series. The International Series in Engineering and Computer Science* (Vol. 740, pp. 181-192).

Erdmann, M., & Rudi, S. (2001). How to structure and access XML documents with ontology. *IEEE Data & Knowledge Engineering, 36,* 317-335.

Ester, M., Frommelt, A., Kriegel, H.-P., & Sander, J. (2000). Spatial data mining: Database primitives, algorithms and efficient DBMS support. *Journal of Data Mining and Knowledge Discovery, 4*(2-3), 193-216.

Euzenat, J. (1995). Building consensual knowledge bases: Context and architecture. In *Proceedings of 2nd International Conference on Building and Sharing Very Large-Scale Knowledge Bases.* Enschede, Amsterdam: IOS Press.

Faatz, A., & Steinmetz, R. (2002). *Ontology enrichment with texts from the WWW.* Semantic Web Mining 2nd Workshop at ECML/PKDD-2002. Helsinki, Finland.

Fayyad, U., Haussler, D., & Stolorz, P. (1996). Mining scientific data. *Communications of the ACM, 39*(11), 51-57.

Fayyad, U., Piatetsky-Shapiro, G., Smyth, P., & Uthurusamy, R. (Eds.). (1996). *Advances in knowledge discovery and data mining.* Cambridge, MA: AAAI / MIT Press.

Fayyad, U.M., Piatetsky-Shapiro, G., & Smyth, P. (1996). From data mining to knowledge discovery, an overview. In U. Fayyad, G. Piatetsky-Shapiro, P. Smyth, & R. Uthurusamy (Eds.), *Advances in knowledge discovery and data mining* (pp. 1-30). Menlo Park, CA: AAAI/MIT Press.

Fensel, S.B. (1998). Knowledge engineering: Principles and methods. *Data and Knowledge Engineering, 25,* 161-197.

Fischer, D.H. (1998). From thesauri towards ontologies? In W.M. Hadi, J. Maniez, & S. Pollitt (Eds.), *Structures and*

Relations in Knowledge Organization: Proceedings of the 5th International ISKO Conference (pp. 18-30). Würzburg: Ergon.

Fiske, S. T., & Taylor, S. E. (1991). *Social cognition* (2nd ed.). New York: McGraw-Hill.

Flouris, G. (2006). *On belief change and ontology evolution.* Doctoral Dissertation, Department of Computer Science, University of Crete.

Flouris, G., & Plexousakis, D.G. (2006). Evolving ontology evolution, Invited Talk. In *Proceedings of the 32nd International Conference on Current Trends in Theory and Practice of Computer Science (SOFSEM 06)* (p. 7). Merin, Czech Republic.

Fortin, S., & Liu, L. (1996). An object-oriented approach to multilevel association rule mining. In *Proceedings of the 5th International Conference on Information and Knowledge Management* (pp. 65-72). New York: ACM Press.

Foskett, D.J. (1980). Thesaurus. In A. Kent & H. Lancour (Eds), *Encyclopedia of library and information science* (pp. 416-463).

Frazier, M.E., Johnson, G.M., Thomassen, D.G., Oliver, C.E., & Patrinos, A. (2003a). Realizing the potential of genome revolution: The genomes to life program. *Science, 300,* 290-293.

Frazier, M.E., Thomassen, D.G., Patrinos, A., Johnson, G.M., Oliver, C. E., & Uberbacher, E. (2003b). Setting up the pace of discovery: The genomes to life program. In *Proceedings of the 2nd IEEE Computer Society Bioinformatics Conference (CSB 2003).* Stanford, CA: IEEE CS Press.

Freitas, A.A. (1999). On rule interestingness measures. *Knowledge-Based Systems, 12*(5-6), 309-315.

Fu, Y., Sandhu, K., & Shih, M. (2000). A generalization-based approach to clustering of web usage sessions. In *Proceedings of the 1999 KDD Workshop on Web Mining* (Vol. 1836, pp. 21-38). San Diego, CA: Springer-Verlag.

Furnkranz, J. (1999). Exploring structural information for text classification on the WWW. In *Intelligent data analysis* (pp. 487-498).

Gabrilovich, E., & Markovitch, S. (2005, August). Feature generation for text categorization using world knowledge. In *Proceedings of the 19th International Joint Conference in Artificial Intelligence* (pp. 1048-1053).

Gal, A., Modica, G., & Jamil, H.M. (2004). OntoBuilder: Fully automatic extraction and consolidation of ontologies from Web sources. In *Proceedings of the 20th International Conference on Data Engineering.* IEEE Computer Society.

Galperin, M.Y. (2006). The molecular biology database collection: 2006 update. *Nucleic Acids Research, 34,* D3-D5.

Gangemi, A., Guarino, N., Masolo, C., Oltramari, A., & Schneider, L. (2002). Sweetening ontologies with DOLCE. In *Proceedings of the International Conference on Knowledge Engineering and Knowledge Management* (pp. 166-181).

Garavelli, J.S. (2003). The RESID database of protein modifications: 2003 developments. *Nucleic Acids Research, 31,* 499-501.

Gauch, S., Chaffee, J., & Pretschner, A. (2003). Ontology-based personalized search and browsing. *Web Intelligence and Agent System, 1*(3-4), 219-234.

Geller, J., Scherl, R., & Perl, Y. (2002). Mining the Web for target marketing information. In *Proceedings of the Collaborative Electronic Commerce Technology and Research (CollECTeR) Workshop.* Toulouse, France.

Geller, J., Zhou, X., Prathipati, K., Kanigiluppai, S., & Chen, X. (2005). Raising data for improved support in rule mining: How to raise and how far to raise. *Intelligent Data Analysis, 9*(4), 397-415.

George, D. G., Orcutt, B.C., Mewes, H.-W., & Tsugita, A. (1993). An object-oriented sequence database definition language (sddl). *protein Seq. Data Anal., 5,* 357-399.

George, D.G., Mewes, H-W., & Kihara, H. (1987). A standardized format for sequence data exchange. *protein Seq. Data Anal., 1,* 27-29.

Gibson, J.J. (1979). *The ecological approach to visual perception.* Boston: Houghton Mifflin.

Gilbert, D.T. (1991). How mental systems believe. *American psychologist, 46,* 107-119.

Gilbert, R., Liu, Y., & Abriel, W. (2004). Reservoir modeling: integrating various data at appropriate scales. *The Leading Edge, 23*(8), 784-788.

Gladwell, M. (2006). Troublemakers. *The New Yorker.*

Globus Alliance (2005). *Globus Toolkit 4.* http://www.globus.org

Globus Alliance, IBM, & HP (2004). *The WS-Resource framework.* Retrieved May 10, 2006, from http://www.globus.org/wsrf/

Glover, E., Tsioutsiouliklis, K., Lawrence, S., Pennock, M., & Flake, G. (2002). Using web structure for classifying and describing Web pages. In *Proceedings of the 11ᵗʰ International World Wide Web (WWW) Conference.*

Gòmez-Pérez, A., & Rojas, M.D. (1999). Ontological reengineering and reuse. In D. Fensel & R. Studer (Ed.), *European Workshop on Knowledge Acquisition, Modeling and Management (EKAW). Lecture Notes in Artificial Intelligence LNAI 1621* (pp. 139-156). Springer-Verlag.

Gómez-Pérez, A., Fernandez, M., & de Vicente, A.J. (1996). Towards a method to conceptualize domain ontologies. In *Proceedings of the European Conference on Artificial Intelligence (ECAI'96)* (pp. 41-52).

Gordon, A.D. (1981). *Classification: Methods for the exploratory analysis of multivariate data.* London: Chapman & Hall.

Gornik, D. (2000). *Data modeling for data warehouses.* A rational software white paper. Rational E-development Company.

Gouy, M., Gautier, C., Attimonelli, M., Lanave, C., & Di Paola, G. (1985). ACNUC: A portable retrieval system for nucleic acid sequence databases: Logical and physical designs and usage. *Computer Applications in the Biosciences, 1,* 167-172.

Govaert, G. (1977). Algorithme de classification d'un tableau de contingence. In *Proceedings of first international symposium on Data Analysis and Informatics* (pp. 487-500). INRIA, Versailles.

Govaert, G., & Nadif, M. (2003). Clustering with block mixture models. Pattern recognition. *Elservier Science Publishers, 36,* 463-473.

Grefenstette, G. (1992). Use of syntactic context to produce term association lists for retrieval. In *Proceedings of the Conference on Research and Development in Information Retrieval (SIGIR)* (pp. 89-97).

Gruber, T. (1993). Toward principles for the design of ontologies used for knowledge sharing. In N. Guarino & R. Poli, (Eds.), *International Journal of Human-Computer Studies, special issue on Formal Ontology in Conceptual Analysis and Knowledge Representation,* LADSEB-CNR Int. Rep. ACM.

Gruber, T. R. (1993). A translation approach to portable ontologies. *Knowledge Acquisition, 5*(2), 199-220.

Gruber, T. R. (1993). Towards principles for the design of ontologies used for knowledge sharing. Formal ontology in conceptual analysis and knowledge representation. *International Journal of Human-Computer Studies, 43,* 907-928.

Grüninger, M., & Fox, M.S. (1995). Methodology for the design and evaluation of ontologies. *IJCAI'95 Workshop on Basic Ontological Issues in Knowledge Sharing,* Montreal, Canada.

Guan, S., & Zhu, F. (2004). Ontology acquisition and exchange of evolutionary product-brokering agents. *Journal of Research and Practice in Information Technology, 36*(1), 35-45.

Guarino, N. (1998). Formal Ontology in Information Systems. Guarino (Ed.), *First International Conference on Formal Ontology in Information Systems* (pp. 3-15). Italy.

Guarino, N., & Giaretta, P. (1995). Ontologies and knowledge bases: Towards a terminological clarification. In N. Mars (Ed.), *Towards very large knowledge bases: Knowledge building and knowledge sharing* (pp. 25-32). Amsterdam: IOS Press.

Guarino, N., Carrara, M., & Giaretta, P. (1994). Formalizing ontological commitments. In *Proceedings of the AAAI Conference.*

Guha, S., Rastogi, R., & Shim, K. (1999b). CURE: An efficient algorithm for clustering large databases. In *Proceedings of ACM-SIGMOD International Conference on Management of Data.*

Gyssens, M., Paredaens, P. & Gucht, D. (1990). A graph-oriented object database model. In *Proceedings of the 9ᵗʰ ACM SIGACT-SIGMOD-SIGART symposium on Principles of database systems.* Nashville, TN: ACM Press.

Haav, H.M., & Lubi, T.L. (2001). A survey of concept-based information retrieval tools on the web. In *Proceedings of the 5ᵗʰ East-European Conference ADBIS* (Vol. 2, pp. 29-41).

Hadzic, F., Dillon, T.S., Sidhu, A.S., Chang, E., & Tan, H. (2006). Mining substructures in protein data. *2006 IEEE Workshop on Data Mining in Bioinformatics (DMB 2006) in conjunction with 6ᵗʰ IEEE ICDM 2006.* Hong Kong: IEEE CS Press.

Hadzic, M., & Chang, E. (2005). Ontology-based support for human disease study. In *Proceedings of the 38ᵗʰ Hawaii International Conference on System Sciences.*

Hafner, C.D. & Fridman, N. (1996). Ontological foundations for biology knowledge models. In *Proceedings of the 4ᵗʰ International Conference on Intelligent Systems for Molecular Biology.* St. Louis: AAAI.

Hahn, U., & Schulz, S. (2004) Building a very large ontology from medical thesauri. In S. Staab & R. Stuber (Eds.), *Handbook on ontologies* (pp. 133-150).

Han, J. (1995). Mining knowledge at multiple concept levels. In *Proceedings of the 4ᵗʰ International Conference on Information and Knowledge Management* (pp. 19-24). New York: ACM Press.

Han, J., & Fu, Y. (1995). Discovery of multiple-level association rules from large databases. In U. Dayal, P.M.D. Gray, & S. Nishio (Eds.), *International Conference on Very Large Data Bases* (pp. 420-431). Zurich: Morgan-Kaufmann.

Han, J., & Fu, Y. (1995). Discovery of multiple-level association rules from large databases. In *Proceedings of the*

21ˢᵗ *International Conference on Very Large Data Bases* (pp. 420-431). Zurich, Switzerland.

Han, J., & Kamber, M. (2001). *Data mining: Concepts and techniques.* San Francisco: Morgan Kaufmann.

Han, J., Koperski, K., & Stefanvic, N. (1997). GeoMiner: a system prototype for spatial data mining. In J. Peckham (Ed.), *ACM SIGMOD International Conference on Management of Data, 26* (pp. 553-556). Tucson: ACM Press.

Han, J., Pei J., & Yin, Y. (2000). Mining frequent patterns without candidate generation. In J. Chen, F. Naughton, & P.A. Bernstein (Eds.), *20ᵗʰ ACM SIGMOD International Conference on Management of Data* (pp. 1-12) Dallas: ACM.

Han, J., Pei, J., Yin, Y., & Mao, R. (2004). Mining frequent patterns without candidate generation: A frequent-pattern tree approach. *Data Mining and Knowledge Discovery, 8*(1), 53-87.

Harman, D. (1992). The DARPA TIPSTER project. *SIGIR Forum, 26*(2), 26-28.

Harmelen, F.V., Patel-Schneider, P.F., & Horrocks, I. (2001). *Reference Description of the DAML+ OIL Ontology Markup Langauge.* Retrieved from http://www.daml.org/2001/03/daml+oil-index.html

Hearst, M.A. (1992). Automatic acquisition of hyponyms from large text corpora. In *Proceedings of the 14ᵗʰ International Conference on Computational Linguistics.*

Heeks, R. (2000). Information technology, information systems and public sector accountability. In C. Avgerou & G. Walsham (Eds.), *Information technology in context* (pp. 201-220). Aldershot, Hampshire: Ashgate.

Heracleous, L., & Barrett, M. (2001). Organizational change as discourse: Communicative actions and deep structures in the context of information technology implementation. *Academy of Management Journal, 44*, 755-778.

Hernandez, N., Mothe, J., & Poulain, S. (2005). Accessing and mining scientific domains using ontologies: The OntoExplo System. In *Proceedings of the 28ᵗʰ Annual International ACM SIGIR* (pp. 607-608).

Hildebrandt, M., & Backhouse, J. (2005). *D7.2: Descriptive analysis and inventory of profiling practices*. FIDIS Future of Identity in the Information Society.

Hoffer, J.A, Presscot, M.B., & McFadden, F.R. (2005). *Modern database management* (6th ed.). Prentice Hall.

Honkela, T., Kaski S., Lagus, K., & Kohonen, T. (1997, June). WEBSOM: Self-organizing maps of document collections. In *Proceedings of WSOM '97, Workshop on Self-Organizing Maps*. Helsinki University of Technology, Neural Networks Research Centre, Espoo, Finland.

Hori, M., & Ohashi, M. (2005). Applying XML web services into health care management. In *Proceedings of the 38th Hawaii International Conference on System Sciences*.

Hornick, F. M., et al. (2005). *Java data mining 2.0*. Retrieved June 20, 2006, from http://jcp.org/aboutJava/community-process/edr/jsr247/

Horrocks, I., & Patel-Schneider, P.F. (2003). Three theses of representation in the Semantic Qeb. In *Proceedings of the Twelfth International Conference on World Wide Web*.

Horrocks, I., Patel-Schneider, P. F., Boley, H., Tabet, S., Grosof, B., & Dean, M. (2004). *SWRL: A Semantic Web rule language combining OWL and RuleML*. W3C Member Submission. Retrieved May 10, 2006, from http://www.w3.org/Submission/2004/SUBM-SWRL-20040521

Hosein, I. (2005). *Researching the ethics of knowledge management: The case of data-mining.* (Working paper). London School of Economics.

Hotho, A., Maedche, A., & Staab, S. (2001, August). Ontology-based text clustering. In *Proceedings of the IJCAI-2001 Workshop of Text Learning, Beyond Supervision*. Seattle, USA.

Hotho, A., Maedche, A., Staab, S., & Zacharias, V. (2002, April 26-27). On knowledgeable unsupervised text mining. In *Proceedings of the DaimlerChrysler Workshop on Text Mining*, Ulm.

Huang, C.C., Chuang, S.L., & Chien, L.K. (2004). LiveClassifier: Creating hierarchical text classifiers through web corpora. In *Proceedings of the 13th International World Wide Web (WWW) Conference* (pp. 184-192).

Huang, Y., Shekhar, S., & Xiong, H. (2004). Discovering co-location patterns from spatial datasets: A general approach. *IEEE Transactions on Knowledge and Data Engineering, 16*(12), 1472-1485.

Huang, Z. (1997). A fast clustering algorithm to cluster very large categorical data sets in data mining. In *Proceedings of SIGMOD Workshop on Research Issues on Data Mining and Knowledge Discovery*.

Humby, C., Hunt, T., & Phillips, T. (2003). *Scoring points: How tesco is winning customer loyalty*. London: Kogan Page.

Huston, D.C., Hunter, H., & Johnson, E. (2003). Geostatistical integration of velocity cube and log data to constrain 3D gravity modeling, Deepwater Gulf of Mexico. *The Leading Edge, 23*(4), 842-846.

ISO SQL/MM Part 6 (2001). http://www.sql-99.org/SC32/WG4/Progression_Documents/ FCD/fcd-datamining-2001-05.pdf

Jagoto, A. (2000). *Data analysis and classification for bioinformatics*. CA: Bay Press.

Jain, A.K., Murty, M.N., & Flynn, P.J. (1999). Data clustering: a review. *ACM Computing Surveys, 31*(3), 264-323.

Jannink, J. (1999). Thesaurus entry extraction from an on-line dictionary. In *Proceedings of Fusion 99*, Sunnyvale CA.

Jasper, R., & Uschold, M. (1999). A framework for understanding and classifying ontology applications. In *Proceedings of the IJCAI-99 ontology workshop* (pp. 1-20).

Johnston, D.H. (2004). 4D-gives reservoir surveillance. *AAPG Explorer, 25*(12), 28-30.

Junker, M., Sintek, M., & Rinck, M. (1999). Learning for Text Categorization and Information Extraction with ILP. In J. Cussens (Eds.), *Proceedings of the 1st Workshop on Learning Language in Logic* (pp. 84-93). Bled: Slovenia.

Kamp, M., Korffer, B., & Meints, M. (forthcoming). Profiling of customers and consumers: Customer loyalty programs and scoring practices. In M. Hildebrandt & S. Gutwirth

(Eds.), *Profiling the european citizen: Cross-disciplinary perspectives* (pp. 181-196). Spinger.

Karoui, L., Aufaure, M.-A., & Bennacer, N. (2004). Ontology discovery from web pages: Application to tourism. *Workshop on Knowledge Discovery and Ontologies (KDO), co-located with ECML/PKDD,* Pisa, Italy, pp. 115-120.

Karp, P.D. (1996). A strategy for database interoperation. *Journal of Computational Biology, 2,* 573-583.

Kaufman, L., & Rousseeuw, P.J. (1990). *Finding groups in data: An introduction to cluster analysis.* New York: John Wiley & Sons.

Kickinger, G., Hofer, J., Tjoa, A.M., & Brezany, P. (2003). Workflow mManagement in GridMiner. *The 3rd Cracow Grid Workshop.* Cracow, Poland: Springer.

Kietz, J.U., Maedche, A., & Volz, R. (2000). A method for semiautomatic ontology acquisition from a corporate intranet. In *Proceedings of EKAW-2000 Workshop Ontologies and Text.* Lecture Notes in Artificial Intelligence (LNAI). France: Springer-Verlag.

Kohavi, R., Rothleder, N.J., & Simoudis, E. (2002). Emerging trends in business analytics. *Communications of the ACM, 45*(8), 45-48.

Kohonen, T. (1982). Self-organized formation of topologically correct feature maps. *Biological Cybernetics, 43,* 59-69.

Kohonen, T. (1998). Self-organization of very large document collections: State of the art. In L. Niklasson, M. Bod, & T. Ziemke, (Eds.), *Proceedings of ICANN98, the 8th International Conference on Artificial Neural Networks* (Vol. 1, pp. 65-74). London: Springer.

Kohonen, T., Kaski, S., Lagus, K., Salojärvi, J., Honkela, J., Paatero, V., et al. (2000). Self organization of a massive document collection. *IEEE Transactions on Neural Networks, 11*(3) 574-585.

Koller, D., & Sahami, M. (1997). Hierarchically classifying documents using very few words. In *Proceedings of the 14th International Conference on Machine Learning (ICML)* (pp. 170-178).

Koonin, E.V., & Galperin, M.Y. (1997). Prokaryotic genomes: the emerging paradigm of genome-based microbiology. *Current Opinions in Genetic Development, 7,* 757-763.

Koperski, K., & Han, J. (1995). Discovery of spatial association rules in geographic information databases. In M.J. Egenhofer, J.R. Herring (Eds.), *4th International Symposium on Large Geographical Databases, 951* (pp. 47-66). Portland: Springer.

Kosala, R., & Blockeel, H. (2000). Web mining research: A survey. *SIGKDD Explorations: Newsletter of the ACM Special Interest Group on Knowledge Discovery and Data Mining, 2*(1), 1-5.

Kotsifakos, E., Ntoutsi, I., & Theodoridis, Y. (2005). Database support for data mining patterns. In *Proceedings of PCI'05* (pp. 14-24). Springer Verlag.

Kuonen, D. (2003). Challenges in bioinformatics for statistical data miners. *Bulletin of Swiss Statistical Society, 46,* 10-17.

Labrou, Y., & Finin, T. (1999). Yahoo! as an ontology: Using Yahoo! categories to describe documents. In *8th International Conference on Knowledge and Information Management (CIKM-99* (pp.180-187). Kansas City, MO.

Lame, G. (2003). Using text analysis techniques to identify legal ontologies components. In *Workshop on Legal Ontologies of the International Conference on Artificial Intelligence and Law.*

Lant, T. (2002). Organizational cognition and interpretation. In J. A. C. Baum (Ed.), *Blackwell companion to organizations* (pp. 344-362). Malden: Blackwell Publishers.

Lassila, O., & McGuiness, D. (2001). The role of frame-based representation on the Semantic Web. Rapport technique KSL-01-02, Knowledge Systems Laboratory, Stanford University.

Lave, J., & Wenger, E. (1991). *Situated learning: Legitimate peripheral participation.* Cambridge: Cambridge University Press.

Lewis, D.D. (1991). Evaluating text categorization. In *Proceedings of the Speech and Natural Language Workshop* (pp. 312-318).

Leymann, F. (2001). *Web services flow language (WSFL 1.0)*. Retrieved September 23, 2002, from www4.ibm.com/software/solutions/webservices/pdf/WSFL.pdf

Li, Y., & Zhong, N. (2006). Mining ontology for automatically acquiring Web user information needs. *IEEE Transactions on Knowledge and Data Engineering, 18*(4), 554-568.

Liebenau, J., & Harindranath, G. (2002). Organizational reconciliation and its implications for organizational decision support systems: A semiotic approach. *Decision Support Systems, 33*(4), 339-398.

Litvak, M., Last, M., & Kisilevich, S. (2005, October). *Improving classification of multilingual Web documents using domain ontologies*. The Second International Workshop on Knowledge Discovery and Ontologies. Porto, Portugal.

Liu, B., Hsu, W., Chen, S., & Ma, Y. (2000). Analyzing the subjective interestingness of association rules. *IEEE Intelligent Systems, 15*(5), 47-55.

Liu, K. (2000). *Semiotics in information systems engineering*. Cambridge: Cambridge University Press.

Liu, K., & Dix, A. (1997). *Norm governed agents in cscw*. Paper presented at the 1st International Workshop on Computational Semiotics, Paris.

Liu, L., Buttler, D.T.C., Han, W., Paques, H., Pu, C., & Rocco, D. (2003). BioSeek: Exploiting source-capability information for integrated access to multiple bioinformatics data sources. In *Proceedings of the 3rd IEEE Symposium on Bioinformatics and Bioengineering (BIBE 2003)*. Bethesda, MD: IEEE CS Press.

Loftus, E. (1979). *Eyewitness testimony*. Cambridge, MA: Harvard University Press.

Loh, S., Wives, L.K., & Oliveira, J.P.M. (2000). Concept-based knowledge discovery in texts extracted from the web. *ACM SIGKDD Explorations, 2*(1), 29-39.

Longley, I.M., Bradshaw, M.T., & Hebberger, J. (2001). Australian petroleum provinces of the 21st century. In M.W. Downey, J.C. Threet, & W.A. Morgan (Eds.), *Petroleum provinces of the 21st century, AAPG Memoir, 74*, 287-317.

Lu, S., Dong, M., & Fotouhi, F. (2002). The Semantic Web: Opportunities and challenges for next-generation Web applications. Retrieved from http://informationr.net/ir/7-4/paper134.html

Lu, S., Hu, H., & Li, F. (2001). Mining weighted association rules. *Intelligent Data Analysis, 5*(3), 211-225.

Lu, W., Han, J., & Ooi, B. C. (1993). Discovery of general knowledge in large spatial databases. *In Far East Workshop on Geographic Information Systems* (pp. 275-289). Singapore.

Luke, S., & Heflin, J. (2000). *SHOE 1.01 Proposed Specification, SHOE Project*. Retrieved from http://www.cs.umd.edu/projects/plus/SHOE/spec.htm

Mädche, A., & Volz, R. (2001). The ontology extraction and maintenance framework Text-To-Onto. In *Proceedings of the ICDM'01 Workshop on Integrating Data Mining and Knowledge Management*. San Jose, CA.

Maedche, A., & Staab, S. (2001). Ontology learning for the Semantic Web. *IEEE Intelligent Systems, Special Issue on the Semantic Web, 16*(2).

Maedche, A., Motik, B., Stojanovic, L., Studer, R., & Volz, R. (2003). Ontologies for enterprise knowledge management. *IEEE Intelligent Systems, 18*(2), 26-33.

Maidak, B.L., Olsen, G.J., Larsen, N., Overbeek, R., Mccaughey, M.J., & Woese, C.R. (1996). The ribosomal database project (RDP). *Nucleic Acids Research, 24*, 82-85.

Majithia, S., Walker, D. W., & Gray, W.A. (2004). *A framework for automated service composition in service-oriented architectures* (pp. 269-283).ESWS.

Mannila, H., Toivonen, H., & Verkamo, A. (1994). Improved methods for finding association rules. In *Proceedings of the AAAI Workshop on Knowledge Discovery* (pp. 181-192). Finland.

Maojo, V. (2004). *Domain specific particularities of data mining: Lessons learned*. Paper presented at the ISB-MDA.

Marakas, M.G. (2003). *Modern data warehousing, mining, and visualization core concepts*. Prentice Hall.

Markman, A.B., & Gentner, D. (2001). Thinking. *Annual Review of Psychology, 52*(1), 223-247.

Martin, D., Paolucci, M., McIlraith, S., Burstein, M., McDermott, D., McGuinness, D., et al.(2004). Bringing semantics to Web services: The OWL-S approach. In *Proceedings of the 1st International Workshop on Semantic Web Services and Web Process Composition.* San Diego, California.

Masseglia, F., Poncelet, P., & Cicchetti, R. (1999). An efficient algorithm for web usage mining. *Networking and Information Systems Journal (NIS), 2*(5-6), 571-603.

Masseglia, F., Tanasa, D., & Trousse, B. (2004). Web usage mining: Sequential pattern extraction with a very low support. *In Advanced Web Technologies and Applications: 6th Asia-Pacific Web Conference, APWeb 2004,* vol. 3007 (pp. 513-522). Hangzhou, China: Springer-Verlag.

Matsuzawa, H., & Fukuda, T. (2000). Mining structured association patterns from databases. *PAKDD, LNAI 1805,* 233-244.

Mattison, R. (1996). *Data warehousing strategies, technologies and techniques.* Mc-Graw Hill.

Maxam, A.M., & Gilbert, W. (1977). A new method for sequencing DNA. In *Proceedings of National Academic of Science, 74* (pp. 560-564).

McBride, B. (2002). Jena: A Semantic Web toolkit. *IEEE Internet Computing,* November /December, 55-59.

McGuinness, D.L., & Harmelen, F.V. (2005). *OWL Web ontology language overview.* Retrieved Feburary 2005, from http://www.w3.org/TR/owl-features/

McGuinness, D.L., van Harmelen F. (2004). OWL Web ontology language overview, W3C Recommendation. Retrieved February 10, 2004, from http://www.w3.org/TR/owl-features/

Mckusick, V.A. (1998). *Mendelian inheritance in man: A catalog of human genes and genetic disorders.* Baltimore: Johns Hopkins University Press.

Meersman, R.A. (2004). Foundations, implementations and applications of Web semantics. Parts 1, 2, 3, lectures at School of Information Systems.

Mervis, C.B., & Rosch, E. (1981). Categorization of natural objects. *Annual Review of Psychology, 32,* 89-115.

Messai, R., Simonet, M., & Mousseau, M. (2006). A breast cancer terminology for lay people. *European Journal of Cancer EJC Supplements. 4*(2), 179-180.

Middleton, S.E., Shadbolt, N.R. & Roure, D.C.D. (2003). Capturing interest through inference and visualization: Ontological user profiling in recommender systems. In *International Conference on Knowledge Capture KCAP '03,* (pp. 62-69). New York: ACM Press.

Miles, A., & Brichley, D. (2005). SKOS Core GuideW3C Working Draft. Retrieved May 10, 2005, from http://www.w3.org/TR/swbp-skos-core-guide/

Miller, G.A. (1988). Nouns in WordNet. In C. Fellbaum (Ed.), *WordNet. An electronic lexical database* (pp. 23-46). MIT Press.

Miller, H.J., & Han, J. (2001). Fundamentals of spatial data warehousing for geographic knowledge discovery. *Geographic Data Mining and Knowledge Discovery,* 51-72.

Mills, D. (2006). *Semantic waves 2006.* Retrieved from http://www.ift.ulaval.ca/~kone/Cours/WS/WS-Plan-Cours2006.pdf

Missikoff, M., Velardi, P., & Fabriani, P. (2003). Text mining techniques to automatically enrich a domain ontology. *Applied Intelligence, 18*(3), 323-340.

Miyazaki, S., Sugawara, H., Gojobori, T., & Tateno, Y. (2003). DNA Databank of Japan (DDBJ). *Nucleic Acids Research, 31,* 13-16.

Mladenic, D. (1998). Turning Yahoo into an automatic web page classifier. In *Proceedings of the 13th European Conference on Artificial Intelligence* (pp. 473-474).

Morris, C.W. (1938/1970). *Foundations of the theory of signs.* Chicago University Press.

Murzin, A.G., Brenner, S.E., Hubbard, T., & Chothia, C. (1995). SCOP: A structural classification of proteins database for the investigation of sequences and structures. *Journal of Molecular Biology, 247,* 536-540.

Mustapha, N., Aufaure, M-A., & Baazhaoui-Zghal, H. (2006). Towards an architecture of ontological components for the semantic web. In *Proceedings of Wism (Web Information Systems Modeling) Workshop, CAiSE 2006,* Luxembourg (pp. 22-35).

Nakagawa, M., & Mobasher, B. (2003). Impact of site characteristics on recommendation models based on association rules and sequential patterns. In *Proceedings of the IJCAI'03 Workshop on Intelligent Techniques for Web Personalization,* Acapulco, Mexico.

Nake, F. (2002). Data, information, and knowledge: A semiotic view of phenomena of organization. In E. Liu, R.J. Clarke, P.B. Andersen, R. Stamper, & E.S. Abou-Zeid (Eds.), *Organizational semitiocs: Evolving a science of information systems* (pp. 41-50). London: Kluwer Academic Publishers.

Narayanan, A., Keedwell, E.C., & Olsson, B. (2002). Artificial intelligence techniques for bioinformatics. *Applied Bioinformatics, 1,* 191-222.

Navigli, R., & Velardi, P. (2004). Learning domain ontologies from document warehouses and dedicated web sites. *Computational Linguistics, 30*(2), 151-179.

Ng, R.T., & Han, J. (1994). Efficient and effective clustering methods for spatial data mining. In *Proceedings of International Conference on Very Large Databases (VLDB'94)* (pp. 144-155). Santiago, Chile .

Ng, S.K , & Wong, L, (2004). Accomplishments and challenges in bioinformatics. *IT Professional, 6,* 44-50.

Nigam, K., McCallum, A.K., Thrun, S., & Mitchell, T.M. (2000). Text classification from labeled and unlabeled documents using EM. In *Machine Learning, 39*(2-3) 103-134.

Niles, I., & Pease, A. (2001). Toward a Standard Upper Ontology. In *Proceedings of the 2nd International Conference on Formal Ontology in Information Systems (FOIS2001).*

Niles, I., & Terry, A. (2004). The MILO: A general-purpose, mid-level ontology. In *2004 International Conference on Information and Knowledge Engineering (IKE'04).*

Nimmagadda, S.L., & Dreher, H. (2006, August). *Mapping and modeling of oil and gas relational data objects for*

warehouse development and efficient data mining. Paper presented in the 4th International Conference in IEEE Industry Informatics, Singapore.

Nimmagadda, S.L., & Rudra, A. (2004c). Applicability of data warehousing and data mining technologies in the Australian resources industry. In *Proceedings of the 7th International Conference on IT,* Hyderabad, India.

Nimmagadda, S.L., & Rudra, A. (2004d). Data sources and requirement analysis for multidimensional database modeling: An Australian Resources Industry scenario. In *Proceedings of the 7th International Conference on IT,* Hyderabad, India.

Nimmagadda, S.L., Dreher, H., & Rudra, A. (2005a, August). Ontology of Western Australian petroleum exploration data for effective data warehouse design and data mining. In *Proceedings of the 3rd International IEEE Conference on Industry Informatics,* Perth, Australia.

Nimmagadda, S.L., Dreher, H., & Rudra, A. (2005b, August). Data warehouse structuring methodologies for efficient mining of Western Australian petroleum data sources. In *Proceedings of the 3rd international IEEE conference on Industry Informatics,* Perth, Australia

Nimmagadda, S.L., Dreher, H., & Rudra, A. (2006, August). *Mapping of oil and gas exploration business data entities for effective operational management.* Paper presented in the 4th International Conference in IEEE Industry Informatics, Singapore.

Novacek, V. (1998). Data mining query language for object-oriented database. In *Proceedings of the 2nd East European Symposium on Advances in Databases and Information Systems* (pp. 278-283). New York: Springer Verlag.

Noy, F.N., & McGuinnes, D.L. (2003). *Ontology development 101: A guide to create your first ontology.* Retrieved 2003 from http://ksl.stanford.edu/people/dlm/papers/ontology-tutorial-noy-mcguinnes.doc

Noy, N. F. , Sintek, M., Decker, S., Crubezy, M., Fergerson, R. W., & Musen, M.A. (2001). Creating Semantic Web contents with Protege-2000. *IEEE Intelligent Systems, 16*(2), 60-71.

Noy, N.F., & Klein, M. (2004). Ontology evolution: Not the same as schema evolution. *Knowledge and Information Systems, 6*(4), 428-440.

Ntoulas, A., Cho, J., & Olston, Ch. (2004). What's new on the web? The evolution of the web from a search engine perspective. In *Proceedings of the 13th International World Wide Web (WWW) Conference* (pp. 1-12).

O'Leary, D.E. (2000). Different firms, different ontologies, and no one best ontology. *IEEE Intelligent Systems,* 72-78.

Ohkawa, H., Ostell, J., & Bryant, S. (1995). MMDB: An ASN.1 specification for macromolecular structure. In *Proceedings of the 3rd International Conference on Intelligent Systems for Molecular Biology.* Cambridge, UK: AAAI.

Ohno-machado, L., Vinterbo, S., & Weber, G. (2002). Classification of gene expression data using fuzzy logic. *Journal of Intelligent and Fuzzy Systems, 12,* 19-24.

Oinn, T. M., Addis, M., Ferris, J., Marvin, D., Senger, M., Greenwood, R. M., et al. (2004). Taverna: A tool for the composition and enactment of bioinformatics workflows. *Bioinformatics, 20*(17), 3045-3054.

Olston, C., & Chi, E. (2003). ScentTrails: Intergrading browsing and searching. *ACM Transactions on Computer-Human Interaction, 10*(3), 1-21.

Omelayenko, B. (2000). Integration of product ontologies for B2B marketplaces: A preview. *ACM SIGecom Exchanges, 2*(1), 19-25.

Open Gis Consortium. (1999a). *Topic 5, the OpenGIS abstract specification—OpenGIS features—Version 4.* Retrieved August 20, 2005, from http://www.OpenGIS. org/techno/specs.htm

Open Gis Consortium. (1999b). *Open GIS Simple Features Specification For SQL.* Retrieved August 20, 2005, from http://www.opengeospatial.org/specs

Open Gis Consortium. (2001). *Feature Geometry.* Retrieved August 20, 2005, from http://www.opengeospatial. org/specs

Orlikowski, W.J. (1996a). Evolving with notes: Organizational change around groupware technology. In C. Ciborra (Ed.), *Groupware and teamwork* (pp. 23-60). London: John Wiley & Sons.

Orlikowski, W.J. (1996b). Improving organizational transformation over time: A situated action perspective. *Information Systems Research, 7*(1), 63-92.

Ostell, J. (1990). *GenInfo ASN.1 Syntax: Sequences.* NCBI Technical Report Series. National Library of Medicine, NIH.

Ott, T., & Swiaczny, F. (2001). Time-integrative geographic information systems. *Management and analysis of spatio-temporal data.* Springer.

Padmanabhan, B., & Tuzhilin, A. (1998). A belief-driven method for discovering unexpected patterns. In *Proceedings of the International Conference on Knowledge Discovery and Data Mining* (pp. 94-100).

Pagel, S., & Westerfelhaus, R. (2005). Charting managerial reading preferences in relation to popular management theory books: A semiotic analysis. *Journal of Business Communication, 42*(4), 420-448.

Páircéir, R., McClean, S., & Scotney, B. (2000). Discovery of multilevel rules and exceptions from a distributed database. In *Proceedings of the 6th ACM SIGKDD International Conference on Knowledge Discovery and Data Mining* (pp. 523-532). New York: ACM Press.

PANDA (Patterns for Next-generation Database Systems). (2001). *Project homepage.* http://dke.cti.gr/panda

Papatheodrou, C., Vassiliou, A., & Simon, B. (2002). C. Papatheodrou, Discovery of ontologies for learning resources using word-based clustering. In *Proceedings of ED MEDIA 2002,* Denver.

Pasquier, N., Bastide, Y., Taouil, R., & Lakhal, L. (1999). In C. Beeri & P. Buneman (Eds.), *7th International Conference on Database Theory, 1540* (pp. 398-416). Jerusalem: Springer.

Patel-Schneiderand, P.F., & Fensel, D. (2002). Layering the Semantic Web: Problems and directions. In *Proceedings of the 1st International Semantic Web Conference.* Springer.

Pazzani, M., & Billsus, D. (1997). Learning and revising user profiles: The identification of interesting Web sites. *Machine Learning Journal, 23,* 313-331.

Pazzani, M.J. (2000). Knowledge discovery from data? *IEEE Intelligent Systems & Their Applications, 15*(2), 10-13.

Pazzani, M.J., Mani, S., & Shankle, W.R. (2001). Acceptance by medical experts of rules generated by machine learning. *Methods of information in medicine, 40*(5), 380-385.

Pei, J., Han, J., Mortazavi-asl, B., & Zhu, H. (2000). Mining access patterns efficiently from web logs. *PAKDD, LNAI, 1805,* 396-407.

Peirce, C.S. (1931-58). *Collected writings*. Cambridge, MA: Harvard University Press.

Piatetsky-Shapiro, G. & Matheus, C.J. (1994). The interestingness of deviations. In *Proceedings of KDD-94: AAAI-94 Knowledge Discovery in Databases Workshop* (pp. 25-36). AAAI Press.

Piatetsky-Shapiro, G. (1991). Discovery, analysis, and presentation of strong rules. In G. Piatetsky-Shapiro & W.J. Frawley (Eds.), *Knowledge discovery in databases* (pp. 229-248). Cambridge, MA: AAAI/MIT Press.

Piatetsky-Shapiro, G. (2000). Knowledge discovery in databases: 10 years after. *SIGKDD Explorations, 1*(2), 59-61.

Pinto, H.S., & Martins, J.P. (2001) A methodology for ontology integration. In *Proceedings of the 1st International conference on Knowledge Captur.* (pp. 131-138).

Pohle, C. (2003) *Integrating and updating domain knowledge with data mining*. VLDB PhD Workshop.

Pohle, C., & Spiliopoulou, M. (2002). Building and exploiting ad hoc concept hierarchies for web log analysis. In Y. Kambayashi, W. Winiwarter, & M. Arikawa (Eds.), *Proceedings of the 4th International Conference on Data Warehousing and Knowledge Discovery, DaWaK 2002, Vol. 2454 of Lecture Notes in Computer Science* (pp. 83-93). Aix en Provence, France: Springer-Verlag.

Pongor, S. (1998) Novel databases for molecular biology. *Nature, 332,* 24-24.

Porter, M. (1980). An algorithm for suffix. *Stripping Program, 14*(3), 130-137.

Portscher, E., Geller, J., & Scherl, R. (2003). Using internet glossaries to determine interests from home pages. In *Proceedings of the 4th International Conference on Electronic Commerce and Web Technologies* (pp. 248-258). Berlin: Springer Verlag.

Psaila, G., & Lanzi, P. L. (2000). Hierarchy-based mining of association rules in data warehouses. In *Proceedings of the 2000 ACM Symposium on Applied Computing* (pp. 307-312). New York: ACM Press.

Pujari, A.K. (2002). *Data mining techniques*. India: University Press Pty Limited.

Qiu, Y., & Frei, H.P. (1993). Concept based query expension. *Conference on Research and Development in Information Retrieval (SIGIR),* (pp. 160-169).

Quinlan, R. (1993). *C4.5: Programs for machine learning*. San Mateo, CA: Morgan Kaufmann Publishers.

Rahm, E., & Bernstein, P. (2001). A survey of approaches to automatic schema matching, *The VLDB Journal*, 334-350.

Ramkumar, G.D., & Swami, A. (1998). Clustering data without distance functions. *Bulletin of IEEE Computer Society Technical Committee on Data Engineering.*

Rawlings, C.J. (1998). Designing databases for molecular biology. *Nature, 334,* 447-447.

Resnik, Ph. (1999). Semantic similarity in a taxonomy: an information based measure and its application to problems of ambiguity in natural language. *Journal of Artificial Intelligence Research,* 11, 95-130.

Ritter, O. (1994). The integrated genomic database. In S. Suhai (Ed.), *Computational methods in genome research*. New York: Plenum.

Rizzi, S., Bertino, E., Catania, B., Golfarelli, M., Halkidi, M., Terrovitis, M., et al. (2003). Towards a logical model for patterns. In *Proceedings of ER'03 Conference*.

Robbins, R.J. (1994). Genome informatics I: community databases. *Journal of Computational Biology, 1,* 173-190.

Robertson, S., Sparck, E., & Jones, K. (1976). Relevance weighting of search terms. *Journal of the American Society for Information Sciences, 27*(3), 129-146.

Roiger, J.R., & Geatz, M.W. (2003). *Data mining, A tutorial — Based primer.* Addison Wesley.

Rosch, E. (1975). Cognitive reference points. *Cognitive Psychology, 1,* 532-547.

Rosch, E. (1978). Principles of categorization. In E. Rosch & B. Lloyd (Eds.), *Cognition and categorization* (pp. 27-47). Hillsdale, NJ: Erlbaum.

Rosch, E., & Mervis, C.B. (1975). Family resemblances: Studies in the internal structure of categories. *Cognitive Psychology, 7,* 573-605.

Rubin, D.L., Hewett, M., Oliver, D.E., Klein, T.E., & Altman, R.B. (2002). Automatic data acquisition into ontologies from pharmacogenetics relational data sources using declarative object definitions and XML. In *Proceedings of the Pacific Symposium on Biology,* Lihue, HI.

Rudra, A., & Nimmagadda, S.L. (2005). Roles of multidimensionality and granularity in data mining of warehoused Australian resources data. In *IEEE Proceedings of the 38th Hawaii International Conference on Information System Sciences.*

Ruiz, M.E., & Srinivasan, P. (1999). Hierarchical neural networks for text categorization. In *Proceedings of the ACM's Special Interest Group in Information Retrieval (SIGIR) Conference* (pp. 281-282).

Saias, J. (2003). Uma metodologia para a construção automática de ontologias e a sua aplicação em sistemas de recuperação de informação (*A methodology for the automatic construction of ontologies and applications in information retrieval systems*). PhD thesis. University of Évora, Portugal (in Portuguese).

Sairafi, S., A., Emmanouil, F. S., Ghanem, M., Giannadakis, N., Guo, Y., Kalaitzopolous, D., et al. (2003). The design of discovery net: Towards open Grid services for knowledge discovery. *International Journal of High Performance Computing Applications, 17*(3).

Salton, G. (1971). *The smart retrieval system.* Englewood Cliffs, NJ: Prentice Hall.

Salton, G., & Buckley, C. (1988). Term-weighting approaches in automatic text retrieval. *Information Processing and Management, 24,* 513-523

Salton, G., & McGill, M. (1983). *Introduction to modern information retrieval.* McGraw-Hill.

Salton, G., Wong, A., & Yang, C. S. (1975). A vector space model for automatic indexing. *Communications of the ACM, 18*(11), 613-620.

Sanchez, D., & Moreno, A. (2004). Automatic generation of taxonomies from the WWW. In *Proceedings of the 5th International Conference on Practical Aspects of Knowledge Management (PAKM 2004). LNAI, Vol. 3336* (pp. 208-219). Vienna, Austria.

Sanger, F., Nicklen, S., & Coulson, A.R. (1977). DNA sequencing with chain-terminating inhibitors. In *Proceedings of National Academic of Science, 74* (pp. 5463-5467).

Sauberlich, F., & Huber, K.-P. (2001). A framework for web usage mining on anonymous logfile data. In Schwaiger M. & O. Opitz (Eds.), *Exploratory data analysis in empirical research* (pp. 309-318). Heidelberg: Springer-Verlag.

Scherl, R., & Geller, J. (2002). Global communities, marketing and Web mining. *Journal of Doing Business Across Borders, 1*(2), 141-150.

Schulze-Kremer, S. (1998). Ontologies for molecular biology. Pacific Symposium of Biocomputing. In *Proceedings of the PSB 1998 Electronic,* Hawaii.

Seaborne, A. (2004). *RDQL: A query language for RDF.* Retrieved May 10, 2006, from http://www.w3.org/Submission/RDQL/

Sebastiani, F. (1999). A tutorial on automated text categorization. In A. Amandi & Zunino (Eds.), *Proceedings of ASAI-99, 1st Argentinian Symposium on Artificial Intelligence* (pp 7-35). Buones Aires.

Seismo-Surfer. *A WebGIS application for integrating, visualizing and analyzing seismic data.* http://www.seismo.gr

Servigne, S., Ubeda, T., Puricelli, A., & Laurini, R. (2000). A methodology for spatial consistency improvement of geographic databases. *Geoinformatica, 4*(1), 7-34.

Shanks, G., Tansley, E., & Weber, R. (2003). Using ontology to validate conceptual models. *Communications of the ACM, 46*(10), 85-89.

Shanks, G., Tansley, E., & Weber, R. (2004). Representing composites in conceptual modelling. *Communications of the ACM, 47*(7), 77-80.

Shekhar, S., & Chawla, S. (2003). *Spatial databases: a tour.* Upper Saddle, NJ: Prentice Hall.

Sidhu, A.S., Dillon, T.S., & Chang, E. (2005). Ontological foundation for protein data models. In *Proceedings of the 1st IFIP WG 2.12 & WG 12.4 International Workshop on Web Semantics (SWWS 2005). In conjunction with On The Move Federated Conferences (OTM 2005).* Agia Napa, Cyprus: Springer

Sidhu, A.S., Dillon, T.S., & Chang, E. (2006a). protein ontology. In Z. Ma & J.Y. Chen (Eds.), *Database modeling in biology: Practices and challenges.* New York: Springer.

Sidhu, A.S., Dillon, T.S., & Chang, E. (2006b). Advances in protein ontology project. In *Proceedings of the 19th IEEE International Symposium on Computer-Based Medical Systems (CBMS 2006).* Salt Lake City, UT: IEEE CS Press.

Sidhu, A.S., Dillon, T.S., Setiawan, H., & Sidhu, B.S. (2004c). Comprehensive protein database representation. In A. Gramada & P.E. Bourne (Eds.), *8th International Conference on Research in Computational Molecular Biology 2004 (RECOMB 2004).* San Diego, CA: ACM Press.

Sidhu, A.S., Dillon, T.S., Sidhu, B.S., & Setiawan, H. (2004a). A unified representation of protein structure databases. In M.S. Reddy & S. Khanna (Eds.), *Biotechnological approaches for sustainable development.* India: Allied Publishers.

Sidhu, A.S., Dillon, T.S., Sidhu, B.S., & Setiawan, H. (2004b). An XML based Semantic protein map. In A., Zanasi, N.F.F. Ebecken, & C.A. Brebbia (Eds.), *5th International Conference on Data Mining, Text Mining and their Business Applications (Data Mining 2004).* Malaga, Spain: WIT Press.

Silberschatz, A. & Tuzhilin, A. (1996). What makes patterns interesting. In knowledge discovery systems. *IEEE Transactions on Knowledge and Data Engineering, 8*(6), 970-974.

Simonet, M., Bernhard, D., Diallo, G., & Gedzelman, S. (2005a). *Building an ontology of cardio-vascular diseases for concept-based information retrieval.* Computers in Cardiology, Lyon.

Simonet, M., Bernhard, D., Diallo, G., Gedzelman, S., Messai, R., & Patriarche, R. (2005b, December 14-16). An environment for ontology design and enrichment from texts. In *Proceedings of SWAP 2005, the 2nd Italian Semantic Web Workshop,* Trento, Italy, CEUR Workshop Proceedings, ISSN 1613-0073.

Sirin, E., & Parsia, B. (2004). *Pellet: An OWL DL Reasoner, 3rd International Semantic Web Conference,* Hiroshima, Japan. Springer.

Sirin, E.B. Parsia, B., & Hendler, J. (2004). Filtering and selecting Semantic Web services with interactive composition techniques. *IEEE Intelligent Systems, 19*(4), 42-49.

Smirnov, A., Pashkin, M., Chilov, N., Levashova, T., Krizhanovsky, A., & Kashevnik, A. (2005). Ontology-based users and requests clustering in customer service management system. In V. Gorodetsky, J. Liu, & V. Skormin (Ed.), *Autonomous intelligent systems: Agents and data mining.* AIS-ADM.

Smith, G., Blackman, D., & Good, B. (2003). Knowledge sharing and organizational learning: The impact of social architecture at ordnance survey. *Journal of Knowledge Management Practice, 4*(3), 18.

Smith, M.K., Welty, C., & McGuinness, D.L. (2004). OWL Web ontology language guide. *W3C Recommendation.* Retrieved February 10, 2004, from http://www.w3.org/TR/owl-guide/

Soergel, D., Lauser, B., Liang, A., Fisseha, F., Keizer, J., & Katz, S. (2004). Reengineering thesauri for new applications: The AGROVOC example, *Journal of Digital Information, 4*(4).

Song, Y.I., Han, K.S., & Rim, H.C. (2004). A term weighting method based on lexical chain for automatic summarization. In *Proceedings of the 5ᵗʰ Conference on Intelligent Text Processing and Computational Linguistics (CICLing)* (pp. 636-639).

Sowa, J.F. (2000). *Knowledge representation: logical, philosophical, and computational foundations.* Pacific Grove, CA: Brooks/Cole Publishing.

SPARQL. Query Language for RDF, W3C Working Draft 4 October 2006. Retrieved October 8, 2006, from http://128.30.52.31/TR/rdf-sparql-query/

Spiliopoulou, M., Faulstich, L.C., & Winkler, K. (1999). A data miner analyzing the navigational behaviour of web users. In *Proceedings of the Workshop on Machine Learning in User Modeling of the ACAI'99 Int. Conf.*, Creta, Greece.

Spyropoulos, CD., Paliouras, G., & Karkaletsis, V. (2005, November 30- December 1). *BOEMIE: Bootstrapping ontology evolution with multimedia information extraction.* 2ⁿᵈ European Workshop on the integration of knowledge, Semantic and Digital Media Technologies, London.

Srikant, R. & Agrawal, R. (1995). Mining generalized association rules. In U. Dayal, P. M. D. Gray, S. Nishio (Eds.), *Proceedings of the 21ˢᵗ International Conference on Very Large Databases* (pp. 407-419). Zurich: Morgan Kaufmann.

Staab, S., Schnurr, H.-P., Studer, R., & Sure, Y. (2001). Knowledge processes and ontologies. *IEEE Intelligent Systems Special Issue on Knowledge Management, January/February, 16*(1).

Stamou, S., Krikos, V., Kokosis, P., & Christodoulakis, D. (2005). Web directory construction using lexical chains. In *Proceedings of the 10ᵗʰ International Conference on Applications of Natural Language to Information Systems (NLDB).*

Stamper, R. (1996). Signs, information, norms and systems. In P. Holmqvist, P. B. Andersen, H. K. Klein, & R. Posner (Eds.), *Signs of work: Semiotics and information processing in organizations*: Walter de Gruyter.

Stamper, R., Liu, K., Hafkamp, M., & Ades, Y. (2000). Understanding the roles of signs and norms in organizations: A semiotic approach to information systems design. *Behaviour and Information Technology, 19*(1), 15-27.

Stein, L.D., Cartinhour, S., Thierry-mieg, D., & Thierry-Mieg, J. (1998). JADE: An approach for interconnecting bioinformatics databases. *Gene, 209*, 39-43.

Stoesser, G., Baker, W., Van Den Broek, A., Garcia-Pastor, M., Kanz, C., & Kulikova, T. (2003). The EMBL nucleotide sequence database: Major new developments. *Nucleic Acids Research, 31*, 17-22.

Stojanovic, L., Stojanovic, N., & Volz, R. (2002). Migrating data-intensive web sites into the semantic web. In *Proceedings of the 17ᵗʰ ACM symposium on applied computing (SAC).* ACM Press.

Suryanto, H., & Compton, P. (2001). Discovery of ontologies from knowledge bases. In *Proceedings of the 1ˢᵗ International Conference on Knowledge Capture, the Association for Computing Machinery* (pp. 171-178). New York.

Tan, H., Dillon, T.S., Hadzic, F., Chang, E., & Feng, L. (2005). MB3 Miner: Mining eMBedded sub-TREEs using tree model guided candidate generation. In *Proceedings of the 1ˢᵗ International Workshop on Mining Complex Data, held in conjunction with ICDM 2005.* Houston, TX: IEEE CS Press.

Tan, H., Dillon, T.S., Hadzic, F., Chang, E., & Feng, L. (2006a). Mining induced/embedded subtrees using the level of embedding constraint. *Knowledge and Information Systems An International Journal*, Submitted.

Tan, H., Dillon, T.S., Hadzic, F., Chang, E., & Feng, L. (2006b). IMB3-Miner: mining induced/embedded subtrees by constraining the level of embedding. In *Proceedings of the 10ᵗʰ Pacific-Asia Knowledge Discovery and Data Mining Conference (PAKDD 2006).* Singapore: Springer.

Tan, H., Dillon, T.S., Hadzic, F., Feng, L., & Chang, E. (2006c) Tree model guided candidate generation for mining frequent subtrees from XML. *Transactions on Knowledge Discovery from Data (TKDD)*, Submitted.

Tanasa, D. (2005). *Web usage mining: Contributions to intersites logs preprocessing and sequential pattern extraction with low support*. PhD thesis, University of Nice Sophia Antipolis.

Tanasa, D., & Trousse, B. (2004). Advanced data preprocessing for intersites Web usage mining. *IEEE Intelligent Systems, 19*(2) 59-65.

Telford, W.M., Geldart, L.P., & Sheriff, R.E. (1998). *Applied geophysics* (2nd ed.) (pp. 100-350 and 600-750).

Terveen, L., & Hill, W. (2001). Beyond recommender systems: helping people help each other. In J. Carroll (Ed.), *Human computer interaction in the new millennium*. Addison-Wesley.

Thatte, S. (2001). *XLANG: Web services for business process design*. Microsoft Corporation, Initial Public Draft.

Theodoridis, Y., Marketos, G., & Kalogeras, I.S. (2004). Collecting and mining seismic data in Greek territory: The seismo-surfer tool. In *Proceedings of the 7th Panhellenic Geographical Conference of the Hellenic Geographical Association (HGA'04)*, Mytilene, Lesvos, Greece.

Trousse, B., Jaczynski, M. & Kanawati, R. (1999). Using user behavior similarity for recommandation computation: The broadway approach. In *Proceedings of 8th International Conference on Human Computer Interaction (HCI'99)* (pp. 85-89). Munich:Lawrence Erlbaum.

Tsalgatidou, A., & Pilioura, T. (2002). An overview of standards and related technology in web services. *Distributed and Parallel Databases. 12*(3).

Tsujii, J., & Ananiadou, S. (2005). Thesaurus or logical ontology, which one do we need for text mining? *Language Resources and Evaluation, 39*(1), 77-90.

Tudhope, D., Alani, H., & Jones, C. (2001). Augmenting thesaurus relationships: Possibilities for retrieval. *Journal of Digital Information, 1-8*(41).

Uschold, M. (1998). Knowledge level modeling: Concepts and terminology. *Knowledge Engineering Review, 13*(1).

Uschold, M., & Gruninger, M. (1996). Ontologies: Principles, methods and applications. *Knowledge Engineering Review, 11*(2).

Uschold, M., & King, M. (1995). Towards a methodology for building ontologies. In *Proceedings of the Workshop on Basic Ontological Issues in Knowledge Sharing at the International Joint Conference on Artificial Intelligence (IJCAI1995)*.

Verde, R., & Lechevallier, Y. (2003). Crossed Clustering method on Symbolic Data tables. In M. Vichi, P. Monari, S. Migneni, & A. Montanari, (Eds.), *New developments in classification, and data analysis* (pp. 87-96). Heidelberg: Springer-Verlag.

Volz, R., Oberle, D., Staab, S., & Studer, R. (2003). *OntoLiFT Prototype*. IST Project 2001-33052 WonderWeb Deliverable.

Wang, B.B., McKay, I., Abbass, H.A., & Barlow, M. (2003). A comparative study for domain ontology guided feature extraction. In *Proceedings of the 26th Australian Computer Science Conference (ACSC-2003)* (pp. 69-78). Adelaide, Australia. Australian Computer Society, Inc.

Wang, H., Azuaje, F., & Bodenreider, O. (2005). An ontology-driven clustering method for supporting gene expression analysis. In *Proceedings of the 18th IEEE Symposium on Computer-Based Medical Systems* (pp. 389-394).

Wang, W., Yang, J., & Yu, P.S. (2000). Efficient mining of weighted association rules (WAR). In *Proceedings of the Sixth ACM SIGKDD International Conference* (pp. 270-274). Boston.

Weimer, P., & Davis, T.L. (1995). Applications of 3D-seismic data to exploration and production, *AAPG studies in geology, No.42, and SEG Geophysical Developments series, No.5*.

Weissig, H., & Bourne, P.E. (2002). Protein structure resources. *Biological Crystallography, D58*, 908-915.

Wertheim, M. (1995). Call to desegregate microbial databases. *Science, 269*, 1516.

Wesbrook, J., Feng, Z., Jain, S., Bhat, T.N., Thanki, N., Ravichandran, V., et al. (2002). The protein data bank: Unifying the archive. *Nucleic Acids Research, 30*, 245-248.

Wielinga, B., Schreiber, G., Wielemaker, J., & Sandber, J.A.C. (2001). From thesaurus to ontology. In *Proceedings of the International Conference on Knowledge Capture.*

Witten, I.H., & Frank, E. (2000) *Data mining, practical machine learning tools and techniques with java implementations.* San Francisco: Morgan Kaufmann.

Witten, I.H., & Frank, E. (2005). *Data Mining: Practical machine learning tools and techniques,* (2nd ed.). San Francisco: Morgan Kaufmann.

Wong, L. (2000). Kleisli, a functional query system. *Journal of Functional Programming, 10,* 19-56.

Wong, L. (2002). Technologies for integrating biological data. *Briefings in Bioinformatics, 3*, 389-404.

World Wide Web Consortium. (2004). *OWL Web ontology language semantics and abstract syntax.* W3C Recommendation 10 Feb, 2004.

Wu, S. H., Tsai, T. H., & Hsu, W. L. (2003). Text categorization using automatically acquired domain ontology. In *Proceedings of IRAL2003 Workshop on Information Retrieval with Asian Languages*, Sapporo, Japan.

Xodo, D., & Nigro, H.O. (2005). Knowledge Management in Tourism. In L.C. Rivero, J.H. Doorn, & V.E. Ferraggine (Eds.). *Encyclopedia of database technologies and applications* (pp. 319-329). Hershey, PA: Idea Group Reference.

Yao, Y.Y., & Zhong, N. (2000). On association, similarity and dependency attributes. *PAKDD, LNAI, 1805,* 138-141.

Yoo, J. S., & Shekhar, S. (2006). A join-less approach for mining spatial co-location patterns. *IEEE Transactions on Knowledge and Data Engineering, 18*(10).

Yuefeng, L., & Ning, Z. (2006). Mining ontology for automatically acquiring web user information needs. *IEEE Trans. Knowl. Data Eng., 18*(4), 554-568.

Yun, C.H., & Chen, M.S. (2000). Mining Web transaction patterns in an electronic commerce environment. *PAKDD, LNAI, 1805,* 216-219.

Zaki, M.J. (2005). Efficiently mining frequent trees in a forest: Algorithms and applications. *IEEE Transaction on Knowledge and Data Engineering, 17,* 1021-1035.

Zaki, M.J., & Hsiao, C.J. (2002). CHARM: An efficient algorithm for closed itemset mining. In *Proceedings of the 2nd SIAM International Conference on Data Mining.* SIAM.

Zaki. M. (2000). Generating nonredundant association rules. In S.J. Simoff & O. R. Zaïane (Eds.), *Proceedings of the 6th ACM SIGKDD International Conference on Knowledge Discovery and Data Mining* (pp. 34-43) Boston: ACM Press.

Zaki., M., & Hsiao, C. (2002). CHARM: An efficient algorithm for closed itemset mining. In R.L. Grossman, J. Han, V. Kumar, H. Mannila, & R. Motwani (Eds.), *Proceeding of the 2nd SIAM International Conference on Data Mining* (pp. 457-473). Arlington: SIAM.

Zhang, T., Ramakrishnan, R., & Livny, M. (1996). Birch: An efficient data clustering method for very large databases. In H.V. Jagadish, & I.S. Mumick (Ed.), *Proceedings of the 1996 ACM SIGMOD International Conference on Management of Data* (pp. 103-114). Montreal, Quebec, Canada: ACM Press.

Zhong, T., Raghu, R., & Livny, M. (1996). An efficient data clustering method for very large databases. In *Proceedings of ACM SIGMOD International Conference on Management of Data.*

Zhou, S., Zhou, A., Cao, J., Wen, J., Fan, Y., & Hu, Y. (1996). *Combining sampling technique with DBSCAN algorithm for clustering large spatial databases.* Springer.

Zhou, X. (2006). *Enhancing web marketing by using an ontology.* Doctoral dissertation, New Jersey Institute of Technology, Newark, NJ.

Zhou, X., Geller, J., Perl, Y., & Halper, M. (2006). An application intersection marketing ontology. *Theoretical computer science: Essays in memory of Shimon Even. Lecture Notes in Computer Science,* Vol. 3895 (pp. 143-153). Berlin: Springer-Verlag.

Zhou, Z., Liu, H., Li, S.Z., & Chua, C.S. (2001). Rule mining with prior knowledge: A belief networks approach. *Intelligent Data Analysis, 5*(2), 95-110.

Zhu, J., Hong, J., & Hughes, J.G. (2002). Using Markov Chains for link prediction in adaptive Web sites. *In Proceedings of Soft-Ware 2002: First International Conference on Computing in an Imperfect World* (pp. 60-73). Belfast, UK.

About the Contributors

Héctor Oscar Nigro received a systems engineer degree from UNICEN (Universidad Nacional del Centro de la Provincia de Buenos Aires), Tandil, Argentina; Magister degree in sociology and political sciences from FLACSO (Facultad Latinoamericana de Ciencias Sociales) and he is PhD from UBA (Universidad Nacional de Buenos Aires). He is a full professor in the Department of Computer Sciences and Systems in the Exact Sciences Faculty—UNICEN. He is the director MERAIS III—Data Mining Ontology Project (UNICEN). Also, he realizes consulting activities related to data mining, data analysis, and knowledge management for the last 15 years. His research interests are in databases, data warehouses, data mining, knowledge management, and OLAP. He has published book chapters and articles presented at various professional conferences on his research activities.

Sandra Elizabeth González Císaro was born in Mar del Plata, Argentina. She received a systems engineer degree from UNICEN (Universidad Nacional del Centro de la Provincia de Buenos Aires), Tandil, Argentina. She is an assistant professor at Department of Computer Sciences and Systems in the Exact Sciences Faculty, UNICEN, and she is also working on MERAIS III—Data Mining Ontology Project (UNICEN). Her research interests are in databases, data warehouses, data mining, knowledge management, OLAP, symbolic data analysis and management expert systems. She has published book chapters and articles presented at various professional conferences related with her research activities. Eng. González Císaro is an IEEE Computer Society member.

Daniel Hugo Xodo received a mathematics-physics sciences degree, industrial engineer degree and master degree in business administration from UNICEN (Universidad Nacional del Centro de la Provincia de Buenos Aires). He is a professor at Department of Computer Sciences and Systems, in the Exact Sciences Faculty, UNICEN, and a professor at UTN (Universidad Tecnológica Nacional, Regional Bahía Blanca, Argentina). He is studies group director on knowledge management (UTN), and is working on MERAIS III Project (UNICEN). His research interests are in data mining, knowledge management, management science, balanced scorecards and operations research. He has published book chapters and has articles presented at various professional conferences related with his researching. In addition, he realizes consulting activities related to his professional field.

* * * * *

Luis Otavio Alvares is a professor at the Department of Applied Computing (Departamento de Informática Aplicada) at Universidade Federal do Rio Grande do Sul (UFRGS), Porto Alegre, Brazil.

He received his PhD in computer science from Université Joseph Fourier, Grenoble, France, in 1988, and his MSc in computer science from PPGC/UFRGS in 1982. He did a postdoctoral stage at Laboratoire LEIBNIZ/IMAG, Grenoble, France, with Yves Demazeau in 1994/1995. He has served as reviewer, organizer, and technical committee member of several conferences and journals. His research interests include artificial intelligence applied to computer games, multiagent systems, geographic information systems, and data mining. He advised 21 MSc and three PhD dissertations.

Marie-Aude Aufaure obtained her PhD in computer science from the University of Paris 6 in 1992. From 1993 to 2001, she was associated professor at the University of Lyon; then, she was integrated into a French research center in computer science (INRIA) for two years. Now, she is a professor at Supélec and scientific partner of the Inria Axis project. From 1998 to 2001, she was a member of the GDR-CNRS I3's direction committee. Her research interests deal with the combination of data mining techniques and ontologies to improve the retrieval process of complex data. Another research interest concerns the construction of a Web knowledge base in a specific domain to improve the retrieval process. She also works on semantic and conceptual context-aware information retrieval. Another topic of interest is about the integration of metadata and ontologies into a whole process, such as data mining. Her work is published in international journals, books, and conferences.

Delphine Bernhard is a PhD candidate in the TIMC Laboratory. Her work is focused on the unsupervised acquisition of morphological knowledge with the aim of building lexical resources. Her research interests include text mining, natural language processing, and the acquisition of semantic knowledge.

Vania Bogorny is currently in a postdoctoral position at the Computer Science Department of the Univerity of Hasselt, Belgium, in the context of the GeoPKDD project. She received her PhD in computer science from Universidade Federal do Rio Grande do Sul (UFRGS), Porto Alegre, Brazil, in 2006, and her MSc in computer science from Universidade Federal do Rio Grande do Sul (UFRGS), in 2001. Research accomplishments include frequent pattern mining in geographic databases, knowledge discovery in spatio-temporal databases using prior knowledge, databases, and data mining.

Thyago Borges is a candidate for a bachelors in information systems in the Catholic University of Pelotas, Brazil. His research interests include ontologies and text mining.

Peter Brezany is a professor at the Institute of Scientific Computing, University of Vienna, Austria. He received his PhD in computer science, in 1980, from the Slovak Technical University Bratislava, Slovakia. Since 1990, he has worked at the University of Vienna on automatic parallelization of scientific and engineering applications for distributed-memory systems, parallel input/output support for high-performance computing, and large-scale parallel and distributed data mining. His current research focus is knowledge discovery and data management on computational Grids.

Ana Isabel Canhoto is a fellow in marketing at Henley Management College, serves as a consultant to a number of leading UK and international organisations, and is a member of the FIDIS Network of Excellence, supported by the European Union. Her primary research interests lie in the role of technology, mental stereotypes and social norms on decision making. Most recently, she has been investigating the mining of large transaction databases, and how that may be influenced by the value judgments and task constraints of the individuals participating in the data mining activity.

Dimitris Christodoulakis was born in Samos. He received a BSc degree in mathematics from the University of Athens in 1975 and a PhD degree in informatics from the University of Bonn in 1980. From 1980 to 1983 he was a researcher at the National Informatics Centre of Germany (GMD, Bonn), assistant and associate professor in computer engineering at Patras University from 1984 to1995. From 1995 until now he is a professor. He is also scientific coordinator in many research and development projects in the followings sections: knowledge and data base systems, very large volume information storage, hypertext, natural language technology for modern Greek. He is author and co-author in many articles published in international conferences, editor in proceedings of conventions, and responsible for proofing tools development for Microsoft Corp. Since 1991 he is vice director at the Research Academic Computer Technology Institute (RACTI). From September 1997 until 2001 he was chairman of the computer engineering and informatics department of Patras University and from 2001 until now he is vice President of the department.

Gayo Diallo is a member of the OSIRIS group at the In3S Laboratory and a part time lecturer in computer science at Pierre Mendès France University in Grenoble. His research interests include ontologies and Semantic Web technologies, data integration, and information retrieval. He received an bachelor degree in computer science from the National Computer Engineering Institute (INI, Algiers) and a master degree in information systems from Joseph Fourier University in Grenoble.

Tharam S. Dillon is currently the dean of faculty of information technology at the University of Technology Sydney (UTS). He is the foundation professor in computer science and engineering. He is the chair of Work Group on Web Semantics (WG 2.12/12.4) in Technical Committee for Software: Theory and Practice (TC2) for International Federation for Information Processing (IFIP). He is an expert in object component-based conceptual modeling, and design, XML modeling, ontology development, and knowledge engineering. He has authored five books and co-edited four books. He has also published over 400 scientific papers in refereed journals and conferences.

Elizabeth Chang is currently director of the frontier technology for Extended Enterprise Centre (Centre for Extended Enterprise and Business Intelligence) at Curtin Business School, Curtin University of Technology, in Perth, Western Australia. She is the vice-chair of Work Group on Web Semantics (WG 2.12/12.4) in Technical Committee for Software: Theory and Practice (TC2) for International Federation for Information Processing (IFIP). Professor Chang has published over 200 scientific conference and journal papers including two co-authored books. The themes of these papers are in the areas of ontology, software engineering, object/component-based methodologies, e-commerce, trust management, and security, Web services, user interface, and Web engineering as well as logistics informatics.

Heinz Dreher is a senior lecturer and research fellow in information systems at the Curtin Business School, Curtin University, Perth, Western Australia. He has published in the educational technology and information systems domain through conferences, journals, invited talks and seminars; is currently the holder of Australian National Competitive Grant funding for a 4 year e-learning project and a four-year project on automated essay grading technology development, trial usage and evaluation; has received numerous industry grants for investigating hypertext based systems in training and business scenarios; and is an experienced and accomplished teacher, receiving awards for his work in cross-cultural aware-ness and course design. In 2004. Dr. Dreher was appointed adjunct professor for computer science at TU Graz, Austria, and continues to collaborate in teaching and learning and research projects with European partners.

Paulo Martins Engel is a professor in the Department of Applied Computing (Departamento de Informática Aplicada) at Universidade Federal do Rio Grande do Sul (UFRGS), Porto Alegre, Brazil. He received his PhD in microelectronics from Technische Universität München, Germany, in 1986, and his MSc in microelectronics Science from Universidade de São Paulo, Brazil, in 1981. He did a postdoctoral stage at Technische Hochschule Darmstadt, Germany, from 1991 to1992. He has served as reviewer, organizer, and technical committee member of several conferences and journals. His research interests include connectionist approaches to artificial intelligence and data mining. He advised 22 MSc and five PhD dissertations.

James Geller received a engineering diploma from the Technical University, Vienna, Austria, in 1979, and the MS degree, in 1984, and a PhD, in 1988, in computer science from the State University of New York at Buffalo. Dr. Geller joined the Computer Science Department of the New Jersey Institute of Technology (NJIT) in 1988. He was granted tenure and promoted to associate professor in 1993. Subsequently, he was promoted to full professor in 2000. Dr. Geller has authored and co-authored about 40 journal papers and over 50 conference papers. These papers are in a number of areas, including knowledge representation, parallel reasoning, semantic modeling in object-oriented databases, medical informatics, medical vocabularies, and auditing of ontologies and medical terminologies.

Nathalie Hernandez is a postdoctoral at the Toulouse II University. She obtained a PhD in computer science, in 2005, with a focus in information retrieval "modeling context in information retrieval using domain ontologies." She is currently working in the field of the Semantic Web, in particular on ontology elaboration and use for document indexing and retrieving.

Ivan Janciak is a PhD candidate at the Vienna University of Technology, Austria and research assistant at the Institute of Scientific Computing, University of Vienna, Austria. He received his MS degree in business informatics, in 2000, from the University of Economics in Bratislava, Slovakia. His research interests include distributed and parallel data and text mining, Semantic Web, Grid computing, and workflow management.

Evangelos Kotsifakos is a PhD candidate at the Department of Informatics, University of Piraeus (UniPi). He was born in 1978 in Athens, Greece, and received his bachelor and master degree in infor-mation systems from the department of Informatics of Athens University of Economics and Business. His research interests include pattern management, data mining and scientific databases. He also has a professional experience in software engineering.

Yves Lechevallier was integrated in 1976 into a French research center in computer science (INRIA). He is now vice-leader of the AxIS research team, which is located at Sophia Antipolis and Rocquencourt (near Paris). His current research interests are on the clustering algorithms (dynamic clustering method, Kohonen maps, divisive clustering method), discrimination problems and decision tree approaches. His work was published in international journals, books and conferences. Since 1998, he teaches at the Paris-Dauphine university clustering and neural network methods and, now, teaches data mining techniques at various engineer schools (ENSAE and ENSG near Paris).

Bénédicte Le Grand is an associate professor at the University Pierre and Marie Curie, in the Computer Science Laboratory of Paris 6 (LIP6). After receiving her engineer diploma in telecommunications from the National Institute of Telecommunications, she got her PhD in computer science, in 2001. Her research interests deal with information retrieval in complex systems, the Web in particular. She works on Semantic Web standards, especially topic maps, in order to propose Semantic Web visualization solutions. She also works on conceptual analysis techniques to extract knowledge from data and automate ontology construction. She published her work in international conferences and contributed to several books.

Daniel Lichtnow is a lecturer and researcher at the Catholic University of Pelotas (UCPEL), Brazil. He obtained a MSc degree in computer science at Federal University of Santa Catarina (UFSC), in 2001. His interests include databases systems, text mining, case-based reasoning, information retrieval, XML, and knowledge management.

Stanley Loh is a professor at the Catholic University of Pelotas (UCPEL) and at the Lutheran University of Brazil (ULBRA), in Brazil. He has a PhD degree in computer science, obtained in 2001, at the Federal University of Rio Grande do Sul (UFRGS). He has done researches in recommender systems, information retrieval, data-text-web mining, and technology applied to knowledge management.

Gerasimos Marketos is a PhD candidate at the Department of Informatics at the University of Piraeus (UniPi), Greece. Born in 1981, he received his BSc, in 2003, in informatics from University of Piraeus and his MSc, in 2004, in information systems engineering from University of Manchester Institute of Science and Technology (UMIST), UK. His research interests include spatiotemporal data warehousing and mining, pattern management and scientific databases. He is member of BCS.

Florent Masseglia is currently a researcher for the INRIA (Sophia Antipolis, France) in the AxIS team. He did research work in the data mining group at the LIRMM (Montpellier, France) from 1998 to 2002, and received a PhD in computer science from Versailles University, in France, in 2002. His research interests include data mining (particularly sequential patterns and applications such as Web Usage Mining) and databases. He is one of the five persons in charge for the French working group on mining complex data. He has co-edited a special issue of the RNTI journal (Cépaduès ed.) about mining complex data, co-chaired the 2nd French workshop on mining complex data, and co-chaired the 6th and the 7th international workshops on "multimedia data mining," in conjunction with the KDD conference. Dr. Masseglia is one of the guest editors of special issues of two international journals: MTAP and the

IEEE Transactions on Multimedia. He is the author of over 30 publications about data mining in journals and conferences and he is a reviewer for international journals.

Radja Messai was trained in computer science (bachelor of science from the University of Batna—Algeria in 2003) and is currently a PhD student at the UJF University in Grenoble. She is working on health-related ontology and terminology services for patients and citizens.

Josiane Mothe is a professor at the teacher training school (IUFM,Toulouse) since 2002, previously Maître de Conference at the Toulouse I University (1995-2002). Teaches information system design and information retrieval. She is part of the Information Retrieval Group of the Research centre in Computer Science of Toulouse. She obtained a PhD in computer science, in 1994, in information retrieval and a habilitation, in 2000, in information retrieval and mining. Currently, she is working on information retrieval and knowledge discovery from semistructured information. Scientific and technical fields of work are information extraction, indexing and mining, definition of interactive information retrieval and discovering strategies and graphical interfaces. She works on applications of these techniques to the Web and other more classical collections. She also supervises several DEA and PhD students in this field. She is a co-Editor of the Information Retrieval Journal (Kluwer) for Europe and Africa and has a scientific role in several European projects for IRIT.

Shastri L Nimmagadda is a senior geophysicist with Wafra Joint Operations Petroleum Company in Kuwait. He previously worked for several petroleum companies in India, Australia, and Uganda. He did his masters work in tech in exploration geophysics from Osmania University and a PhD in the exploration of geophysics from the Indian Institute of Technology in Kharagpur, India. He obtained a master of information technology with distinction from the Curtin University of Technology, Australia. Dr. Shastri is interested in data processing, interpretation, knowledge mapping, and exploration data integration. Dr. Shastri is working with a research project on "ontology based warehousing approach for mining of exploration and production data of oil and gas companies."

Alexandros Ntoulas holds a PhD in computer science from the University of California Los Angeles (UCLA). His area of expertise is databases and Web information retrieval. His research interests are in the study of systems and algorithms that facilitate the monitoring, collection, management, mining, and searching of information on the World Wide Web. Dr. Ntoulas has received an MSc degree from the University of California Los Angeles in 2003, and an M.Sc and BSc degree from the Computer Engineering and Informatics Department (CEID) of the University of Patras, Greece, in 2003, and 2000 respectively. He has published a number of research papers in international conference proceedings and he recently received the Best Paper Award for the ICDE 2005 conference. Dr. Ntoulas has co-founded Infocious, a Web search engine that applies linguistic analysis techniques in order to provide highly relevant results and a better search experience to the user.

Minh Hai Pham is currently a PhD candidate in LAVOC laboratory of the Swiss Federal Institute of Technology, in Lausanne. His work now is concentrating on traffic data processing. During his internship for the master degree in computer science, he did research on text mining within OSIRIS group. His research interests include machine learning and data mining.

Gustavo Piltcher has a bachelors degree in computer science, obtained at the Catholic University of Pelotas in 2006. His research interests include clustering algorithms, ontologies, data structures, and computer theory.

Amandeep S. Sidhu is a structural bioinformatics researcher at in the faculty of IT at the University of Technology Sydney, with expertise in protein informatics. He is currently working on a protein ontology project with Professor Tharam S. Dillon. His research interests include: biomedical ontologies, structural bioinformatics, proteomics, XML enabled Web services, and artificial intelligence. His work in these fields resulted in 27 scientific publications.

Michel Simonet, PhD, is the head of the knowledge base and database team of the TIMC laboratory. His group works on the design and the implementation of knowledge bases and databases, and currently on the integration of information systems by using the tools and methodologies they have developed. They work on two main projects: a database and knowledge base management system, named OSIRIS, and a system for database conception and reverse engineering based on original concepts and a new methodology. Ontologies have become central to their work, both as a particular case of a knowledge base and as the starting point of database design. Ontologies have been applied to the Semantic annotation of texts and to the automatic clustering of texts.

Sofia Stamou is a postdoctoral researcher in the Computer Engineering and Informatics Department at Patras University, Greece. She received both her PhD and MSc degrees in computational linguistics from Patras University, in 2006 and 2002, respectively, and a diploma in linguistics from the University of Ioannina, Greece, in 1999. Her research interests focus on the linguistic processing of Web data, Web data classification, semantics and information retrieval. While being a postgraduate student, Sofia has been invited to spend a year as a visiting researcher at the Department of Linguistics of the University of California, Los Angeles. From October, 1999 until present she has been a member of the Databases Laboratory of Patras University, where she also teaches the undergraduate course "Language Technology." Sofia has published numerous articles in international scientific journals and conferences and she has served as a reviewer to several international conferences on language technology.

Yannis Theodoridis is an assistant professor with the Department of Informatics at the University of Piraeus (UniPi). Born in 1967, he received his B.S. (1990) and PhD, in 1996, in electrical and computer engineering, both from the National Technical University of Athens, Greece. His research interests include spatial and spatiotemporal databases, geographical information management, knowledge discovery, and data mining. Currently, he is scientist in charge for UniPi in the EC-funded GeoPKDD project (2005-08) on geographic privacy-aware knowledge discovery and delivery, also involved in several national-level projects. He has co-authored three monographs and over 50 articles in scientific journals (such as Algorithmica, ACM Multimedia, IEEE TKDE) and conferences (such as ACM SIGMOD, PODS, ICDE) with over 400 citations in his work. He participates in the steering committee for the International Symposium on Spatial and Temporal Databases (SSTD) and in the editorial board for the International Journal on Data Warehousing and Mining. He is member of ACM and IEEE.

A Min Tjoa is a full professor and the head of the Institute of Software Technology and Interactive Systems at the Vienna University of Technology. He received his PhD in engineering from the University Linz in Austria. Since 1999, he has been president of the Austrian Computer Society. His research interests include Semantic Web, e-commerce, advanced and scalable data management, and data analysis solutions for management information systems and decision support.

Brigitte Trousse received her PhD in computer science (artificial intelligence and computer-aided design) from the University of Nice—Sophia Antipolis. In 1990, she was a permanent research scientist at INRIA Sophia Antipolis, in France, and in 2003 the scientific leader of the AxIS Project-Team there. Her research interests deal with knowledge discovery from databases (KDD) in the context of a global approach of knowledge management in designing complex systems: in particular her work aims the use of usage mining in addition with content and structure mining in order to evaluate or (re)design information/knowledge systems such as Web sites. Her research topics include artificial intelligence (AI) in design, information systems, adaptive recommender systems, information retrieval, knowledge management, KDD, Web mining, case-based reasoning, and Semantic Web. She has published her work in over 60 articles in journals, books, and conferences and was co-editor or guest editor for few journals, proceedings and books on mining complex data and on AI in Design. She has also an intense reviewing activity for international and national conferences and journals.

Xuan Zhou is currently working as a software engineer at VPIsystems Corporation located in Holmdel, New Jersey. Dr. Zhou received his PhD in computer science, in 2006, from the New Jersey Institute of Technology (NJIT) at Newark, New Jersey. Dr. Zhou also received the Master of architecture and Bachelor of architecture from Hunan University at Changsha, Hunan, P.R.China, in 2000 and 1997, respectively. Dr. Zhou's research interests include ontologies, data mining, algorithms, and architectural terminologies, about which he has published several papers.

Index